The Literate Revolution in Greece

PRINCETON SERIES OF COLLECTED ESSAYS

This series was initiated in response to requests from students and teachers who want the best essays of leading scholars available in a convenient format. Each book in this series serves scholarship by gathering in one place previously published articles representing the valuable contribution of a noted authority to his field. The format allows for the addition of a preface or introduction and an index to enhance the collection's usefulness. Photoreproduction of the essays keeps costs to a minimum and thus makes possible publication in a relatively inexpensive form.

The Literate Revolution in Greece and Its Cultural Consequences

Eric A. Havelock

Princeton University Press
Princeton, New Jersey

Contents

Acknowledgments

THE AUTHOR wishes to thank the publishers of the following papers for permission to reprint them here:

"Spoken Sound and Inscribed Sign," "The Pre-Greek Syllabaries," "The Technology of the Greek Alphabet," and "Aftermath of the Alphabet" are reprinted from Eric A. Havelock, *Origins of Western Literacy*, Toronto, The Ontario Institute for Studies in Education, 1976. Copyright © 1976 by Eric A. Havelock. Reprinted by permission of The Ontario Institute for Studies in Education.

"Transcription of the Code of a Non-Literate Culture" and "The Character and Content of the Code" are reprinted from Eric A. Havelock, *Prologue to Greek Literacy*, Lectures in Memory of Louise Taft Semple (University of Cincinnati Classical Studies, Vol. 2). Copyright © 1973 by University of Oklahoma Press.

"The Ancient Art of Oral Poetry" is reprinted from *Philosophy and Rhetoric*, Vol. 12, No. 3 (Summer 1979), pp. 187-202. Copyright © 1979 by The Pennsylvania State University Press.

"The Alphabetization of Homer" is reprinted from *Communication Arts in the Ancient World*, edited by Eric A. Havelock and Jackson P. Hershbell, pp. 3-21. New York, Hastings House, 1978. Copyright © 1978 by Hastings House, Publishers.

"The Preliteracy of the Greeks" is reprinted from *New Literary History*, Vol. 8 (1976-1977), pp. 369-391.

"Thoughtful Hesiod" is reprinted from *Yale Classical Studies*, Vol. 20 (1966), pp. 61-72. Copyright © 1966 by Cambridge University Press.

"Preliteracy and the Presocratics" is reprinted from *Institute of Classical Studies Bulletin* No. 13 (1966), pp. 44-67. Copyright © 1966 by University of London, Institute of Classical Studies.

"The Oral Composition of Greek Drama" is reprinted from *Quaderni Urbanati di Cultura Classica* No. 35 (1980), pp. 61-113. The author is grateful to Professor Bruno Gentili for kind permission to reprint this article.

The Literate Revolution in Greece

Johnson called the East-Indians barbarians.

BOSWELL: You will except the Chinese, Sir.

JOHNSON: No, Sir.

BOSWELL: Have they not arts?

JOHNSON: They have pottery.

BOSWELL: What do you say to the written characters of their language.

JOHNSON: Sir, they have not an alphabet. They have not been able to form what all other nations have formed.

BOSWELL: There is more learning in their language than in any other, from the immense number of their characters.

JOHNSON: It is only more difficult from its rudeness; as there is more labour in hewing down a tree with a stone than with an axe.

The Oral and the Written Word: A Reappraisal

ALTHOUGH THE PAPERS collected in this volume address themselves to a common theme, their previous publication has been scattered unevenly over a period of twenty years, and by no means in the order in which they now appear. If some sequence of historical chronology and continuity of argument now presents itself, this has only slowly emerged as the materials were variously explored and composed. The result as now laid before the reader merits some prefatory explanation.

An author may express thanks to his publisher as a matter of custom and formality. In the present instance, a debt owed to the authorities of the Princeton University Press calls for more than formal acknowledgment. Disciplines of knowledge tend to conduct themselves so as to reflect the influence of a presiding establishment which sets general objectives and helps to determine among a variety of scholarly opinions and researches what shall be considered sound and unsound. The natural sciences have won those recent advances which are so striking largely at the price of continual defiance of this elitist rule. In the more restricted field of classical learning, there is a strong disposition to accept authority. Perhaps this is inevitable, given the antique flavor of the material. At any rate, what is here collected and reprinted has proved to be unusually contentious, and among my professional peers there are surely some who would prefer not to see it reprinted at all. My gratitude to the Press and its readers is all the more sincere for taking a different view of the matter.

Behind these various papers lies a series of related propositions which if accepted would require some rewriting of the history of Greek literature and thought in the archaic and high classical periods. They have ascended only slowly to the level of conscious recognition during a course of research and reflection which has extended itself over a period of over fifty years. These propositions are summarized at the beginning of the chapter on "The Preliteracy of the Greeks," and there is no need to repeat them in full here. They can, however, reasonably be viewed as offering some offense to a view of antiquity which has long been traditional and deeply rooted in the cultural consciousness of "the West" (as it is often loosely termed). Some explanation of why this is so may be in order.

The glory that was Greece, so far from being diminished by the advent of industrialism, has if anything gained fresh luster from its supposed contrast with some less acceptable aspects of modern life. Can it be seriously proposed that the people who invented what became an ideal were at the time of the invention illiterate, and had been for centuries? Scholars of the written word, who spend their lives upon the documentation of Hellenism, are likely to find such a thought repugnant. "No aspect of the Greek Dark Age is more poignant than illiteracy."[1] The condescension implicit in these words, reflecting as it does the values of a literate culture, is perhaps misconceived and misdirected. Once the term "illiteracy," hallmark of a personal failure, is replaced by "nonliteracy" or "preliteracy," a different historical perspective becomes possible.

The Greek authors in question, responsible for works widely regarded as ideal specimens of the literary art, range from Homer to Euripides. They were inscribed at the time of composition (Homer perhaps being an exception) or else we would not have them. They have been painstakingly copied and recopied, printed and reprinted, over a span of two and a half millennia. Is it plausible to argue that these authors were not authors or writers in any sense that would be understood today? We may digest, however uncomfortably, the conclusion that the Homeric poems despite their obvious sophistication obey the formulaic rules characteristic of oral composition with all this may imply of oral improvisation. But as we painstakingly peruse the Presocratic philosophers or the Greek dramatists, annotating them line by line, can we bring ourselves to believe that what we are doing is from a historical standpoint an artificial exercise imposed upon linguistic arrangements which were framed to catch the attention of the ear but not the eye, and responded to the acoustic sensibilities of audiences who would listen to and remember some of what they heard, but never expected to read it or judge it as a written work of literature?

Oral composition as practiced by the early Greek masters is not in fact to be thought of as a matter of improvisation, in the manner of Yugoslavian singers, nor is its character to be understood in terms restricted to the stylistic. It was by definition rhythmic, and we can say therefore "poetic," though it would be more appropriate even if clumsier to call it "poetized." "Poetic" and "poetry" as we think of them are like "literate" and "literacy." They exemplify a language that places a value judgment on what is named, in this case derived from the value system of a literate culture. Poetry is the name of an ideal use of language, superior in some ways to the expressive powers of prose. While the latter can become the language of art (as in the novel, to give only one example) it is used much more commonly as the language of information and instruction, of history, law, technology and the like, and its value is estimated primarily in terms of content. If style is added, so much the better, but whereas style is the essence of poetic art, it is incidental to the vast body of prose composition. To argue as I have done that the original Greek masters pursued and performed an instructional function for their community, that this was their essential role as agents and instruments of the oral tradition, can seem like a willful attempt to downgrade the poetry of the ideal as though it were the prose of the commonplace. It flies in the face of that impressive body of critical interpretation which would estimate these works as "literature," to be judged by the light of norms that are aesthetic rather than functional and didactic. No wonder that such a nonliterary viewpoint can be stigmatized as "irritating" and regarded as irrelevant to their proper understanding.[2]

The demand made by what is here reprinted is historiographical, in the sense that it calls for these early masterpieces to be measured by being placed in anthropological time rather than just classical time. It is argued first that their composition with accompanying alphabetization must have been preceded by a continual production and perishing of oral prototypes in the nonliterate centuries. The forms of Greek literature were not suddenly invented after 700 B.C. Secondly, and more drastically, the kind of oral composition the Greeks indulged in, and we may say perfected, must have had a millennial history stretching back into the experience of all preliterate but civilized societies, and its fundamental rules are rooted in this history. The curious power of the early Greek classics is primarily due not to inspiration but to their share in the technique and purpose of such prehistoric composition. Obviously it is impossible to prove such a thesis by positivistic methods: oral language does not fossilize.

The Greek alphabet, by way of contrast, is here introduced, when it impinges on the Greek scene, as a piece of explosive technology, revolutionary in its effects on human culture, in a way not precisely shared by any other invention. Uniqueness is claimed for it in the fact that, while emerging from a process of experimentation which covered perhaps three previous millennia, it constituted the terminus of the process. Once invented, it supplied the complete answer to a problem, and there has never been need to reinvent it. The Roman and Cyrillic variants are just that, and no more. The problem had been to devise a system of "shapes" (as the Greeks properly called them) of required small sizes, with maximum economy, (so far, the Phoenician achievement) such as would, despite the economy, when seen (or as we say, "read") in endless variety of linear arrangements automatically trigger an acoustic memory of the complete spoken speech indexed by the shapes. The Greek device, because of its success in solving the last stage of the problem, brought into existence what we call "literature" in the modern, i.e. postalphabetic, sense. It can even be argued (below chapter 13) that the device furnished a necessary conceptual foundation on which to build the structures of the modern sciences and philosophies.

From two rather different points of view, this estimate of the role of the Greek alphabet may seem at best exaggerated, at worst obnoxious. The mathematician rightly regards his craft as esoteric and intellectually demanding. If it can be shown, as seems probable, by decipherment of prealphabetic documents, that pre-Greek societies achieved a measure of mathematical sophistication unattained by the Greeks themselves, it is tempting to extend by analogy this sophistication to linguistic documentation as well. If they could achieve quadratic equations, surely they were capable of producing a sophisticated literature.

On their side, the scholars of oriental languages who have spent their lives deciphering the remains of hieroglyph, cuneiform, and Semitic script, tracing the continuities in the progress of the writing art, well-aware of the debt owed by the Greeks to the proximate stage of development, may feel justified in protesting a claim of uniqueness for the final stage of the process. They may prefer to designate what was really a "breakthrough" as nothing more than an "improvement" upon previous systems. "Alphabet," a Greek word invented in the Christian era to describe simplistically and quite properly a Greek device, is now commonly and loosely transferred to describe prealphabetic systems, particularly the Phoenician, just at the term "literate" is transferred backward to describe the earlier societies which used these systems, and the term "literature" with all its European connotations is applied to what scholars of Near Eastern systems of writing are able to decipher and retranslate into a modernized vocabulary. In this volume, it is argued that the limitations of prealphabetic scripts prevented their content from ever reaching that standard of sophistication characteristic of Greek and post-Greek literatures.[3]

In the main, the studies in this volume confine themselves to investigating the material conditions surrounding a change in the means of communication between human beings, social and personal. Underlying the analysis, and for the most part unstated but perceptible, lies the possibility of a larger and more formidable proposition, that the change became the means of introducing a new state of mind—the alphabetic mind, if the expression be allowed.[4] Here again, a claim is put forward which to many will seem inflated, violating as it does some widely held preconceptions about the character of the human mind. How such a change could or might come about is best understood by appreciation of a physical fact: the alphabet converted the Greek spoken tongue into an artifact, thereby separating it from the speaker and making it into a "language," that is, an object available for inspection, reflection, analysis. Was this merely a matter of creating the notion of grammar? It is true that Greek originally had no word for a word singly identified, but only various terms referring to spoken sound,[5] and that syntactical categories and parts of speech first became subjects of discourse toward the end of the fifth century, after nearly three hundred years of alphabetic usage.[6] But something deeper was also going on. A visible artifact was preservable without recourse to memory. It could be rearranged, reordered, and rethought to produce forms of statement and types of discourse not previously available because not easily memorizable.[7] If it were possible to designate the new discourse by any one word, the appropriate word would be conceptual. Nonliterate speech had favored discourse describing action; the postliterate altered the balance in favor of reflection. The syntax of Greek began to adapt to an increasing opportunity offered to state propositions in place of describing events. This was the "bottom line" of the alphabetic legacy to postalphabetic culture.

Such a sweeping conclusion is bound to encounter resistance at three different levels. It proposes that both law and ethics as understood today, meaning verbalized structures stating principles and describing applications, came into existence as the result of a change in the technology of communication. What had preceded them was procedure rather than principle,[8] embodied in forms of social habit and commemorated in rhythmic speech. Prealphabetic societies were not immoral but in a conceptual sense nonmoral. Moral philosophers are not likely to relish such a conclusion, nor the further conclusion that philosophy as an intellectual discipline is a postalphabetic invention: that much of the story of early Greek philosophy so-called is a story not of systems of thought but of a search for a primary language in which any system could be expressed.[9] Nor are idealists easily to be conciliated by a historical interpretation that argues in effect not only that "the medium is the message," that is, the content of what is communicated is governed by the technology used, but that this same technology may have a causative function in determining how we think.

Oral theory applied to Homer, with analogies drawn from Balkan oral poetry, has encouraged the habit of regarding oral and literate practice as mutually exclusive. The literate, it is presumed, invades the genius of oral composition and corrupts it so that oral originality gives way to mechanical repetition. This portrait of what took place in Greece is borrowed from the example of colonial administrations equipped with the perfected technologies required to produce literacy who invade nonliterate societies and take them over.[10] Such is not the thesis of this book. Chapter 8 on the alphabetization of Homer offers the suggestion that even the *Iliad* and *Odyssey* are complex compositions reflecting the beginning of a partnership between the oral and the written, which proved creative. Those who suppose that I offer a narrowly oralist version of Greek literature extravagantly extended to the death of Euripides lend themselves to an error of oversimplification. If the main stress in these articles falls on the oralist element, this is because a novel thesis requires a restricted emphasis to be put across. But in larger perspective, the complete genius of the literature and philosophy here placed under inspection is understandable as neither oralist nor as a flaccid compromise between the oral and the literate but as the product of a dynamic tension between them. Put in terms of compositional technique, and simplified as much as possible, the process is one in which language managed acoustically on echo principles is met with competition from language managed visually on architectural principles. What occurred has been called "an alteration in the ratio of the senses."[11] After Plato, the balance tilted irrevocably in favor of the latter, a tilt in which Plato plays a decisive role, even though his own discourse retains some of the hallmarks of previous oralism. Demosthenes' speeches (which lie beyond the range of this volume) are typical of the change. Their syntax is essentially conceptual, and might even be styled Platonic. The statesmen of the fifth century, it is to be supposed, used a much more Homeric idiom. There is no way of proving this since their utterances have not survived—a lack, one would have thought, that itself provides indirect testimony to the oral character of communication at the time. Indirect testimony has to be sought in the speeches composed by Thucydides, which again lie beyond the scope of this volume, but provide a fascinating study of the interweave between oral and written styles of vocabulary and syntax. In accounting for the complexities of actual practice as between "orality" accompanied by memorization on the one hand and documentation also accompanied by memorization on the other, I have made use of the term "craft-literacy," to distinguish the period ending about 430 B.C. from that which succeeded it. One of the very few insights offered by a Greek author on current communication technique is a phrase used by Herodotus, but unfortunately in an Egyptian rather than a Greek context. The priests from whom he gathered his information on the land and its people "practiced memory," as they communicated with him.[12] Literate commentators would like to render this as meaning the reading of written records. There is, however, no mention of documents in the context though elsewhere Herodotus reveals he is well aware of their existence. The phrase can only mean that the priests told verbally and from memory tales or reports (*logoi*) which they may or may not have previously read. If they had read them, what relationship did the recitation bear to what we think of (but they did not) as the "text"?

The reader attuned to the styles of a Homer, a Pindar, a Plato, who passes on to peruse the literature of the Hellenistic age, is liable to succumb to a feeling of nostalgia, that something which happened once can never happen again. The basic reason for this, I suggest, is that he has passed through a major cultural transition, from the word still orally shaped and heard and shared communally to the word read in silence and solitude. Not that oral recitation or performance ceased— they obviously did not—but in Greek experience they no longer enjoyed overall priority. High culture had become alphabetized or more correctly, alphabetization had become socialized. What was now written was not worse but different. To probe the quality of the difference would be a fascinating study lying beyond the limits of this volume. Scholarship has indeed offered some comparisons, usually at the expense of the Hellenistic period, and unguided by the technological criteria here proposed. By the time of Aristotle's death, the alphabetic "book" has come into its own and was soon to translate itself into a second but friendly tongue. It is quite appropriate that the word "literature" should base itself on Latin usage, not Greek. With literacy there also arrives the literate consciousness. Poetry becomes increasingly segregated from the mainstream of cultural record and custom, and is converted into an exercise in aesthetic sensibility and private insight. In parallel, the intellectual man tends to be recognized as a type participating in the body politic but not of it. His conceptualized written language no longer expects to command the direct sympathy of nonliterate listeners. He ceases to be a bard and becomes a "thinker."[13] The first beginnings of this latter process become perceptible before the end of the fifth century, in the era of the early Sophists. Those proto-intellectuals who were invited from overseas to the court of Pisistratus in the sixth century were still poets working in the oral tradition. Those who gathered at the court of Dionysius II at Syracuse in the fourth century were prose writers. Each group in its generation was involved in the performance of a didactic function, but in two different modes of discourse.

So much by way of an overview of the historical context which has controlled the writing of these papers. Exigencies of printing costs, requiring photographic reproduction, have left some duplication and prevented revision. A few observations are offered here by way of correction and supplement.

An understanding of the alphabet's phonetic technology (below chapter 4) makes it impossible to believe that any prior system could have successfully symbolized the language of the *Iliad* and *Odyssey*. This puts out of court any hypothesis that would regard existence of the Linear B of Mycenae as having any relevance to the text of Homer. Respectable authority has maintained otherwise, as in the statement "For Wolf it became a central thesis that the poet could not write. The view is no longer tenable since our discovery of the early use of writing in Greece."[14] Such a statement confuses the issue by a loose use of the word "writing," as though all types of script completely accomplish a single invariable result, just as "literacy" and "literate" are used without differentiation to argue that the Greeks of the Mycenaean age having once become "literate" could never thereafter have forgotten this capacity.[15] The more recent authority of the *Cambridge Ancient History*[16] has fortunately come to the rescue of common sense, by dismissing any Homeric possibilities for Linear B script as lying beyond the competence of its catalogue type of notation.[17]

While I have sought to expose the theoretic reasons for the technical breakthrough represented by the alphabet (chapter 3), some may properly ask the question: What can have been the immediate and material motive for its invention, since such innovations are not usually prompted by theoretic considerations? It may be appropriate here to mention the answer to this question which has been supplied by Professor Robb.[18] The Greek device, he suggests, arose as a procedure of inscription carried on at places or in areas (Cyprus being the favored candidate) where bilingual Greeks, neighbors to the Phoenicians, cultivated the oral art of composing versified ritual dedications—a standard practice in all preliterate cultures. They were able to observe and, being bilingual, to understand the parallel practice of their Phoenician counterparts, but they also observed the Phoenician ability to inscribe symbols of their compositions upon the dedicatory offerings. This provoked emulation. But Phoenician oral composition required the manufacture only of cadences expressive of standard parallelisms and antitheses, rhythmic but not strictly metrical, so that decipherment, by using some guesswork, was possible even within the limitations of the script used. The Greek hexametric measure was much more exacting, requiring the oral enunciation of carefully measured vocalic lengths. The difference required the Greek imitator to supply five marks to symbolize these lengths and so render adequately the metrics of his own dedication. He had to learn the Phoenician abecedarium, i.e. the list of names of the Phoenician signs, in order to start applying the Phoenician consonants to his own Greek purposes. As he did so, and still obeying his epigraphical authority, he transferred some signs of "weak consonants" to function as symbols of vocalization because listening to them suggested some approximation to what he needed. Their new acoustic values came into existence as the Greek hexameter was pronounced. Such an explanation has the great advantage of asserting that principle of intimate partnership between oral and written practice which in my own view continued to operate and control the transition toward full literacy in the next three hundred years.

It is argued below that on the epigraphical evidence, the original inscribers of alphabetic statements were craftsmen, though the purposes for which the inscribing was done were not commercial. The hypothetical bilingual Greek was still likely to have been a stonecutter who worked with his hands, rather than a bard, for it was hand and eye that moved to emulate the Phoenician marks. The virtuosity of the bard relied on mouth and ear.

The general reader of Homer no less than the scholar will always find it difficult to accept a thesis which places *Iliad* and *Odyssey* in an exclusively oral setting. When all is said and done, the analogy drawn with the recorded songs heard from surviving singers in the Balkans cannot be extended to cover any parallel with Homer's sophistication, not merely of structure overall but of rhythmic virtuosity and vocabulary. Chapter 8 has tried to meet this problem—the perennial Homeric problem—by arguing that there must be something to the later tradition which reports either assemblage of Homeric texts or organization of Homeric recitation, or both, occurring in the era of Pisistratus at Athens. Respectable authorities have dismissed the tradition, mainly, one suspects, because it suggests the poems assumed their present order at an uncomfortably late date. To restore credibility to the tradition— Cicero himself is a chief source, but it can be traced backwards to the classical era[19]—is to admit that the methods of proto-literacy played a part in the final composition. These masterpieces may owe a good deal to the use of the eye, and since it is essential to the thesis of these pages to suppose that ear was continuously seduced into collaboration with eye during the high classical period, and that the result was a distinctive type of creative composition which straight literacy could never duplicate, it would follow that creative epic composition may well have continued for perhaps a century after the inscription of parts of Homer had begun.[20] But how, originally, had the siren learnt to sing in this way? By what process of development had the hexameter and its formulas, so fine-tuned and elaborate, won their perfection? (chapter 7). Long afterwards, in the context of a literate society, Aristotle was to point to the intimate partnership between "music" and "education"[21] (as indeed had Plato before him, but to serve more ideological purposes). Can an explanation of the Homeric sophistication be furnished by transferring the social equation described by Aristotle backwards to the preliterate centuries? That is to say, the Greek city-states of the ninth to the sixth centuries perfected a system of oral instruction in dance, instrumental music, and recitation, by which certain works of oral composition were selectively memorized, recited, expanded, but in a disciplined manner imposed by the seniors upon the young as part of their initiation into an oral society which was to command their allegiance. To these performances a status was given which called forth the energies of bards and musicians to perfect their art in the social interest. Homer in short is a monument of oral education, not simply of artistic achievement. Some such picture of what went on in the so-called "dark" age seems required to explain the unusual linguistic virtuosity of Homeric and archaic Greek, as though vocabulary and formulas had been refined over a long period of time by careful enunciation controlled by musical measures carefully observed. The society failed to devise a viable system of musical and choreographic notation. That part of the curriculum is irretrievably lost. It did, after some centuries of oralism, invent a successful notation for the recited word, the one we still read. "Literature" was born. But the major works of this literature in its earlier alphabetized forms continued for some time the previous oral function of reporting, conserving, and recommending the unwritten ethos of Greek social, civic, and personal behavior. In these pages, this last conclusion is defended as it may apply to Greek drama (chapter 12). For an extensive testing of it against Homer's text, the reader is referred to my *Preface to Plato* (chapter 4) and *Greek Concept of Justice* (chapters 6 to 10).

The approximate date of the alphabet's invention is stated here (chapter 9) as about 700 B.C. "plus or minus." This may to some experts appear incautiously late; on the other hand, a view that would relegate it to early in the first half of the eighth century or even at the end of the ninth[22] is rash and unsupportable. Any conclusion depends on intricacies. By common consent, the earliest alphabetic inscription is a Greek hexameter line, followed by a second, imperfect and incomplete, scratched on the shoulder of a late geometric wine jug, found in Attica before the days of scientific archaeology.[23] A date for its manufacture has been proposed by an expertise which associates it with a group of five of similar style. These in turn are fitted into a chronological series of groups of pots stylistically classified, in a relative position which yields a date of circa 740 B.C.[24] The scholarship of geometric pottery is fine-tuned. The original provenance of the pot being unknown, its date is fixed by analogy with others. It is of routine manufacture and decoration, certainly late geometric. To quote the opinion of Miss Davison as expressed in the course of a personal conversation, "It could have been in household use for a generation before someone scratched that verse on it—there is no way of telling."[25] Partisans of an early dating for the inscription may point to the cheapness of the ware to argue that it would not have been treasured for long but one would have thought that any pot of this period would have had some value regardless of decoration. Was it in fact picked up and filled with wine to make an improvised present for a competitor in an informal competition? (Below p. 193.) It remains an interesting fact that in all discussions of this famous pot which have come to my attention, no scholar has so much as mentioned the obvious possibility that the inscription postdates the manufacture. In this omission one is justified in detecting a deep-seated desire to spare even the geometric age the stigma, as it is supposed, of "illiteracy." The character of this prejudice, and some of the evidence that should remove it, are discussed more fully in the third chapter of my *Preface to Plato*.

One of the important factors that foster the prejudice turns on the presumed date for composition of the Homeric poems. For oralists of all persuasions a late date for alphabetic transcription presents no problem. But for those to whom *Iliad* and *Odyssey* are works of "literature" in the traditional sense, fully formed in writing, a date at least as early as the beginning of the eighth century is devoutly to be wished for. Given the uncertainty, however, surrounding the chronological relation of the graffiti on the jug to the period of manufacture (with some residual uncertainty as to when precisely manufacture occurred) it is of more importance to notice that the other few but genuinely early alphabetic inscriptions (below pp. 190-97) all group themselves round the end of the eighth century, perhaps (but not certainly) beginning as early as 720 B.C. There are not enough samples within this narrow period to chart a development of letter styles. The inscription on the jug may reasonably have occurred within the same general period.

The written composition of Homer was truly com-position (below pp. 181-82) and began to occur after 700 B.C. Central elements in the report he gives of maritime life and civic and military behavior can be placed in the seventh and even early sixth centuries, as I have sought to demonstrate elsewhere.[26] Not that such "Ionian" material enjoys a monopoly of the text, since the poems contain a growing amalgam of orally conserved traditions. But its presence in the text means that the era of creative oral composition overlapped with the era of documentation, and reached its zenith precisely during the time of overlap.

While these articles extend themselves from Homer to Greek drama in order to demonstrate a continuity in the partnership between oral and written to the close of the fifth century, they pass over early lyric and Pindar. As to Pindar, it will be appreciated that he occupies a mediating position between Homer and drama, that is, so far as his relationship to the literate revolution is concerned. In the words of one of his editors, "It is probable that he did not write his odes"[27]—perhaps too radical a statement, but one that correctly identifies him as an "oralist" poet. In this view, his didacticism is not a product of personal temperament, but a response to that functional role expected of a poet part of whose task was both to recommend and to conserve the ethos of an oral society. The task had achieved something close to conscious recognition much earlier in the two poems ascribed to Hesiod. Chapter 10 of the present volume reprints a preliminary study of a new style of linguistic managment attempted by the poet as a result of his becoming a reader while remaining an oralist. It now needs to be supplemented by that more extensive analysis of "The Spoken and the Written Word" which occurs in chapter 13 of my *Greek Concept of Justice.*

The term "lyric" as used today is post-classical,[28] often applied to identify the fragmentary remains of a group of poets ranging from Archilochus to Simonides. It can have misleading overtones, best understood when the social conditions in which the poetry was produced are understood. The poetry was multifarious, not the product of any one specialized craft. Literate analysis can classify it by types, into cult hymns addressed to a deity, festival songs, including processional songs and dancing songs, marriage songs and funeral dirges, birthday songs, children's songs (including begging songs), lullabies, military and campfire songs, epitaphs, elegies and elegiac homilies—covering all kinds of social communication beyond the casual converse of the vernacular. In oral societies, "musical" ability, meaning the ability to improvise versification and accompaniment, is more widely distributed than in literate ones, and a vast body of oral "lyric" must have circulated which had ephemeral value. The scraps that we have represent the work of those poets who were lucky enough to live late enough to be inscribed and whose manuscripts were deemed worthy of preservation. Their oral ancestry must have been as sophisticated as that of Homer. But because alphabetized, they entered the realm of "literature." It is absurd to suppose in the manner of histories of Greek literature that the forms of "lyric" were suddenly invented in all their perfection at the point where the Alexandrian canon begins in the seventh century B.C.

These poets were not read in their own day but listened to. In order to achieve any degree of what we think of as "publication," their "works" had to be not written but performed *before* audiences, large or small, and often performed *by* the audiences as well, who became participants, as in dances and work songs. The composer's fame, frequently commemorated as a treasured objective, rested solely on this condition. Literate poets can afford to discard the expression of a passionate desire for fame. Their publishers will look after this for them—and their reviewers.

Such fame rests on recollection, which is assisted when music and dance become the companions of the words. Of the three kinds of instrument available, strings, percussion, and wind, only the first two allowed of solo performance, as in epic. Wind always required at least one reciter and one player (unless music was reserved for interludes), and the latter, until the days of achieved literacy, was at the service of the former. This situation helps to explain why, as musical performance in our sense of "musical" began to emerge as an art form in its own right, toward the end of the fifth century (where it might be expected, as readership of poetry began to increase), it emerged in the form of flute performance. The flutist, always an individual separated from the recitation, began to take over on his own.[29]

The social occasion therefore, whether public or restricted, furnished an essential condition without which important lyric could not exist. To be sure, the songs were transcribed, presumably in the poets' own lifetimes. Both Archilochus and much later Xenophanes seem to refer to written communication with other poets.[30] But the interchange of scripts remained narrowly limited; what evidence there is supports not a wide or general circulation, but the reverse. The act of composition is itself oral. The language is "melic,"[31] to use the correct ancient term. It is framed to be sung.

Cult performances, public and processional festivals and the like are self-evident inspiration for the content of the choral "lyrics" composed for such occasions. This same genre, with all its didactic overtones recommending the proprieties of the society, became incorporated in stage drama,[32] itself an essentially public performance. One restricted institution, a permanent feature of Hellenism, remains to be noted, crucial

to the composition of love poetry but not confined thereto—
the symposium, chief vehicle of private social intercourse.
Here again the necessary means of publication was provided
in the persons of the participants who shared in recitation
and acceptance of each other's "works." The most famous
record of such an occasion was composed in the fourth century, and it is characteristic of this date that lyric performance,
now relegated to the status of entertainment, is discarded
altogether in favor of prose rhetoric. As late as the fifth century, the performance expected from participants was still
"musical." A song could be addressed to a favorite reclining
on the same couch. Even a tyrant's dinner table could furnish
an appropriate occasion. A high proportion of Sappho's verse
can be read as symposiastic poetry, and the rest as cult hymns
and processional songs. Varieties of the symposiastic occasion
were furnished under military conditions in the barrack room
and around the campfire. Kipling's ballads, though themselves a writer's poetry, exploited an age-old genre which goes
back to Archilochus, as is also true of marching songs, a variety
of work song. The compositional form of much that survives
of Archilochus, especially his invective and his bawdy, fits this
situation. He is, in fact, the lyric voice of the common soldier,
the good soldier Schweik of his generation.

Elegiac, like lyric, was a functional component of orally
preservable communication. Neither genre in its early forms
ever lost touch with the didactic requirements that had to be
met. The elegiac distich, lending itself as it does to the framing
of aphorism, reveals the didactic function more obviously as
it indulges in protreptic and meditative wisdom. But wisdom
is not absent from the lyric of Archilochus and Sappho, and
is prominent in Simonides.

Archilochus and Sappho are appropriate examples to cite,
if only because they are the favorite authors of those historians
who would see in Greek lyric the emergence of a purely private poetry of the personal consciousness. The impression is
fostered by the fact that the verse is often though by no means
always spoken in the first person, and perhaps addressed to
a second person. But the psychology of composition cannot
be understood within the limits set by the personal pronouns.

Conditions of publication were socially oriented, and this inevitably controlled the intentions of the poem's content, which are not those that can become introspective, as is possible in a literate situation. Greek lyric is commonly estimated by the light of canons derived from the romantic poets of the late eighteenth and nineteenth centuries. What requires to be understood is that the exercise of the private imagination, one of the hallmarks of romanticism, implies a valuation placed upon the personal and private which is post-Hellenic. This is as true of Greek sculpture as of Greek verse. Romanticism in literature was given full opportunity to express itself when technology not only of the written word but of the printing press allowed the circulation of written poetry (and then prose) to escalate and so be read without benefit of a participating audience, even an audience of one. When Shelley wrote:

> I arise from dreams of thee
> In the first sweet sleep of night

his composition is an act of private imagination. He did not need to speak to his love in the flesh, or even have such a love absent but addressable at the moment of composition. His inspiration could be self-engendered unaided by a working relationship to an external object presently felt, whether a single person or a thousand. Greek poetry is immune to this kind of private idealization. Its style and substance is "other-oriented," not in any abstract sense, but in the sense that the other is an audience, a "public" external to the speaker, often symbolized in the vocative as a single person, but always palpably felt as a listener who is a partner in the poetry. This came about because the poetry was first nurtured in societies of oral communication which also were "other-oriented."

For further exploration of the oral context of early lyric, the reader is referred to the studies of Gentili and Cerri who have extended the same kind of attention to Greek historiography.[33] In the overview contributed by this volume, both Herodotus and Thucydides are omitted, the latter reasonably so as an author who (in contrast to Herodotus) is prepared to recognize himself as a writer. Although the events of his history belong to the last third of the fifth century, much of the written composition must have been carried out after the Peloponnesian War was over. The works of both authors celebrate in effect the replacement of poetry by prose as the appropriate vehicle of preserved record. It is to be inferred that they are responding to an increase in readership, which is cancelling out the previous acoustic demand for oral publication in suitably oral, i.e. poetic, style. History is now to be given substance and survival as a written artifact and for this purpose prose is adequate. Thucydides, the Attic author, confirms by his position in the chronology of the transition the thesis that Athens was becoming "literate" only as late as the period of the Peloponnesian War. Herodotus of Halicarnassus, composing in Ionic fifty years earlier, reveals by his priority a fact supported by other evidences, that literacy in the Ionian cities and islands had a head start over the mainland. In all likelihood, Herodotus attended a primary school that taught letters and expected to have readers created by the same curriculum, at a time (the period just after the Persian Wars) when similar instruction at the primary level was not yet available in Athens. Turning to his self-appointed task as a historian, and extending his composition by degrees to many rolls of writing, he is not likely to have engaged in such an enterprise for mere self-edification. He surely expected a public of readers who would prefer to read him in Ionic, not Attic, even though emigration to the mainland later gave him (like the Sophists) an Attic audience. Epigraphy may supply an interesting if indirect support for such a supposition. Comparative study of epigraphic letter-shapes indicates the early influence in Ionia exercised by the practice of writing cursively instead of monumentally, a habit that would be encouraged by increasing use of papyrus rolls and the need to increase speed of writing on them.[34] The alphabet applied epigraphically represents a relatively labored process of incision, even when scratched, or else a careful use of paint. The use of papyrus presumably increased in parallel with readership; the latter had to be supplied by instruction given not in adolescence but at the elementary level (below p. 83). It is not inappropriate to infer that the earliest fully effective writing schools developed not on the mainland but in Greece overseas, where the alphabet itself had been born.

As readership increased, anywhere in the Greek world, the pressure to compose historical record in poetry would decrease. Following this rule of thumb, Hecataeus of Mïletus, predecessor of Herodotus, emerges precisely at that time and in that place which would be expected of the first prose historian. Earlier historical record was poetic (or as I prefer to say poetized) and therefore recitable, as in the case of the *Ktiseis*,[35] local histories of city-states in which the composers lived. Achieving alphabetization, in a period restricted to craft literacy, these "histories" were able to survive. Preceding compositions lacking this advantage would have enjoyed only an ephemeral existence, the character of which can be gauged by analogy from the reported experience of a nineteenth-century explorer of the Sudan:

> After some initial wariness Mek Nimmur's followers . . . went back to their leader with the white man's gifts. A few days later a musician arrived to welcome the strangers into the Leopard King's domain. . . . The musician himself astounded Baker by an immaculate and dandified appearance in such wild surroundings. He rode on a snow-white mule and wore skin-tight white pantaloons. . . . Playing on a kind of violoncello called a rababa . . . the visitor sang a long paean in praise of Baker, recounting many bold deeds never in reality performed; one of these was the rescue of Florence from a tribe which had kidnapped her, a feat during which the carnage was immense. 'He sang of me as though I had been Richard Coeur de Lion' wrote Baker, who was less pleased when one of the Arab hunters said it was the custom to pay heavily for such unusual tributes. . . . Sam gave short shrift to a second musician who arrived a few hours later to repeat the performance.[36]

We do not have to assume that this performance reached any kind of Homeric standard in order to realize the presence of Homeric themes. Baker and his bride may or may not have had the requisite classical background to understand that they were being cast in the roles of Menelaus (or even Achilles) and Helen. The episode has elements of extravagance which are distinctly un-Greek—at least as we like to think of the Greeks. But as it describes literate Europe encountering non-literate Africa, it serves as a useful reminder of the fact that oral record of what is supposed to have been the past represents an act of free composition, not less so when cast in epic form. It can never be historical in our sense. The true parent of history was not any one "writer" like Herodotus, but the alphabet itself. Oral memory deals primarily with the present; it collects and recollects what is being done now or is appropriate to the present situation. It reports the institutions of the present, not the past. It is not likely to reach backward for detail further than the grandfather, and perhaps not that far in societies of short life expectancy. What it preserves of the past is partial and incidental, and is woven into coherence by the use of fantasy, like the Mycenaean background emplaced in the Homeric poems.

In the eyes of the Greeks, their original historian was Homer. The *Iliad* and *Odyssey* gained a monopoly over their early imagination, exercising a power that was accepted by Hesiod and the lyrists in the seventh century and extended itself to Aristotle in the fourth, when he was writing his *Ethics*.[37] Though the influence reflected the genius of the original, one can reasonably infer that it also had a technological basis, through the head start gained by the papyri in which the poems were inscribed. Homer's alphabetization was first in the field. In an age of craft literacy, his successors in composition, no matter in what genre, could read him when their public still did not, or at least could hear him recited from a text which was gaining status as a corpus and a canon. The poets of the epic cycle adopted the role almost of commentators upon a preexistent text, supplying stories to fill out its historical context, by way of introduction, supplement, and conclusion.

The dominance of what should be imagined as an alphabetic presence is relevant to the historiography of both Herodotus and Thucydides. Their concept of history as military and heroic is adopted from Homer, and their execution of the concept is guided by Homeric norms. Herodotus for his part desires to emulate Thucydides, a more self-conscious author, to replace an influence from which neither could escape. For delineation and defense of this view of them, I must refer the reader to my *War as a Way of Life in Classical Antiquity*.[38] Here I need only record an impression, gained after much comparative reading of both authors, that behind the prose of Herodotus as he describes the epic contest between Greeks and Persians on the mainland one hears the epic hexameters as they were recited—meaning that he was remembering them—whereas in the Archaeology of Thucydides we view a reader of a Homeric text who looks carefully for detail in order that he may correct it. The point to be made is that both historians compose in very special styles, the one a little closer to the oral mode, the other closer, and perhaps aware he is closer, to the written. This came about precisely because of their relative historical positions in that cultural transition we style the literate revolution.

Their kind of meditative chronicling is written in a freedom from the past, a freedom we cannot easily imagine, one untrammeled by great complexities of evidence, unburdened by great accumulation of documentation. They could create as their successors could not, precisely because of their intermediate position at a transition point in the changing technology of communication.

The same creative energies, as opposed to what we think of as historical fidelity and scrupulous scholarship, came to be deployed in the area of biography. The life of a dead contemporary was to be thought of as a subject not for reporting but for redrafting within the parameters of the writer's own preconceptions, who however assumed a continuity between his subject and himself, and identified with it. It was a mimetic relationship, not unlike the continuity that the two historians felt between Homer and themselves. It is this kind of relationship that inspires the composition of the Socratic dialogues of the fourth century. In the nature of the case they are composed in innocence of prior documentation, and if robbed of such innocence they could never have become what they are. It is a curious and interesting fact that Plato, as the fourth century wore on, wishing to produce credentials for composition appropriate to a literate epoch, feels free to invent a fifth century documentation for his own writing which could never have plausibly existed.[39]

It is to Alexandria one turns to discover the beginnings of a literary attitude which we might call biographical in the modern sense. Alphabetic transcription, effecting a slow accumulation of documented speech, created in the Hellenistic age a past that could separate itself from the present, and from the present consciousness. The reader could look back (and the word "look" is not merely metaphorical), as his oral counterpart could not and never wanted to. The age of Alexandrianism was ushered in on the basis of a technological revolution now completed. The time had come to collect, to annotate, to correct, to explain and to reflect, standing apart from what prior men had done and said, and compare it with what was to be said now, and to use the comparison for a new type of literary creation. In Latin authors, the new style comes of age. Whether poets or prose authors, they inherited the revolution's effects without experiencing that slow press of increasing tensions between oral and written which had characterized its previous history in Greece. They learned to read quickly because their predecessors had taken so much more time over it.

The separation between past and present which found expression in literature had its analogy in the plastic arts. The archaistic style in sculpture is in a true sense a Hellenistic one.[40] It had to be, for its aesthetic intention rested on that same separated Hellenistic consciousness which documentation had created. We can even say it was in this sense the first truly "literary" style—not in the sense of representing narrative, a habit which went back to the oral period—but because it depended upon a sense of past versus present created by literary means. It is true that sculpture, unlike the contrived word, had always provided something to look back to, so that a retrospective style combining past and present was theoretically possible in the classical period. But to concentrate on such an objective and refine it by manipulating the relationship between past and present styles was surely the hallmark of later Hellenism and let us say an alphabetized Hellenism.

The ninth chapter in this collection, reviewing some evidences from epigraphy, tries to make the point that the occurrence of writing as such does not enable us to make concurrent assumptions about the practice of reading, its quality or extent. One or two footnotes can be offered by way of supplement to the examples cited. Subsequent to the alphabet's invention, letters could be variously written on artifacts as voices, as pictures, or as messages. In the absence of a large corpus of inscribed discourse which could be circulated and read continuously, there was a growing body of customers who for various reasons liked to see letters placed on objects of use. One example was the habit, oral in inspiration, of naming names (below p. 191), the earliest example of which is furnished by part of a list of names inscribed on two sherds, fragments of the same cup, found in Corinth (if indeed this collection can by stratification be dated back to the close of the eighth century or early seventh).[41] Another occurs in artistic form on the surface of the well-known François Vase of circa 570 B.C., elaborately decorated with a variety of mythological scenes and actors, to whom are attached a plethora of personal names.[42] The manner in which spaces are filled up suggests a decorative intention which could be appreciated by non-readers. It does not occur to a fully literate population to use mere writing in such a way. The motive (though not the writing) could in a rather special sense be called calligraphic (below pp. 326ff.). Calligraphy properly understood appears in a sophisticated form in the fifth century practice of arranging the letters of public inscriptions in vertical rows without reference to their relationship to actual words. The practice makes its first appearance very early on the surface of a piece of pottery found at Cumae, on which some Greek— very likely the potter himself—has started practicing his A B C.[43] There may even have been two inscribers, for a lower row of letters is better managed in an altered style. Both rows read left to right, but in the top row those letter-shapes not symmetrical are written "backwards," with omission of alpha and any vowel sign after delta. The writer's visual memory of his A B C seems faulty. Both rows give up after zeta; the upper having six signs and the lower eight. What is interesting is that the writer of the lower row writes with the intention of arranging his letters vertically below the upper ones, starting backwards so that zeta, delta, and tau in both rows get lined up as vertical pairs—but since he has eight letters to accommodate against six, symmetry breaks down, and his alpha, beta, gamma get crowded in below beta. It is not so much that this kind of writer is unpracticed as that he is thinking of his letters not phonetically but artistically: he is not really "reading" them but arranging them decoratively. The public engravers of the *stoichēdon* inscriptions in the fifth century, for all their sophistication as engravers, were thinking of the alphabet in the same way, making letters pleasurable to see rather than read. Such a pleasure could be purchased only at the cost of indifference to the "sense" (which depends on acoustic reference); the public for whom this device was designed was not primarily interested in a quick reading of an important statement, because (so I infer) they could still rely on hearing it uttered in order to be informed.

I have frequently stressed the dependence of "literacy," as the term is commonly used, upon the introduction of letters at the primary level of schooling, and have argued that this did not begin to occur before circa 440-430 in Athens. Some literary evidences bearing on this point, as on the general question of the use and circulation of documents, are reviewed in the third chapter of my *Preface to Plato* and are supplemented in the chapter of the present volume devoted to Athenian drama. A different interpretation, using as evidence illustrations of book-rolls in vase painting, has been stated in the following terms: "a development is clearly discernible, beginning with the use of books as school texts, continuing with the literary pursuits first of youths, then of women, and culminating in the pairing of the roll and lyre as symbols of Apollonic poetry."[44] The difficulty with this summation, which is intended to cover the whole of the fifth century, is twofold. Of thirty-four illustrations of book-rolls, six are datable in the first half of the century and thirty to the last half, six of these being assigned circa 450. Quantity intensifies near the chronological point at which on other grounds I have placed the introduction of primary schooling in letters. Secondly, the

statement as it is applied to the fifth century can be supported
by only two school scenes which include book-rolls; in fact,
school scenes of any kind, in the plethora of available vase
paintings, are too rare to support the view that they represent
a tradition derived from "the great vase painters of the turn
of the century."[45] The two examples available are painted so
as to associate the roll respectively with music plus recitation
(below p. 202) or with recitation alone, on the part of youths
not boys. The latter example, not included in my text, occurs
on an Attic red figure cup of some elegance painted about
thirty years after the earlier one and carries three scenes commonly identified by the title "school boys."[46] The single figure
on the interior is of a young man walking and holding by the
handle folded tablets bound together. On each of two external
scenes, two standing pupils, one behind the other, approach
a third who is taken to be an instructor. All figures are of the
same size. The two pupils are as tall as the instructor. Can
they really be "children playing at school"? Or are they less
fancifully adolescents (ephēboi), one of whom indeed holds a
walking stick? None of them is reading. What then are they
doing? In scene one (so identified for convenience) the pupil
seems to be reciting to a seated instructor the contents of the
scroll he is holding. It is held unopened: he has had to memorize it, or more probably use it to check his practicing of
poetry already memorized. In scene two, the instructor has
got up to extend an accolade to the reciter who, his assignment
completed, is holding out his scroll to restore it to the instructor's possession. Such objects were not yet in general circulation. The accolade is accompanied by the gift of a spray of
olive or myrtle appropriate for a poetic performance. The
two scenes are complementary.

The cause of literacy has advanced since the earlier Duris
cup was painted. Pupils can now handle scripts themselves.
The emphasis of the curriculum still falls on recitation and
therefore also on listening to recitation. Memorization and
mousikē remain at the core of the curriculum, but within ten
to twenty years after this, reading at the primary level of
education will have won an equal place with recitation, or even
replaced it.

Greek literary criticism begins with Aristophanes, but of a

special kind (below chapter 12). His critique of rival styles and substance, as between Aeschylus and Euripides, can be interpreted as turning on issues created by the literate revolution. Why then does it not occur to him to state through his characters explicitly that such a revolution is taking place? The hints in the text of the *Frogs*[47] which point in this direction are only hints. The question poses an obstacle to acceptance of the thesis that such a revolution did in fact occur. Strict scholarship prefers conclusions drawn from explicit statements and material facts, including artifacts. The physical existence of a statue of a scribe or of an illustration of a book-roll, or of a relief representing a reader (below pp. 200, 204) can inspire confident dogmatisms on the topic of Greek literacy where a more complex interpretation would take account of what is not there as well as what is, of silence as well as statement. The truth is that the revolution was something spread over many generations too gradually for its participants to be aware of its technological basis and what they were doing with it.[48] Such unconsciousness is not uncharacteristic. A student of our own era a thousand years hence would gather from our surviving published literature that we were experiencing some alteration in the status and role of women, but it is unlikely he would find explicit recognition of those technological inventions, ranging over more than a century, which have cumulatively made this possible. Unawareness extended itself through the Alexandrian and Roman periods. Even a perception of the essentially oral character of the formulaic Homeric hexameter escaped the notice of the ancients. More generally, the rise of a historical consciousness separating past from present was not strong enough to isolate the original oral character of the culture now inherited. The fact is understandable when one realizes that alphabetic technology is of a kind which ceases to be recognizable as a technology. It interweaves itself into the literate consciousness of those who use it so that it does not seem to them that they could ever have done without it. Moreover, later antiquity never wholly discarded oral habit, and so was prevented from recognizing its separate historical existence. Even the solitary reader read aloud to himself, and writers still sought audiences.

The book as an institution has gripped the historical imagination, to the degree that it is accepted as a necessary instrument of civilized existence in defiance of the historical evidence. Nowhere is this truer than in classical scholarship, which in spirit is Alexandrian, not Periclean. Could it indeed as scholarship hope to be otherwise? If it is sometimes willing to recognize the unstated or the ignored, and to draw upon the inferential or the speculative, this will be when what is so recognized accords with current values or preferences. The object that is investigated—namely Hellenism—is by definition assumed to be an ideal one expressive of the intellectual values of modern Europe as these have been nurtured by philosophic idealism and literary romanticism. They are perceived to be in the trusteeship of an intelligence that is literate. There is a touch of snobbery in this view but it is genuinely and deeply felt, and it cannot help being offended by a proposal to deny to early Greece those tools of the trade on which professional and popular culture alike seem to depend. The United States furnishes a less bookish, one may say less literate, climate of opinion for the scholar to grow up on. It may not be just accident that the two men who respectively established the oral composition of Homer and the late date of the alphabet were both Americans.

The ground of my own readiness to accept what might follow from these findings—if I may be allowed to close this account on a personal note—was laid during my Cambridge days nearly sixty years ago, in a classroom in Trinity College. The reminiscence is pertinent to the contents of the eleventh chapter in this volume. F. M. Cornford was giving a course of lectures on the Presocratics to that small group who were taking ancient philosophy as their special subject in the Tripos. A remark by the lecturer offered early in the course caught my notice: it was a quotation from William James, to the effect that the historian of ideas faces the problem of understanding foreign states of mind. The textbook recommended for the course in those days was not the magisterial one of Diels, in which the *ipsissima verba* of the Presocratics are presented in isolation from the tradition that reports them, but a work we called "*R-P*," edited by Ritter and Preller, in which originals and doxography were compendiously intermingled in such a way as to place the former under the control of the latter. Perusing the text, I was struck over and over again by a disparity between the vocabulary and idiom of the actual quotations and that of the interpretation surrounding them, beginning with Aristotle and extending through Hellenistic, Roman, and early Christian authors. Cornford himself drew attention to the apparent lack of certain philosophical terms in these early thinkers, and some possible errors in the transmission. His treatment in this context of the Milesians and of Anaxagoras[49] was seminal for me. Becoming a college teacher myself after graduation, I became aware of how modern histories of the period wrote of those far-off men in the idiom of the later tradition about them, which was also essentially a modern idiom.

Through later years, it began to dawn on me that an explanation of the difference might lie in a Homeric and partly nonphilosophic quality latent in early speculation. I also groped my way toward concluding that Presocratic rhythms and syntax which were either poetic or smacked of the poetic were matters not of style but substance and reflected a social situation in which listening audiences prevailed over a reading public. But the notion that these philosophers still lived in an era of mainly oral communication seemed too radical to me, because I had been schooled from my youth to assume that Greek literature began with a written Homer, and that Homer wrote in the tenth or ninth centuries. While at Toronto, by good fortune I described my problem to some archaeological friends[50] who promptly referred me to Rhys Carpenter's seminal articles on the date of the alphabet. Soon afterwards, I encountered Milman Parry on the oral character of the Homeric poems. A union between the two fructified in my mind, with results now exposed to view in this volume. While teaching at Harvard I was able to test my own growing interpretation of the genesis of early Greek thought against the minds of several generations of Harvard students, young, bright, and without prejudice, and also acquainted with Greek. To their spoken comments and written critiques in response to my own lectures, I owe a considerable debt. But I was becoming increasingly aware that I was likely to threaten the status of some sacred cows in my profession, and so published what now appears in these pages only slowly and with due deliberation and caution which has surely been justified. It has been written of the physical sciences that novel theories in this field are never automatically accepted. The process appears to require that contemporaries in the course of nature be replaced by the fresh minds of a new generation. The contents of this volume are accordingly entrusted to future judgment.

1. J. N. Coldstream, *Geometric Greece* (New York, 1977), p. 295.
2. Review of *The Greek Concept of Justice* in *Greece and Rome* 26 (1979): 210-211. (P. Walcot), where the work is characterized as "the latest effusion."
3. Below, pp. 70-73. The use of the term "alphabet" to designate prealphabetic scripts continues to gain popular currency; as for example in Sarah B. Pomeroy, *Goddesses, Whores, Wives and Slaves* (New York, 1975), p. 32: "adapting the Phoenician alphabet to the requirements of the Greek language."
4. The alphabet was "a technology of the intellect": Jack Goody, *Domestication of the Savage Mind* (Cambridge, 1977), p. 10.
5. *Epos, logos, muthos, phatis, rhēsis, phthegma, rhēma* (the last two post-Homeric) all signify "utterances" of various types. "Feathered epē" are phrases which penetrate the listener's attention like arrows (not birds); the arrow metaphor is common in Pindar. The notion of articulation of language "*epos* by *epos*" emerges in Aristophanes' *Frogs* (below p. 290). The early philosophers (Heraclitus B 23, 32, 67; Parmenides B 8.38 and 53; Empedocles B 8; Prodicus A 16) identified the *onoma* as a vital component of language, but it is questionable whether the isolation of the individual "word" as the basic building block of language is achieved before Plato.
6. Protagoras A 1, 53-54; cf. A 24-28.
7. Havelock, *The Greek Concept of Justice* (Cambridge, Mass., 1938), chapter 12, "The Spoken and the Written Word."
8. Ibid., index s.v. "Principle."
9. Havelock, *Preface to Plato* (Cambridge, Mass., 1963), pp. 300-301.
10. "A newly literate population (sc. of Africans) will read anything," apparently even a telephone directory; so a reviewer in *Times Literary Supplement*, 3 December 1971.

11. I borrow this expressive phrase from Walter J. Ong.
12. Herodotus, II, 77. What they recite *ek bublou* (II, 100) is a catalogue of 330 names; continuities of lineage are demonstrated (II, 143) by appeal to a series of colossal statues, not documents.
13. Havelock, *Greek Concept of Justice*, pp. 212-213.
14. Albin Lesky, *A History of Greek Literature*, trans. J. A. Willis, 2nd ed. (London, 1966), p. 36.
15. A.J.B. Wace, Foreword to *Documents in Mycenaean Greek* by Ventris and Chadwick (Cambridge, 1950), p. xxxii, "It is incredible that a people as intelligent as the Greeks should have forgotten how to read and write once they had learnt how to do so. It is more probable that the Linear B script continued in use and perhaps overlapped the first appearance of the Greek adaptation of the Phoenician alphabet."
16. Sterling Dow, writing in the revised edition of Volume II, "The Linear Scripts and the Tablets as Historical Documents" (Cambridge, 1971), pp. 25-26. "Verse such as the Homeric, but even much simpler verse, would be impossible in Linear B."
17. The thesis that Homer could have been inscribed in Linear B c. 1350 and transcribed alphabetically c. 750 was proposed in 1967 by G. Kahl-Furthmann, *Wann lebte Homer?* (Meisenheim, 1967).
18. "Poetic Sources of the Greek Alphabet" in *Communication Arts in the Ancient World*, edited by Havelock and Hershbell (New York, 1978), pp. 21-36. The explanation offered renders improbable the hypothesis of alphabetic experiment on papyrus prior to epigraphic application—a hypothesis which would seem to be a necessary resort for those who wish to move the date of the invention backwards (below, n. 22). The inscriber, as I argue in the next paragraph (see also below pp. 190-197 on the earliest Greek verse inscriptions) worked to the dictation of the oral "rhymster."
19. Isocrates, *Panegyr.* 159; (Plato) *Hipparchus* 228b-c, Lycurgus *in Leoc.* 102; cf. Plato, *Timaeus* 21b.
20. *Rhapsōdos* and *rhapsōdeō* are used ironically and pejoratively in fourth century literature (Plato's *Ion* a conspicuous example). This might be expected in a period when increasingly literate habits would render the practice of formal recitation obsolete. There is no hint of this sense in Pindar's phrase *rhaptōn epeōn aoidoi* (*Nem.* 2.2) nor in *rhapsōdos* as used in Herodotus and Sophocles; *rhapsōdia* is applied by Aristotle (*Politics*, 1447b 22)

to poetic composition in general. If the rhapsode was indeed originally a singer of "stitched" poems (*L S J* s.v. *rhapsōdos*) this would lend color to the explanation of Homer's "written" composition put forward below pp. 181-182. For the contrary view, sharply distinguishing creative oral composition from the mechanical style introduced by the use of writing, see Kirk, *Songs of Homer* (Cambridge, 1962), p. 71: ". . . *Iliad* and *Odyssey* are oral poems, composed according to an elaborate system which is quickly weakened when the poet begins to compose by writing"; p. 87: "literacy destroys the virtue of an oral singer."

21. *Politics*, VIII, 4,1339a 11ff; VIII 6.1340b 20ff stresses educational value of actual performance. See also W. D. Anderson, *Ethos and Education in Greek Music* (Cambridge, Mass., 1966).

22. J. N. Coldstream, *Greek Geometric Pottery* (London, 1968), p. 359; "a date of c. 775-750 seems most reasonable for the birth of the Greek alphabet"; *Geometric Greece* (New York, 1977), p. 296: "In the present state of our knowledge, then, the birth of the Greek alphabet is most likely to have occurred somewhere within the first half of the eighth century." In popular currency, the date gets moved back still further, as for example in Pomeroy, *Goddesses*, p. 32. "By 800 B.C. writing had been reintroduced into the Greek world." The *C.A.H.* (above n. 16) says that the interval of "illiteracy" after Mycenae "is lengthy, at most ante-1200-c. 725 B.C.; at least 1100-post-800 B.C."

23. Below pp. 192-194.

24. Jean M. Davison, "Attic Geometric Workshops," *YCS* 16 (1961), a main source for Coldstream's *Greek Geometric Pottery* (above n. 22). Davison however (pp. 5 and 8) notes the reservations of Chamoux deprecating use of terms Master and Workshop: "the one implies the existence of a personality which is in fact unverifiable, and the other indicates an actual place of work, the existence of which is equally unascertainable." Coldstream's own treatment indicates that the warning has been judged unnecessary.

25. In Boston, December 1979, during a meeting of the American Philological Association.

26. *Greek Concept of Justice*, chapter 4: "The Society Reported by Homer."

27. C.A.M. Fennell, *Pindar the Olympian and Pythian Odes* (Cambridge, 1893), Introduction, p. xvii; "Metrical literature was not committed to writing for nearly a generation after the Persian Wars, i.e. not until Pindar was an old man; so that it is probable

that he did not write his odes." Fennell's paper "On the First Ages of Written Literature" was published as early as 1868, by the Cambridge Philosophical Society, anticipating in a general sense my own conclusions by nearly one hundred years. I gratefully acknowledge his priority. Internal evidence of the odes we have could support the view that the poet occasionally sent either a papyrus of the poem for performance overseas, or one or more musicians who had memorized the poem, or did both.

28. Below n. 31.

29. The establishment by Pericles of the Odeum as an arena designated specifically for "an agōn of music" at the Panathenaea (Plut. P⌣r. 13.6) suggests the possibility that melodic performance was gaining separate recognition apart from the poetry that it had accompanied and whose servant it had been. The specifically "musical" (in our sense) theories of Damon were being promoted in the same period. Luigi Rossi, "Asynarteta from Archaic to Alexandrian poets" *Arethusa* 912 (Fall 1976) recalls Wilamowitz' notice of a trend from separation to unification of poetic cola and argues that "music" (in our sense) gradually gained control over words, blurring the boundaries between cola.

30. Archilochus 185 (West) Xenophanes B 6 (if exchange of cuts of meat symbolizes an exchange of poems).

31. Pindar (*Ol.* 9.1) speaks of the *melos* of Archilochus and the usage recurs in classical authors; *melopoios* in *Frogs* (below p. 272) designates the "lyric" composer. Plutarch much later (2.348b and 120c) applies the adjective "melic" to poiesis, and to Pindar, but *lurikē* to the *technē* of lyre playing (2.13b).

32. Below chapter 12.

33. B. Gentili, "Lirica Greca arcaica e tardo arcaica" in *Introduzione allo studio della cultura classica* (Milan, 1972), pp. 57-105. B. Gentili and G. Cerri, *le teorie del discorso storico nel pensiero Greco e la storiographia Romana arcaica* (Rome, 1975); see also M. Finley, "Myth, Memory and History," in *History and Theory*, vol. 4, no. 3 (1965); A. Momigliano, *The Development of Greek Biography* (Cambridge, Mass., 1971); B. Gentili, "L'idea di biografia nel pensiero Greco," *Quad. Urb.* 27 (1978).

34. L. A. Jeffery, *The Local Scripts of Archaic Greece* (Oxford, 1961), pp. 57 and 327-328. The phenomenon shows up in the second quarter of the sixth century, in a contrast between eastern Ionic lettering and contemporary mainland lettering which Miss Jef-

fery attributes to a growing use of *diptherai* in Ionia. To the Ionian head start in the provision of elementary reading and writing schools I would ascribe the original use of Ionic for the first "literary" prose, employed even when the subject matter might be Athenian or Attic, as was the case with Pherecydes of Leros and Ion of Chios; the latter is also credited with a title *Chiou Ktisis*, cf. note 35 below.

35. The title *Ktisis Colophōnos* is attested for Xenophanes, as also a poem on the *apoikismos* which founded Italian *Elea* (D. L. IX 19). Early verse of the same historical type now lost included the *Corinthiaca* (Eumelus), the *Naupactica* (Carcinus), the *Phoronis* (anonymous), and in the early fifth century the *Ionica* (Panyassis). The concerns of the polis had been central to the "elegies" of Callinus and Tyrtaeus and remained so in much so-called "lyric." Composition in the archaic period continued to reflect the didactic function expected of poetry in societies of oral communication.

36. Richard Hall, *Lovers of the Nile* (New York, 1980), pp. 58-59.

37. M. Bowra, *Landmarks of Greek Literature* (London, 1960), pp. 58-59. For Aristotle see *E. N.* I caps 9-10, 1100a5-1101a8, where illustration for a crucial philosophic dilemma in eudaemonistic moral philosophy is sought in the concluding books of the *Iliad*.

38. Vanier Lectures, 1970-1971, "Classical Values and the Modern World," ed. E. Gareau (Ottawa, 1972). On Herodotus' use of Homeric catalogues as historical model see G. K. Armayor "Herodotus' Catalogues of the Persian Empire in the Light of the Monuments and the Greek Literary Tradition," *TAPA* 108 (1978): 1-9.

39. *Theaetetus*, 142d-143c. The introduction to the *Phaedo* (58d, 59c) presumably earlier (but equally artificial?) assumes oral conditions of transmission.

40. Christine Mitchell Havelock, "Archaistic Reliefs of the Hellenistic Period"; "The Archaic as Survival versus the Archaistic as a New Style"; "The Archaistic Athena Promachos in Early Hellenistic Coinages," *AJA* 68 (1964) 43-58 with plates; 69 (1965) 331-340 with plates; 84 (1980) 41-50 with plates.

41. Jeffery, *Local Scripts*, pp. 120-121 (where the difficulties surrounding the dating are exposed), 130, and plate 18. Professor John Barron (to whom I am indebted for comments on a number of points in this introduction) has in conversation observed to me that if these sherds date to late eighth century, this would

fit possibility of transcription of Eumelus' *Corinthiaca* (above n. 35) in the same period, (perhaps the first work of Greek written "literature"?). I would myself not regard the use of letters for naming as necessarily indicating a practice of transcribing discursive speech: the inscription was done by the potter himself.

42. Jeffery, *Local Scripts*, p. 77; Arias and Hirmer, *Greek Vase Painting*, trans. and rev. by Shefton (London, 1962), plate 42 and commentary. R. M. Cook, *Greek Painted Pottery* (London, 1960), p. 255 notes presence of some quite superfluous labels ("well house," "water pot," "chair"). Such virtuosity I suggest springs not from literacy but the reverse; the word inscribed is a novelty to be exhibited.

43. I follow here Miss Jeffery's reading, *Local Scripts*, pp. 116-117.

44. H. B. Immerwahr, "Book Rolls on Attic Vases," *Classical, Mediaeval and Renaissance Studies in honor of B. L. Ullman*, ed. C. Henderson, Jr., 2 vols. (Rome, 1964), 1: 36. This work is indispensable to any treatment of Greek literacy, regardless of whether all its conclusions are accepted.

45. Immerwahr, "Book Rolls," p. 23. In reviewing 5th century B.C. "school scenes" which include book-rolls, I have disallowed no. 2 in Immerwahr's book-roll list but have added his no. 6.

46. Richter and Hall, *Red Figure Athenian Vases in Metropolitan Museum*, 2 vols. (New Haven, 1936), 1: 136: also Immerwahr, "Book Rolls," p. 21.

47. Below pp. 286-290.

48. The letters (*grammata*) of the alphabet came to be recognized as representing the elements (*stoicheia*) of language (Plato, *Cratylus* 424d, al.). If the atomists extended this usage by analogy to illustrate a general theory of atomism (Arist. *Met.* A4 985 b 4 ff) they may be viewed as having insensibly come near to recognizing the alphabet's revolutionary potential. On the oral side, the attention given by Hippias to mnemonics (A2, 5a, 11, 12) might be regarded as betraying an awareness of memory as a recording function (cf. Aesch., *Prom.* 461), now falling into partial disuse because of increasing literacy and so needing reinforcement. The alphabet also received his attention (A11, 12, 14).

49. "Anaxagoras' Theory of Matter" and "Innumerable Worlds in Presocratic Philosophy," *CQ*, 24, 1 and 2 (1930); 28, 1 (1934). These papers had been anticipated in the lectures. They can be said to have raised questions which were answered in the

critical examinations of the Aristotelian and doxographic tradition undertaken by Cherniss and McDiarmid (see also Havelock, *Preface to Plato*, [Cambridge, Mass., 1963], Introd., p. viii).

50. Homer and Dorothy Thompson, from whom I first understood what philosophy can learn from archaeology.

Spoken Sound
and Inscribed Sign

One of the notable poems of the English language is addressed by Edgar Allan Poe to a woman whom he called Helen. Was she indeed an intended embodiment of Homer's princess? However that may be, he told her in his poem that her beauty was more than mortal and personal. Contemplating it, he was aware of returning to an experience of things past, which were still present and familiar to him, for he had been brought home

> To the glory that was Greece
> and the grandeur that was Rome

The lines have become a cliché, expressive of what is taken to be an irreversible partnership between the past and the present. Here were two cultures, the Greek and the Roman, which having joined together in antiquity to create a common civilization continue to exist as a historical fact within our own contemporary culture. The classic still lives and moves and has its being as a heritage which supports our own sensibilities. Poe certainly believed this and it is possible that what he believed is still felt by us obscurely to be true, though unacknowledged.

If Greece and Rome were for Poe a kind of house with familiar rooms that he liked to live in, if they still have some present reality for ourselves, this state of affairs is grounded upon one small technological fact. The civilization created by the Greeks and Romans was the first on the earth's surface which was founded upon the activity of the common reader; the first to be equipped with the means of adequate expression in the inscribed word; the first to be able to place the inscribed word in general circulation; the first, in short, to become literate in the full meaning of that term, and to transmit its literacy to us.

A demonstration of this statement relies upon a history of the written word which begins before the Greeks, but is mainly concerned with the invention of the Greek writing system and its impact on Greek culture, before it was transmitted to the rest of Europe. It is a story too complex to be included in these lectures. But since misconceptions exist concerning the whole subject of literacy and its role in human civilization it seems worthwhile before indicating even in outline the course and direction which a history of literacy might take, to prepare my audience for the removal of certain prejudices and the clarification of certain confusions that have long bedeviled this subject. These are nourished, as such confusions often are, upon the use or the misuse of terminology, and I shall first address myself to what in effect are a series of definitions or of redefinitions. If, as I believe, much of what is written in this area of research is in need of correction, the trouble can be traced in part to a looseness in the way we have used words.

"Illiterate," "non-literate," "pre-literate"
It comes as something of a shock to realize that the Greeks in what is sometimes called the High Classical period, in

the age of Pericles and the three Greek dramatists, do not seem to have employed any terms for these notions. They spoke only of men who were musical or unmusical, educated or uneducated, and with good reason. It was sensed that literacy and cultivation were not necessarily synonymous. The Greek word *grammatikos* came into use only in the fourth century, to mean a man who could read, without necessarily implying that this skill was synonymous with education. The Romans, a more bookish people, who relied for their higher education on a knowledge of Greek, a language they read strenuously, whether or not they could speak it, exploited the concept of the *litteratus*, "the man of letters," that is, a reader of letters, and also of his converse the *illiteratus*, a man without "literary" culture. In a modern Western society, "illiterate" is used to identify that proportion of the population which, because they cannot read or write, are presumed to be devoid of average intelligence, or else underprivileged. It is therefore pejorative, signifying those who have been left behind in the battle of life, mainly because they are not bright enough. Nor do we hesitate to enlarge this significance of the term to cover whole societies of men. If they happen to be underprivileged economically in comparison with the industrial nations, then their poverty and "backwardness" must be due to their "illiteracy." This kind of thinking is not confined to the learned. The following quotation, from an editorial writer of liberal views, appeared in the *New York Times*[1] in October 1970:

"Between a third and a half of the world's people suffer from hunger and malnutrition. The people of the undeveloped world are the majority of the human race, and are breeding faster than the people of the Soviet Union, the United States, or Western Europe. There are one hundred million more illiterates in the world today than there were twenty years ago, bringing the total to about eight hundred millions."

It will be noted in these words how "hunger," "malnutrition," and a state of underdevelopment on the one hand are automatically linked with a condition of illiteracy on the other. A formal distinction within society based on these lines would not have occurred to the Greeks, and this fact should bring us up short. For a term which is used pejoratively to describe a presumed minority within modern literate societies is not permissibly or properly applied to describe whole cultures which may be "non-literate" without being "illiterate." Human society existed long before literacy, either partial or complete, was achieved. The illiteracy of individuals today should not be confused in any way with the "non-literacy" or "pre-literacy" of human societies that preceded our own.

The pre-literacy of the Greeks

But it often is, and so the view is encouraged that non-literate societies are somehow barbarian, crude or primitive, thus denying cultural significance to oral cultures — cultures, that is, of the spoken word — which in effect are regarded as non-cultures. Even the Greek example, confined though it is within narrow historical limits, is sufficient to show how false this is. The Greeks between say 1100 and 700 B.C. were totally non-literate: the evidence of epigraphy on this point is now irrefutable. Yet it was precisely in these centuries that Greece invented the first forms of that social organization and artistic achievement which became her glory.

Perhaps the start was slow, and from about 1100 to 900 the achievement did not amount to much. Archaeology has made evident the physical ruin of the Mycenaean palace-complexes and it is usually deduced that with this went also the destruction of those political and social arrangements which had previously rendered commerce, art, and a settled way of life possible. Even this hypothesis of a totally dark age supervening upon the Mycenaean period has been lately questioned. Whatever the truth of it, there is no reason to doubt that, as Professor Geoffrey Kirk has recently emphasized, the centuries after 900 were "Dark" only in the sense that so much about them is unknown. If we consider the period from 900 to 650 as a chronological unit, it is obvious that we view in this period, however obscurely, the genesis of that classical culture which becomes evident to documentary inspection only in the sixth and fifth centuries. In what forms had this genesis appeared? The primary one was institutional, embodied in the formation of those corporate identities known as *poleis*, the Greek city states. All the essential features of this Greek way of life seem to have been organized and functioning by the tenth century. Professor Kirk remarks on the settlements of the Anatolian sea-board which followed the early migrations: "This [viz. some social stability] the Ionian towns with their aristocratic form of government and their federal system had probably achieved to a high degree by the ninth century and to a moderate degree before that."[2] Ionia, it is now agreed, did not become wealthy, in comparison with the mainland, before the seventh century. A fortiori, the towns of mainland Greece must be deemed already capable by the tenth century of supporting forms of social life which went well beyond the limits of village existence. At the level of technology, these communities were capable of forging iron, and presumably of smelting it, a feat beyond the competence of the Mycenaeans. Their activities in commerce and navigation may not have exceeded Mycenaean standards. Their temple architecture not later than the end of the eighth century can be shown to have anticipated in wood the conceptions and refinements of the archaic age now partially preserved for us in stone. In the realm of the arts, this period saw at its inception the invention and perfection of the geometric style of decoration, followed by the introduction of naturalistic motifs in the so-called orientalizing period which began, appropriately enough, about the time that the Phoenician letters were put to Greek use. Finally, and irrefutably, it was this period that fostered the verbal art of Homer.

In the face of these facts, a conception which identifies cultural sophistication with a degree of literacy must be discarded. A culture can somehow rely totally on oral communication and still be a culture.[3]

The Greek experience, whether it belongs to history or to prehistory, is contained within that small moment of human time with which the ancient historian is able to deal. It is only a typical fragment of an immense history of human culture which extends backwards for uncounted millennia. From the standpoint of human evolution a perspective on the "orality," if I may use that term, of the human animal requires us to recognize that oral language is fundamental to our species, whereas reading and writing wear the appearance of a recent accident. It is a curious kind of cultural arrogance which presumes to identify human intelligence with literacy. It won't do to assume, for example, that the Athenian democracy had to be literate in order to function.[4] One would have thought that even the example of modern India would have disposed of this presumption. Our skulls achieved their present cubic capacity through processes of natural selection extending over perhaps a million years. The brains inside them cannot be measurably different from those of our ancestors of say ten thousand years ago. If we are equipped to use language for communication, so were they. Such a capacity does not merely identify us as human beings; it is the foundation of all human cultures. These have existed as oral systems from prehistoric times. The age of script, of the successive stages of a growing literacy, is by comparison a mere moment in the history of our species.

If the history of literacy is to come under inspection, a phenomenon which still has its roots in the operation of human language, then its own laws, conditions, and procedures can be fully comprehended only by first comprehending the laws and procedures of the spoken language in those cultures of oral communication which preceded the invention of reading. In present-day America we encounter difficulty in teaching our children to read. Is this possibly because we do not take the pains concurrently to teach them the art of oral recitation? Unless the developing child is first grounded in the oral culture of his ancestors for which his developing brain has been formed to cope, how can he be expected successfully to take the artificial step of converting his oral recognition of language into a visual act?

In the specific case of the Greeks, the advance towards literacy should in the first instance be viewed as an act of interpenetration of letters into an oral situation. Age-old habits of non-literacy were to be invaded by new habits of literacy, whatever those should prove to be. Placed in this perspective, Pindar and Plato were very close to total non-literacy. Can their contrived words, as they have survived in script, be properly understood without reviewing the procedures of oral composition and record? Admittedly an oral society by definition leaves no linguistic record. But luckily in the case of the Greeks, for reasons to be explained later, this is not quite so. Behind any account of the literate revolution in Greece lies an examination of the oral culture of

Greece, and this will have to be a priority in our own examination.

Symbols of number versus symbols of language
Mathematical skill, as it is practiced today, calls for a degree of intellectual sophistication which appears to lie beyond the competence of the majority of literate populations. To estimate the presence of mathematical aptitude, as a prerequisite for advanced study in the exact sciences, is a commonplace of academic procedure in the university. It seems empirically proven that good mathematicians, like good musicians, are born not made, and constitute a minority of even the so-called educated population. This has encouraged the historical view that the invention of the written word was an easier accomplishment than the invention of the written number, with the corollary that if an ancient civilization — the Babylonian being one particular example — was on the epigraphical evidence able to handle an arithmetic superior to anything that the Greeks could manage, this proves that the Babylonians had first to be literate in at least as full a sense as the Greeks were. But a general review of inscribed artifacts, wherever they have occurred in the world and been discovered, will I think support the conclusion that our ancestors learned to count long before they learned to read. In other words, the visual symbolization of quantities originally came easier than the symbolization of speech. And this is surely reasonable since quantities are visual entities, whereas speech sounds are not. Moreover many of the "objects" that are described even in common speech are not such as to be easily visualized. Measures of wheat or phases of the moon are alike phenomena which the hand can encompass or the eye can watch, and watching them, the eye and the hand can make motions in parallel, to trace visible symbols of what

has already been seen, in clay or stone or bone. If Egyptian geometry was prior to the Greek (not a demonstrable fact), if Babylonian arithmetic could solve quadratic equations with a system of enumeration certainly far in advance of anything available to Plato, if the Roman numerical system remained remarkably clumsy and ineffective when compared with Babylonian numbers invented centuries earlier, this need not mean that therefore the Egyptians and the Babylonians had to be as literate, as the Greeks or Romans were literate, in order to do this. Many of us may even feel that in our own childhood we have recapitulated the earlier stages of human development in this respect, when we have learnt to do sums in our heads or on paper with comparative fluency long before we have mastered a vocabulary which could be styled fully literate.

To be sure, the so-called Arabic numerals, which perhaps were really Indian, did not appear on the European scene to make modern calculation possible until about 1100 A.D., long after literacy had come into existence in Greece. Without this later invention the industrial and scientific age in which we live would not be possible. Ancient literacy, unaided by it, therefore had its cultural limits. It was in a certain fundamental sense only proto-technological, only proto-scientific. But its major achievement still stands: the imprisonment of spoken language in a system of visual symbols which did not in fact constitute a real prison but rather provided a fresh release, a freedom for language and its resources to expand beyond previous oral standards.

Speaking versus reading
Because spoken language consists of what we call words, and words can also be "written down," as we say, and because of that mental block that we experience when we try to think

of a culture as non-literate, it has become quite common to confuse a spoken language with the script in which it happens to be written. The term "word" carries the double meaning of linguistic sound and a visible object spelled out on a material surface. Kemal Ataturk by decree abolished the Arabic script previously employed for the Turkish language and replaced it by the completely different Romanized script. This was done without altering the spoken language; it merely increased the accuracy with which sound was transcribed, making the transcription more flexible and fluent. One would have thought that this fact of recent history would have taught us the difference between speech and the visible symbols of speech. But apparently not. It is scarcely possible to discover any linguistic discussion, popular or learned, in which the writer does not at some point slip into this confusion.

The confusion goes back to antiquity, for it is found in Aristotle who, in a discussion of the function of the lips and tongue in pronunciation, "clearly uses the term *gramma* in the sense of 'minimal unit of sound.'" But, as is pointed out by the authority (Professor Zirin) whom I am quoting, "the plain meaning of *agrammatos* (the privative adjective) is 'not having letters' either in the sense 'not consisting of letters' or in the sense of 'not knowing letters,' illiterate." The Greek term *gramma*, literally indicating a letter, shaped or inscribed, is therefore "often employed by Aristotle in an extended sense." This way of putting it is kind to Aristotle, perhaps kinder than he deserves. Such an "extended" use of the word can lead to confusion. A term designating a visible inscribed shape is being used to denote an invisible sound. The habit of thinking of language as existing only in its written form has already begun. The beginnings of this error of nomenclature are discernible in

Plato's *Cratylus*, a pioneering analysis of the nature of language, though in the more technical portions of this dialogue he avoids it. The error is forgivable, inasmuch as the invention of the alphabet was probably a prerequisite to the recognition that speech consists of discrete units of sound rather than a continuous flow, so that it came natural for *gramma* to be used for that unit which a "letter" can represent, since it was precisely this representation that led to the perception of the sound-units.

The confusion, which has become habitual, could arise only in the minds of members of a culture which takes literacy for granted. It shows up continually in two areas of modern discussion, dealing respectively with the education of small children and with the difficulties encountered in learning certain foreign languages. A child's capacity to learn to speak is habitually treated as identical with his capacity to read. The basic "learning problem" for children is classified as a reading problem rather than as a problem of oral vocabulary. To quote a recent newspaper article, purporting to cite experts in the field of education: "Four areas of difficulties have been identified: how sensory information is received, how it is put together, how it is stored as memory, and how it is expressed as written or spoken language." To equate written with spoken and to give priority to the written eloquently betrays an unconscious but wholly mistaken notion that the human animal is by nature a reader, or ought to be, and that his language exists primarily for him as it is written down. Among the foreign languages with which an English-speaking individual may be required to cope are those like Arabic or Chinese which are not only foreign but happen to employ a non-alphabetic script. This latter element superimposes a second difficulty upon the initial task of oral mastery of the language, but it is a difficulty which is *sui generis* quite distinct from the linguistic one. But the two difficulties are continually treated as though they were one, as though the Arabic script was an inherent element of the Arabic dialects. The character of the script may indeed have had some effect upon linguistic usage, but only indirectly. Any language owes its basic existence to an arrangement of sounds, not script.

The biological-historical fact is that *homo sapiens* is a species which uses oral speech, manufactured by the mouth, to communicate. That is his definition. He is not, by definition, a writer or reader. His use of speech, I repeat, has been acquired by processes of natural selection operating over a million years. The habit of using written symbols to represent such speech is just a useful trick which has existed over too short a span of time to have been built into our genes, whether or not this may happen half a million years hence. It follows that any language can be transliterated into any system of written symbols that the user of the language may choose without affecting the basic structure of the language. In short, reading man, as opposed to speaking man, is not biologically determined. He wears the appearance of a recent historical accident, and the same can be said of whatever written symbols he may choose to use. This makes for caution in estimating the relationship between script and language. Whatever be the laws of the spoken tongue, it is likely that the writing system, if the tongue is "written down," should have only approximate relevance to those laws. This may be an unpalatable conclusion for scholars who have to work with those inscribed symbols which furnish the only evidence we have for what a given language was or is. To give an example from Greece again: even admitting the standardization of the Greek alphabet which was achieved in the Hellenistic age, we have no real means of knowing how words in Homer were spelled when Homer was first written down, and we can be sure that the orthography, the shapes of the letters used, would show very important variations from Hellenistic and Byzantine scripts. This would make no difference whatever to the expressive meaning of the spoken tongue. Between the measure of what words "say" when they are spoken and their "meaning" when they are written down there will always be a gap of some sort, of varying dimensions, depending on the script used.

The example of Chinese may be thought to constitute an exception to the rule which insists that writing and language represent completely separate functions, and indeed increasing acquaintance in the West with Chinese has encouraged the mental confusion between a language and its script. This is because Chinese script is logographic, that is, a sign represents a whole word, not its phonetic components, and by combining signs into larger units or "characters" individual words can be "hyphenated" so to speak with each other to convey a meaning which each by itself would not convey. Because of this "plus" effect, it is tempting to classify the Chinese system as "ideographic" as though it was being used to symbolize "thoughts" or "concepts" directly. There is a sense in which a word when pronounced becomes an idea, though idealist philosophers would presumably reject such a view with vehemence. The possibility of entertaining it is responsible for much argument between those who insist that Chinese is logographic and those who maintain it is ideographic.

The three points to be emphasized here however are simply these: (i) because of the correspondence between signs and spoken words, taken as wholes, the unwary can be deluded into thinking of the characters as fully "phonetic" in the Greek sense and (*ii*) into thinking that spoken Chinese and the written characters in which it is expressed together constitute two aspects of a single language system; (*iii*) since a sign represents a whole word, and the character a combination of whole words, and since the words of any language are theoretically infinite, it is clear that the Chinese system cannot meet the requirement of economy in the number of signs, a requirement which any system which endeavors to symbolize the phonemes of a language however approximately can readily meet. The net result is that the *average* Chinese, as opposed to the specialist, is limited in the number and variety of statements he can read easily, because his ability to accommodate the shapes of a variety of symbols in his memory is also limited. If the aphorisms of Chairman Mao with their restricted vocabulary and syntax are acceptable to the Chinese masses as a guide to attitude and action, this is precisely because they are both easily read and orally memorizable.

For a literate Chinese to increase his reading vocabulary (using the term "literate" in its Chinese but not its European sense) requires a stringent discipline in, among other things, the memorization of inscribed shapes. Can this be said to have reversed the normal course of evolutionary development? The common conventions of language as encoded in our brain are acoustic, not visual. Man's ability to think is correlated biologically with his ability to speak, and to communicate in oral speech in whatever dialect his language group have chosen to use, that is, to share with each other. Is it even possible that the dominance of Mandarin, which makes unified communication available by nonacoustic means, may have inhibited any tendency to draw the spoken dialects closer to each other, a tendency which alone could furnish China with a spoken *lingua franca*? This may

explain the familiar paradox of a China both highly civilized
and yet curiously "backward" in a very special sense, and
also the continuing difficulties which China is likely to encounter in being "understood" by other cultures. Could it be
argued that if the Chinese revolution seems to be a response
to the needs of rural society, whereas the Russian is an urbanized phenomenon, this difference corresponds to that
which exists between the users of two different forms of
written communication, the one archaic, the other alphabetic? For the purposes of this study, at any rate, the Chinese
script is a historical irrelevance.

In European systems of writing, whether Semitic or Greek,
the letter shapes behave phonetically, and their shape is only
incidental to this function. Yet it has been historically true
that even so, the shapes of letters as they have come into existence have exercised a curious if illogical fascination over
the artistic imagination of the users. Strictly speaking, written orthography should behave solely as the servant of the
spoken tongue, reporting its sounds as accurately and swiftly
as possible. It need not and should not have a nature of its
own, and the Greek system when it was invented seemed to
have conformed to this specification. But, as we shall see,
the artistic fascination of the Chinese with the calligraphy of
the ideogram has had its counterpart in the development of
scripts and their elaboration in European and Arabic countries. This visual development of the written signs has
nothing to do with the purpose of language, namely instantaneous communication between members of a human
group. On the contrary, in Arabic as in Latin, the elaboration of the script as a visual object, carried out in competing
local centers of calligraphy, has narrowed the field of expertise which can recognize and use the script. It is a sign
of the arrival of modern scientific and socialized man that

calligraphy as an art form has largely expired. This is a welcome development. The practice would not have flourished to the degree that it has but for the recurrent tendency to confuse the properties of a language with the properties of its script.

Diverse meanings of the word "write"

The history of writing and the written word is often treated simplistically as though the term "writing" identified a single invention which has operated with more or less uniform effects from ancient Egypt to modern Europe. This reflects that prejudice which would divide all history into two epochs, the illiterate and the literate. In fact, the term "writing" describes a series of technological devices which, regardless of the varying instruments and materials used to write with or on, have been historically distinguishable by their widely varying capacity to perform their basic function: namely, to assist the user in an act of recognition. The visual experience of a given inscribed shape or sign was originally used to connect with and to trigger a "thought" which somehow "belongs" to the shape or "goes with it." Such use of markings on stone or bone would appear to go far back into prehistory, especially if the so-called art of the cave dwellers be regarded as a form of writing. Markings on bone of very great antiquity have been interpreted by archaeologists to denote the passage of time as measured by the phases of the moon. The later use of writing on a systematic scale seems to have originated at those sites of human settlement where society first became urbanized, creating a social situation which can be interpreted as requiring some more sophisticated method of recording information than was available in oral speech. The date for such a development, so far as at present ascertained by artifacts uncovered by the spade, would be around the fourth millennium before Christ, and it seems to have occurred in the deltas of Egypt and Mesopotamia, and perhaps, though not certainly, somewhat later in the valley of the Indus, as well as in those areas of the Near East which are intermediate between Mesopotamia and India. Did it occur in all these places independently? Argument over the possible interconnection between the Egyptian and the Mesopotamian systems of writing is inconclusive.

In their very earliest forms these systems do not belong in our present account. Their examination may even furnish distraction. For in the beginning they were used to symbolize three different psychological operations: first, counting up and comparing quantities; second, observing physical objects as such in the external world; third, the act of naming these objects and the art of relating names and therefore objects to each other. The shapes were used to symbolize these mental acts directly. They went straight to the psychological processes inside the brain. In a sense they were too ambitious. They were not content to deal solely with phonetics. Finally came the systems that sought only this limited aim, of "copying" linguistic noises. It is with the last, and only this last, that our examination of literacy is concerned. All systems which use scratching or drawing or painting to think with or feel with are irrelevant, though they have had long histories. A successful or developed writing system is one which does not think at all. It should be the purely passive instrument of the spoken word even if, to use a paradox, the word is spoken silently.

To speak therefore of writing in the abstract, or attempt to discuss it as a general phenomenon, is a mistake. There are only specific systems of writing, each of which has its own specific effect within a particular social system.

The priority of reading over writing
Oral speech and written word are both acts, or represent acts, which seek to communicate. But the essential act of communication does not take place unless the speech is heard and the writing is read. The operation is completed only in the act of sharing between two or more persons, in which one vocalizes or inscribes and the other receives and recognizes the effect produced. Sometimes it is necessary to state the obvious, especially in tackling the concept and problems of literacy. For whereas historians who have touched upon literacy as a historical phenomenon have commonly measured its progress in terms of the history of writing, the actual conditions of literacy depend upon the history not of writing but of reading. In dealing with the past, it is obviously much harder to be certain about the practice of reading, its conduct and extent, than about writing. For the latter can simply exist in an artifact, whatever its use or application may have been. In antiquity this existence is measurable by records inscribed on stone or clay, with a meager supplement from Egypt provided by both wrappings and papyrus fragments. From the late Middle Ages the documentation provided by perishable materials, parchment and paper, takes over in quantity. But reading is an activity, not a material artifact, which is why scholarship has paid relatively little attention to the presence or extent of reading in historical cultures. An inscriber or "writer" can imprint on a material marks which are not intended for communication at all. The activity can be solipsist, as in the case of children who will write "letters" to themselves in imitation of adult practice in shapes that only they can decipher. For an adult, inscription can serve solely as a self-reminder. He can scan the marks he has made to refresh his own memory before communicating orally

with someone else. This admittedly is an extreme situation, though in my opinion some ancient writing, so-called, is nothing more than this. But once we consider the theoretic possibility of the solipsist use of writing and theoretically extend its boundaries, we begin to realize that whereas the use of writing for solitary recognition represents a rare and untypical practice, it cannot have been at all rare or untypical for the recognition of writing to be shared by a comparatively few persons. The systems current before the Greek alphabet were all in various measure restricted in their circulation. They were practiced by experts or elites for reading by experts or elites, serving as reminders, as mnemonic devices for recapitulating bodies of information or belief which for whatever reason it was desirable to preserve in this form. Argument to support this conclusion can be postponed. I state it now only to illuminate the truth that literacy cannot be defined as coterminous with the historical existence of writing in Egypt or Mesopotamia or Mycenae or Greece. Literacy, though dependent on the technology employed in inscription, is not to be defined by the simple existence of that technology. It is a social condition which can be defined only in terms of readership.

If readership is not a phenomenon easily amenable to examination and measurement, the fact should not be used as an excuse for ignoring it. If evidences are available at all, they are indirect, to be gathered by inference. In the case of the Greeks, they can be supplied by some references in literature which are incidental, some usages in inscriptions which permit inference as to the public that was expected to read the inscription, and some portrayals in art, which usually, however, portray recitation and very rarely portray reading. The truth is that the act of reading passes virtually unnoticed by the authors and artists of any culture where reading occurs. The same is not true of oratory, or music, or playing games, or fighting, or eating, or running, or even sleeping or dying. Of all the activities of mankind which we now take to be ordinary, reading is historically the one which is most sparsely recorded. But we know it goes on now and that it went on in antiquity, but to what extent, and under what conditions?

These difficulties in providing precise answers should not withhold us from establishing certain propositions which are axiomatic, and upon which any consideration of literacy should base itself. Whereas we can apply the term "literate" to an individual, its operative meaning derives from the fact that his literacy is shared by a given number of people, all of whom are readers; not only do he and his fellows exercise a common skill employed upon a common material, but in exercising it they place themselves in automatic communication with each other. First, he is literate in so far as he reads documents and also does so as a matter of habit, not painfully deciphering them, but fluently and rapidly recognizing what has been written. Second, this body of writing would not exist for him to be read if it had not been composed for others to read as well. A Robinson Crusoe could theoretically step onto his island equipped with a small library to refresh his solitude, but this artifact could never have come into existence for him alone. Its "authors" had created it solely in the expectation of its use by a reading public.

It is the numerical ratio of this reading public to the total population using the spoken tongue which determines the degree to which "literacy" and the "literate man" have come into existence at any given historical moment. In short, literacy is not a term with a single determinant; to take on meaning, it has to be qualified quantitatively to indicate the extent of the readership within which the individual act of

reading takes place. In the cultures that immediately preceded the Greek, if I may anticipate, the limitations enforced
on readership require us to speak of pre-Greek literacy as
craft literacy. When Greece acquired her own writing system
after 700 B.C., superior as it was to previous systems, the
term craft-literate should still be applied to her culture for
at least a century and a half after this date. Thereafter the
increasingly rapid extension of reading habits in the late
sixth and fifth centuries permits us to describe periods of
semi-literacy, of recitation literacy, and finally of scriptorial
literacy, achieved as Hellenic culture extended itself over
the Mediterranean world at the beginning of the fourth
century. Waiting in history's anteroom there was still typo-
graphical literacy, dependent upon the invention of movable
types, and it should be noted that in the intervening centuries, after the fall of Rome, most of Europe reverted to
what in effect was a period of craft literacy employed by
clerics. The same was to hold true in the Eastern Empire
when conquered by the Turkish language and script.

1. See also the discussion in E. A. Havelock, "Prologue to Greek Literacy," in *Lectures in Memory of Louise Taft Semple*, University of Cincinnati Classical Studies, vol. 2 (University of Oklahoma Press, 1973),
pp. 347–348.
2. G. S. Kirk, *Songs of Homer* (Cambridge University Press, 1963), p.
49.
3. Cf. Havelock, loc. cit.
4. For the contrary view see F. D. Harvey, "Literacy in the Athenian
Democracy," *Revue des Etudes Greques*, 29 (1966) : 585–635.

The Pre-Greek
Syllabaries

The more readers in ratio to the population, the more literate a given population becomes. This quantitative conception once proposed seems obvious and easy to accept. What is not so obvious is that the quantitative dimension is likely to depend historically upon qualitative factors, namely the efficiency of the script used. What do we mean here by "efficiency"?

The act of recognition
Reading, to repeat, is an act of recognition whereby inscribed shapes are matched against their agreed counterparts. In phonetic reading, these counterparts are elements of sound usually meaningless in themselves, though the brain of him who is visually scanning the script recollects them as elements of language. If this procedure, for whatever reason, is so arranged that it is rather complex and difficult, it will remain in the status of a craft, a special skill. Decipherment is the word we would then apply to the act of reading. If the procedure becomes easy and swift, not requiring specialized attention and time, then it can cease to be a craft and is available to the common reader to practice.

What are the required qualities in a script which will produce this result?

The conditions to be met are ideally three, each distinct from the other. First, the coverage of linguistic sound offered by the writing system should be exhaustive. The visible shapes (I avoid here the term "letters" because of its association with the uniquely Greek invention) must be sufficient in number or character to trigger the reader's memory of all sounds of the language which are distinctive in the language. Conveniently, these noises can be reduced in any language to a given number and identified by the modern term "phoneme." Ideally there should be no exceptions to be supplied by guesswork from context.

Second, this function should be performed unambiguously. That is to say, any one shape or combination of shapes must trigger the memory of one and only one phoneme. Again speaking from an ideal standpoint, there should be no room for a requirement imposed upon the reader to make choices in his attempt to recognize the sound represented.

Third, the total number of shapes must be held to a strict limit to avoid overburdening the memory with the task of mastering a large list of them before the process of recognition, that is of reading, can even begin. It is to be remembered that it is not enough for the brain to catalogue the shapes with precision. It is also required to associate them with a corresponding series of sounds and to be prepared to recognize the connection not in the tidy, constant sequence of the letters of a memorized alphabet, an "abecedarium," but in the thousand eccentric combinations which make up words and sentences. The brain has been biologically encoded to contain a memory of these varieties as they occur acoustically in a spoken tongue. It has not been encoded to manage a corresponding variety of shapes.

The fewer the shapes, the less is the burden on the brain to memorize them. To be sure, the trained memory can accommodate a very large number, as the example of Chinese illustrates. But the history of human cultures since the introduction of writing encourages the empirical conclusion that the degree of participation by a given population in the skill of reading (referring this degree not only to actual numbers who read at all, but to the variety of the material read) varies in inverse proportion to the number of signs employed; and that a number between twenty and thirty has in fact proved to be the "ideal" number for the "democratization" of reading. This number however may bear some relation to the fact that the phonemes of Indo-European lie within these limits.

When and only when this last requirement is met can a fourth and final condition of literacy come within reach. This occurs when a system of instruction is devised to impose the habit of recognition upon the brain before it has fully concluded its growth; that is, in its developmental stage before puberty. More precisely, the habit must be formed in that period when the brain is still engaged in the task of acquiring the oral language code for which it is biologically equipped. It would appear that the two codes necessary for speaking and then for reading have to meld together at a time when mental resources are still in a plastic condition — to use a loosely conceived but convenient image — so that the act of reading is converted into an unconscious reflex. In short, a population is rendered literate when an educational apparatus can be brought into being which is able to teach reading to very young children before they have been introduced to other skills. The adult who learns to read after his oral vocabulary is completed rarely if ever becomes as fluent.

Alphabet versus syllabary

To meet these three qualitative conditions simultaneously in a linguistic sign system has proved extraordinarily difficult for mankind and indeed was achieved only after 700 B.C. and only in Greece. The instrument provided was the Greek alphabet, and in the following pages the term "alphabet" will be restricted to this invention. A wider application of the word is, however, very common. The Phoenician system, for example, which immediately preceded the Greek and from which the Greek borrowed many of its letters, is commonly identified as an "alphabet." The Phoenician script, in turn, can be demonstrated to be one variety of the Northwestern Semitic systems of script invented in the second millennium before Christ. This has encouraged the notion that these also were "alphabets." The basis of the claim rests simply on the fact that these systems were the first to cut down the number of signs to twenty-two, regardless of their ability, or rather, lack of ability, to symbolize phonemes accurately.

This claim for them is made and can be seen fully operative in a two-volume work on the alphabet, wholly uncritical but lavishly illustrated, which has circulated in the United States in a revised and enlarged edition since 1965. The author David Diringer describes his subject in a subtitle as "A Key to the History of Mankind." After devoting Part One of this work to the identification of non-alphabetic systems of writing, the author, without apology or explanation, launches what he calls the "alphabet" into history with the following statement, delivered, as it were, *ex cathedra*: "Anyone wishing to study the history of the alphabet must take as the starting point the earliest known inscriptions written in the fully developed system which we know as the North Semitic alphabet. In our present state of knowledge only this can be considered the true ancestor of the alphabet." If this alleged system was "fully developed," one may well ask why it is also described as merely the "ancestor of the alphabet." The two statements seem contradictory, and the author likewise is forced to remark somewhat ruefully that the term "alphabet" did not come into existence until the Christian era. What the author regards as the "decisive achievement" of the North Semitic system was in his words "not the creation of signs. It lies in the adoption of a purely alphabetic system which denoted each sound by one sign only." This confused and tendentious statement exactly reverses the truth. It was the previous syllabic systems which had at least tried to denote "each sound by one sign only." This got them into trouble through the multiplication of signs. The Semitic script simply cut the number of signs drastically to twenty-two at the price of assigning one sign to several linguistic sounds and throwing the responsibility for the correct choice upon the reader. As we shall see, it was only the Greek system that was to solve this crucial problem of ambiguity. As if to confess the muddle that he has got into by committing himself to such a statement, the author on the next page feels compelled to explain and define the supposed Semitic "alphabet" in terms which are Greek, namely *grammata* (letters) and *stoicheia* (elements) and *syllabai* (syllables).[7] None of these came into existence for at least a thousand years after the supposed invention that Mr. Diringer is describing, nor could they have existed until the Greek system had become current, for they analytically seek to define the components of that system, namely a true alphabet.

Stanley Morison, that authority on the European alphabetic scripts, written and printed, in his Lyell lectures on "Politics and Script" delivered at Oxford in 1957 put the matter correctly when he said: "To scrutinize Western script . . . it must first be observed that the letters we now use are an inheritance which originated in Greece some twenty-five centuries ago . . . secondly, that these were appropriated by Rome two or three centuries later. If the print before the reader needs to be thought of in accurate terms it is correct to say that it is a composition using the 'Graeco-Roman' alphabet."

A reviewer in the *Times Literary Supplement* of September 1, 1972, perhaps in debt to Mr. Diringer, sought to put Mr. Morison right. "In fact the alphabet was created centuries earlier in the second half of the second millennium B.C. by the Northwest Semites and was adopted by the Greeks about 1000 B.C. and passed to the Romans through the Etruscans. So if the print now before the reader really needs to be thought of in accurate terms it is correct to say that it is a composition using not the Graeco-Roman but the Northwest Semitic Graeco-Roman-Etruscan alphabet."

It was not however Morison who stood in need of correction, but his reviewer, who, wishing to give the term "alphabet" such an extended application, in effect sought to perpetuate a notion as widespread as it is erroneous. The reader in search of expertise in this crucial problem surrounding the history of scripts is better advised to consult I. J. Gelb, who in his *Study of Writing*[8] would identify all North Semitic systems as syllabaries, in contradistinction to the true Greek alphabet.

The Greek system was a true alphabet because it was the first and only system to achieve concurrently the three conditions for reading that I have previously analyzed. How did it manage to do this? As I have said, the difficulty of the achievement for the human mind is indicated by the lateness of the date of the invention. The very long history of writing that precedes the Greek alphabet demonstrates a series of trial and error attempts to manage what proved for millennia to be unmanageable. This previous series includes the Phoenician system, of which so much has been made, and indeed all the so-called North Semitic scripts from which Persian, Sanscrit, Aramaic, Hebrew, and Arabic have descended. The technological gulf that intervenes between all of these systems and the Greek cannot be overemphasized. That is why a restrictive term is essential to describe the Greek accomplishment, and since the word "alphabet" is simply shorthand Greek for the names of the first two letters of the Greek system, it seems wholly appropriate that this Greek term should be reserved to describe the Greek system and its descendants as these have been used in Western Europe, Russia, and America.

The Phoenician, on the contrary, has been well described as an "unvocalized syllabary," as also were its kindred, the North Semitic systems.[9] The psychological "pressure" (if that is the best word) in favor of recognizing the presence of vocalization made itself felt even in these systems, but sporadically, as when they made room for some partial representation of vowels. The majority of the cuneiform writings, in which the so-called "literatures" of the Near East are inscribed, were fully vocalized syllabaries, as is the so-called Linear B (if its decipherment holds up) used by the Cretans and the Mycenaeans. So also is modern Japanese script, apparently devised in complete independence of antique models.

The understandable but crucial difficulty encountered by man in successfully symbolizing linguistic sound for reading purposes becomes explicable when the technology of the syllabary is compared with that of the Greek alphabet. The technology of the syllabary itself proceeds through two stages, the earlier being exhibited in the cuneiform and the later in the Northwest Semitic. If we keep steadily before our minds the fact that a language consists of sounds, not symbols or letters, and then reflect how these sounds are actually made, we can perceive that the basic elements of a language as it is pronounced — the linguistic noises so to speak — are formed by combining two physical operations. There is the vibration of a column of air in the larynx or nasal cavity as it is expelled past the vocal chords and modified by them, and there are the controls, restrictions, and releases imposed upon this vibration by the interaction of the tongue, teeth, palate, lips, and nose. The vibration by itself can produce a continuous sound which is modifiable simply by altering the shape of the mouth. These modified vibrations we call vowels. The rest of the physical equipment can also be used, to start the vibration or to stop it, or to do both. When this occurs, the representation of the start or stop is called a consonant. Although both "vowel" and "consonant" seek to describe sounds, they were coined only after the Greek alphabet made these sounds "visually" recognizable as "letters," and strictly speaking vowel and consonant, though derived from the Latin, denote types of letters of the Greek alphabet.

The more exact terminology of linguistic science, remaining faithful to the oral character of language, identifies the theoretic units of a spoken tongue as phonemes, meaning the minimal acoustic constituents distinctive from each other out of which a given tongue is constructed. We can say that the Greek system, by "atomizing" linguistic sound into theoretic components, approached a system which aimed in principle at identifying phonemes, though with only relative success.

The syllabaries on the other hand are so called because they seek to represent syllables, which again is a confusing term, so far as it purports to describe a given type of linguistic noise but in fact describes a combination of written letters which represent this noise. The type consists of a vowel started and/or stopped by a consonant or consonants. It is therefore in one sense phonetic, but the phonetic analysis has not been carried far enough.

Yet it is more empirically based than any true alphabetic system, for what it tries to do is to represent without too much ambiguity units of speech as they seem actually to issue from the mouth in what we call "syllables." The syllables into which a spoken tongue can be divided are far more numerous than are the ultimate units of linguistic sound; and moreover, a syllable can embrace two and sometimes three consonant noises occurring together, as tongue, palate, and teeth combine in a joint movement. The syllabary by insisting that a written symbol represent a single consonant plus a vowel gets into immediate trouble in representing combinations which do not fit this pattern, as for example the first word of the Odyssey, *andra*.

In sum, the syllabic system builds itself on the principle of symbolizing each of the separate sounds in a given language which are actually pronounceable. Its theoretical objective is to represent these visually on a one-to-one basis. The result could be a sign system which might run into hundreds. This can be done, and the resulting shapes can be memorized, but the pressure on the brain to cut down the number is very great. The reason for this may lie in the complex nature of the psychology that is employed in the act of reading and which I have earlier sought to analyze. If I may repeat what has been said, the brain's memory, built by natural selection, is encoded to hold an enormous variety of acoustic units and combinations thereof. It is not encoded to hold anything like a corresponding variety of visual shapes, and so the procedure of matching shape with sound requires very great effort, which can be mitigated only by visual economy, by cutting down drastically the number of shapes that require to be held in the memory. But in the case of the syllabaries as the process of economy is pursued, the range of ambiguity of recognition is inevitably extended. One sign has to represent several sounds and the open choices left to the reader, which are acoustic, become extensive. The attempt to transliterate the language from sound into shape has partially broken down.

The Greek alphabet dissolves the syllable into its acoustic components — we might almost say its biological components in so far as these are actually effects produced by movements of different parts of the human body. It therefore scrapped the syllable as a graphic unit and substituted a quite different type of unit, essentially theoretical. Looked at in this way, the Greek invention looks like a quantum jump. But this is misleading. The jump occurred in two steps, one of which was supplied by Phoenician, the chief representative of that family of scripts known as Northwest Semitic. In Phoenician, the syllable has been retained in thought as the ultimate unit of speech, which it is not. But it has been realized that syllables fall into "sets" which can be grouped according to a common feature, namely the consonantal noise which starts them off. That is to say, Phoenician grasps the principle that "ba be bi bo bu" constitutes a set of "b" syllables. Previous syllabaries would have used five unrelated signs for these five sounds. Phoenician uses one, the consonantal "index" of the set. In a sense therefore Phoenician prepares the way for the recognition of the consonant as a theoretically separate element of speech, and the system is able to reduce the number of signs used to something over twenty, and this is why it is often hailed as an "alphabet." But its obvious drawbacks are: (*i*) it is less flexible than the Greek system, being designed to index only syllables beginning with a consonant; (*ii*) it is much more ambiguous, since it requires the reader to infer whether vocalization has to be supplied and if so how much. The Greek word *andra* again offers a case in point; it is as intractable for Phoenician as for syllabic script. It should also be remembered that the syllabaries had carried analysis far enough to identify the vowels as separable components of speech, treating them as syllables to be included in the sum of consonantal syllables. The Phoenician and its descendants, the Aramaic and Hebrew scripts, abandoned this discovery, only to be forced to reintroduce it later, but in a very limited way as a kind of supplement. The grammar of Semitic tongues, it is claimed, makes it relatively easy for the reader to make the correct guesses. There is however the possibility that if a script is inherently ambiguous, this may encourage the users insensibly to simplify the grammar of what they wish to say. However that may be, the margin of guesswork was wide enough, as is seen by subsequent attempts to supply vocalizations, like using the letter jod for the vowel *i*, and vau for *u*. In short, non-vocalized syllabaries require a little more effort, a little more time, on the part of the reader who deciphers accurately, than does the Greek system. To that extent, even at their best they are less efficient reading instruments.

Literacy and literature

However, they are also forced to operate under a limitation much more severe than this, which has not received the attention it deserves hitherto from scholars or laymen alike. In all documentation which is pre-alphabetic the speed with which the correct guesses and choices are made by the reader is governed by a factor of familiarity with the material which he is expected to read. The content of what is placed in the script requires to be governed by his previous expectations. The translated versions of Egyptian and Near Eastern texts that are available are commonly described as "literatures." A term originally applied to describe the written products of alphabetic literacy is transferred backward to the products of pre-alphabetic cultures. Is this a proper application of the word, or rather one more instance of the intellectual confusion which has intruded into all consideration of writing and its relation to reading?

If a speaker be imagined as the voice behind a given pre-alphabetic script, he is required to address to the reader such statements and sentiments as fall into an idiom easily recognizable. They will tend to partake of the formulaic, and this is as true of a modern Hebrew or Arabic newspaper as of the Old Testament even if the modern equivalent of the ancient formula becomes a slogan. One can state a general law which governs the operation of all types of script as follows: the range of ambiguity in decipherment stands in inverse ratio to the range of possible coverage supplied by the content. If you want your reader to recognize what you intend to say, then you cannot say anything and everything you might want to. You must fit your intended meanings to meanings that he will be prepared to accept. The specific effects of this will register themselves in an unconscious limitation imposed upon vocabulary and upon syntactical arrangement of vocabulary and upon the subjects treated in the vocabulary. The written language, in short, will fail to exhibit the full possibilities of the spoken tongue. Ambiguity being inevitable, it is better to minimize it by minimizing the possible expectations of the reader, so that he can slide as it were into well-tried themes.

To illustrate these conditions in actual operation we need only turn to the so-called literatures of the ancient Near East as they have been translated for us. We have first to discount the inevitable tendency of the modern translator to over-translate his original, relieving its verbal repetitions, for example, by variation, and removing ambiguities by using his version to impose a single choice among many possible ones. But even so, we gain an overall impression that we are being asked to read a rather formalized version of what went on, what people actually said and did and believed. A few central stories, legends or myths recur, usually focused upon the careers of a limited number of persons. Story and person alike have become familiar in retelling. Rituals in regular use are described, parables and proverbs abound. But when all allowance is made for simple grandeur of conception or refinement of design, the basic complexity of human experience is not there. The full report of oral utterance is missing; we are being treated to an authorized version. It is no doubt the very virtues inherent in these limitations, namely, a certain monumentality of composition and simplicity of style, which tempt scholars to describe many of these works as "literary masterpieces." But they are not literature in the Graeco-Roman sense. Even the tales of common life which can be found in these collections avoid the eccentricities of specific detail in their descriptions. They tend to deal with action and thought in typical situations and use a style which is formulaic and repetitive. One need only compare what is narrated in the so-called Epic of Gilgamesh with what is narrated in Homer, or, for that matter, expounded in Hesiod, to realize the difference.

The common reader can test this evaluation for himself by taking up the Old Testament. The older parts of this compendium were inscribed and so preserved in a version of the Phoenician shorthand syllabary. To be sure, some theological editing of these records occurred in the period after the Second Temple was founded, which restricted the realism of the original narratives. But even allowing for this, it remains true that these originals and their surrounding sentiments are syntactically repetitive, that typical situations recur, that the relationships between the characters are relatively simple and their acts take on an almost ritual quality. We feel the simple rhythm of the record as it unfolds. It is precisely these limitations imposed upon the possible coverage of human experience that give to the Old Testament its power of appeal, as we say, to "simple people."

The record of a culture which is composed under these restrictions is likely to center upon religion and myth, for these tend to codify and standardize the variety of human experience so that the reader of such scripts is more likely to recognize what the writer is talking about. It is therefore no accident that the cultures of the Near East which preceded the Greek and are recorded in hieroglyph, cuneiform, or Semitic shorthand, seem on the basis of the record to be peculiarly occupied with such matters. We normally take it for granted that such preoccupation was an inherent characteristic of these cultures, and it is often put down to the fact that they were at a more "primitive" stage of development. The reason I am suggesting is rather to be sought in a fact of technology. If it is tempting for modern research to discover archetypal myths in these so-called literatures, may this not reflect the fact that the original transcribers, given the limitations of the medium they were using, found it equally tempting to confine themselves to archetypes, to gain assurance that they would be read easily and correctly?

To enter the world of what we call "Greek literature," from Homer on, is to encounter a larger dimension of human experience, so much more diverse, personal, critical, subtle, humorous, passionate, ironic, and reflective. This remains true even when all allowance is made for the limitations imposed by the oral poetic form in which so much of this literature is cast. If we ask ourselves the reason why this may be so we usually look for the answer in what is assumed, perhaps unconsciously, to be a racial superiority. The Greek genes conferred upon the adult Greek a better equipment with which to achieve creative effort in art and intellect. But I doubt whether such a racial hypothesis has any more scientific foundation when applied to the Greeks than it has had when applied to the Germans. If the clue to the selectivity of content found in Near Eastern texts resides in the nature of their orthography, may it be true that the comparatively greater richness of content in Greek texts is correspondingly due to the superior technical resources of Greek orthography?

The control of technology over content
It may be objected that to ask this question at all brings one closer to accepting that modern doctrine or slogan which states that "the medium is the message." Though coined to apply to electronic and audio-visual means of communication recently invented, there is indeed some truth in the dictum as it can be applied backwards to the medium of script. The coverage and content of the message depends upon the efficiency of the script used, and efficiency is measured by accuracy and speed in the act of recognizing or as we say "reading" what the script intends to "say."

There is a further element of control likely to intrude into the content of all pre-alphabetic scripts, one which operated independently of writing. Not only was the content required to be limited and familiar. To meet this requirement it was likely to have been put together orally before being inscribed, and put together according to the laws of composition which would tend to preserve the statement in its oral form. These laws are rhythmic. Orally preserved statement has to be "poetized statement." It is scarcely to be doubted that the older portions of the Old Testament were in their original version poetic and the same would hold true of the Near Eastern literatures. The inscribed versions that we have are often summaries or paraphrases. Rhythmic speech has its own limitations of idiom and statement as opposed to what we call prose, but that is not to suggest that pre-alphabetic texts are limited simply because their genius is poetic. The documents we identify as Homeric epic or Greek drama, for example, are poetic, but their coverage of human experience is much more extensive, analytical, and varied. The scripts of the Near East had to be cut down to the coverage of their own oral poetry, but of this poetry itself they offer what I have called an authorized version essentially simplified, not the original epics, nor the songs of the people, not the full record of their hopes, fears, aspirations, and emotions. Ambiguities of the script, in short, would be bound to encourage a selectivity practiced at the expense of the oral originals, one which concentrated upon central facts and sentiments at the expense of the more unique, eccentric, and we might say the more personal element in the oral repertoire. The former were more easily accommodated to or matched with the script, the latter more difficult to document adequately and more difficult to recognize when documented. Syllabic scripts in this way produced paraphrases of oral originals rather than the originals themselves, with some tendency to standardize syntax and vocabulary. In short, they supplied overall a simplified orthodoxy of statement and acceptability of narrative readily recognizable and easily deciphered by those skilled in using the system.

Expected and recognizable discourse becomes highly traditional both in form and content. Such traditionalism is characteristic of a craft, the secrets of which are carefully nurtured by its practitioners. The scribes who used these syllabaries were practitioners of this sort. The so-called literacy that they represented was craft literacy. The scripts were readable by elites. This was true of the so-called alphabets of the North Semitic systems no less than of the previous syllabic systems. For in North Semitic the task of expertise became not memorization of a large number of signs, but interpretation of a smaller number now offered to the reader. Given the range of possible ambiguity, the interpreter had to be prepared to pronounce what the script might say and this gave him and his peers authority to dictate the interpretation. The "scribe" of the time of Christ was still the required and recognized exponent of scripture, because the script used was precisely of that kind which required the services of an interpreter. That is to say, the Palestinian culture, even at that date, was according to our previous definition only craft-literate. As for the parables and sayings which constitute the bulk of the teaching of the three synoptic Gospels, their Aramaic originals were cast in oral form to be addressed to audiences who did not read but listened and memorized and orally repeated what they had heard. In this strictly technological sense the three gospels are "Homeric." Meanwhile the expert who was reading in the synagogue from the books of the law addressed himself to a script which required a series of choices basically acoustic in nature but which would, however, reflect mental decisions as to what the text ought to mean. Scholars of the Old Testament have pointed out how in the period of stabilization and canonization of the text there was room for scribes to interpret the unvocalized script in different ways according to their theological inclinations. Once a given reading became orthodox, the need to guard it against alteration stimulated the production of commentaries. One of the reasons for the lore and learning which has accumulated round the books of the Judaic law lies in the original ambiguities of the script.

7. David Diringer, *The Alphabet: A Key to the History of Mankind*, 3d ed., vol. 1 (Funk and Wagnalls, 1968), pp. 160–165.

8. I. J. Gelb, *Study of Writing*, rev. ed. (University of Chicago Press, 1963).

9. Gelb, op. cit., pp. 147ff.

The Greek Alphabet

We recall the three theoretic requirements for a true alphabet to be met concurrently in the same system. First, coverage of all the phonemes in the language is to be exhaustive, second, the letter shapes are to be restricted to between twenty and thirty, and third, individual shapes are not asked to perform double or triple duty. Their acoustic identities must be fixed and unchanging.

The pre-Semitic syllabaries tried to achieve the first of these, but the nearer they came to success by multiplying the syllabic signs the further they removed themselves from the second requirement. The Semitic unvocalized syllabaries met the second requirement at the cost of abandoning the third. The Greek met all three, but how did it do it?

The problem, we remind ourselves, is both visual and acoustic: the sense perception is visual but the triggered memory is acoustic. The solutions available can be illustrated by a linguistic-visual model of the simplest sort. Let us take the nursery rhyme "Jack and Jill went up the hill, etc." The problem begins at once with the first three words. How are they to be transcribed? The fact that they use the phonemes of English rather than of Assyrian or Phoenician makes no theoretic difference to the problem. First, we convert the arbitrariness of the English spelling to get the true alphabetic transcription:

JAK AND JIL   (Example 1)

This consists of a total of nine signs, of which seven are unique. They yield instant recognition of the correct linguistic noises to anyone who has mastered this particular alphabet, that is, has been trained to "read," as we say.

How would a syllabary transcribe these sounds? It would do it only with overkill, so to speak. Let us choose for convenience a syllabary which tries to index all possible "open" syllables of the language, as many syllabaries do.

JA and JI would offer no difficulty. They would be represented by two different syllabic signs. Let us make them up as

ЈА and **ЈІ**

Let us also allow our syllabary to have signs for vowels, as is claimed to be true of Greek Linear B.

Then the A of AND will give us no trouble.

For the rest, that is the terminal consonantal stops and the double consonants, the syllabary could only supply more than is needed — excess sound, so to speak, since every sign in the system contains a vowel. Let us assume that when this occurs the vocalic type that is chosen will be that which repeats the vowel of the previous syllable, so that K in this instance will be represented by the sign for the sound KA, N by NA, D by DA, and L by LI.

These will all possess their separate symbols in the syllabary. Let us make them up as

KA NA DA LI

The whole phrase would then read as follows:

ЈА КА А ИА ФА ЈΙ Ц (Example 2)

A total of seven signs, all unique.

The Semitic system then takes over and cuts the whole thing down to

J K N D J L (Example 3)

Only six letters, of which five are unique.

It is obvious that Example 3 is the most economical in terms of the amount of writing involved, and thus easy to see how such a system tempts its interpreters to hail it as the great alphabetic breakthrough. But it is equally obvious that neither Example 2 nor 3 will yield instantaneous recognition of the linguistic sounds of the oral original. How then can they be read? The answer lies in the familiarity of the original linguistic statement; its rhythm and rhyme is there at the back of our memory and once we get used to handling an unvocalized system like the Semitic its six consonants will ring a bell in our acoustic memory and we supply the missing vocalics in Example 3. More laboriously, as we work on Example 2, we will be encouraged to recall the same rhythm and so discard the redundant vocalics. Both systems design themselves to fit the task of triggering memory not merely of sounds but of whole meanings, arrangements of sounds that are previously known and recognizable.

Why is JAK AND JIL so superior a vehicle of recognition? So superior as to be a revolutionary invention? We note first that it is the least economical of the three, employing a total of nine signs to trigger the correct acoustic memory as against seven and six in its earlier rivals. If we were to continue the transcription of the line through "went up the hill" etc., we would find this disparity increasing. The actual number of signs used per word would continue to increase over both Examples 2 and 3. Number 2 would include an increasing number of *unique* signs, however, requiring separate cataloguing in the memory. Numbers 1 and 3 would keep repeating a restricted stock.

In Example 1 something important has happened. What is it? The usual answer given is that the Greek system invented signs for the five vowels. But this cannot be the real answer. Example 2 can index vowels as well as vowels in combination with consonants. Indeed as a system it is very fully vocalized. The real answer begins to emerge when we ask the further question: why do the imperfect systems, numbers 2 and 3, use fewer signs than the perfect one to index the same number of phonemes? The answer to this one is that they assign or attempt to assign one symbol and only one to each phoneme; that is, the linguistic units of the spoken language are indexed as it were or copied empirically on a one-to-one basis. Example 3, even though it is in shorthand, essentially retains this intention but the intention is most evident in Example 2. The technique of Example 1, however, calls our attention to the basic analysis of what a linguistic unit is, namely, a vibrating column of air which is also started or stopped, or both started and stopped, as in the word "JAK," by the action of lips, palate, tongue, and teeth. It is the combination of these two physical acts which constitutes an actual linguistic unit, that is, an actual noise which can be made separately from other noises. The starts and the stops created by the action of the lips and so forth, which we think of as "consonants," can by themselves produce no sounds at all. A consonant is a non-sound and was correctly so designated over two thousand years ago by Plato. The pre-Greek systems set out to imitate language as it is spoken in these syllabic units. The Greek system took a leap beyond language and beyond empiricism. It conceived the

notion of analyzing the linguistic unit into its two theoretic
components, the vibrating column of air and the mouth
action imposed upon this vibration. The former could exist
by itself in language, as in exclamations like "Ah." The
latter could not. It was therefore an abstraction, a non-
sound, an idea in the mind. The Greek system proceeded to
isolate this non-sound and give it its own conceptual identity,
in the form of what we call a "consonant."

Once achieved, this step led automatically to the principle
that any given linguistic unit except an isolated vocalic
requires at least two and possibly three or four signs for effective symbolization, and that is why Example 1 uses more
signs than its rivals. Whereas all syllabic systems, including
the Semitic shorthand, aim to reproduce the actual spoken
units on a one-for-one basis, the Greek produces an atomic
system which breaks up all units into at least two abstract
components and possibly more. Now, since the number and
variety of vibrations is limited and the variety of starts and
stops is also strictly limited in any language, the resultant
system, while less economical in a mere quantitative sense
than the Semitic one, could provide a complete coverage of
all possible phonemes while keeping the required letter signs
under a total of thirty. A combination of two to five of these,
forming diphthongs and double consonants, could identify
with precision any linguistic noise that the mouth chose to
make.

The Greeks themselves perceived that the twenty-three or
so signs of their own invention now furnished a table of
elements of linguistic sound, and accordingly when their
philosophers later came to propose an atomic theory of
matter, thus explaining the variety of physical phenomena
as the result of a combination of a finite number of primary
elements, they saw the analogy with what the alphabet had

done to language and likened their atoms to letters. The consonant represented an object of thought, not sense, just as the atom did to those who first proposed its existence. The one was invisible and the other we might say inaudible, although this is an exaggeration. More strictly, some like the "s" sound can be prolonged and so are "semi-pronounceable," others are unpronounceable except with the assistance of vocalization. Hence the original Greek term *aphona* — "voiceless elements" — used by Plato was later replaced by a more accurate classification into *hemiphona* — "semisonants" — and *sumphona* — "con-sonants," elements voiced "in company." Atomism and the alphabet alike were theoretic constructs, manifestations of a capacity for abstract analysis, an ability to translate objects of perception into mental entities, which seems to have been one of the hallmarks of the way the Greek mind worked.

The results of the invention

The introduction of the Greek letters into inscription somewhere about 700 B.C. was to alter the character of human culture, placing a gulf between all alphabetic societies and their precursors. The Greeks did not just invent an alphabet; they invented literacy and the literate basis of modern thought. Under modern conditions there seems to be only a short time lag between the invention of a device and its full social or industrial application, and we have got used to this idea as a fact of technology. This was not true of the alphabet. The letter shapes and values had to pass through a period of localization before being standardized throughout Greece. Even after the technology was standardized or relatively so — there were always two competing versions, the Eastern and the Western — its effects were registered slowly in Greece, were then partly cancelled during the European

Middle Ages, and have been fully realized only since the further invention of the printing press. But it is useful here and now to set forth the full theoretic possibilities that would accrue from the use of the Greek alphabet, supposing that all human impediments to their realization could be removed, in order to place the invention in its proper historical perspective.

It democratized literacy, or rather made democratization possible. This point is often made, but in simplistic terms, as though it were merely a matter of learning a limited number of letters, that is, learning to write them. Hence even the Semitic system has often been erroneously credited with this advantage. If Semitic societies in antiquity showed democratic tendencies, this was not because they were literate. On the contrary, to the extent that their democracy was modified by theocracy, with considerable prestige and power vested in priesthoods, they exhibited all the symptoms of craft literacy. The Greek system by its superior analysis of sound placed the skill of reading theoretically within the reach of children at the stage where they are still learning the sounds of their oral vocabulary. If acquired in childhood, the skill was convertible into an automatic reflex and thus distributable over a majority of a given population provided it was applied to the spoken vernacular. But this meant that democratization would depend not only upon the invention but also upon the organization and maintenance of school instruction in reading at the elementary level. This second requirement is social rather than technological. It was not met in Greece for perhaps three hundred years after the technological problem was solved, and was abandoned again in Europe for a long period after the fall of Rome. When operative, it rendered the role of the scribe or the clerk obsolete, and removed the elitist status of literacy characteristic of craft-literate epochs.

Have the outward social and political effects of full literacy really been as important and profound as is sometimes claimed? Our later examination of oral cultures and the way they function may throw some doubt on this. What the new script may have done in the long run was to change somewhat the content of the human mind. This is a conclusion which will not be argued fully here. But this much should be said at once. The acoustic efficiency of the script had a result which was psychological: once it was learned you did not have to think about it. Though a visible thing, a series of marks, it ceased to interpose itself as an object of thought between the reader and his recollection of the spoken tongue. The script therefore came to resemble an electric current communicating a recollection of the sounds of the spoken word directly to the brain so that the meaning resounded as it were in the consciousness without reference to the properties of the letters used. The script was reduced to a gimmick; it had no intrinsic value in itself as a script and this marked it off from all previous systems. It was characteristic of the alphabet that the names of the Greek letters, borrowed from the Phoenician, for the first time became meaningless: *alpha, beta, gamma*, etc. constitutes simply a nursery chant designed to imprint the mechanical sounds of the letters, by using what is called the acrophonic principle, in a fixed series on the child's brain, while simultaneously tightly correlating them with his vision of a fixed series of shapes which he looks at as he pronounces the acoustic values. These names in the original Semitic were names of common objects like "house" and "camel' and so on. Uncritical students of the history of writing will even make it a reproach against the Greek system that the names became "meaningless" in Greek. The reproach is very foolish. A true alphabet, the sole basis of future literacy, could only become operative when its components were robbed of any independent meaning whatever, in order to become convertible into a mechanical mnemonic device.

The fluency of reading that could result depended upon fluency of recognition and this in turn as we have seen upon the removal so far as possible of all choices upon the part of the reader, all ambiguities. Such an automatic system brought within reach the capacity to transcribe the complete vernacular of any given language, anything whatever that could be said in the language, with a guarantee that the reader would recognize the unique acoustic values of the signs, and so the unique statements conveyed thereby, whatever they happened to be. The need for authorized versions restricted to statements of a familiar and accepted nature was removed. Moreover the new system could identify the phonemes of any language with accuracy. Thus the possibility arose of placing two or several languages within the same type of script and so greatly accelerating the process of cross-translation between them. This is the technological secret which made possible the construction of a Roman literature upon Greek models — the first such enterprise in the history of mankind. For the most part, however, this advantage of interchange between written communications has accrued to the later alphabetic cultures of Europe. By way of contrast, the historian Thucydides in the Greek period records an episode where the documents of a captured Persian emissary had to be "translated" into Greek. That is how the word is interpreted by the commentators who explain this passage. But Thucydides does not say "translated." What the would-be translators had first to do was to "change the letters" of the original syllabic script into the Greek alphabet. How could they have done this? I suggest that it was done only with the previous assistance of the spoken tongue, not the written. That is, an orally bilingual Persian who was also craft-literate in the Persian sense, that is, knew his cuneiform, would read aloud what the document said, translating as he went into spoken Greek. His opposite number would then transcribe from his dictation into the Greek alphabet, unless there was a Persian available who could use both cuneiform and alphabet. Then the Persian dispatch, now in Greek alphabetic form, could be carried to Athens and read there. In the United Nations today some such procedure is still required for cross-communication between the alphabetic cultures and the non-alphabetic ones like the Arabic, Chinese, and Japanese, leading as it often does to ambiguities and even misunderstandings of a special sort that do not arise between the alphabetic cultures, misunderstandings which can even have political consequences.

These effects, to repeat, were theoretically attainable. For reasons to be explained later, the full vernacular was not in fact the first thing to be transcribed. The alphabet was not originally put at the service of ordinary human conversation. Rather it was first used to record a progressively complete version of the "oral literature" of Greece, if the paradox may be permitted, which had been nourished in the non-literate period and which indeed had sustained the identity of the previous oral culture of Greece. Although today we "read" our Homer, our Pindar, or our Euripides, a great deal of what we are "listening to" is a fairly accurate acoustic transcription of all the contrived forms in which oral speech had hitherto been preserved. This phenomenon as it occurs in the formation of what we call Greek literature has been imperfectly understood and will be explored in depth when the Greeks are at last allowed, as they will be, to take over the course and direction of this history.

And yet, though fluent transcription of the oral record

became the primary use to which the alphabet was put, the secondary purpose which it came to serve was historically more important. I could say that it made possible the invention of fluent prose, but this would be misleading, since obviously the larger component of oral discourse even in an oral culture is prosaic. What it effectively brought into being was prose recorded and preserved in quantity. To interpret this innovation as merely stylistic would be to miss the point of a profound change occurring in the character of the content of what could be preserved. A revolution was underway both psychological and epistemological. The important and influential statement in any culture is the one that is preserved. Under conditions of non-literacy in Greece, and of craft literacy in pre-Greek cultures, the conditions for preservation were mnemonic, and this involved the use of verbal and musical rhythm, for any statement that was to be remembered and repeated. The alphabet, making available a visualized record which was complete, in place of an acoustic one, abolished the need for memorization and hence for rhythm. Rhythm had hitherto placed severe limitations upon the verbal arrangement of what might be said, or thought. More than that, the need to remember had used up a degree of brain-power — of psychic energy — which now was no longer needed. The statement need not be memorized. It could lie around as an artifact, to be read when needed; no penalty for forgetting — that is, so far as preservation was concerned. The mental energies thus released, by this economy of memory, have probably been extensive, contributing to an immense expansion of knowledge available to the human mind.

These theoretic possibilities were exploited only cautiously in Graeco-Roman antiquity, and are being fully realized only today. If I stress them here in their twofold sig-

nificance, namely, that all possible discourse became translatable into script, and that simultaneously the burden of
memorization was lifted from the mind, it is to bring out
the further fact that the alphabet therewith made possible
the production of novel or unexpected statement, previously
unfamiliar and even "unthought." The advance of knowledge, both humane and scientific, depends upon the human
ability to think about something unexpected — a "new
idea," as we loosely but conveniently say. Such novel thought
only achieves completed existence when it becomes novel
statement, and a novel statement cannot realize its potential
until it can be preserved for further use. Previous transcription, because of the ambiguities of the script, discouraged
attempts to record novel statements. This indirectly discouraged the attempt to frame them even orally, for what
use were they likely to be, or what influence were they likely
to have, if confined within the ephemeral range of casual
vernacular conversation? The alphabet, by encouraging the
production of unfamiliar statement, stimulated the thinking
of novel thought, which could lie around in inscribed form,
be recognized, be read and re-read, and so spread its influence among readers. It is no accident that the pre-alphabetic
cultures of the world were also in a large sense the pre-
scientific cultures, pre-philosophical and pre-literary. The
power of novel statement is not restricted to the arrangement of scientific observation. It covers the gamut of the
human experience. There were new inventible ways of
speaking about human life, and therefore of thinking about
it, which became slowly possible for man only when they became inscribed and preservable and extendable in the alphabetic literatures of Europe.

THE TRANSCRIPTION OF THE CODE OF
A NON-LITERATE CULTURE

A GENERATION AGO, there existed a consensus among scholars in the field of antiquity[1] that the Greek alphabet must have come into use by the Greeks not later than the tenth century and perhaps earlier. This dating could not be supported by any evidence from epigraphy; the inscriptions which could reasonably have been expected to survive from such a period are non-existent. Nor does Homer's text supply any references to alphabetic writing.[2] If such a date seemed reasonable, the evidential grounds for accepting it lay in the history not of the Greeks but the Phoenicians. A majority of the Greek letter-shapes and their names were borrowed from the script used by this people, a script which was certainly in use in Mediterranean lands by that date. A variant of it must have been borrowed for example by the Hebrews[3] to transcribe the content of the earliest documents of the Old Testament in the eleventh or tenth century.[4] More recently, archaeology has demonstrated that it was in use in Palestine much earlier.[5] It therefore seemed plausible to conclude that the Greek adaptation[6] should have occurred in the same period or a little later.

The Phoenicians were not the only people living on the littoral

[1] Earlier opinions on this question are reviewed by H. J. Lorimer, "Homer and the Art of Writing," *AJA* 52 (1948), pp. 11-19: vid. also Rhys Carpenter (below n. 12).

[2] The two possible allusions are *Il.* 6.155ff. and 7.175, 187, 189, both dismissed by Lilian Jeffery in *A Companion to Homer*, ed. Wace and Stubbings, London 1962, p. 555.

[3] David Diringer, *Writing*, N.Y. 1962, observes (p. 125) that both the Phoenician and the Early Hebrew scripts are branches of the North Semitic alphabet.

[4] Authorship of the original "Biography of David" has been ascribed to a younger contemporary of the king, i.e., to the tenth century: vid. R. Pfeiffer, *An Introduction to the Old Testament*, N.Y. 1948, p. 342ff., who asserts (p. 357) that the author is "the father of history in a much truer sense that Herodotus half a millennium later." The "Song of Deborah" (Judges 5), originally an oral composition, describes an event of the eleventh century.

[5] Pfeiffer, *op.cit.*, p. 73, deduces that Phoenician script was invented c. 1500 B.C.; vid. also Diringer, *op.cit.*, p. 131 and Carpenter (below n. 12).

[6] Adaptation of Phoenician letter-shapes in the formation of the Greek alphabet is discussed by Nilsson, "Die Uebernahme und Entwicklung des Alphabet durch die Griechen": *Opuscula Selecta*, Lund 1952, vol. 2, pp. 1029-1056: but vid. also Carpenter (below n. 12).

of the Mediterranean who in the pre-Homeric period used script.
For a generation now, it has been known that the Mycenaeans used
a writing system identified by scholars as Linear B, apparently
adapted from a Cretan prototype. Its decipherment though only
partially successful was achieved on the hypothesis that the Mycenaeans spoke an early form of Greek.[7] The system, judging from
the content of the records that have been deciphered, was used for
very limited purposes, but its existence has supplied a second excuse for believing that the Greeks between the eleventh and eighth
centuries B.C. used writing. If Linear B, so this assumption runs,
was in use before 1150, it must have continued in use after 1100.
Was it credible that a people who had used such a tool of commerce
and civilisation would ever forget it?[8] But alas! the epigraphical
evidence for the survival of Linear B is equally non-existent.[9] In
dealing with the question of Greek literacy, the supposed "literacy" of the Mycenaeans has proved to be a red herring drawn
across a problem which is not soluble on these lines.

The fact that the problem exists is a reflection in part of that
state of mind in which we as members of a literate culture approach
the study of the civilisation of the Greeks. Behind the reluctance to
trust the negative influence of epigraphy it is possible to discern the
influence of an assumption, or set of assumptions, working in the
unconscious mind of scholars and historians, which run something
like this: Any civilised culture worth the name has to be a literate
culture, and while we recognise such a culture by many hall-marks,
the chief one is the production of a sophisticated literature, and
this is particularly true of the Greeks. In the field of literature,
composition takes place most readily in prose, even though much
of the prose does not aim at high literary pretension and is consequently ephemeral. Superimposed, so to speak, upon the prosaic

[7] John Chadwick, *The Decipherment of Linear B*, London 1967, describes the
procedure followed. Cautionary qualifications are set forth in G. S. Kirk, *Songs
of Homer*, Cambridge 1962, pp. 24-28.
[8] This is the argument put forward by G. Kahl-Furthmann, in *Wann lebte
Homer?*, Meisenheim am Glan 1967, who proposes that the Homeric poems were
originally written in a refined Linear B script, but much later transcribed in
the Greek alphabet in the eighth century.
[9] "There is no evidence available that knowledge of the script survived the
'dark age' which followed the end of the Mycenaean period"—so J. A. Davison
in *A Companion to Homer* (above n. 2), p. 217.

sub-structure of the culture are the works of poetry. They represent a form of composition of an exceptional sophistication and refinement, a supplement to the prose literature. A civilisation in short includes as part of its equipment both a literature of prose and a literature of poetry, but the prose has priority and is more extensive. The Greek literature that has been preserved begins with Homer and Hesiod, followed by the lyricists, Pindar, and the Greek dramatists. Here is a poetic literature as sophisticated as any the world has seen. It must therefore represent the refined product of a culture which had begun its ascent to supremacy a considerable time before these works appeared, one which indeed must have rested on a foundation of discourse written in prose, even if most of it has been lost. Such poetic refinement presupposes a long previous period of development in the art of the written word. It is therefore incredible that the Greeks who either preceded Homer or were contemporary with him were completely non-literate.

This argument so far as I know has not been explicitly formulated by scholars. In stating it as I have done,[10] I have tried to make explicit what was there by implication in the way in which they have viewed the history of Greek literature and have written about it. The argument of the following pages, as it step by step unfolds, may lead to the conclusion that such premises are mistaken; that in fact, given the conditions under which Greek civilisation developed, the order of priorities should be reversed.

Between the years 1928 and 1938 there came to light the results of two investigations in the field of classical antiquity, which in retrospect can be seen to have intimate connection, but which at the time were pursued in separate areas of scholarship and in independence of each other. It is perhaps noteworthy that the authors of both were Americans. In 1928 Milman Parry published, initially in a French thesis, his analysis of the metrical and verbal structure of the Homeric poems, drawing the conclusion that the *Iliad* and *Odyssey* were examples of a strictly oral composition which employed a formulaic and highly traditional language. The 'author' or 'authors', terms henceforth to be placed within quotation-marks, were therefore bards who were non-literate, who composed from

---

[10] Vid. also Havelock, "Pre-Literacy and the Pre-Socratics," in *Institute of Classical Studies*, Univ. London Bulletin no. 13, 1966, pp. 44-45.

memory in their heads, for audiences who listened but presumably did not read.[11]

In 1933 and again in 1938 Rhys Carpenter published his demonstrations that the Greek alphabet could not have been invented earlier than the last half of the eighth century.[12] I have adverted elsewhere[13] to the reluctance with which this conclusion, reached on epigraphical grounds, has been accepted by students of language and literature.[14] Clearly the presupposition that Greek literature presented the full flowering of a literate culture which had already been incubating for some centuries was put in jeopardy. Carpenter's date meant that prior to the last half of the 8th century, and very probably during the last half itself, any composition in Greek that we would style "literary" had to be oral anyway. This would still leave a choice of dates for "Homer," using his name as a convenient shorthand for that process of composition, whatever it was, of which the *Iliad* and *Odyssey*, much as we have them, were the end products. Either "he" composed earlier, perhaps much earlier, than the last half of the eighth century, and the poems were then memorised and so preserved more or less intact until they could be written down at the close of the century: or else "he" composed very near the time that the alphabet was introduced, so that "his" composition could be given documentary form either in "his" life time or soon after "his" death.

At this point the oral theory, supplemented by previous research into the language and content of the Homeric poems, determined the choice that should be made. The formulaic technique, carried only in the living memories of bards, was shared and transmitted between the generations. Since it was never frozen in documented form, its language could slowly respond to dialectical changes over periods of time, and the content of what was sung could reflect not only memory of the remoter past but experience contemporary

---

[11] See now *The Making of Homeric Verse*: The Collected Papers of Milman Parry, edited with introduction by Adam Parry, Oxford (Clarendon) 1971.

[12] Rhys Carpenter, "The Antiquity of the Greek Alphabet," *A.J.A.* 37 (1933), pp. 8-29, and "The Greek Alphabet Again," *A.J.A.* 42 (1938), pp. 58-69.

[13] Havelock, *Preface to Plato*, Cambridge, Mass. 1963, p. 49 n. 4.

[14] Vid. most recently Kirk, *op.cit.*, pp. 69-71, who is willing to assign the transmission of the Greek alphabet from the Phoenicians to the early eighth century, while noting that none of the inscriptions can be dated before the last decade of the eighth.

with the time of the singer. Homer's dialectical forms, and the report which his poems give of historical and social conditions, are demonstrably an amalgam which ranges forward from Mycenae as far down as the conditions in which the Ionian Greeks spoke and lived in the eighth century. Previous efforts to separate these chronologically disparate elements and allot them to different portions of Homer's text had failed. The Homeric mixture is so to speak chemical not mechanical.[15] Recognition of the flexibility of response inherent in the oral technique had now solved Homeric problems which had previously seemed insoluble. Equally, it was now demonstrated that the creative process, which produced Homer, had ended only at that point, or shortly before it, when the Greek alphabet was invented.[16]

There were some peculiar merits enjoyed by the Greek alphabetic invention, when it is compared with all previous writing systems.[17] The issue here does not lie between ideographic and phonetic systems. All the nearest competitors of the Greek system were already phonetic, though it is indicative of the comparative "backwardness" of Linear B that it still employed some ideograms.[18] But at the level of phonetic invention, the issue still lay between systems which were content to symbolise actual sounds which any mouth makes when it speaks, and a system like the Greek which analysed such sound into abstract components. An actual linguistic sound is produced either by the vibration of a column of air in the larynx, or by this vibration as it is variously restricted, controlled and released by the tongue, teeth and lips. The former

---

[15] M. P. Nilsson, *Homer and Mycenae*, London 1933, found elements in the poems ranging from the Mycenaean to the beginning of the Orientalising period (and especially pp. 158-59): these are "inextricably mixed." Kirk, *op.cit.*, pp. 179ff., reviews the "cultural and linguistic amalgam," containing dialectical forms aı d reports of customs and objects from widely divergent periods, fused to a degree which allows "the identification of only a few elements in the amalgam." (p. 181).

[16] Kirk, *op.cit.*, p. 180, notes that in the case of certain elements incorporated by oral tradition there is a *terminus post quem* of about 750 B.C.

[17] For general discussion of the alphabet and particularly of the Near Eastern scripts from which the Greek alphabet was adapted, see D. Diringer, *The Alphabet*, London 1948, and *Writing* (above n. 3) (esp. pp. 123ff.), as well as C. F. and F. M. Voegelin, "Typological Classification of Systems with Included, Excluded and Self-sufficient Alphabets," in *Anthropological Linguistics* III (1961).

[18] Vid. Ventris and Chadwick, *Documents in Mycenaean Greek*, Cambridge 1956, pp. 48ff.

in simple terms is equivalent to a vowel, the latter to a combination of a vowel with consonants either preceding, following, or enclosing. We can think of all these sounds actually made as syllables, whether they consist of vowels alone or vowel-consonant combinations.

The systems of writing including the Phoenician which had been in use in the Near East in the period preceding the Greek invention were themselves all syllabic. That is, they sought to represent the sounds actually made by the mouth as these are put together in words. Mostly these were vowel-consonant types, but also vowels alone, as we can see for example from the practice of Linear B[19] (if the decipherment be accepted). Their achievement therefore was empirical. They took the language so to speak as they found it and sought to objectify the actual sound-units as these existed in pronunciation.

But this effort to create a one-to-one correspondence between signs and speech-sounds produced an inherent difficulty. The distinct syllables into which any given language can be divided might theoretically run into the hundreds, especially if the language uses vowel-consonant combinations not only in pairs but in triplets. A spoken tongue is probably always looser, richer, and more idiosyncratic than the rules of its transcription would imply, however perfect a copy they be, but in the case of the syllabaries, the gap between what the system might indicate was being said and what actually had been said could be very considerable.[20] To symbolise what might actually be said with approximate fidelity might mean multiplying the number of different signs to an unmanageable extent. Or else, the number could be cut down to manageable size, with the result that a single sign had to serve double or triple duty. Ambiguity in decipherment became inevitable, in varying degree. All these sign systems were placed in a theoretic dilemma: either to increase the register of symbols to achieve a one-to-one correspondence with possible syllables, and so achieve relative acoustic accuracy, or to cut down the register to a manageable number, at the cost of increasing ambiguity. The Phoenician system alone

[19] Ventris and Chadwick, op.cit., pp. 76ff.
[20] By way of example, in Documents, p. 170, a word deciphered as e-so-to is interpreted as either esto ("let there be") or essontoi ("there shall be").

achieved maximum economy, which is why it is sometimes falsely likened to an alphabet, but in fact it provided what has been correctly described as an "unvocalised syllabary,"[21] which still left the reader to make the correct choice of possible vocalic combinations.

These inherent difficulties would seem to have placed some important limitations upon the actual use of such systems. Their management called for a degree of professional skill restricted to a class of specialists who had the ability and leisure to master it. In cases where the signs had accumulated in the interest of acoustic fidelity, the skill called for special training in the memorisation of the system. So far on the other hand as the system practised economy, the skill needed was one of interpretation. The "scribe" of the time of Christ was still the required and recognised interpreter of scripture, in the first place because he was prepared to say what a given transcription "meant," that is, in practice, what choices to make of key syllables where choice was possible.[22] To read such a script required a series of decisions basically acoustic in their nature. This should call our attention to the fact, usually neglected, that in the history of writing systems the relative degree of success obtained is tested not in the act of writing, but in the act of reading.

It follows that pre-Greek systems of writing in their application could not be democratised. Their management remained in the hands of experts, lay or priestly. It is a question whether, if we apply the term literacy to such cultures as employed them, we are not mis-using the term.[22a]

But while reflection on these technological difficulties makes it easy for us to realise how restricted the expertise might be, it is not at first so easy to recognise that similar restriction would apply

---

[21] By F. Householder in review of Emmett Bennett and Others, *C.J.*, 54 (1959), 379-83. For further discussion of this question, see Havelock, *op.cit.* (note 13), p. 129, n. 6.

[22] Pfeiffer, *op.cit.*, pp. 73ff., notes how, in the period of stabilisation and canonisation of the text, there was room for scribes to interpret the unvocalised script in different ways according to their theological inclinations.

[22a] A small flat rectangular piece of stone found at Thera has been interpreted by Prof. Marinatos (in his catalogue of the Thera exhibit in the National Museum at Athens) as "the earliest example of the present day slate used by school children on which they scratched designs and learnt their first letters." My own recent inspection of this object (in show case No. 7) reveals with clarity, as he himself notes, only a drawing of a lily-flower.

not only to the people who could use the system, but also to the kind of material they were likely to put into it. If the number of those who could read and write remained limited, so also did the content of what was transcribed. When used to record catalogues and numerical quantities, such systems functioned without much ambiguity. But when it came to transcribing discursive speech, difficulties of interpretation would discourage the practice of using the script for novel or freely-invented discourse. The practice that would be encouraged would be to use the system as a reminder of something already familiar, so that recollection of its familiarity would aid the reader in getting the right interpretation. And to be familiar, this something would resemble material already on the lips of people, independently of any existence in writing, and so independently "known." It would in short tend to be something— tale, proverb, parable, fable and the like—which already existed in oral form and had been composed according to oral rules. The syllabic system in short provided techniques for recall of what was already familiar, not instruments for formulating novel statements which could further the exploration of new experience.

The rules of oral composition themselves laid strict limitations on the kind of statement which could be made, if it was to be preserved. Precisely what these were will be examined later. It is sufficient for the moment to recognise that they existed in order to recognise a further restriction which was placed upon the range and scope of oral statement when it came to be encased in the syllabaries. Ambiguities of the script would be bound to encourage a selectivity practised at the expense of the oral originals, a selectivity which concentrated upon central facts and sentiments, at the expense of the more unique, eccentric, and we might say, the more personal element in the oral repertoire. The former were more easily accommodated to or matched with the script, the latter more difficult to document adequately and more difficult to recognise when documented. Syllabic scripts would tend to produce paraphrases of oral originals rather than the originals themselves, and even to simplify somewhat their syntax and vocabulary.

A glance at the literatures so called preserved in hieroglyph, cuneiform or Phoenician will confirm that these characteristics of content do exist, characteristics for which I have sought explanation in the technological difficulties created by the writing systems in use. We gain an overall impression, as these documents are translated for us,[23] that we are being asked to read a rather formalised version of what went on, what people actually said and did and believed. A few central stories or myths recur, usually focussed upon the careers of a limited number of persons. Story and person are alike familiar. Rituals in regular use are described, parables and proverbs abound. But when all allowance is made for simple grandeur of conception or refinement of design, the basic complexity of human experience is not there. The full report of oral utterance is missing. We are being treated to an authorised version. The common reader can test this statement for himself, by taking up the Old Testament. The older parts of this compendium were inscribed and so preserved in a version of the Phoenician Syllabary.[24] To be sure, some theological rewriting of these records occurred in the period after the Second Temple was founded.[25] But it remains true that the original narratives and the surrounding sentiments are syntactically repetitive, that typical situations recur, that the relationships between the characters are relatively simple, and their acts take an almost ritual quality. We feel the simple rhythm of the record as it unfolds.

It is precisely these limitations imposed upon the possible coverage of human experience that give to the Old Testament its power of appeal, as we say, to simple people. The record of a culture which is composed under these restrictions is likely to center upon religion and myth, for these tend to codify and standardise the variety of human experience so that the reader of such scripts is more likely to recognise what the writer is talking about. It is therefore no accident that the cultures of the Near East which precede the Greek and are recorded in hieroglyph, cuneiform or Phoenician seem on the basis of the record to be peculiarly occupied with such matters. We normally take it for granted that such pre-

[23] As for example, in the case of that kind of material assembled in *Ancient Near Eastern Texts Relating to the Old Testament*, ed. J. B. Pritchard (2nd ed., Princeton 1955).

[24] Above, notes 2 and 3. Pfeiffer, *op.cit.*, pp. 72 ff., observes that the Samaritan Pentateuch was written in an ornate form of the Phoenician letters and preserved in that form, while in the case of the Masoretic Pentateuch a different and more developed script was used.

[25] Pfeiffer, *op.cit.*, p. 56.

occupation was an inherent characteristic of such cultures, and it is often put down to the fact that they were at a more primitive stage of cultural development. The reason, I am suggesting, is rather to be sought in a fact of technology. If it is easy for modern research to discover archetypal myths in these so-called literatures, may this not reflect the fact that the original transcribers, given the limitations of the medium they were using, found it equally easy to write down the archetypes with some assurance that they would be read easily and correctly?[26]

To enter the world of what we call Greek literature, from Homer on, is to encounter a larger dimension of human experience, so much wider, more diverse, personal, critical, subtle, humorous, passionate, ironic and reflective. This remains true even when all allowance is made for the limitations imposed by the poetic form in which so much of this literature is cast. If we ask ourselves the reason why this may be so, we usually find the answer in what is assumed perhaps unconsciously to be a racial superiority. The Greek genes conferred upon adults a better equipment with which to achieve creative effort in art and intellect. But I doubt whether such a racial hypothesis has any more scientific foundation when applied to the Greeks than it has when applied to the Germans. If the clue to the selectivity of content found in Near Eastern texts resides in the nature of their orthography, may it be true that the comparative richness of content of Greek texts is correspondingly due to the superior technical resources of Greek orthography?

Pre-Greek systems, we recall, sought to symbolise the actual sounds which a mouth makes when it adds sound to sound to produce speech. They therefore were empirical inventions which sought to copy linguistic sounds on a one-to-one basis. Although they analysed words into their syllabic components, they still provided as it were visual reproductions of language rather than analytic definitions of the elements of linguistic noise. The Greek invention, which perhaps betrays the application to language of a mathematical type of reasoning, consisted in pursuing the analysis of linguistic sound to the level of complete abstraction. It is commonly said that the Greeks accomplished this by inventing signs

---

[26] Possible implications, as they bear on the structuralist theories of Lévi-Strauss and his followers, cannot be pursued here.

for vowels.[27] This is not a true statement of what actually happened. The trick of symbolising vowels, as previously noted, had already been tried and achieved, for example, in Linear B.[28] What the Greeks did was to invent the idea that a sign could represent a mere consonant, a sound so to speak which does not exist in nature but only in thought. It requires an effort of reflective analysis to realise and recognise that the movements of teeth, tongue, palate, and lips are ineffective, considered as linguistic sound, except when accompanied by vocalic breath of varying compression. Strictly speaking, a consonant is a non-sound. When we memorise our consonants by repeating our ABC we have to add vocalic values to them to make them pronounceable, which is another way of saying that alphabets taught orally by rote to children still have to be taught as syllabaries. The Greek alphabet, when it took over the Phoenician signs, made the crucial decision of restricting the function of most of them to the symbolisation of non-sounds. The syllables actually pronounced in any language were broken down and dissolved into abstract components. These, so far as they were what we call consonants, were objects of intelligence, not units of actual speech. At a stroke, by this analysis, the Greeks provided a table of elements of linguistic sound not only manageable because of its economy but, for the first time in the history of homo sapiens sapiens, also accurate.

The term accurate must not be pressed to an absolute degree. It may be doubted whether any given sign system inventible by man could accommodate without ambiguity all the possible noises made in the course of speaking a given language. All systems depend for effective functioning upon the principle that agreed acoustic values are attached to given inscribed shapes. We can posit that the Greek alphabet embodied the first system in which in all cases one and only one acoustic value was theoretically attachable to one given shape. From this fixed rule there followed a second: any actual sound could be achieved only in combinations of two or more shapes. It is theoretically possible that this principle of uniform orthography as it is pursued in literate cultures has encouraged some reduction in what might be called erratic language sounds.

[27] Thus Kirk, *Songs*, p. 70 and Diringer, *Writing*, p. 152.
[28] Above note 19.

Modern French, to a foreigner at least, seems to be a tongue which
in the course of centuries has submitted to some acoustic rationalisation induced by the fact that a given spelling may have a tendency
to mould a pronunciation to correspond. This, if true, reverses the
rationale which guides the science of linguistics, which as a science
has to presume that acoustic usage in a given language is logical
and invariable and which may even enlarge the presumption into
a belief that a common rationale is discoverable behind all languages. Such conceptions are assisted to become pervasive to the
degree that we are compelled to study languages in written versions of what was once spoken. I offer this as a speculative aside.
The sometimes erratic orthography of Greek inscriptions and graffiti[29] should at least alert us to the possibility, not that the writers
were unskilled, but rather that the linguistic sounds they were
transcribing did not always fit neatly and unambiguously into the
agreed values of the marks they were obliged to use.

Subject to these qualifications, we can still say that the sign-
system used in the Greek alphabet, thanks to its ability to identify
the abstract components of syllables, provided in theory an instrument of unique efficiency for transcribing any language, and in
practice one of peculiar efficiency for transcribing the Greek language, a tongue in which the vocalic component of a syllable was
enlarged in comparison with the usage of Semitic tongues, and
which therefore encouraged a more ready identification of the difference between a vowel and its consonantal accompaniment. While
the practical effect was to insist that a consonantal syllable required
at least two signs for its transcription, the signs employed, because
of the level of analysis now applied were not only economical in
number but by permutation and combination could provide exhaustive coverage. Thus was revealed the fact that the complexity
and variety of linguistic noise is achieved by combinations and
permutations of a few theoretically fixed elements.

When therefore it came to transcribing a given oral statement,
the signs employed, through the abstract values attached to them,
produced a relatively clear, unambiguous and economical register
of the exact sounds of what had been said. The reader therefore—

29 Vid. below note 32.

and it is in the act of reading rather than writing that the secret of the alphabet subsists—the reader of any transcription who had previously memorised the proper values could acquire automatic and rapid "recognition"—the Greek word for the act of reading— of what was being said.

The invention therefore brought within the reach of any people using it a degree of fluency and ease in reading which had hitherto been unknown. A sign-series which numbered thirty or less placed the act of memorisation of the system within the competence of a majority of men, and for the first time made it possible to democratise its use. Whole populations could theoretically become literate, if by the term literacy we mean to identify a situation of socialised readership. And if we do, it is proper to apply the adjective literate only to those cultures which used or adapted the Greek invention.[30]

This kind of literacy depended not merely upon the invention, but upon its application in a system of programmed instruction for children. This in turn depended upon the accumulation and availability of alphabetic documentation in sufficient quantity to make it worth while for children to be taught to read. As they were taught, the alphabetic skills would be convertible into an automatic reflex, not something laboriously mastered in maturity. These developments towards literacy in a meaningful sense involved social and institutional changes covering the manufacture and distribution of script and the introduction of a reading curriculum at the school level with an adequate instructional base. No doubt informal starts were made in this direction on the model of the village dame-schools of England a century ago. But these would take a great deal of time. The Greeks were unlikely to organise programmed instruction in reading in order to facilitate the decipherment of a few inscriptions. Even the political device of ostracism initiated in the first quarter of the fifth century called for nothing more than the ability to inscribe and therefore to spell a personal name which had perhaps already been announced in

[30] For a discussion of what degree or diffusion of readership constitutes literacy, vid. Jack Goody and Ian Watt, "The Consequences of Literacy," in *Literacy in Traditional Societies*, Cambridge 1968, pp. 27-68.

previous voting.[31] Many groups of voters found it more feasible to have even this office performed for them by someone else.[32]

In 700 B.C., at the time when the alphabet first came into use, the conditions of socialised literacy lay far in the future. But something can be said immediately about the unique role which at its inception this invention was called upon to play in the documentation of Greek culture. During the centuries immediately preceding, this culture had been totally non-literate. Yet it was a culture, a civilisation; I shall later defend the use of this term as applied to the period in question. It must therefore have devised and relied upon its own forms of linguistic record. These must have been oral, and relied on oral rules for their preservation and transmission. These again are matters to be explored later. The Near Eastern cultures were equipped to inscribe their own oral records, but at the cost of selectivity and simplification.

The alphabet's intrusion at this point into the history of homo sapiens sapiens introduced not literacy, but a permanently en-

---

[31] This is A. W. Gomme's suggestion, *O.C.D.* s.v. "Ostracism," but it is omitted in Vanderpool's account (next note).

[32] See now Eugene Vanderpool, *Ostracism at Athens*, Semple Lectures (1969), University of Cincinnati. His statement (p. 15) that "obviously the very existence of a law such as the law on ostracism presupposes that the electorate was largely literate" reflects what has been *communis opinio*. He supports it by appeal to a sentence in Plutarch (Aristeides VII.5) who, however, could only interpret the institution in the light of the literate expectations of his own day, as do we. The tabulations and descriptions of actual *ostraka* in this admirable monograph would seem to point to an opposite conclusion. (a) Uncertain orthography and spelling is fairly frequent. Was this commoner in the earlier samples? (b) evidence that some of the graffiti were "prefabricated," Vanderpool suggests by scribes, for voters presumably non-literate. This presumption, now necessary to cover some of the finds in the Kerameikos (Vanderpool, p. 11), would seem to be extendible to the case of the "Themistocles" collection (Vanderpool, pp. 11-12 and fig. 30) whether or not the common hands there discernible represent an attempt at "ballot-stuffing." There are three general considerations usually ignored in this question which should have some weight in favour of at best a "semi-literate" condition when the institution was first used: (i) The choice of sherds presupposes absence of any ready supply of appropriate writing materials, and *a fortiori* of a reading and writing public. Vanderpool (p. 12) notes the tediousness of the operation; (ii) In semi-literate societies, the first and often only thing you learn to write is personal names, your own and those of others, needed for legal signature; (iii) the writing down of a man's name recalled magical practice. You could put a curse on him by naming his name and putting the curse on the name, or by drawing his picture or his "sign" and cursing it.

The institution may indeed have been inspired by this ancient practice. The little drawings noted by Vanderpool are therefore not "doodlings" (p. 29) and the curses (some metrical) are not an indulgence but a "making sure."

graved and complete record of the ways of non-literacy. That is the paradox. Because of its phonetic superiority, it provided an instrument in which for the first time the full complexities of an oral tradition could be adequately revealed, for in theory any linguistic noise could now be automatically recognised in transcription. Previous writing systems had reported a muffled version of what went on in pre-Homeric cultures. Where on the one hand oral composition still survives into modern times, and has been recorded, as in the Balkans and elsewhere, it can give us only what lingers on as entertainment on the margins of cultures which administer their affairs by literate methods. As for the true oral cultures which have enjoyed isolated survival in Polynesia and elsewhere, these can be transcribed only in anthropological reports which are compelled to use the vocabulary and thought forms of that literate culture in which the anthropologist was trained.

On the other hand, the documentation furnished by the Greek alphabet, juxtaposed as it was, by the accident of technological invention, against the immediately preceding oral culture, constituted as it were an act of precipitation in which the identity of that culture could crystallise and preserve itself to an unusual degree in unusual purity. It made visible the rules by which personal intercourse was regulated, how its members thought and felt, the consciousness in short of the people concerned. Such documentation, as I shall later seek to demonstrate, should not be understood as completing itself with the appearance of the Homeric poems.

What was the character of this culture of pre-literate Greece? Before an answer is attempted, it is well to recognise that it could not have automatically terminated itself at the date of the introduction of the alphabet. Greece must have remained largely non-literate till at least 650 B.C. "The alphabet," says Denys Page, summarising the epigraphical evidence, "was not in common use anywhere until the life time of Archilochus, and indeed we have no right whatever to believe that the use was common even then."[33] My own more radical view would urge that there are serious reasons for postponing its common use to a date much later

[33] Fondation Hart Entretiens X: "Archiloque" Vandoeuvres-Genève 1963, p. 121.

than this. But on a conservative showing, the Greeks between 1100 and 650 achieved what they did without the help of any script whatever.

Perhaps from about 1100 to 900 this achievement did not amount to much. Archaeology has made evident the physical ruin of the Mycenaean palace-complexes and it is usually deduced that with this went also the destruction of those political and social arrangements which had previously rendered commerce, art and a settled way of life possible.[34] Even this hypothesis of a totally dark age supervening upon the Mycenaean period has been lately questioned. Whatever the truth of it, there is no reason to doubt that, as Professor Geoffrey Kirk has recently emphasised, the centuries after 900 were "Dark" only in the sense that so much about them is unknown. If we consider the period from 900 to 650 as a chronological unit, it is obvious that we view in this period, however obscurely, the genesis of that classical culture which becomes evident to documentary inspection only in the 6th and 5th centuries. In what forms had this genesis appeared? The primary one was institutional, embodied in the formation of those corporate identities known as *poleis*, the Greek city states. All the essential features of this Greek way of life seem to have been organised and functioning by the 10th century. Professor Kirk remarks on the settlements of the Anatolian sea-board which followed the early migrations: "This (viz. some social stability) the Ionian towns with their aristocratic form of government and their federal system had probably achieved to a high degree by the ninth century and to a moderate degree before that." Ionia, it is now agreed, did not become wealthy, in comparison with the mainland, before the seventh century. A fortiori, the towns of mainland Greece must be deemed already capable by the tenth century of supporting forms of social life which went well beyond the limits of village existence. At the level of technology, these communities were capable of forging iron, and presumably of smelting it, a feat beyond the competence of the Mycenaeans.[35]

[34] Thus, for instance, A. W. Lawrence writes, in *Greek Architecture*, London 1957, p. 83: "The Bronze Age ended in wholesale destruction, about 1100 B.C., after which four centuries of poverty ensued." The "Hellenic" civilisation, he assumes, begins only when they terminate.
[35] Vid. Kirk, *Songs*, p. 130.

Their activities in commerce and navigation may not have exceeded Mycenaean standards. Their temple architecture not later than the end of the eighth century can be shown to have anticipated in wood the conceptions and refinements of the archaic age now partially preserved for us in stone.[36] In the realm of the arts, this period saw at its inception the invention and perfection of the geometric style of decoration, followed by the introduction of naturalistic motifs in the so-called orientalising period which began, appropriately enough, about the time that the Phoenician letters were put to Greek use.[37]

In the face of these facts, a conception which identifies cultural sophistication with a degree of literacy must be discarded. A culture can somehow rely totally on oral communication and still be a culture. The contrary presumption, as I said earlier, was originally responsible for reluctance among scholars to accept a late date for the alphabet. But this kind of thinking is not confined to the learned. Parenthetically, its effect may be noted in our own discussions of modern problems, educational, social, and political, as these arise in the world at large today. Consider, for example, the following quotation from a recent editorial by a vice-president of the *New York Times*:

"Between a third and a half of the world's people suffer from hunger or malnutrition. The people of the undeveloped world are the majority of the human race, and are breeding faster than the people of the Soviet Union, the United States, or Western Europe. There are one hundred million more illiterates in the world today than there were twenty years ago, bringing the total to about eight hundred millions."[38]

It will be noted in these words that hunger, malnutrition, and backwardness, on the one hand, are automatically linked with a

[36] Admittedly the surviving evidence for public or religious architecture before 700 remains meager. For a list of nine structures identified as "early," vid. G. Becatti, *The Art of Ancient Greece and Rome*, London 1968, p. 56. Of these the Heraeum at Samos and the temple of Artemis Orthia at Sparta are dated to the eighth century by Lawrence, *op.cit.* (above n. 34), pp. 88ff. On wooden structure, metopes, entablature, etc. in the seventh century yielding to stone vid. Becatti, *op.cit.*, p. 57.

[37] For a convenient review of these developments vid. Becatti, *op.cit.*, pp. 14, 27-28.

[38] James Reston, *New York Times*, October 16, 1970.

condition of non-literacy on the other. It has in fact become a fashion in the Western industrialised countries to regard all non-literate cultures as non-cultures. This, in spite of the fact that a segment of our own population never learns to read, and a significant segment never learns to read fluently. Yet somehow we manage. In considering the Greeks, we had better come to terms at once with the fact that their civilisation began in non-literacy. An oral culture deserves to be considered and studied in its own terms, so far as these can be recaptured.

Technology at varying levels supplies the necessary basis for all cultures modern and ancient. We have detected its presence in the non-literate period of Greek culture as applied to architecture, metallurgy and navigation. The ability to document a spoken language is itself a technological feat, one on which the cultures which preceded the Greek placed some reliance, and which has become essential in post-Greek cultures. This brings us to ask an important question in the following terms: Failing a technology of the written word, did non-literate Greece rely on any technology of the spoken word? Was oral communication formulated in any contrived fashion to assist that preservation of record which is more obviously achievable by the use of writing? Were any methods available for managing ephemeral speech in such a way as to render it less ephemeral?

The answer to such a question is more easily perceived when it is placed within a larger context supplied by the science of anthropology. The non-literate character of Greek culture before 650 B.C. reproduced conditions of immense antiquity. These bore some resemblance to those which had obtained in the pre-Greek cultures of the Middle East, so far as these had remained unaffected by the limited use of inadequate writing systems. Non-literacy had been the rule for tens, nay hundreds of thousands of years during which homo sapiens became homo sapiens sapiens. This creature—the prototype of ourselves—achieved that condition of culture which we can identify as societal and humane only after his achievement and mastery of language. The emergence of human culture is often identified, in the popular mind at least, with the invention and manipulation of tools. It does not appear however that this capacity in itself is the hall-mark of our particular species among the animals. The more correct view can be illustrated by quotation from that classic work by Ernst Mayr, *Animal Species and Evolution*:

"It has been claimed that the skillful use of tools set up a strong selective pressure for increased brain size until the brain was large enough to enable its owner to manufacture his implements himself. The discovery of stone cultures among rather small-brained hominids forces us to modify our ideas. It now seems probable that the use of tools is an ancient hominid trait, an assumption supported by the readiness with which, for instance, chimpanzees adopt implements." Mayr also points out that many anthropologists are unaware of the widespread use of tools in the animal kingdom, of which he cites many examples, and he then continues:

"The assumption that rather small-brained hominids were experienced tool users and manufacturers raises at once the question of the nature of that (tremendous) selection pressure which caused an increase of brain size during the mid-Pleistocene at an unprecedented rate. Average cranial capacity rose from a thousand to 1,400 cubic centimeters in less than one million years. . . . It seems likely that the ability to make tools contributed far less to this selection pressure than did the need for an efficient system of communication, that is, speech. Foresight and capacity for leadership would be greatly enhanced by an ability for articulate communication. Many aspects of intelligence and planning would have little survival value without a medium of communication far more efficient than that of the anthropoid apes."[39]

To achieve a capacity for enunciating that complex register of sounds which are represented in a language required the evolution of a physical apparatus suitable for making them. If we may amend a statement attributed to the Greek philosopher Anaxagoras,[40] "Man is intelligent not because he has hands but because he has a mouth." In modern scientific language, which I again borrow from Ernst Mayr, we read this lesson as follows:

"The hominid line was well preadapted for the development

[39] Ernst Mayr, *Animal Species and Evolution*, Cambridge, Mass. 1963, pp. 634-35.
[40] D.-K. 59 A 102.

of speech, owing to the low position of the larynx, the oval shape of the teeth row, the absence of diastemas between the teeth, the separation of the hyoid from the cartilage of the larynx, the general mobility of the tongue and the vaulting of the palate. . . . The transfer of the food-uptake function from the snout to the hands further facilitated the specialization of the mouth as an organ of speech. Speech does not fossilize, and all we can say about the origin of language is pure conjecture. Yet it is evident that a superior ability for communication and the possession of associated brain functions to make such communication optimally effective would add enormously to fitness. The hominid evolution is an impressive example of the chain reaction of evolutionary change that results from key innovations such as bipedalism and speech."[41]

An animal can bark, bellow, grunt, and whine, and a bird can warble. Man's mouth represents an apparatus which, by using tongue, palate, teeth and lips to impose closure upon various pitches of vocalic vibration, can produce an enormous supply of diverse sounds suitable for organisation in human language. This instrument of communication was perfected over a long span of time—was it 30,000 years or 3 million years? A satisfying answer to this particular chronometric problem does not seem to be forthcoming, so far as I can discover. But its perfection came about—and this is the point crucial to our present investigation—before it ever occurred to our species to enlist the hand and eye in the service of the mouth and ear so as to inscribe a code of visible signs which should correspond to the sounds of any language in use. The non-literate condition of Greek culture between 1100 and 650 B.C. was one which responded to immemorial habits and needs, compared with which the history of literate habits, even if we include the Egyptian and Near Eastern civilisations, is a mere moment in time.

Language is an act of management of sound, not an arrangement of letters. But it does not consist in the mere enunciation of sounds by the mouth, however extensive these may be. It comes into existence only as these sounds are arranged in patterns with corresponding signification. But signification cannot take place

[41] Mayr, loc.cit.

unless the patterns are shared between members of a group, and to be shared they must be standardised. So they become a code, of fantastic complexity. But this code can function as a code only as it is embedded in the memories of all the individuals using it. It is there stored up for continual re-use, and memorised with that complete accuracy which will alone make it an effective means of shared and instant communication. Men do not gather grapes from thorns and figs from thistles. More correctly, they do not allow themselves to speak that way. To do so is to break the code. This requirement of memorisation, I suggest, lay behind those selective pressures which accelerated the growth of the brain, at such a fantastic rate, as noticed in a previous quotation from Mayr. Without the memory, communication was impossible. The human brain is a computer which far outdoes any imaginable artifact turned out by IBM.

The central role played by memory in the achievement of culture by man should alert us to the fact that the significance of language as a historical phenomenon does not lie primarily in its function as communicator: or rather, that communication is only half the story. It does not in itself define the peculiar resources which are made available.

Every species of animal has its own intra-specific method of communication, for mating, food gathering, migration, defense and the like.[42] Some of the sensory apparatuses are superior to anything human, as I can note by walking out of my house quietly to observe a woodchuck a hundred yards away. My appearance will be an intrusion to him because he can sense it, but if our roles were reversed, I would not recognise his presence with the same automatic response. Aside however from the advantage which animals have over man in scent, hearing, and sensitivity to light, air pressure, and so forth, the plain fact is that man, considered as a single species, has in the invention of language developed one intensive type of communication at the price of destroying another more general type. The best that language can do is to function within separate groups within the species. We live in a tower of Babel. Language in the singular has become languages in the plural, and these, so far from improving communication within

42 Vid. N. Tinbergen, *Social Behaviour in Animals*, London 1953.

the species, taken as a whole, have disrupted it. This violation of what seems to be one of the rules of effective speciation may help to explain those aspects of human culture which seem self-defeating, especially its tendency to self-destruction by war. A given animal species is protected against self-destruction by the fact that its individual members recognise each other by using a common communication system. In man, the fragmentation of the communication system has the effect of splitting the single species into apparent sub-species which can become alien to each other.

A common language is the first prerequisite for a given human culture, and a common language is built on a common memory. This memory finds its existence not in some vague tribal consciousness but in the living brains of all individual members of a species. Its function is to codify a pattern of behaviour on the part of the mouth. The code thus programmed in the memory can be regarded as a body of information hoarded up and stored for continual re-use. The primary purpose of speech however as it is produced by the mouth is to direct action and effect response between two or more individuals of the species. To speak of talking to myself is to use a metaphor. Talk is sponsored by the need to programme some mutual activity, which is the essence of communication. The information stored in language thus becomes a means of programming a continual series of acts. The purpose is not merely informational but directive.

The validity of the concept of linguistic storage when it is used to explain the initial phenomena of human civilisation lies in the fact that it supplies continuity with man's pre-civilised history, that is, his physical evolution. Biological information is stored in the genes, where it is programmed to produce the biological behaviour of all individuals of a given species. This procedure has recently been opened to scientific inspection.[43] It determines not only the colour of our eyes and skin, but how we are born, grow, eat, sleep, and die.

With the achievement of language, our species was placed in a position to invent a supplement to the genetically imprinted code. A second form of informational storage became available for man

[43] The spectacular discovery of the structure of D.N.A. is recounted autobiographically by James Watson in *The Double Helix*, New York 1968.

to use, and this enabled him to some extent to take charge of his own further evolution. Instead of adapting to his environment, he acquired the ability to change it, and also to change himself. The first initial use to which this ability was put was to devise the primary structures of human society. These grew up as they were incorporated in the language of a linguistic group, the individuals of which were required to memorise behaviour patterns shared by all members of the group. By the act of communicating in accordance with these memorised codes, mere herds and tribes gave way to societies with socially conditioned habits, customs, laws, history. All of this information had to be transmissible between the generations to ensure continuity. The biologist's description of this procedure reads as follows:

"Through the higher mammals, and most strikingly in man, there has been a trend towards replacing rigidly genetically determined behaviour patterns by behaviour that is subject to learning and conditioning. The closed programme of genetic information is increasingly replaced in the course of its evolution by an open programme, a programme that is so set up that it can incorporate new information. In other words, the behaviour phenotype is no longer absolutely determined genetically, but to a greater or lesser extent it is the result of learning and of education.

This involves not only a capacity for learning but also a readiness to accept authority. 'The newborn infant has to be ready to believe what he is told.' It is this system of non-genetic determination of the behavioral phenotype that permits the development of religious dogmas (based on revelation), and of ethical codes. The capacity to accept concepts, dogmas, and codes of behavior is one of the many forms of imprinting. The greater the amount of parental care and education, and the more highly developed the means of communication, the more important becomes "conceptual imprinting." The acceptance of ethical systems and religions is as much testimony to this as is the success of demagogues and of the mass media."[44]

Some rather crude illustrations may suffice to illustrate the difference between genetic encoding and cultural encoding. A child

[44] Mayr, *op.cit.*, pp. 636-37.

is genetically equipped to stoop and pick up a pebble and throw it at a target which attracts his vision, say, a glass window reflecting the light. The cultural code, transmitted in language, will direct him however not to destroy property, and so inhibits the action that might otherwise be taken. Common sense recognises the difference when we say that stone-throwing is a habit we grow out of. Genetically coded behaviour at first predominates in children, until it is by degrees overlaid by the cultural code imprinted through language and teaching. After puberty, the genetic code will propel us at physically appropriate times to attempt to reproduce ourselves by sexual union. The culturally transmitted code will surround this procedure with a whole set of social regulations, the pattern of which will vary from culture to culture, depending on the family structure. This example indeed furnishes a case where under our eyes a further addition to the cultural code is slowly being formulated, when we recognise something we call today the Population Explosion and formulate a need to control it. The very phrase as it stands carries directive force suggesting further conditions which should surround the act of reproduction. We call these artificial, these proposed regulations, but from a strictly scientific point of view, and considered in relation to the genetic codes of behaviour, they are neither more nor less "artificial" than familial and social regulations which have governed in this area for millennia. They remind us that the storage of information which man now carries out for himself in language is carried out according to an open programme, not the closed one which is characteristic of genetic encoding.

So far, the terminology I have used, and which professionals in the field of anthropology also use, to describe the function of language as a builder of culture has assumed that language takes documentary form. Words like code and programme, information and storage, imply a visible or physical existence. When applied, however, to an oral culture they become only metaphors which disguise from us the interesting question, rarely if ever asked: How does cultural storage take place in a non-literate culture? How is it built up in language as ephemeral as the spoken word?

An initial answer seems to lie in the mere fact that a given language exists. I mean that by existing it maintains a usage of vocabulary which incorporates, at an unconscious level, a good deal of information and direction which covers the behaviour of the group that uses the language. The words employed identify not merely objects but fields of meaning surrounding the objects. They carry associations, as we say, and are customarily arranged in syntactical situations which express these associations. This quite fundamental aspect of language as itself a conserver of culture-pattern lies beyond my present limits. I can give it only cursory attention as a preparation for the next step in our analysis. Once more, illustration crudely chosen will have to suffice.

In the vocabulary of monogamous culture, polygamy and promiscuity are dirty words, fidelity and faithfulness are approval words. These latter, though borrowed from the terminology of contractual relationships, become synonymous with the maintenance of monogamy. You do not need to be told what to do and what to avoid doing. The tonal inflexion of the words as they are pronounced and used carry the directive message. To give a more sophisticated example: any given culture group will codify the procedures of marriage, child-rearing, and property holding within a given family structure. The words for cognates and relatives within this patterned structure come into existence in obedience to the kind of pattern of relations that is set and assumed. They will themselves carry associations which automatically denote appropriate status and prescribe mutual behaviour. An unusually striking example of the way this works can be supplied from Homer's own text. It is found in that moving lament for Hector which on the lips of Helen brings the *Iliad* towards its close. The modern translator renders the relevant terms that she uses as follows:

Hector, of all my lord's brothers dearest by far . . .
I have never heard a harsh saying from you, nor an insult.
No, but when another, one of my lord's brothers or sisters, a fair-robed
wife of some brother, would say a harsh word to me in the palace,
Or my lord's mother—but his father was gentle always, a father
indeed—then you would speak and put them off and restrain them
by your own gentleness of heart and your gentle words.[45]

[45] *Iliad* 24.762, 767-773, translated by Richmond Lattimore, Chicago 1951.

The English formulas, my lord's brothers, lord's sisters, wife of some brother, my lord's mother, his father, are renderings of five single Greek words, each distinct from the others and all specific, denoting definite relationships in which these people stood to Helen, and she to them. In the English version they have all been translated into appendages of her husband. The Greek vocabulary denotes that Helen, by marrying Paris, became a member of a complex family group system with which she would normally enjoy complex relations and from which she could normally expect support, for they all have specific roles to play vis-à-vis her, and the roles are indicated by the words. The pathos of her isolation is that she has been rendered a woman without a family. The marriage therefore has not worked, but its failure is not one we would understand in modern terms. It does not concern herself and Paris alone. This kind of vocabulary implies a set of proprieties quite unfamiliar to Western or English manners and mores, and as it implies them, it also recommends, as it were, the maintenance of such relationships and of the behaviour that goes with them, which, as they become incorporated into the language structure, are also incorporated into the tradition of the culture. We realise this when we come up against our failure to translate. We cannot do it because the vocabulary of our language is programmed to express a set of directives, legal and social, covering the family which are quite different from the Greek directives.

A non-literate culture, then, could maintain some basic identity for itself simply by maintaining the stability of its vocabulary and syntax. The vernacular can do this. Using such a vocabulary you acquire from childhood the information whom to marry and whom not, whom to consort with and whom not, whom to love, whom to hate, what to eat, what to wear; you learn automatic responses to given situations; your cultural expectations are supplied to you. In using the term 'stored information' we include both description and prescription. The two modalities overlap. To describe the done thing is also to prescribe it. The necessary information, at this level, to repeat, is storable in any brain which is equipped to memorise a linguistic convention of the necessary complexity.

But will this be enough to supply a culture with that degree of self-consciousness, of awareness of identity, which entitles it to be called anything except primitive? How does a culture become a civilisation? Admittedly, to put a question of this sort in this form involves the use of terminology which is imprecise. What are the meanings of primitivism versus self-consciousness when applied to a total culture? I suggest that the operative meaning appears at that theoretical point when a linguistic group ceases to be satisfied with the encoding of its folkways at the unconscious level, and instead seeks to devise a special statement of what these are in order to identify them. If such a statement is to be special, it must lie outside the casual usage of the vernacular, for at the conversational level language is ephemeral.[46] To be effective as a statement, however, it must be preservable, and to be preservable it must rely, like the language itself, on the resources of memory. But whereas the ability to memorise a language has been genetically encoded in our species by a million years of selective evolutionary pressures, the unconscious resources of the brain stop there. To what extent we are programmed biologically to memorise special statements without conscious effort seems uncertain and ambiguous. What is certain is that to formulate, hoard, and transmit such statements will require extra efforts of memory, and for this some assistance will be required. These statements when formulated, and however they are formulated, will express the cultural code of the group. Today we can see this code in all its increasing complexity as it is accumulated in documentary form, in literature, philosophy, theology, law, science. But how is it to be documented, so to speak, in an oral culture?

The essential fact in the preservation of record which is carried out by documentation is that a given statement remains unchanged, and this means that the syntax or order of words in the statement remains unchanged. This is automatic in the case of any inscribed statement. We can change it only by an act of physical destruction which substitutes another piece of documentation in its place. If then we ask how, in an oral culture, can statements be preserved, we are asking what device is available to guarantee the preservation of a fixed syntax and word order. There is only one way of

[46] Historically this has been true, prior to the invention of recording devices.

doing this, by the arranging of words in a rhythmic sequence which is independent of the words, but to which they have to respond acoustically. Even the word "arrange" suggests a literate metaphor, as though language were something we could touch and move on a chessboard. More accurately, the mouth, which has learnt to arrange speech sounds to conform to the grammar of a linguistic code, must now learn the further trick of so selecting these sounds that they not only make sense, but set up a kind of music in the ear—both of speaker and listener—which is governed by rhythmic periods which repeat themselves.

It will be realised now that I am pointing to what we call poetry —I prefer to call it poetised speech—as a device contrived to produce what might be called paradoxically the oral documentation of a non-literate culture. It is not in genesis a sporadic activity of inspired persons who did it for fun, but a serious instrument—the only one available—for storing, preserving, and transmitting that cultural information which was felt to be important enough to require separation from the vernacular. Poetic composition therefore formed an enclave, so to speak, constructed within the vernacular of a given non-literate culture, and provided the culture with its cultural memory.

Rhythm as a principle of composition is more extensive than meter. It is the genus of which meter is a species. At the acoustic level it can be set up by assonance, alliteration and the like, and at the level of meaning it can be generated by parallelism, antithesis and the simpler figures of speech like chiasmus. These principles are all evident in the construction of what we call, quite correctly, a "saying," whether this takes the form of proverb, aphorism, maxim, adage, epigram. Parenthetically it will be noted that here too our terminology while seeking to describe phenomena of oral communication is often induced to borrow metaphor from the practice of inscribed speech.

I select the saying as being for theoretical purposes the primary form of preserved oral speech because of its obvious role as the container of directive information which is placed in linguistic storage for repetition, that is, for re-use. An appropriate illustration can be cited from the saying which happens to head the collection known as the Book of Proverbs in the Old Testament:

My son hear the instruction of thy father
and forsake not the law of thy mother
for they shall be a chaplet 'of grace unto thy head
and chains about thy neck.

The rhythmic devices which at the acoustic level contribute to
the memorisation of this statement, and hence to its survival value,
can be properly observed only in the original. But even the English translation brings out the system of balances, parallelisms and
contrasts which at the thematic level contribute to the total rhythm
of the saying. The sentiments are arranged in pairs: the first couplet
lists two directives referring to two parallel figures, father and
mother, while at the same time exploiting the antithesis between
father and son, and the correspondence between instruction and
law. The second couplet lists two parallel statements which are
linked to the two preceding directives as a commentary upon them
and are put together with the aid of similar parallelism and antithesis. (Once more it will be noted that our attempt to analyse a
strictly oral-acoustic procedure is forced to borrow its metaphors
from the conditions of inscription.) This saying provides an example of particular appropriateness in the context of my present
argument, for it happens to identify that cultural procedure which
guarantees the life of the saying itself. It is indeed like a chain
placed round the neck, for the child, in order to acquire the cultural tradition, has to respond to adult instruction. The convenient
adult, chosen by most if not all cultures for this purpose, is the
parent. There is no other way in which the identity of the tradition can be preserved, for being wholly oral it is carried solely
in the personal memories of individuals in the succeeding generations as they memorise it.

It is unlikely that extensive collections of sayings like the Book
of Proverbs would come into existence without the aid of inscription, even though the component parts are formed according to
oral rules. It is essential to the rhythm set up in a saying that it is
complete in itself and does not allow of extension. It does have
relatives, so to speak, in the oral repertoire which are somewhat
longer, like the parable, the fable, and the ritual incantation. Very
often, as in the case particularly of the fable, the versions now in

circulation in literate cultures are themselves the product of literate
paraphrase in which some of the original rhythmic elements have
been suppressed. This was very likely true for instance of the
fables of Aesop as they were available for literate Greece, though
if their models were Egyptian, these would have been inscribed at
a time when Greece was still non-literate, and so attained the form
of prose paraphrase at an early date.[47] But even in prose versions,
the thematic rhythm of parable and fable persists, reminding us of
their genesis and function in an oral culture. Nor must the humble
nursery rhyme be forgotten, which can sustain a single memorised
narrative statement, but within its own unique metric. The readiness of children to memorise this form of speech suggests that it may
have served from time immemorial as a training in the handling
of rhythm. The child thus becomes accustomed to managing the
acoustic aids to memorisation. They are the oral equivalent of instruction in reading. Hence the proclivity observable in children
to indulge in nonsense-language chosen for its sound values as a
mnemonic. The nursery rhyme has proved ephemeral so far as the
cultural record is concerned, though indications of its wide use can
be found in some corners of surviving Greek literature. Considered in terms of its length and self-containment, it resembles an
extended saying. It can be regarded as a preparation for more
meaningful and lengthy efforts of memorisation which are to come
later as the capacity of the brain is more effectively mobilised.

The rhythms of all these forms of preservable speech whether
acoustic or thematic are governed by an important limitation. They
are self-contained and complete in themselves. The parable or fable
comes to a stop. If it did not, its unique rhythm would be destroyed. The meter of a nursery rhyme is unique to itself. None
of them admit of extended statement; none of them are open-
ended.

Yet a culture which had reached the stage of seeking to incorporate its traditions in memorisable speech would surely wish them
to take the form of an extended statement, a connected report, we
might say, which would command attention and provide a verbal

---

[47] An examination of the relationship between the Greek fables attributed to
Aesop and the fable-tradition of the Near East is promised by B. Perry in the
"Preface" (p. VII) to Vol. 1 of his *Aesopica*, Urbana 1952.

nexus round which the consciousness of the culture could rally. The saying or the parable can furnish clues to the consciousness of a people, but not the key to that consciousness. To achieve extension of statement required the invention of an extendible rhythm. This could be achieved by simplifying and formalising rhythm, converting it into a repetitive meter, which produced, we might say, a series of sayings of roughly equal acoustic lengths, which could follow one another like a series of waves in extended duration. The oral memory could then be led on to recall the sequences, and so retain a coherent and extended statement, a program of instruction, so to speak, in the accumulated cultural information. Such, I suggest, was the genesis of the epic as it has subsisted in all oral cultures. It arose in response not to artistic impulse but functional need. It constituted a massive attempt at oral storage of cultural information for re-use.

The time has come to draw together the two threads of my argument: on the one hand the peculiar powers possessed by the Greek alphabet for the accurate and fluent transcription of oral speech; on the other hand, the measures taken by a non-literate culture to preserve its corporate tradition in an enclave of language existing apart from the vernacular, metrically contrived to preserve an extensive statement in the memories of the members of the culture. To transcribe this enclave became the first business to which the alphabet was put. And so we reach in the first instance the poems that pass under the name of Homer. The notion that they represent survivals of a form of entertainment marginal to the day's work must be abandoned. They require to be estimated in the first instance as a report on the day's work, and to be understood in terms of their function rather than their contribution to the aesthetics of literature. Such a revaluation is bound to meet with considerable resistance from the advocates of a purely literary and aesthetic approach to these poems, and may take a long time to achieve.

But Homer constitutes only the first installment, albeit the purest, of that act of precipitation as I have called it which brought the oral tradition of Greece into corporate documentary form. He is followed by Hesiod, the lyricists, Pindar and Attic drama. Should we not in these works also be prepared to view the presence of a continuous transcription of that enclave of contrived language which had nourished the previous oral culture? This is not to say that new facilities of composition opened up by the written word remained uncultivated. Authorship in the literate sense was becoming possible, for the novel statement, poetic or prosaic, could now be assured of adequate transcription, and also of recognition once a reading public had been supplied. But it was not supplied at once, and in any case cultural habits survive their technical obsolescence.

Given the fact that the composition of verse to serve functional ends was a skilled procedure of great antiquity, universal among non-literate cultures, is it credible that with the arrival of the alphabet, the procedure would be quickly abandoned? Is it not much more likely that for a long time after the resources of transcription became available, they would be used still to transcribe what had previously been orally composed, that the transcription would be made in the first instance for the benefit of the composers themselves rather than their public, and that the products of the Greek poets who followed Homer would be devised for memorisation by listening audiences, not for readership by literates? And is it not therefore also likely that the didactic and public purpose of such oral composition would not be lost sight of, that the poetry of Greece even as late as the death of Euripides can still recall in varying degree the stylised storage of cultural information which had been poetry's immemorial function? This, I feel convinced, is a clue to that peculiar quality which we identify as classic in the antique sense of the word.

Homer's documentation however was the alphabet's first gift to the Greeks as to ourselves. His orality need not now be defended. Scholarship with the aid of comparative studies has established it on linguistic and metrical grounds. The distance between his contrived dialect and the vernaculars of Greece, no less than the Mycenaean memories in his tales, attest his ultimate attachment to pre-literate Greece. His survival on the other hand, carefully guarded in the memories of the citizens of the Greek states, ensured that the paradox of complete preservation of orality by a non-oral device persisted into the classical age. Side by side with the new forms of prosaic expression slowly made possible by growing literacy, there existed in Homer through Greek history a completely articulated transcription of the old pre-literate ways of speaking. This transcription was read and recited for centuries, becoming a partly foreign language in competition with the forms and idioms of current speech. It is scarcely to be doubted that the tension thus built up between oral and written proved fruitful in helping to release those post-Homeric energies, mysteriously creative, which remain the secret of Greece in the archaic and high classical epochs.

THE CHARACTER AND CONTENT
OF THE CODE

IF THE ORIGINAL use to which the Greek alphabet was put
had to be the transcription of that tradition which had previously enshrined the code of a non-literate culture, then the
first documents of what we call Greek "literature" could not be
compositions freely invented by individual artists. They would
rather be in the nature of what I have elsewhere described as
"tribal encyclopaedias."[48] This view of them is a good deal easier
to accept in the case of Hesiod than in that of Homer. If the *Iliad*
and the *Odyssey* are transcriptions of oral information framed and
stored for cultural re-use, why do they insist on disguising this central fact by telling stories of the *Wrath of Achilles* and the *Home-
coming of Odysseus?* This is the crucial problem with which we
are now confronted, and which demands urgent solution. The
Homeric poems have invited decades of critical admiration and
dissection, guided by the assumption that the tale was the thing,
and that the poet's primary intention was to entertain rather than
instruct. Any attempt to reverse this priority will invite disbelief.

As a preface to any explanation of why the tale is to be treated
as a disguise for something else, I will ask the reader temporarily
to suspend his disbelief, in order to consider that view of the matter which was taken by the Greeks themselves. The earliest stated
opinions concerning character or function of the Greek epics are
found in the philosophers Xenophanes and Heraclitus in the archaic period, and in Herodotus, Aristophanes and Plato during the
classical period. When the quotations are tabulated, certain features recur with surprising consistency:

Xenophanes contributes two statements as follows:

> (i) Since from the beginning according to Homer all men
> have been instructed that . . .
> (ii) All things to the gods did Homer and Hesiod assign
> which among human beings are a reproach and shame
> thieving, adultery and telling lies

Heraclitus likewise contributes two statements:

---

[48] Havelock, *op.cit.*, p. 66 and *passim*.

(iii) Of the most is Hesiod instructor
   Him they conceive to know most
   who did not recognise day and night.
   They are one.

(iv) . . . what Homer deserves is to be flung out of the
   assemblies and beaten up (and Archilochus too).[49]

Cross comparison of these sayings, brief as they are, reveals an estimate which agrees in the following features: Homer and Hesiod are epic partners between whom no distinction is drawn; they are partners in an enterprise which is viewed as the instruction of Greece; this instruction deserves severe criticism.

Between fifty and seventy years later, Herodotus committed himself to the following:

(v) As to whence the gods severally sprang, and whether all of them were eternal, and the several shapes of some of them—it was a manner of speaking only yesterday that the Greeks formed a clear idea about these matters. For in my opinion, the generation of Hesiod and Homer preceded me by not more than four hundred years, and it was they who composed divine genealogies and assigned the titles and distributed the privileges and skills over which the gods preside, and indicated their respective shapes.[50]

This opinion seems unequivocal: it agrees with those previously considered in treating Hesiod and Homer as partners in a didactic enterprise undertaken for the benefit of Greece as a whole, and agrees with Xenophanes in identifying one element of this enterprise as theological instruction: they were the first to document the Greek pantheon.

The judgment voiced by Aristophanes, as the fifth century drew to its close, still insists that they are teachers, and enlarges the dimension of what they taught:

(vi)   Consider from the beginning
   How the master-poets have been the poets of utility:
   Orpheus published our rituals and the prohibition against homicide
   Musaeus published medical cures and oracles, Hesiod
   Works of tillage, seasons of harvest and ploughing; as for
           divine Homer

[49] See Havelock "Pre-Literacy" (above note 10) from which these translations are taken. They pertain to D.-K. 21 B 10, 11; 22 B 57, 42.

[50] Herodotus II 53. The criticisms elsewhere directed against Homer as a historian, as also by Thucydides, underscore the didactic view of his function.

Surely his honour and glory accrued simply from this, that he
gave needful instruction
In matters of battle order, valorous deeds, arms and men.[51]

Homer and Hesiod are again paired together, but their spheres
of instruction are now distinguished, as pertaining to agriculture
and warfare respectively, in company with religious ritual, oracular
wisdom, moral guidance and medical lore, which are parcelled
out among two other traditional authorities. Taken together, these
items bear some resemblance to a summary of that kind of information which an oral culture required to be placed in storage for
re-use. This fact seems to be half-acknowledged in the emphasis
which is placed upon the utilitarian function performed by such
poetry.

The overall debate between Aeschylus and Euripides of which
this passage forms a part extends itself to the larger and still more
surprising assumption that all poetry is didactic and utilitarian, and
that its success as poetry is to be judged by this criterion. Such a
perspective extending from oral epic into post-Homeric literature
offers a prospect which must here be postponed for later examination. But precisely this assumption, some twenty years later, provides the starting point for Plato's proposals to reform the Greek
educational system.

(vii) What is to be this education? It is difficult to devise one any better
than that which tradition has discovered for us. This of course means
"gymnastic" for the body and "music" for the soul. . . . The content
of music is discourse . . . factual and fictional . . . you realise of
course that initially we start children with tales, mostly fictional, in
part factual. . . . Looking at the greater tales, we shall see the models
for minor ones. . . . The greater ones are those told by Hesiod and
Homer, as well as other poets. They were the composers of fictions
related by them to mankind, and which continue to be related.[52]

The fact that the philosopher proceeds to recommend censorship
of these two epic composers, far from denying them the role assigned by tradition, only places them ever more firmly in the category of didactic poetry, a category which Homer once more shares
with Hesiod in a partnership affirmed even to the extent of using
the verb of which they are joint subjects in the dual number. And

[51] Aristoph. *Frogs* 1030-1036.　　[52] *Republic* 2. 376e2.

it is now on the epic tale itself rather than on incidental material contained in the tale, that the philosopher confers the didactic function.

At a later stage of the same treatise, Plato's position hardens: censorship is no longer enough; the poets must be banned altogether. Plato is now legislating not for schoolboys but for the prototype of a university. Once more, his hostility to the role of epic in Greek society only serves to make plain what that role in fact was.

> (viii) It is now time to consider tragedy and its master Homer, because we are sometimes told that "they" are masters on the one hand of all technology and on the other of all humane matters pertaining to virtue and vice, not to mention divine matters. . . . There are matters of supreme importance on which Homer proposes to speak, warfare, military command, civic management and a person's education. . . . If Homer were really competent to educate persons and render them better . . . would he not have acquired a company of disciples, just like Protagoras or Prodicus. . . . If Homer were of utility to men in gaining virtue, would his contemporaries have been content to let him, and Hesiod too, make their rounds as reciters, rather than attaching themselves to them as precious objects, to be retained in their households, or failing that, to be followed around by themselves as their pupils until sufficiently educated?[53]

These eight notices extend over a period of perhaps a hundred and fifty years. If the earlier ones are brief, they are not ambiguous, and their full effect is spelled out in the pages of Plato. For those who lived within three hundred years of the invention of the alphabet, Homer stood with Hesiod as the original teacher of Greece. The instruction for which he is given credit is not literary or aesthetic, but sociological and utilitarian. It covers technology, including both military skills and (in the case of Hesiod) agricultural, and also civic conduct, morals, and religion. He is viewed in short in those terms which I have already indicated to be appropriate to the documentation of an oral tradition, in which the epic has served as an exercise in the storage of cultural information for re-use.

Is it possible to formulate more precisely what kinds and types of information an oral culture was required to preserve? The indications given in the Greek notices are not systematic or exhaustive,

[53] *Republic* 10. 598d-600d.

nor intended as such. To attempt a more formal classification would appear useful as a preface to further examination of the epic structure and content, if indeed the epic is to be estimated as an encyclopaedia. The easy and tempting path of investigation would seem to direct itself in the first instance towards Hesiod, viewed as Homer's partner, for in him the didactic function is perfectly evident. Information covering the gods on the one hand, as noted by Herodotus, and agricultural procedures on the other, as noted by Aristophanes, is presented in catalogue format. Nevertheless, to read backwards towards Homer from the example of Hesiod is to distort the priorities. There are serious reasons for thinking that direct didacticism is a reflection of post-oral development, that is, it exhibits some of the new possibilities inherent in the use of visible script; that the indirect or disguised didacticism of Homer himself provides a more reliable model of the mode in which a strictly oral culture preserved its traditional lore.

Technological procedures, though they would seem to be those items of information most easily identifiable, need not in fact be stored as such, orally that is, with any precision or detail. The reason lies in the material and visible character of their products. An artifact, say a house, a ship, or a pot, once constructed constitutes a model for the artist to reproduce or to modify, and it remains a visible example for the apprentice to follow. The transmission of skills in such a culture can therefore proceed by copying, to which the necessary detailed verbal instructions form an adjunct. These have no need of incorporation in that enclave of memorized and poetic speech. They can rely on the use of the vernacular because the formula, so to speak, is there visible before the eye and has no need of verbal incorporation. Yet even so, the epic is not innocent of technological formulae. For example, heroic confrontations are often preceded by "arming scenes"[54] which provide samples of military instruction covering the warrior's equipment; or again, that embassy by sea which restores Chryseis to her father in the first book of the *Iliad* provides occasion for four passages describing the voyage which "preserve a complete and formulaic report on loading, embarking, disembarking and un-

[54] J. I. Armstrong, "The Arming Motif in the *Iliad*," *AJP* 79 (1958), pp. 337-54.

loading."⁵⁵ And yet these, and similar reports, do not go into detail. They fail to incorporate the dozens of minutiae which an experienced warrior or a skilled navigator would observe in the course of such operations. Rather do they set up the general order of procedure; they describe what we might call the proprieties of the operation. This applies to all technological information formulaically stored in the epic, not least in those many Homeric similes drawn from contemporary life. Overall, this kind of information forms an exercise in general education, not in the specifics of skilled performance. Some specifics occasionally get into the formulae but seem to linger there by accident. Their presence is not functionally necessary.

But while in the case of the manufacture and management of artifacts the material model serves as embodiment of the tradition, it is otherwise in that area of information which covers human relations, opinion, and belief. To be sure, even here, if artifacts are employed, for example in the service of cult, the appropriate behaviour is supported by the existence of the priestly equipment or even the shape of the temple architecture which may suggest, and help to conserve, appropriate processional formalities or sacrificial operations. Nevertheless, the religion, law, and custom, the ethical and historical consciousness of an oral culture are not in themselves capable of incorporation in visible models. Their close conservation depends upon strictly verbal description handed down between the generations. Description here passes into prescription. What is done becomes what ought to be done. It is the storage of such social directives *par excellence* which is entrusted to the enclave of contrived and memorised speech, and in particular to the epic.

In outline, these constitute the affairs of men, their doings and dealings.⁵⁶ Primary among such is the role of the familial structure of any given culture, comprising in the first instance relationships between children and parents, and also those of the mature but younger generation towards the elders. Both sets of relationships require the management of an educational process whereby tradition is transmitted by indoctrination, and the epic is likely to memorialise with some emphasis the respective deportments and

⁵⁵ Havelock, *Preface*, p. 84.   ⁵⁶ Cf. Plato, *Republic* 10.603c4-7.

attitudes which guarantee this: the choice of a wife, the status of the concubine, the acknowledgement of legitimacy, and the inheritance of property—all these are matters which cannot be left to the vernacular for conservation. They require embodiment in contrived speech. This is particularly true of the procedures to be followed at death, covering the choice of mourners, and content of the lament, and type of offerings at the tomb, which indirectly acknowledge the heir or heirs and guarantee orderly succession of authority.

Outside the family, there is the larger political structure of a people, less deeply rooted in tradition, looser and less formulaically determined. Nevertheless, it will comprise, and so sanctify, some description of the status of the ruler and the subject, the procedures for reaching and implementing decisions for war or for peace or for legal arbitration. It will perhaps include indication of some hierarchy of rank and privilege governing communal relations within and beyond the village precinct.

As for the economic support of the society, so far as it is pastoral its procedures will be described in terms of the rearing and protection, the breeding and the use of flocks and herds. So far as it is agricultural, it will require some kind of annual calendar governed by motions of the stars and sun, and a general account of the basic operations of raising crops, the management of the vintage, and the like. It is less the technical details of such that is called for in memorised and verbal form, but rather the social management and distribution of such resources.

Finally, there is what we might term the historical consciousness of the group embodied in the first instance in its cult and religious practices. The gods are its ultimate ancestors and arbiters of its destinies; they set the geographic and temporal borders within which the group discovers itself and finds its identity. Cult hovers over that entire body of custom law previously described, regulating and regularising everything from family relationships to harvesting the grapes. The role of religious practice is to protect and conserve the culture pattern as well as to give it a historical and perhaps cosmic dimension.

The burden of instruction thus entrusted to the muses of oral verse was summed up in the post-Homeric generation by Hesiod who described the content of their song as "the custom-laws of all, and folkways of the immortals."[57] Both terms employed in this quotation signify usage as predetermined by a given culture pattern to which the members are bound to conform. But whereas *nomos* indicates usage in its aspect of what we would call public law, *ethos* focusses more on private practice and personal habit. In an orally preserved tradition, it is difficult for a split to develop between these two. They remain separable aspects of a single custom-law-and-ethic.

In the Socratic period there developed an intellectual movement which sought to rationalise these patterns to discover uniform principles which might lie concealed within them. It is therefore not surprising that the dialogues of Plato are preoccupied with the centrality of *nomos* in the structure of any society and the way that it sanctions in particular the family structure and civic identity.[58] On the other hand, the earlier dialogues, as they seek to focus on the *ethos* of men, attempt to reach precise definition of the demands made on the members of a *polis* by, respectively, piety (the proper practice of cult), by courage (the military posture required for defense of the society), by temperance (the proper relationship between the generations, and particularly between parents and children), by intelligence (the proper direction of skillful management and the methods of reaching correct decision), by justice (the proper determination of reciprocal responsibilities to preserve social cohesion), and in general by education itself viewed overall as that enterprise which maintains a culture pattern by watching over its transmission, either within the family or as an undertaking of professionals.[59] From the matrix of traditional *ethe*, these are now emerging as "ethical norms," constituting separate objects of knowledge, at a level of consciousness of which the oral culture itself was innocent.

The oral enclave of contrived speech therefore constituted a body of general education conserved and transmitted between the generations. In addition, any organized society, and the Homeric

[57] *Theog.* 66.
[58] This is a constant Platonic preoccupation, from *Crito* through *Republic* to *Laws*.
[59] *Euthyphro* (piety), *Laches* (courage), *Charmides* (temperance), *Meno* and passim (intelligence), *Republic* (justice), *Protagoras* and passim (education).

one was no exception, stood in constant need of "short term direc- tives and legal formulas which, though designed to suit specific occasions, were nevertheless required to have a life of their own in the memories of the parties concerned for varying periods of time, or else the directive failed through lack of fixity in trans- mission, or the legal formula became unenforceable because the parties concerned had forgotten what it was or were in dispute because of variant versions. Such directives could therefore remain effective only as they were themselves framed in rhythmic speech of which the metrical shape and formulaic style gave some guar- antee that the words would be both transmitted and remembered without distortion. The colloquial word of mouth which in our own culture is able to serve the uses of even important human transactions remains effective only because there exists in the back- ground, often unacknowledged, some written frame of reference or court of appeal, a memorandum, or document, or book. The memoranda of a culture of wholly oral communication are in- scribed in the rhythms and formulas imprinted on the living memory."[60]

These short term directives combined precedent with current application, or more precisely tended to frame a judgment or order addressed to an immediate occasion within the confines of formulas sanctified by tradition. In both legal and governmental spheres such oral pronouncements were styled *themistes* and *dikai*, and those with social authority to pronounce them had their corresponding titles. They might require promulgation by herald as the agent whose task it was publicly to repeat a directive for re- tention in the popular memory. In post-Homeric times such oral directives were often styled *kerugmata*, that is "heraldings." An illustrative example of the practice as it survived into the post- Homeric period can be drawn from Sophocles' *Antigone*. There one of the dead brothers has received burial, rightfully, says Antigone, which in the context means with propriety. This does not require any special rescript and none is mentioned; the act of burial responds to the unwritten *nomos* of the society. But in the case of the other brother, if his corpse, and therefore his name, are to be dishonoured, normal social procedure must be interrupted.

[60] Havelock, *Preface*, pp. 106-7.

This requires a special instruction promulgated by herald, a *kerugma* which has already been issued as the play opens. To be effective, it must be remembered and repeated by the citizens. So it is reported as what "they say," not what the herald has said.[61] Its content is naturally framed in metrical terms to conform to the diction of drama. But the verbal arrangement of the proclamation in Sophocles' text employs repetition, parallelism, consonance and assonance, in a manner which recalls precisely those formulaic peculiarities which in a society of oral communication would help to guarantee memorisation and so fidelity. Moreover, the instruction is clinched, or sealed as it were, by an embellished version of the fourth and fifth lines of the *Iliad* itself:

> They say that to the citizens has proclamation been made;
> Cover not up in tomb the corpse nor cry lament for it
> Leave it unwept, untombed, for the observing birds
> A treasury delicious to gratify their forage.[62]

When we turn to Homer's epics, all these things are there embedded in the narrative sweep as it proceeds, and they are there over and over again. Agamemnon demanding that he retain his prize-woman memorialises the accepted role of the concubine, and in the same breath itemises the requirements which are to be met in choosing a wife. The disputants mirrored on the sculptured scenes on Achilles' shield perform the proper ritual of debate and decision before the judges which will settle a blood feud. Penelope and her son confront the suitors to protect the inheritance of the missing husband and father. The gods rise up as Zeus enters for dinner, to give an example of table manners. Achilles' repeated memories of Peleus and his interview with Priam furnish the archetypal pattern which governs the relationship of father and son, as does the return of Telemachus to his father's side. The obsequies of Patroclus or Hector are carefully itemised and identify the chief mourners as heirs to the memory and fortunes of the dead. The lament, the offering, the encomium, the burial procedure are all there. The counsels of Nestor enshrine the authority of the elders to direct policy and provide advice and precedent. The demeanor and courage of the warrior are presented in a

---

[61] Soph. *Antig.* lines 23, 8, 27.   [62] *Ibid.* lines 28-30.

hundred episodes as examples, while on the other hand, Penelope and her staff furnish the paradigm of the proper management of a household economy. Even when the tales, in order to heighten dramatic interest, describe situations which violate these norms—the reflections of Achilles as he withdraws from war in Book 9, or the illegal rapacity of the suitors in the *Odyssey* are conspicuous examples—the listener is still reminded all the more forcefully of what the basic paradigms are. As for cult and sacrifice and ritual hymn, their presence and procedures pervade the narrative with repetitive, and one might say, affectionate familiarity. In a hundred similes we are told how to fish and hunt, to protect cattle, to snare birds, to weave and to plant and to reap.

And yet the tale remains the thing. This great accumulation of precedent, custom, and propriety is memorialised by indirection in the things that men and women are saying and doing, in those recurrent narrative situations in which the poet chooses to place them, and which call for them to say and to do. It is not spelled out in treatise form. It is not even catalogued. Why did it have to be this way? Why was it essential for this contrived enclave of oral speech that it should achieve its task of storage of information for re-use only by disguising essentially what it was doing? To this last question I now address myself.

A first step towards an answer is to consider the formidable effort on the part of the human brain which is required to memorise extensive portions of discourse. We are aware, are we not, that over two thousand years of literate habit has robbed us—or robbed the average man—of this capacity. The psychology which is required to explain this loss I do not intend to explore in this place. I would suggest however that if those conditions of social pressure, exerted on the unconscious, were ever revived, in which the act of memorisation as a means of cultural storage was again required, then the capacity for the act would revive also, and the act itself once more be performed. I have earlier pointed out that the retention of discourse in a fixed word order could be achieved only by placing discourse in rhythmic shape, of which the epic supplies the most regular and continuous example, suitable for framing a content which shall be lengthy yet coherent. But is an epic any easier to memorise than a book of Thucydides? If it is, what are the psychological reasons for this?

We take a second step towards a solution to our question when we recognise that human energy becomes available for performance of necessary functions as it is accompanied by a feeling of pleasure. This linkage between function and pleasure received an analysis in Aristotle's *Ethics* twenty three hundred years ago which still seems adequate. However, the argument can be made directly pertinent to our present context, without benefit of classical authority, if I revert once more to a consideration of the genetic and pre-cultural level of behaviour.

The human organism, in order to develop, live, and perpetuate itself, is called upon to perform elementary but necessary biological functions; to ensure their performance, a pleasurable feeling is genetically encoded to accompany the performance; eating, drinking, excretion, and copulation are obvious examples. We indeed automatically link these experiences with appetite which requires "gratification," as we say. The infant, as he sucks, enjoys sucking. The operation requires some output of energy which the organism has to supply. Pleasure expected and savoured guarantees the response.

The management of a language, the ability, that is, to store and speak a language system even at the vernacular level, makes a severe call upon the energies of the enlarged brain. We would therefore expect that the performance of a language, an ability which is genetically encoded, would be assisted by an accompanying pleasure so that the effort of recollection involved in using the vocabulary and syntax would be encouraged by response to pleasurable stimuli of the same automatic character as accompanies biological functions. The behaviour of children indicates that this is so. The child indulges in linguistic noises before he can properly speak as well as after, and often converses with himself in private manipulations of linguistic sounds. Children chatter to children to a point which wearies an adult and they enjoy the repetition of words, questions and answers which to an adult seem mechanical and unnecessary.

The same principle would surely have to apply to the mastery of contrived speech above the vernacular level, that is, to the retention of words in a fixed order to achieve perpetuation of fixed meaning. But at this level the effort of memory is no longer automatically assisted; that is, we can distinguish between the use of the mouth to speak a vernacular, an ability which is genetically encoded, and so has its encoded pleasure, and the ability to speak a poetised tongue of artificially contrived speech for which it would appear genetic coding is not available, or is minimal. The art of the contrived metrical word will require the invention of further pleasures to supplement those that already accompany the use of language *per se*. For the degree of memorisation now required to hold words in fixed succession requires a new order of mental effort.

The necessary concomitant pleasure is discerned in the operation of rhythm itself. Rhythmic speech involves a repetitive modulation of the motions of the mouth. This dance, so to speak, performed in fractions of seconds by the combined manipulation of larynx, tongue, teeth and palate can be further accentuated by a parallel movement of the body, often imperceptible, but capable of further mobilisation by being incorporated in gesture and dance in which arms and legs become fully involved with torso in the performance of motions which are accompaniments to the rhythm of the mouth and proceed in parallel with it. Finally, it became possible to devise instruments, the drum, the strings, the pipe, which if manipulated either by the reciter or an acolyte would still further reinforce the rhythms already described.

I do not have to argue for the instinctive pleasure felt in rhythm. It is a matter of common observation, and indeed the possibility of rhythmic ecstasy may suggest that the rhythmic pleasures, of all available gratifications, are the most complete. At any rate, while we have hitherto viewed metre as a functional device to hold the words in a fixed order, so as to freeze, as it were, a given statement and therefore a given meaning, the users of metre in the oral culture were much more aware of the ecstatic emotions which accompanied this function. And rightly so, we may say, for while the informative function was socially useful, the emotions aroused to assist memorisation were immediately sensible to the individual who listened and to the poet who manipulated them. So far as dance and melody were added to the performance, the awareness of pleasure was reinforced. It therefore need not surprise us if Homer, in the incidental notices of the bard's activity which occur in his poems, pays more attention to his power to evoke emotion than to his didactic authority. Hesiod as we have seen does attempt some rationalisation of the instruction which the Muses make available, but he too emphasises over and over again the pleasure that they give.

"One of the Muses, indeed is called The Enjoyable. Metaphors like 'sweet dew' and 'honeyed utterance' which 'pour' or 'gush' or 'are spread' suggest the sheer sensuality of those responses which the technique could evoke from its audience. Both the dance and the chant are labelled 'desireful' (*himeroeis*) and Desire, as well as the Graces, has her dwelling near the Muses. The beat of the feet and the voices speaking or singing are likewise linked by epithets with *eros*, and another of the Muses is named Erato—the 'Passionate' . . . The language . . . is highly emotive and suggestive. It allows us, as it were, to hear the actual performance, the effects of which are all-pervasive, for they not only . . . 'rejoice the *noos* of Zeus', but also . . . seem to constitute the atmosphere in which we live, as when 'the halls of the gods laugh' and 'the surrounding earth rings aloud' . . . In one of his most melodious lines the poet signalises oral poetry's hypnotic and curative powers:

A forgetting of what is bad and a respite from anxieties.

The listener may have

Grief in a spirit newly wounded
And endure drought in his heart's anguish

but once he listens to the minstrel

Straightway he does forget his dark thoughts nor are his cares
Remembered any more."[63]

Oral poetry therefore constituted a didactic entertainment, and if it ceased to entertain, it ceased to be effectively didactic. The paradox is well exposed and expressed in the usage of the Greek word *mousike*, evocative at once of the charms of the poet's art

[63] Havelock, *op.cit.* (n. 55), pp. 154-55.

and the sterner requirements of educational discipline. It blends the aesthetic with the didactic, but keeps the aesthetic subordinate. Music in the melodic sense is only one part of *mousike*, and the lesser part, for melody remained the servant of the words, and its rhythms were framed to obey the quantitative pronunciation of speech, and this meant it also obeyed the syntax of speech. Its function so far as it was employed to assist the preservation of the metrical enclave contrived within the vernacular was to assist in imprinting that syntax on the memory by maximising the pleasure in reciting it.

Today, after music in a narrower and more technical sense has been separated off from the verbal art and identified in its own right as a separate discipline, we reverse the relationship and lay words on the rack to suit the rhythms of the melody, as any opera or church service will demonstrate. It is entirely possible that the ability of melodic music to disentangle itself from verbal control, to emerge in its own right, and so undergo those formal developments which give it its present character, depended on the achievement of literate storage of information, in which the functional aspect of melody as a preservative was no longer required. Correspondingly, it was in that era which saw the beginning of literate storage of information that Aristophanes and Plato were able to realise with sharp clarity the informative role which traditional poetry had served hitherto.

So far, I have analysed the concomitant pleasure as restricted to the enjoyment of sound, verbal or melodic, and bodily motion. Can the same type of pleasure become attached also, by some act of transference, to the verbal content of sound, the meaning? To ask this question in this form and after this preparation is to approach at last the crucial puzzle: Why does *epic* oral storage of cultural information have to take narrative form? Why is the storage carried out by indirection?

The pleasures of rhythm are motor responses, they accompany actual motions of the body and mouth. This means that the process of recitation and of remembrance is itself a performance, a doing, a series of rhythmically co-ordinated actions. In choosing the statement which is to be recorded in this way the composer-reciter—no functional distinction should be drawn between them—would insensibly prefer that type of statement which lends itself to a parallel enactment so that he can act it out in imagination, and even in gesture. This means that the preferred form of statement for memorisation will be one which describes "action." But acts can be performed only by "actors"; that is, by living agents who are "doing things." This can only mean that the preferred format for verbal storage in an oral culture will be the narrative of persons in action, and the syntax of the narrative will predominate.

The actions of any actor in narrative can also comprehend his utterances. These are, in fact, acts of speech, part of his continual, flexible, dynamic response to the actions or speech of others. The more rhetorical the form in which these are cast, the more they will tend, as it were, to express argument in action. Not a sequence of propositions, couched in the syntax of the verb to be, logically employed, but a stream of simile, metaphor, instance, and example, angry defiance, fear, despair, sorrow—these are what issue forth in the mouths of Homeric orators, and as they issue they become themselves part of the narrative, in which the speaker remains an actor in action even as he speaks. Such epic utterances, filled as they are with incidental instruction, will therefore be as congenial to the memoriser as the narrative of action itself. Moreover, what a speaker says will not be reported in the syntax of *oratio obliqua*, but kept vividly before the memory as actual utterance. The syntax of Caesar's *Gallic Wars*, with its elaborate resort to the reportage of the gist of a speaker's words or thoughts, reflects the wholly different modalities of speech which become possible as it is written down and stored for literate readers. Homer's rhetoric is a recitation: Caesar's reports are for visual reference and consultation.

Contemporary experience can still supply evidence to support this view of the matter, if we turn to a homely illustration. The gossip which provides all classes of a community with a recurrent pleasure, which as we say is "all too human," reveals that type of discourse in which narrative of event and act and of actual quotation predominates over more sophisticated forms of reporting. "He says to me, he says, and do you know what she did? Of course I can't repeat everything that went on, but I know he was seen going into the house . . ." and so forth.

Gossip, by definition, dealing as it does with the current, and familiar, also deals with the insignificant and the ephemeral, and is not for the record. The personalities who are talked about are liable to be contiguous to the speaker, that is, his neighbours or relatives. When we consider the mnemonic necessities which govern the choice of a medium for speech preserved for the record, it is possible to see that the pleasure principle, as I may call it, is extendible to the choice of special personalities who perform the acts in the narrative. They are not the ordinary topics of gossip. The spectacle of personal importance, status, power, evokes a wonder from *homo sapiens* which seems to be instinctive. If we feel we like the person, we feel admiration; if we are repelled by him, or are frightened by him, we feel awe. But the verbal report of either is pleasurable. Do I need to cite once more, from the area of common-sense observation, the universal habit of turning to illustrations of people in a newspaper, or our preference for descriptions of even the trivial acts of important persons, or persons who have been rendered important by involvement in bizarre or catastrophic action. If such types are pleasurable to the imagination to contemplate, rather more than the actions of my next-door neighbour, then the effort to retain in the memory a tale of action will be further assisted if the actors are such as to excite awe or admiration, envy or fear, and occasionally, affection, though it should be noted that this latter emotion, which presumes some equality between audience and actor, is less likely to produce memorable narrative if indulged in too freely.

This psychological principle, when applied to the construction of memorisable narrative, will favour the choice as actors of gods, demigods and heroes, persons of some exotic status, whose acts and utterances will excite awe because of this special status, or importance, or power, or vigour. So that the contemplation of the status adds to the pleasure of memorisation.

The hedonistic advantage possessed by gods and heroes reacts in turn upon the function of the narrative as a vehicle for cultural information. So far as the stored information of what is done is also a prescription for what should be done, its embodiment in narrative in the acts of status-personalities encourages the listener to regard the tradition with reverence. The actors in the narrative become paradigms round which the tradition clusters.[64] This does not mean they become copybook exemplars of the proper way to behave. Narratives of ideal types would fall far short of stimulating the necessary pleasure in memorisation. A hero can memorialise the correct procedures and attitudes by what he rejects or refuses just as much as by what he performs. What he does is to shed a lustre on the overall context of hoarded information within which he is described as operating.

The syntax of memorised rhythmic speech is therefore not friendly to that type of statement which says "The angles of a triangle are equal to two right angles" or "Courage consists in a rational understanding of what is to be feared or not feared." It is not friendly precisely to that kind of statement which the Socratic dialectic was later to demand, a statement which prefers its subject to be a concept rather than a person, and its verb to be an "is" verb rather than a "doing" verb. Neither principles nor laws nor formulas are amenable to a syntax which is orally memorisable. But persons and events that act or happen are amenable. If a thing always is so, or is meant to be so (or not so), it is not a living (or dead) man or woman, and it is not to be discovered in action or situation. It is not a "happening." Orally memorised verse is couched in the contingent: it deals in a panorama of happenings, not a programme of principles. Parenthetically, it can be noted that the hostility to motion expressed in early philosophy as it became a separate discipline was based not on physical but syntactical grounds. Once you tried to talk about reality in an abstract sense, a form of speech was required which discussed properties and relationships, not the areas of activity in which these were implicit, and the statements about these had to be made to "stand still," as the Platonic Socrates graphically puts it.[65] Whereas information stored purely in the oral memory subsisted there as a series of actions and movements. It followed that the didactic function of oral storage was carried on through the use of concrete examples furnished in the actions and reactions of specific men and women. To be sure, Homer's syntax can accommodate aphorism and proverb, and occasionally includes programmed statements which have the appearance of "truths." But the saying itself is usually cast in narrative

[64] Cf. Aristoph. *Frogs* 1040-1042.   [65] *Euthyphro* 15b.

terms: its subjects are specific, rarely abstract, and if abstract, they still "behave" rather than just "are."

The memory then requires that it be confronted with acts and events for its accommodation, so that all remembered statements be cast as far as possible in this form. This ensures a narrative format for the encyclopaedic epic as a natural consequence, and a grammar of connection which is correspondingly paratactic, rather than syntactic. Action succeeds action in running sequence, and subordination of cause to effect, of condition to consequence, in periodic sentences, is discouraged. But memorisable epic narrative is not simply paratactic;[66] that is, it does not proceed in linear fashion to add item to item in a theoretically endless sequence. Herodotus is much more paratactic in this sense, because he is a writer who is able to compose for the eye as well as the ear: his composition does not rely for its preservation solely upon the resources of individual memory.

The Homeric epic reveals the fact that it does so rely not merely by the use of those formulae, which have recently received extended study from scholars, nor merely by those verbal and physical rhythms on which I have laid such stress. To assist the retention of the material in the memory, the principle of rhythm may be said to have extended itself to content, producing patterns of reverse correspondence as the tale unfolds, mainly of the prototypes ABA or ABBA and extensions of these. Like the formulaic structure of the Homeric line, these have recently received the attention and study they deserve.[67] If I mention them here, it is because I think their cause and character have been misunderstood. Scholars who have otherwise given allegiance to the doctrine of the oral character of Homeric verse have sought explanation for thematic symmetries not in oral but visual terms. They have been explained as exhibiting a geometric design corresponding to that of the visual art of the period. But if the psychology of the poet is oral, this connection is impossible. The correspondences in Homeric narrative must be explained not on visual but acoustic principles. They are not patterns, in short, but echoes.

[66] Vid. J. A. Notopoulos, "Parataxis in Homer," *TAPA* 80 (1949), 1-23.
[67] C. H. Whitman, *Homer and the Heroic Tradition*, Cambridge, Mass. 1958, pp. 259f. Vid. also the critique by Kirk, *Songs*, p. 261-64.

This is not the place for an exhaustive examination of this aspect of epic technique. But enough must be said to demonstrate that, as an epic habit, its source lies in mnemonic necessity, in order to complete the analysis here offered of the epic format as built up out of a series of devices to ensure oral preservation of the cultural encyclopaedia.

The psychological reason for correspondences and symmetries lies in the difficulty of remembering an adequate connection between statements which are novel and which therefore have minimal connection with each other. The problem confronting memory is to remember a host of what we would call "facts" or "data" which in separation cannot be remembered. Therefore one fact must be connected with its predecessor; therefore it must be framed in such a way as to recall its predecessor; therefore, while itself a "new" fact, it must nevertheless resemble its predecessor, as an echo resembles its original.

This is putting it retrospectively. As the metaphor of "retrospect" implies, we are once more using visual terms to try and understand an operation which is responding to acoustic laws. The eye can review, that is, retrospect: the ear and mouth cannot. The composer-reciter works steadily forward, and only forward, and the memory that repeats the composition works forward also. This means that what we are tempted to call correspondence or symmetry is really a process of continual anticipation. The composer has to hint or to warn or to predict what the next thing he says is going to be like, or the next after that, even in the moment when he is saying the thing in front of it. So that the memory as it absorbs statement A is half-prepared to move on to statement B. This produces an effect of continuous recall in the narrative, as names, and adjectives and verbs repeat themselves, evoking situations in series which are partly novel, partly duplicates of each other. Surprise, in short, is anathema to the oral composer, because it is anathema to the oral memory.

Consequently the epic is not only permeated by prophecies which continually but gradually expand the disclosure of forthcoming narrative; it not only arranges sequences of episodes which seem to resemble each other thematically. It also introduces anticipation and therefore echo into the warp and woof of the detailed narrative itself. We can call this method if we choose thematic rhythm: supplementing and extending the mnemonic principles already present in metrical rhythm. Meter leads on the memory by the sheer force of repetition, while admitting the inclusion, within the pattern of sound as it is repeated line by line, of a new set of sounds which as words constitute partly novel statement. The novel is thus remembered as it is contained within the frame of the familiar, working from line to line. The repetition of names, phrases and syntactical situations can achieve a similar result in working from episode to episode.

It is easy to expose this mnemonic technique as for example it operates to open up the story of the *Iliad*. To the listener the Homeric verse introduces the theme of quarrel (*eris*) between a pair of persons and then verbally repeats it (lines 8 and 10). So he waits for it to erupt. He has been alerted as to what to expect in the verses that follow, and will the more easily remember the progress of the sequence. Between lines 11 and 14 he is made aware of the presence of Apollo, and Apollo's priest, and of the fact of insult, of the intention to release a daughter, and of the offer of ransom. Thus alerted he is prepared to anticipate as possibilities in the story the refusal of ransom, the acceptance of ransom, the renewal of insult, the withdrawal of insult, the retention of the girl, the release of the girl. All these are subsequently acted out, to the completion of this portion of the narrative at line 457. The thematic names and words Apollo (and his variant titles), Chryses, Chryse, Chryseis, honour, release, ransom, are either repeated, or echoed in their opposites, over and over again. The prayer of *damnatio* when the girl is retained leads into the prayer of *expiatio* when she is returned, and in the repetition the memory gratefully accepts a verbal duplicate.

Agamemnon confronting the priest had added insult to injury by dismissing him in anger. As the Greeks assemble, Achilles proposes the presence of another priest to solve the problem of the plague. So the first priest, a foreigner, provides the cue for the second, a Greek, who is first offered anonymously, merely as a proposal in the mouth of Achilles, a cue to which Chalcas then responds by getting up. "Yes, here is the priest," but he does not abruptly propose the solution. Instead, he recalls the fact that a powerful but angry man is present, an object of fear. Is it Aga-memnon? Yes it is, and so the listener is led on by this connection towards a solution to the problem, but only by way of a recapitula-tion, in the mouth of the priest, of the angry scene already described.

There is one break in the narrative where the scene and the action shift, and where the rule of anticipation might seem diffi-cult to apply. This is where Achilles resorts to an interview with his mother, who is not part of the mis-en-scène. But as he goes to her, a goddess, alone and prays to her on the sea shore, the listener is ready for the scene. He has been prepared for it for he has already listened to the verses which describe the priest alone on the sea shore praying to his god. The cue has been given, and the device allows a new character, Thetis, that is a novel "datum," to be introduced to the memory within the framework of a datum already present there.

In this way, the psychology of oral memorisation enters into the warp and woof of the epics, no matter which epic or what book is considered. It explains for example their remarkable consist-ency of characterisation, which has invited aesthetic appreciation from literary critics but is not motivated by aesthetic reasons. The naming of a given name, directly or by title, whether god or hero, Zeus, Apollo, Patroclus, Achilles, Helen, acts as a kind of prompter. It requires that in the memory there be provoked recollection of sets of actions and sentiments previously attached to this name. They will vary as the situation varies, yet stay within the type, which has been standardised sufficiently so that when the poem is rehearsed, the lines of speech or description which accompany a given name can to some extent be anticipated and so more easily recalled in recitation.

The review undertaken in these pages of the cultural context in which the Homeric poems are to be placed is now complete. They help to answer the question: How does a human culture maintain an identity when its means of communication are pre-literate? This is achieved in all cultures as information is stored for re-use. Only this procedure makes possible the accumulation of technologies, of arts, of social structures, and of codes of be-haviour. But in a pre-literate society, the conditions of which are very difficult for a literate person to imagine, this storage, apart from its presence in the shapes of artifacts, can occur only in the living memories of individuals, and for this purpose it is expressed in a specially contrived language which I have described as an enclave subsisting within vernacular usage.

The classic civilisation of Greece began its career under these conditions, and we are able to grasp the way in which they operated, through the intrusion of what may be viewed as a fortunate historical accident. In the last half of the eighth century, and possibly at the end of that century, a writing system was invented, superior to any of its predecessors, capable of transcribing linguistic sound with economy and accuracy, so that the full complexity of this enclave of contrived language could be exhibited in documentation. In the orally composed verse thus made available for inspection can be traced the operation of certain laws of composition which are mnemonic. They are at first sight unexpected, but they do explain an equally surprising fact, that under oral conditions of communication that body of cultural information necessary to the culture comes to be stored in narrative epic. Memory, as the Greeks themselves said, was indeed the Mother of the Muses.

In making transition from Homer to the Greek authors who succeeded him, one is tempted to turn over a new page of Greek history in order to view that first chapter which begins after the invention of the alphabet. For historians, themselves literate, it is a relief to get into a period which is documented adequately, as it is supposed, by writers, rather than one which is open only to inspection by what I may call the informed imagination. Were not the necessities surrounding oral storage of information, the pre-literate conditions which required that society codify its traditions in an enclave of contrived language—was not all this swept away after 700? When we reach authors after Homer, cannot we deal with them as authors in our sense, rather than in the Homeric sense?

Yet our impatience may be premature. The utilisation of the rhythmic and contrived word as a mnemonic to accumulate directive information in personal memory was a habit that had been cultivated and applied for tens of thousands of years, and had been shared by total populations in varying degree. It controlled the ordinary expectancy of "authorship," if the term may be used to describe the compositional activity of a singer and reciter. If I may repeat a question which in an earlier context of this essay I have already asked: Is it likely that this expectancy would collapse at once before the onset of a new technology? The impact to be sure was formidable. A collision between old and new was inescapable. Precisely what form it took, cannot be considered in these pages. It is sufficient for the moment to note that the contrast between a technique of acoustic storage which depended on personal memory and one which depended on visual recognition of a script which could be stored outside the memory and could be re-used without any consumption or wear and tear, theoretically forever—this contrast was fundamental. The new technique still depended on that ability to encode a language which is basic to our species, but at a stroke the need for a further stimulus of memorisation achieved within the confines of a contrived linguistic rhythm was abolished.

Or rather, we should say that this was true in theory. The historian, looking back from an experience of over 2,000 years of literacy, has the advantage of retrospect. He can afford to be logical and clear sighted. Is it likely, in the known ways of things, the human ways, that men of the centuries that immediately followed the alphabetic invention would be equally logical? Is it not more likely that habits of oral conservation which had proved viable from time immemorial would seem to retain their viability with some persistence, that the possibilities of the new technique would meet with resistance from the users of the old? Was the professional skill of the rhythmic composer likely to yield with grace to the activity of the scribe? Had not the magisterial status of the composers of rhythmic speech been long acknowledged and entrenched? Were these same people likely to turn their energies to literate composition, or if they did, were they in a position to expect a public which would read their written compositions rather than listen to their recital?

Literacy, when finally achieved, presented a profound change in methods of communication. But the technology of the change was unusually complex. Many revolutionary inventions, perhaps most, supply a new tool or source of energy which has no organic connection with the means of production that has been displaced.

Horse-power, on the one hand, and the steam engine on the other, are quite disparate sources of energy. But in the present case, both old and new depended still on a manipulation of language, and the encoded ability to remember a language remained basic to both. The issue arose not over creating a new language, that is, over a new system of communication as such, but only over the best method of achieving storage and re-use of existing communication. The result was that the usage of the old and the usage of the new in the three following centuries continued to overlap. Composers of the contrived word originally, it is to be guessed, allowed their compositions to be taken down by a listener. Later they took to writing them down themselves at dates which cannot easily be settled. But whichever they did, their initial proclivity would be to use the script now available only to record what was already previously composed according to oral principles. That is, the oral habit would persist and would remain effective to a varying degree, even in the case of composers whom we would style writers. This habit, after all, had not been personally chosen by themselves; it was a conditioned response to the needs of an audience who still demanded of the compositions offered that they be memorisable.

This auditory expectation was not going to change overnight. Indeed, the problems surrounding the creation of a reading public to replace the previous listening public would be formidable. Their exploration, again, lies beyond the limits of the present essay. Consequently, it is likely that for a long time a classical author, aside from his personal proclivity to retain the Homeric habit of composing wholly in his head, would compose under audience control. He would perhaps be able to write, and so document his activity, and he was no doubt quickly aware of the advantage of this kind of permanence to assist his fame, if nothing else. But would he not continue to expect that his fame would mainly depend on the memories of audiences who would transmit his compositions by word of mouth, so that only slowly would he come to recognise the possibility of composing that kind of statement which need not be memorised?

To demonstrate that these probabilities were indeed fulfilled in the history of what we call Greek literature, one need only turn to a survey of its general course and character. Under non-literate conditions, poetic speech was the only preservable speech, that is, it constituted the oral "literature" of the time. Vernacular prose was by definition ephemeral. It lived only a temporary life in the memory of either speaker or listener. The literature of Greece which is documented after 700, down to the lifetime of Euripides, remains peculiarly poetic. The earliest prose attested by extant quotation is Ionic, dating from perhaps 500 or a little earlier.[68] The earliest work of prose literature that has survived in its own right is that of Herodotus. It also is in Ionic and dates from after 450 B.C. In the last third of the fifth century there possibly appeared a very few of the treatises in the Hippocratic corpus, a very few philosophical treatises, all short, and a very few sophistic essays, equally short. These again were composed in Ionic. The first surviving prose composition in the Attic dialect is a short anonymous and ill-written essay on the politics of the Periclean democracy. The first magisterial composition in Attic, equalling in length the achievements of epic poetry, was the history of Thucydides. Thus, while the last half of the fifth century begins to see the acceptance of prose as a viable means of publication, acceptance does not become complete until the fourth. This is three hundred years after the invention of the alphabet had rendered the monopoly exercised by poetry over the contrived word theoretically obsolete.

The arrival of prose composition, as it marked the growing expectation of readership, also signalised a growing distance between the composer and his public, a distance which the writer seeks to bridge by adding a signature like an inscription to his work. The two signatures of Herodotus and Thucydides in their respective differences cast some light upon the mode of the literate revolution now underway.

"Here is information acquired by Herodotus of Halicarnassus, now published to prevent what has happened from departing in the course of time from memory among men, and the mighty and marvellous deeds recorded of Greeks and barbarians from being deprived of their fame."[69]

---

[68] I exclude the Milesian philosophers whose *ipsissima verba* are beyond recall. Cf. Havelock, "Pre-Literacy," p. 51.

[69] Herod. *Proem.*

We observe in these words both his proximity to the epic role of storage, guarding the cultural memory, and yet the essential difference that separates him from Homer. The Greek term which I have paraphrased by the word "published" really indicates an oral performance for an audience, but the performance so indicated would now consist of reading aloud from a manuscript, not intoning an oral address. In terms of the technology of the communication, Herodotus occupies a position poised midway between complete non-literacy and complete literacy. But Thucydides, the historian of the Peloponnesian War, while still a bard in the sense that he is a celebrant of the great deeds of heroes, is himself modernised and literate, a singer no more but now a self-styled writer. As a writer he is able to insist on a new version of the bard's role, and on a revised conception of the bard's methods. The famous promise that his work will constitute an eternal possession, rather than a transient entertainment,[70] still asserts the traditional bardic claim upon the memory of posterity, and reinforces it by competitive disparagement of rivals in terms reminiscent of Pindar. The methods by which the claim is to be executed are different; the work in question is conceived as a written volume which can become a piece of property on a shelf, what he calls a *ktema*, rather than a performance offered in oral competition, the meaning of the word *agonisma* with which he points up the contrast. The effect of oral performance is ephemeral, but a document continues to exist in time, a second contrast to which he also gives expression.

And so, as the fifth century passes into the fourth, the full effect upon Greece of the alphabetic revolution begins to assert itself. The governing word ceases to be a vibration heard by the ear and nourished in the memory. It becomes a visible artifact. Storage of information for re-use, as a formula designed to explain the dynamics of western culture, ceases to be a metaphor. The documented statement, persisting through time unchanged, is to release the human brain from certain formidable burdens of memorisation while increasing the energies available for conceptual thought. The results as they are to be observed in the intellectual history of Greece and of Europe were profound. Their examination lies beyond the compass of my present inquiry, and indeed would be

---

[70] Thuc. 1. 22. 4.

premature until the poetic literature of Greece between Homer and the death of Euripides has itself been re-evaluated. The paradox of the conditions of its composition, poised as it was between two cultures, the oral and the literate, and forming a bridge between them, was in the nature of things unique and can never recur. It was probably this, even more than the genius of the race, which called into existence those peculiar qualities in Greek literature, at once responsive to us and yet remote from us, which we identify as "classical." But this too must remain a vista for further exploration.

The Ancient Art of Oral Poetry

Eric A. Havelock

Among poets of consequence in the history of European literature, no name is more familiar than Homer's. Millions who have
never read a word of him know he existed. Two reasons have
supported a unique status for him: he is massive and monumental, and also, inexplicably, he is there, present at the beginning,
the first, the oldest, the archetype. Over the last half century,
this general esteem has gained a new dimension. He can now be
read, or rather listened to, as the prototype of the poetic word
orally composed and orally recited without benefit of writing.

This discovery, if that be the right word for an explanation of
his style which now seems obvious, originated in a study of the
formulaic and repetitive character of the text in which the style
is preserved. Theory deduced from this fact was then confirmed
by empirical evidence gathered in the Balkans, by observing and
recording the formulaic and thematic practices of certain oral
"singers of tales" in the villages and countryside, these performances being regarded as contemporary survivals of an ancient
art. Comparative studies supplied further analogical evidence,
drawn from the styles of early "epic" or "heroic" poetry preserved in other areas of the world. In the meantime, two related
disciplines, one extending from the nineteenth century, the other
formed very recently in the twentieth, have been converging
upon the same problem. Anthropology, responding in particular
to the intellectual leadership of French science and scholarship,
has studied in increasing quantity the oral "literatures" and
"myths" of preliterate societies, in areas of Africa and the
Americas, where these have survived long enough to be recorded by literate investigators. In America, the proliferation of
new media of mass communication has encouraged a new interest in communication as such. What are its modes, its methods,
and its aims? Within the range of these problems, an investigation of the modes and effects of oral communication plays an

increasingly prominent role. If, as the writings of McLuhan and Ong suggest, the culture of our own generation is seeing a revival of orality as a viable mode of communication with a long historical ancestry, a mode moreover which has advantages over the "linear" methods of the literate word, are we to look into Homer for additional light upon this important question?

The Winged Word,[1] Berkley Peabody's important contribution to the study of "Oral Theory and the Epos" (the title of the first section of his first chapter), brushes in close contact as it were with these larger questions, while avoiding any involvement with them. But he does confront and attempt to solve one "Homeric question" which it is fair to say many classical scholars, let alone the general public are scarcely aware of. What precisely was this meter in which Homer composed? Or rather, since it is easy to define each "line" on paper as a "hexameter," marked off and and divided by written symbols into six "feet," each "foot" adding up to two "long" syllables or one "long" plus two "shorts," with each hexameter always adding up to the equivalent of 24 "shorts," neither more nor less—How did it come about that such an unusually formal and rigorous system of,counting, standardized within a fixed number of possible variations, could impose itself upon the rhythms of the Greek tongue? The hexameter is so familiar, so neat in its careful elaboration, so manageable, that its essential strangeness escapes notice, especially as the Roman poets adapted it to Latin, in which tongue it had until recently been known and scanned and translated by generations of schoolboys. What of the other meters of Greek poetry? Do they exhibit the same kinds of elaborate fixity? Does any known verse of other cultures combine such complexity with such regularity?

The question was asked and an answer proposed (though not dogmatically) in the first quarter of this century by the French scholar Antoine Meillet. The hexameter he suggested was a "foreign" meter (deriving from whatever source "foreign" might indicate) not native to Indo-European tongues. Some proof of this is visible in the manipulation which the Greek vocabulary has had to undergo to fit into the meter, producing "epic" forms which are artificial. Peabody grounds his own exposition of oral theory in a firm rejection of this suggestion. The hexameter, he argues, like other Greek meters, developed within a general metrical tradition which was Indo-European. Its particular prototypes can be seen in the earliest surviving poetries of Persia ("Iranian") and India, the ancestors of classical Sanskrit poetry. As we examine the relationship between the Greek verse and these "eastern" prototypes, we are on the way to discerning also the general principles of phonetic association upon which all genuinely oral composition proceeds, anywhere in the world.

Peabody pursues the proof of this thesis, in general perspective and closely reasoned detail, with conviction and commitment and, it might be said, a degree of fanaticism. Both method and conclusions are vulnerable to criticisms of a kind which I shall describe later. But his book overall is too close to the realities of the oral situation, it contains too many insights which penetrate into the character of the oral-linguistic medium and the secrets of the mentality that uses it, to be brushed aside or ignored as the work of a specialist with limited appeal to a narrow audience. Yet Peabody makes few concessions to his readers. To follow his argument is a formidable exercise. His text (pp. 1–272) is convoluted, occupying less space than notes and appendices (pp. 273–562). The notes supply a wealth of reference and information which often read more easily and are more convincing. The usefulness of the book is crippled by the lack of a general index. Bibliography can be traced through a name-index of authorities, but laboriously. Stylistically the work suffers from being overwritten with frequent complexity of jargon which has the effect of concealing from view an analysis which, presented in simpler terms, would have more immediate effect. Yet I know of no treatise which seeks to engage so intimately with the phonological and phonetic substance of the oral compositional process. Peabody is not the first to explore the components and continuities of the Greek oral style. But as one reads the competing theories of previous exponents of descriptive metrics, especially as applied to the Homeric sphere of colometric theory, formula analysis, geometric patterns and "monumental" composition, one receives a continual impression of a critique which is still reading a text, looking at it as a visible body to be dissected or assembled. What Peabody does is to try to listen, to see if he can catch the incantation of the verse and somehow describe its own acoustic laws and methods.

The work deserves to be recommended to an informed audience who are unlikely to have the patience to read it through. The summary which follows may help to perform this service. Its length seems necessary if I am to avoid doing violence by omission of essential detail to the careful continuity of Peabody's argument.

Chapter One, styled "The Approach," opens with the argument that there is a specific oral style of composition, distinct from literate styles, which has a necessary existence as the vehicle of the "oral tradition" by which the continuities of a culture are maintained. Actual presence of the style in a given text is detectable by criteria defining five types of "redundancy" or "regularity" in the language. These are phonemic patterns, like rhyme or assonance, formulaic patterns, occurring in recurrent "morphemic clusters," periodic or syntactic patterns, thematic patterns (by which Peabody appears also to identify the repetition of similar syllables in different words) and finally the "Song Test" (1–8). Chapters Three to Six, the reader will discover, in effect explore the substance of these tests, in the order given, explication of the Song Test being reserved for the last chapter. The remainder of Chapter One with Chapter Two explores the problem of the Greek hexameter, as used by Hesiod in what Peabody assumes to be its earliest available Greek form (9–11). Greek is an Indo-European tongue; its meters other than the hexameter have Indo-European analogies. The hexameter is no exception, being a form developed from the meter used in the Iranian Gathas ("Songs") preserved in the collection known as the Avesta, and the Vedas of India (20–29). Chapter Two, "The Shape of Utterance" (30–65) examines these "eastern" prototypes. They are used to express religious utterance, in the form of rituals, incantations, hymns and the like, indicating the original purpose of metrical speech and hence the general character of the oral tradition out of which the Greek epos developed. Narrative style intruded on these forms only later as a gloss (30–

31). The Gathas are composed in "lines" of between eight and twelve syllables. These are syntactically separate units and form a series of padas ("feet," the term being used in an extended sense). The padas combine in twos or threes to form verses, and the verses combine in twos or threes to form stanzas. The Vedic meters have a similar base but are more regularized and in some Vedic "lines" quantity (rather than mere syllable count) begins to emerge as a factor at the end of the line; "the rules are the same as for Greek" (37). In later classical Sanskrit verse, quantity extends over the whole line; the rule of a "long" as equivalent to two "shorts" emerges and the caesura, hitherto a feature of these eastern meters, as of Greek, begins to be eliminated through the process of "Sandhi," a blurring of junctures between words (38–45). However, syllable count still remains fundamental. The line of development from Avesta to the Vedas to classical Sanskrit can be discerned in parallel within the structure of the Greek hexameter. While its syllable count varies between eleven and seventeen, the "mora" count (in which a long syllable equals two short ones) is a constant twenty-three or twenty-four. This has been achieved by combining two padas of 12 syllables each or three of eight, the original junctures being indicated by the Greek caesuras (45–51). The "irregular" quantities encountered in hexameter verse indicate that the original base of the meter was syllabic and not quantitative (51–55). The "long" syllables came about through "syllable collapse" (55–64), so that the hexameter is not that artificial rhythm rigidly controlled by the quantity rule which it is often envisaged to be. The Avestan, the Vedic and the Greek metrical developments are alike (65).

Guided by this view of the ancestry of the Greek epos, Chapter Three, "The Form of Words" examines the structure of the hexameter in terms of the colon (66–96) and the formula (96–117). The text of Hesiod's *Works and Days* (referred to in this review henceforth as "Hesiod") will constitute the basic evidence for such a study (66). The cola are the initial units of composition, being "groups of syllables" (forming a whole word or words) usually but not necessarily four to a hexameter. Their arrangement governs the caesura, not vice versa. The last one is habitually lengthy and reflects the eight-syllable pada of Avestan verse. The cola can group themselves into two pairs, each pair forming a hemistich which recalls the twelve-syllable "line" of Avestan. Hesiod's verses are tabulated according to types of distribution of syllable units. Twelve such types account for three quarters of the Greek total (66–70). The quantities (as opposed to syllable counts) of the meter are created at "juncture points" (72–73). Cola are "single" or "compound," sometimes "eccentric." The final long one takes various forms. These varieties are tabulated statistically (73–95).

"Formulas" (rendered familiar to students of oral theory by Milman Parry's work) are examined colometrically, as consisting of single cola or aggregates of such. The longer ones usually form hemistiches (104–106). There is a separate category of "set phrases" (107–110). These various components of the verse enable the singer to sing, assisted by the fact that idioms and rhythms of ordinary speech (as learned for example by children) are reflected in his composition (110–113). The cola are the basic raw material of composition. The composer moves on from one colon to the next. There are up to five possible "points of decision" for him in the verse (114–116).

Cola are units of rhythm, not in themselves meaningful until combined into "syntactical periods," "clauses," or "sentences." These become the subject of Chapter Four ("The Extension of the Clause" 118–167). The compositional process advances by accretion: first the pada, then the metrical "line" of the eastern prototype. This is also a "clause," and is itself composed of two elements. Padas are then combined to form "utterances" or "sentences," the largest of which becomes the "stanza" (119). These patterns appear in the Avesta and the Vedas and indeed in all Indo-European prototypes and are reproduced in Greek stanzaic construction (120–121). The internal structure of the hexameter is equivalent to a combination (as has been said) of two or three padas. Hexameters frequently combine into couplets, each equivalent to four padas of the Avesta (122). However, the hexameter often behaves internally as though these padas were "enjambed" or fused together. This is a Greek and not an Eastern phenomenon (123). In Hesiod only

165 hexameters are "syntactically separate," about 20%—a figure also true of Homer. In the majority of these a two-clause construction or something like it is perceptible. Such "coincidence of pada and clause periods" reflects Eastern metrical tradition (125). As for the larger "stanza," this also is related to Eastern prototypes, showing a long term trend moving from simple two-clause "incantations" to "sets" of paratactic clauses, a trend demonstrable in Hesiod's text (126–129). However, hexameters also enjamb with each other (135–143), another exclusively Greek habit. Thus while Hesiod yields only 165 single (syntactically separable) hexameters, he yields 250 formed into 125 couplets and 413 yielding larger "periods" of three or more hexameters (143). The single type can under analysis be seen to compose a prototypical "stanza" of hexameter length (147). The structural terms "haploid" and "diploid" (introduced as headings of sections at 143, 152, but not otherwise mentioned or explained till 155) describe ascending stages of "incremental" stanza construction in which the metrical unit is one hexameter, itself formed as a "two or three pada verse" (155), then increased to a hexameter couplet, then to three-and four-hexameter groups, in which the couplet becomes the new "unit," so that historically the epos grows incrementally, using one-cola formulas, then compound formulas, then compounding formulas into a pada, then combining two or three padas into a hexameter, then combining two of these into a couplet (a "haploid" stanza), then fusing couplets into "diploid" stanzas (161). Yet the haploid construction remains dominant; only one quarter of Hesiod is "diploid" (165).

Chapter Five moves on to consider "The Responsions of Thought." The true "thought" or content of oral epos is traditional, to be found in the formulaic and stanzaic patterns of the text, not in the conscious intentions of the singer-composer. "The thought of an oral tradition belongs properly to the discourse of that tradition and not to any individual" (172). The singer controls only "phenomenalised meaning" (179), in the form of narrative features. The thought is the "wisdom" or the "message" of the oral composition (168, 170). It expresses itself in the patterns of "theme" and stanza. The thematic structure can be illustrated by a passage (Hesiod 427–440) in which syllables of words and word themselves are found echoing each other as the verse proceeds, as in *gar . . . arousin . . . bousin . . . aroun . . . heteron . . . heteron* etc. (179–183). The epos in this way is always presenting an "immediate present idea" (188). Phonetic redundancy of diction, producing alliteration, anaphora, chiasmus, and the like, expresses "responsions of thought" (189–192). There is also present that assistance to the "Song" produced by musical instruments. Traditional composition has been associated with "hand activity" (197; this would apply particularly to drum and strings). Phonetic echoes are vital to oral composition. The fable of The Hawk and The Nightingale (Hesiod) and the episode of The Building of the Raft (*Odyssey*) exemplify this (198–206). On the other hand the larger structures of narrative proper are secondary, a "superstructure" imposed upon the original padas and stanzas (206–213). The "thought" of the tradition is found in the "theme"; it resides in a "generalised memory," while the tale told by the singer is deployed at a second "diachronic level" of the memory; the song is a "feedback" (213–215).

It comes therefore as no surprise when Peabody in his last chapter, "The Flight of Song," argues that the story told in the epos is a secondary feature. It is not here that we look for basic clues to the character of oral composition. Nevertheless, "song" (his preferred term) is "what the singer remembers as the truth," which means "the memory of songs sung." It cannot therefore be "imaginative"; it is less essential to traditional discourse than theme; it "regulates" theme like a kind of "super-ego"; it is "remembered experience" (216–218). Yet song can apparently take over from theme, or restrict it and "garble" it (220). The two would seem to interplay with each other. It is wrong to perceive "theme and song patterns only in rapid narrative" (221). Yet in fact the two (theme versus song) are difficult to separate. Thematic units can grow into short narratives, by introduction of narrative formulas (222) and "thematically salient" formulas "fade into the general phenomenalisation of the song." In examples like the Raft Building (*Odyssey*) and the Generations of Man (Hesiod) wé can see "semantic decorum" becoming "the first shadow of song," usually after extending beyond four or five verses (223). At greater intervals of about eleven verses "phonic echo" forms an "interlacing web," though not always predictably. The time span of such phonic responsion systems is about one minute. Possibly they represent "a mental process which synthesises our phenomenalized reality" (224).

Connections beyond this span are achieved by song alone (224). To identify these "song patterns" one first identifies and eliminates all formulaic and thematic features. "Song" is what is left (225–227). To explicate song as a superstructure, Peabody turns to the extended episode of Achilles' Shield (*Iliad* 18). In its context it is "unusual" (231) and indeed the mission which elicits it, the visit of Thetis, Achilles' mother, to Hephaestus to obtain arms for her son, is "all but needless" (234). What has happened is that the singer improvising as he goes commits an initial "accident" (231) by letting Achilles say "I will return to battle" (*Il.* 18, 114) when he logically cannot do so, being without armour; the statement is "accidentally premature." The singer realises his mistake as he sings, but is unable to undo it— "a verse once uttered cannot be recalled" (234)—so his verse stumbles (*Il.* 18, 115–126) and then recovers by retracing and re-singing in reverse order what he had related to this point. But, alas, he then commits a blunder by letting Achilles be prematurely re-armed (*Il.* 18, 165–214). This results from over-recollecting and re-using an inappropriate formula from Book Eleven, a "crucial Homeric nod" (233–234). He then proceeds to re-sing (in summary form) parts of Book One, so as to bring Thetis to Hephaestus (who is substituted for the Zeus of Book One). By this route he reaches the theme of "arms" (*entea, tenchea*), picked up from before the point where the original "accident" occurred. "Retrogression is an important song feature" (232) used in this instance to remedy the "loss of song" and supply its "recall" (233).

In Peabody's concluding pages (266–272) this rationale of Homeric composition is applied to Hesiod, whose text offers an initial difficulty: "The several sections . . . are developed to a size that makes them like complete songs in themselves" (237). Even in the "Strife Passage," Hesiod's first section, "the narrowing of semantic scope . . . does not occur in a gradual, even way . . . rather in a series of steps or plateaus . . . " (239). Nevertheless, the poem overall must have that kind of associative continuity proper to oral composition. Disconnection is only apparent. It disappears when one perceives the singer employing those twin devices of the *Iliad,* "retrogression" and "remembered song" (243–245). Their employment appears internally within the initial Strife Passage (245) and also supplies linkage between the subsequent main sections of the entire poem, which Peabody here identifies as "The Pandora Myth, The Kings, The Harangue on Justice, and the great Catalogue" (244). The Shield of the Iliad, functioning as remembered song—Peabody is thinking in particular of the description in it of a legal dispute—supplies the recollection required to assist composition of the Harangue; or, putting it the other way round, "the re-emergence of dik- in the Harangue prepares the way for the development of the Shield Scene clump" (255). A second major influence in Hesiod's overall composition is supplied by the "Paris Song" (245). The identity of this portion of the *Iliad* (in Book Three and a large part of Four) is defended in an important note (480). It "casts a peculiar shadow on the Works and Days" (245), supplying such "thematic" recollections as *neikos* (quarrel), Helen (equals Hesiod's Pandora), and congruent names like Paris-Perses, Pandarus-Pandora (246). Even Hesiod's Generations of Man is introduced (at line 106) by a thematic linkage with the same fourth book of the *Iliad,* which turns on the word "crest," as well as by the theme of "strife" (248–250). Recollection of some song passages in the *Odyssey* explains linkage between Hesiod's Hawk and Nightingale and his Pandora (251–252), and reveals that the two birds represent rival singers (253). The Harangue is followed by Hesiod's "Principal Section," amounting to two-thirds of the poem and containing "two calendar catalogues one of seasons and one of days" (256). The second of these revives thematic material recollected from the Strife Passage (258–259), and also "relates directly to the first section of the Harangue" (260). Peabody admits however that "sections" of the Song of the Seasons follow "a strict non-linguistic chronological sequence" (260), recollection of the Paris Song having already "faded away" (258). The final Catalogue of Days "depends directly on the Harangue" even though Perses is no longer mentioned (262–263).

The poem overall is unified by the "controlling 'theme' " expressed in the proem to Zeus. This "dominates all sections" (264). Its effect is reinforced by recollection of a passage in Hesiod's *Theogony* describing the offspring of Zeus' marriage with Themis. Pairing of names, like Zeus with Themis, has significance for oral composition; so also the "pair of names" Hesiod and Perses, implying contest between rival singers, only one of whom is Zeus-inspired. Possibly Perses recalls the "wise Perses," a Titan in the *Theogony,* Prometheus (a figure in both poems) being also a Titan (265–266). To be sure, "the peculiar feature of the controlling theme is the personal aspect," which is connected with "contests of singers," so that the whole poem becomes a "Contest-Song" (267–268). The existence of this contest genre of oral poetry is supported by comparative evidence (270–271). However, "the principal song form . . . is difficult to assess . . . there is little to identify" (268–269). Possibly it is "a specialised type of religious song" with an analogue in the Homeric Hymn to Hermes (269). Or is it like "a speech from a giant heroic-epic" (270)?

The poem was however sung in a culture "more and more dependent on material technology for its survival . . . Somehow the song is overly aware . . . ." Through its words "we take a very terrible look deep within the dying eyes of a tremendously brave and ancient past" (272).

To construct this account Peabody has drawn on a large apparatus of previous scholarship, mastery of which is sufficiently indicated in the "Notes" and "Bibliography." Immediately evident is his reliance on the fundamentals established by Milman Parry: oral poetry is a phenomenon *sui generis,* and its composition is formulaic. The researches of Albert Lord have added emphasis to the "theme" as a larger component of the style (one which had already begun to attract Parry's attention). For Peabody, thematic structures become based on phonemic patterns—an important advance in scope and precision. Colometric analysis derives from the work of American scholars who

followed Parry (O'Neill and Porter; the importance of cola had
however already been recognized by Wilamowitz and H. Fraen-
kel). Contributions from a century of scholarship, chiefly Ger-
man and French, have been drawn on to support the thesis that
the Greek epos must be understood as belonging in a larger
historical context. In order to pursue a simpler "eastern" prototype for the Greek hexameter, he revives the "developmental"
approach to problems of Greek metrics first proposed and promoted in Germany in the nineteenth century (Bergk and Usener,
and later Wilamowitz). French scholarship (Meillet) and Slavic
(Jakobson) are drawn on to explicate the syllabic basis of Indo-
European verse, even while rejecting the parallel notion that
verse rhythm responds to quantitative variation (Meillet). An
imaginative analysis of the psycho-dynamics which inform the
mental processes of the oral composer recalls French investigation of this problem. (Jousse; the relevance of much of this
European scholarship had of course been noted by Parry himself.) Almost as an aside, Peabody applies to the Greek epos a
lesson from linguistics, drawn from the influential perception
that in the rhythms of poetry we hear echoes of the "phonological patterns" of ordinary language (Jakobson). Insistence on the
fact that the "thought" of an oral tradition (as opposed to
"idea") is "inherent in its actual linguistic practice" is supported by recent behavioristic theory (Skinner). The resources
of Sanskrit scholarship (Arnold, Macdonell, Winternitz, Tara-
porewala, Keith) are drawn on to supply a foundation for placing the Greek hexameter in a context of the Avestan and Vedic
meters. This resumé indicates only the range of sources and
authorities cited, not their volume. Regrettably, Adam Parry's
edition of his father's writings (*The Making of Homeric Verse,*
Oxford, 1971) is ignored, as also is my own *Preface to Plato*
(Harvard, 1963) though both appear to have been drawn on.

Peabody handles the Greek texts with agreeable dexterity.
Desire to press his thesis can betray him into some slips of
translation and twists of interpretation. This is particularly true
of his management (the best word) of the Shield episode in
Homer's *Iliad,* intended to demonstrate "accident" and "mistake" on the part of the singer. The demonstration retains

doubtful validity, despite its imaginative reconstruction of a singer's mental processes. But errors in philology—and there are not many—are a minor matter. It is more important to inquire whether there are larger criticisms to which this account of the Greek epos is vulnerable, and which go to its heart.

Spoken language does not fossilize. The student of orality cannot, like the archaeologist, rely on the "hard" evidence of artifacts. His explorations, when all is said and done, even after making full use of comparative materials, have to rely very considerably on a mixture of psychological intuition and common sense, avoiding if possible a commitment to dogma. Criticisms, however fundamental—as in this case they seem to me to be—are best framed in the interrogative mood.

1. Hesiod's *Works and Days* is presented as a "Song," representing the closest we can get to the original forms of Greek oral composition. It is "archaic" in the sense in which Homer's epic tales are not. Can we really be sure of this? Peabody himself is perhaps not quite certain. Chronology for one thing scarcely supports it. Quite recently textual proof has been offered (in my *Greek Concept of Justice,* Chapter Eleven) that Hesiod's treatment of justice, oral as its style may be, nevertheless draws upon certain episodes of both *Iliad* and *Odyssey*.

2. Hesiod's asserted priority over Homer supports the important conclusion that narration as such is only a secondary element of oral composition, a "superstructure" imposed upon material of a different character, as seen in Hesiod, whose "song" is committed to singing "Wisdom," not (for the most part) telling a story. If however Hesiod's priority over Homer is doubtful, so also is the thesis that narrative is a secondary characteristic of the oral style. May it not after all be the primary one?

3. A considerable part of Hesiod is catalogue poetry, as Peabody admits. The rest of the poem is made up of "sections" which are identified as a "Strife Song," a "Pandora Song," a "Generations of Man Song," a "Fable," a "Harangue," a "Song of the Seasons." There are also groups of verses ("stanzas") retailing aphorisms, proverbs and the like. Associative connection is sought, sometimes rather desperately, between

these apparently disparate elements to demonstrate that the whole poem is one continuous "song" (though in his conclusion Peabody seems to back away a little from this). But is the poem not more plausibly to be perceived as a congeries of materials, in which the singer is deprived of those "continuities" which assist the progress of genuinely free composition? Is not the attempt to unify the poem, in the sense that Homer's narratives are unified, an artificial exercise?

4. The poem's intentions are overtly didactic. This was recognized in antiquity. Its content is indeed "wisdom" as Peabody defines it. What real support is there for the opinion, widely if unconsciously shared among scholars, including Peabody, that "wisdom literature" constitutes the most antique form of oral composition? that catalogues, religious and moral maxims, and ritualized statements were in circulation as free compositions anterior to epics?

5. The presumption that they were leads Peabody easily to the Sanskrit material as prototypical of oral composition. Much of it is indeed "incantation," religious in tone, even "mystical." For Peabody, it is in these religious hymns that the genius of oral song was born. The barriers of chronology to be climbed in order to reach this conclusion are formidable. The surviving Iranian material postdates the far eastern conquests of Alexander the Great. Tradition in fact asserts that what existed prior to this date was destroyed. As for the Vedas, scholars are free to postulate ancient originals if they choose but no Indian poetry that we have can predate the earliest evidence for Indian writing, in the third century B.C., and most of it is much later. How is one to be sure whether this body of Sanskrit verse responds to the rules of a strictly oral style, rather than to rules which have been modified by literate (or more accurately proto-literate) practice?

6. Must not the same doubts surround the allegedly oral character of Avestan and Vedic metrics? Peabody's model for the hexameter is found in a combination of two or three "padas"; their latent presence in the Greek verse is traced with an ingenuity that is often convincing. But, putting aside the chronological difficulty, can we be sure that the rather mechanical formalism

of the pada measures in the texts we have genuinely reproduces the metrics of an oral style, whether Iranian or Indian, in its original freedom?

7. In fact, when it comes to reconstructing the kind of psychological process which the singer undergoes when he sings, Peabody is guided by the Balkan examples rendered so familiar by Lord's work and illustratable in the Parry collection at Harvard. Overall, the Greek epos is explained in terms of two competing models. On the one hand there are the Jugoslav recitations which offer narrative without benefit of wisdom; on the other there is the "eastern" poetry which offers wisdom without benefit of narrative. In Homer it is possible to perceive the two in combination. May his epics not offer the true original models both of oral style and oral function and purpose in a truly oral culture? This is not a possibility which Peabody considers.

There remains however the genuine problem of Homer's meter (and Hesiod's), which Peabody confronts and for which he offers a carefully thought-out solution. Another can be proposed, of quite a different kind, though it is one for which Peabody denies that any evidence exists. The metrical term "foot" is Greek, and most naturally refers to a dance step. The Greek "chorus" defines a group of dancers, not singers, or else the dance itself. The "strophes" and "antistrophes" into which the stanzas they sing are divided are "turns" and "counterturns" of dance movements. Even the word *metron* ("meter") can apply to a measure spaced out on a surface. Is it possible that the origins of the hexameter—as possibly of other Greek meters— were choreographic? that it was a dance measure (in two-four time?) the tempo of which accompanied elocution? In a literate culture like our own, in which choreography has become a separate and silent art, such a notion may seem bizarre. But might not an oral culture encourage such a partnership, in order to reinforce the task of memorizing the uttered word? Rhythmic pleasures, that is to say, (including those induced by musical instruments), were mobilized to assist in the difficult task of placing the traditional wisdom in orally remembered storage. Whatever the truth of this socially motivated explanation, the epos may have originated in dramatic performances of greater antiquity, later developing its own identity as an independent recitation, but retaining rhythm and music. The reasons for thinking such a theory is plausible lie beyond the limits of this review. What one can say of Peabody's exposition of the problem is that, despite doubts which may surround his particular solution, he cleaves firmly to the phonemic realities which underlie a genuinely oral compositional process. He listens to the singer compounding cola into formulas, formulas into thematic clusters, enclosing clusters in hexameters and hexameters in stanzas, following the lead of the phonetic shapes of the words, by a kind of psychological automatism. It is in these, not in the formation or pursuit of "ideas," as Peabody continually and correctly stresses, that the secrets of oral composition lie. These are the nuts and bolts of the process. Precisely however as one's ear is tuned to hear such rhythms, rather than just see them inscribed on paper, one is tempted to look for analogues, not in the groomed and rather monotonous verses of Sanskrit poetry but in the drumbeat of African and Polynesian recitals, or even the ritualized performance of a rock and roll concert.

Sterling Professor Emeritus
Yale University

NOTES

[1]Berkley Peabody, *The Winged Word. A Study in the Technique of Ancient Greek Oral Composition as Seen Principally through Hesoid's* Works and Days (Albany: State University of New York Press, 1975), pp. xvi + 562.

The Alphabetization
of Homer[1]

by ERIC A. HAVELOCK

SOMEWHERE between 700 and 550 B.C. the *Iliad* and the *Odyssey* were as we say "committed to writing." This way of putting it describes an operation which under modern conditions occurs ten thousand times an hour all over the literate world. The original act was rather different; it was something like a thunder-clap in human history, which our bias of familiarity has converted into the rustle of papers on a desk. It constituted an intrusion into culture, with results that proved irreversible. It laid the basis for the destruction of the oral way of life and the oral modes of thought. This is an extreme way of putting it, intended to dramatize a fact about ourselves. We as literates, inheritors of 2500 years of experience with the written word, are removed by a great distance from the conditions under which the written word first entered Greece, and it requires some effort of the imagination to comprehend what these were and how they affected the manner in which the event took place. More accurately, rather than speak of destruction, we should say that what set in with the alphabetization of Homer was a process of erosion of "orality," extending over centuries of the European experience, one which has left modern culture unevenly divided between oral and literate modes of expression, experience, and living.

All societies support and strengthen their identity by conserving their mores. A social consciousness, formed as a consensus, is as it were continually placed in storage for re-use. Literate societies do this by documentation; preliterate ones achieve the same result by the composition of poetic narratives which serve also as encyclopedias of conduct. These exist and are transmitted through memorization, and as continually recited constitute a report—a reaffirmation—of the communal ethos and also a recommendation to abide by it. Such were the Homeric poems, enclaves of contrived language existing alongside the vernacular. Their contrivance was a response to the rules of oral memorization and the need for secure transmission. Linguistic statements could be remembered and repeated only as they were specially shaped: they existed solely as sound, memorized through the ears and practiced by the mouths of living persons. This sound-sequence was suddenly brought into contact with a set of written symbols possessed of unique phonetic efficiency. An automatic marriage occurred between the two; or, to change the metaphor, upon a body of liquid contained in a vessel was dropped a substance which crystallized the contents and precipitated a deposit upon the bottom.

The spoken and remembered word had after millennia of experimentation with devices we call "writing"—a process abandoned in Greece after the fall of Mycenae—found at last the perfect instrument for its transcription. And therefore in "Homer" we confront a paradox unique in history: two poems we can read in documented form, the first "literature" of Europe; which however constitute the first complete record of "orality," that is, "non-literature"—the only one we are ever likely to have: a statement of how civilized man governed his life and thought during several centuries when he was entirely innocent of the art (or arts) of reading.

The alphabet applied to the Homeric tongue constituted an act of "translation" from sound to sight. It is the completeness of the art which must first be emphasized, and therefore the completeness of the coverage of human experience. Phonetic efficiency meant the removal of that ambiguity of recognition which had limited all previous writing systems in their application.[2] Let us suppose—the supposition is unfounded—that knowledge and use of "Linear B" had survived into early Hellenism. The epic "report" on the Hellenic life-style and mores would have continued to be practiced and recited among the predominantly oral population. The scribes, servants of palace or temple bureaucracies, would have produced what we might call epitomes of this epic material, simplified versions accommodated to the limitations which were inherent in the difficulty of recognition and would require economy and repetitiousness of vocabulary with minimum variation in types of statement. Catalogues and quantities would abound, psychological analysis would be absent. Though meter might be retained, performance would be not popular but liturgical, reserved for high occasions. Meanwhile "Homer" would have continued in composition and recitation among the people, but with the likelihood that the quality of oral art practiced would have suffered because the linguistic brains of the community were being drained off into the scribal centers. Homer's formulaic complexity, unique among the surviving remnants of oral poetry, bespeaks a culture totally non-literate, in which a monopoly of linguistic sophistication was vested in the bard.

A flood recorded in cuneiform

We do not have any Linear B "epic" to support the hypothesis just proposed. Could it be supported by any comparison with syllabic documents of other cultures, documents, that is, which were pre-alphabetic? There is a passage in the *Epic of Gilgamesh* which achieves a degree of narrative vividness not to be matched elsewhere in the poem. This seems due to the employment of an unusually rich vocabulary of words describing acts and occurrences which are very concrete and specific—we might say detailed. Such at least would be the inference which a scholar ignorant of cuneiform—as is the present writer—would allow himself to draw from the English translation that Near Eastern scholarship has provided.[3] The narrator is one Utnapishtim, the Babylonian Noah; his account of the Flood is recognizable as the model for the parallel story in the *Book of Genesis*:

> With the first glow of dawn
> A black cloud rose up from the horizon
> Inside it Adad thunders
> While Shullat and Hanish go in front
> 5 Moving as heralds over hill and plain.
> Erragal tears out the posts;
> Forth comes Ninurta and causes the dikes to follow.
> The Anunnaki lift up the torches
> Setting the land ablaze with their glare.
> 10 Consternation over Adad reaches to the heavens,
> Who turned to blackness all that had been light.
> [The wide] land was shattered like [a pot]:
> For one day the south-storm [blew].
> Gathering speed as it blew [submerging the mountains].
> 15 Overtaking the [people] like a battle.
> No one can see his fellow,
> Nor can the people be recognized from heaven.

!

> The gods were frightened by the deluge,
> And shrinking back, they ascended to the heaven of Anu . . .
> 20 Six days and [six] nights
> Blows the flood wind, as the south-storm sweeps the land
> When the seventh day arrived,
> The flood [-carrying] south-storm subsided in the battle
> Which it had fought like an army,
> 25 The sea grew quiet, the tempest was still, the flood ceased.
> I looked at the weather: stillness had set in
> And all of mankind had returned to clay.
> 28 The landscape was as level as a flat roof.

What variety of vocabulary has been packed so to speak into this passage? Obviously a translation does not of itself provide an accurate word-count of the original. As a general rule it will be a little richer, indulging in the temptation to provide variants in varying contexts for what are really equivalents. However, for what it is worth, a word-count can be made: prepositions and conjunctions can be ignored, also inflections, and the names of the gods can be counted as a single unit, representing a catalogue. With these provisos, the passage in translation furnishes a total of 90 words, of which 69 are unique; the repetitions are counted as follows:

doublets: black . . . blackness (2, 11); go-in-front . . . forth-comes (4, 7); all (11, 27); battle (15, 23); people (15, 17); can (16, 17); six (20); still . . . stillness (25, 26)

triplets: land (9, 12, 21); heavens (10, 17, 19); day (13, 20, 22); blew (13, 14, 21); south-storm (13, 21, 23)

quadruplet: deluge and flood (if equivalent) (18, 21, 23, 25).

The percentage of non-unique words to the total is 23.3.

More significant (because less liable to distortion through translation) are duplicated statements, not necessarily equivalent, but expressive of meanings which paraphrase each other. This phenomenon does not occur in the first 12 lines. But then it is as though the verbal "originality" of composition begins to exhaust itself, and we get the following series of repetitive sequences:

(a) 13 for one day the south-storm blew
    14 gathering speed as it blew
    20 six days and six nights
    21 blows the flood wind as the south-storm sweeps the land
(b) 16 no one can see his fellows
    17 nor can the people be recognized
(c) 18 the gods were frightened
    19 and shrinking back
(d) 15 overtaking the people like a battle
    23 subsided in battle
    24 which it had fought like an army
(e) 25 sea grew quiet, tempest was still, flood ceased
    26 stillness had set in.

The description of the Flood is interrupted by a digression of 13 lines describing the conclave of the frightened gods. It intervenes between lines 19 and 20 of the passage as we have printed it, and runs as follows.

> The gods cowered like dogs
>   Crouched against the outer wall.
> Ishtar cried out like a woman in travail,
> The sweet-voiced mistress of the [gods] moans aloud:
> 5 "The olden days are alas turned to clay,
> Because I bespoke evil in the assembbly of the gods.
> How could I bespeak evil in the assembly of the gods,
> Ordering battle for the destruction of my people!
> When it is I myself who gives birth to my people!
> 10 Like the spawn of the fishes they fill the sea!"
> The Anunnaki gods weep with her,
> The gods, all humbled, sit and weep,
> Their lips drawn tight, [. . .] one and all.

The repetitive, not to say ritualistic character of this passage is obvious: line 7 repeats line 6; the word gods recurs six times in 12 lines; six of the verbs fall into three pairs of variants: cowered—crouched; cried out—moans aloud; weep with her—sit and weep; and there are repetitions of motifs contained in the storm passage.

A flood recorded in the alphabet

It is now appropriate to compare a description of a flood producing similar consequences as it occurs in the text of Homer. In the twelfth book of the *Iliad* the poet himself undertakes to explain why it is that the fortifications built by the Greeks to protect their camp are in his day no longer extant:

> 12.17 Then indeed Poseidon and Apollo devised
>   the wall to demolish, by intruding the might of rivers
>   as many as from Idaean mountains seaward flow-forth
> 20 Rhesus and Heptaporos and Caresus and Rhodius
>   Granicus and Aesopus and divine Scamander
>   and Simois, where many oxhide-shields and helmets
>   tumbled in mud and the generation of demigod men;
>   of them all the mouths together Phoebus Apollo turned
> 25 and nine-days against the wall directed the flow; and Zeus rained
>   continually, that sooner he might set the walls sea-born;
>   himself the earth-shaker having trident in hands
>   went-before, and all foundations discharged upon-the-waves
>   of logs and stones, that the toiling Achaeans had-set
> 30 and made [them] smooth beside full-flowing Hellespont
>   and again the great foreshore covered with sand
>   the wall having-demolished; the rivers he turned to run
> 33 down their flow, whereby formerly they directed [their] fair-flowing water.

Ignoring the Greek particles, counting Poseidon-Apollo as one term, but Zeus separately, and counting the river-catalogue as one, this passage provides a total of 71 words, of which 61 are unique; the repetitions being counted as follows:

doublets: demolish (18, 32); rivers (18, 32); directed (25, 33); turned (24, 32); set (26, 29); flow (25, 33); all (24, 28);
one quadruplet: wall (18, 25, 26, 32).

The percentage of non-unique words to the total is 14%.

Of these two epic descriptions of similar events, the Greek one has managed a variety of vocabulary proportionately greater. The difference between 14% and 23% may not seem very great but it assumes significance when it is borne in mind that the concrete vividness of the Babylonian is untypical of what is mostly offered in the translated version of the epic, whereas the Greek passage is typical of Greek epic. When we look, in the Greek, for duplicated statements not necessarily equivalent but expressive of meanings which paraphrase each other, we discover only one:

18 the wall to-demolish
32 the wall having-demolished

It is true that three variant phrases all describe the assault of the flood waters:

18 intruding the might of rivers
24 the mouths together turned
25 against the wall directed the flow

But what these do is to divide the assault into three successive stages, spelling out details which are not repetitive of each other, but logically cumulative. As for the two concluding hexameters (32, 33), though they carry echoes of lines 19, 24 and 25, their vocabulary and syntax have been carefully manipulated so as to describe a reversal of previous action.

It is fair to conclude that the alphabetized Greek description of a flood is less tautological, less ritualized than the cuneiform. A vocabulary arrangement is applied to the task which is more expressive, as we would say, because it is richer in variety of nouns, verbs and adjectives, and less given to repetitive syntax, that is, to variations of the same essential statements. Both versions are of orally composed speech and therefore formulaic and repetitive to a degree which is uncharacteristic of literate discourse. But admitting this, in the Greek version we are brought into more direct contact with the complexities of human descriptive speech at its most concrete level; the Babylonian version by contrast simplifies the report, reducing it to a kind of archetypal statement, what can be called an "authorized version".[4]

A critic schooled in the ways of literacy would trace the difference to two differing views of "poetics," to two different poetic conventions or "styles" which a given language chooses to adopt, and would use the repetitive charac-

ter of the Babylonian as an excuse to assign to it qualities of solemnity, grandeur, spiritual simplicity and the like. But a quite different explanation is possible, one which relies on the phonetic superiority of the alphabet over the
cuneiform. According to this view, the deficiencies of cuneiform as an instrument of acoustic-visual recognition have discouraged the composer from
packing into his verse the full variety of expression which such a description
calls for: the alphabet on the other hand applied to a transcription of the same
experience places no obstacles in the way of its complete phonetic translation.

If this is true, a further conclusion probably follows: the ability to describe
the human experience fully in adequate language was surely available to the
citizens of all urbanized cultures of the Near East, no less than to the Greeks.
This capacity however was expressible orally and would not be available to
writers. We must presume therefore that behind the scribal version of the flood
which is all we have lies hidden forever, and lost to us forever, a far richer epic,
linguistically speaking, or series of epics, which, obeying the law of cultural
storage, performed for those cultures the functions that Homer performed for
pre-literate Greece. This would be the poetry of the people, on their lips, in
their memories, composed by Mesopotamian bards using formulaic rhythms
comparable with the Greek, though as we have pointed out probably less
sophisticated. What we have in cuneiform is not their words as they were
spoken, but epitomes transcribed for recital on formal occasions, even though
the Gilgamesh epic is classified by scholars as a secular poem.

The limits of expressive speech which impose themselves upon the Gilgamesh poem are shared by the entire "literature" so called of the Near East. If
we may quote from an authoritative judgment: "The first shortcoming in texts
from Mesopotamia is the consistent absence of any expression of that civilizations's uniqueness in the face of an alien background. . . . The second and
closely related negative characteristic is the absence of any polemic in cuneiform literature. There is no arguing against opposing views; we find here none
of the revealing dialogue which in Greek life and thought finds expression in
court, in the theater, and in the lecture room. This might well be the main
reason why we know so little about Mesopotamian attitudes towards the *realities of the world around them* (my italics) and so much about the Greek . . .
No effort is made to relate within one conceptual framework differences in
outlook or evaluation. Hence, all cuneiform texts have to be carefully interpreted with these *curiously inhibiting* and ultimately falsifying constraints in
mind."[5]

What might the Greek account of the Homeric flood have become if committed to a syllabary instead of an alphabet? Obviously we have no means of
knowing; it is impossible for us to recreate the mental processes of a Mesopotamian scribe or a Mycenaean one. If Linear B had survived to be used for
Homer, one can only suggest some ways in which this might have been done.
A narrative too rich for the script could be brought under control by a simplification of vocabulary and syntax while retaining the essentials. A transcription

of the first four lines of our passage might offer few difficulties of recognition, for the sequence runs easily and the mind of the decipherer would readily make out the correct acoustic guesses. The catalogue might have the formulaic ring of an accepted list. A shorthand version however might be tempted to sacrifice the sense of line 19 since no loss of essentials is involved, and would certainly be tempted to omit lines 22 and 23 which interrupt the description by a new thought which momentarily transfers mental attention elsewhere. The senses of lines 26, 32 and 33 would likewise be expendable. The motive for such omissions would be to reduce the effort of recognizing not only new words but new arrangements of words and it would be no less powerful for being unconscious. Such suggestions are offered only by way of speculation, but the fact that simplification of discourse when transcribed in pre-alphabetic systems did occur is not in itself a speculative matter.

So we return to that unique paradox: an alphabetized Homer. By applying a new technology of the written word, there is made available in documented form the first complete report of an undocumented culture, not only the first of its kind, but for all time unique, for some infection of literacy has since invaded all oral cultures wherever experienced, robbing the investigator of that complete confrontation with total orality provided by the Homeric text.

The primary advantage offered by the alphabet over previous writing systems was to provide the power to document the oral report fluently and exhaustively. The language of the two poems is as compendious as their content. As the narrative proceeds, the *nomos* and *ethos* of a whole society are acted out. The nearest analogue in this respect would lie not in the surviving pockets of oral poetry practiced on the fringes of literate bureaucracies, as for example in the Balkans, in Russia, in Finland. For this kind of poetry does not carry encyclopedic responsibilities. The analogues would lie if anywhere in the epics recoverable from African or Polynesian societies if uncontaminated by documentation. Yet the analogues are necessarily imperfect; the societies which have yielded such pure specimens of orality appear to be relatively simple in structure compared with the Greek and thus the requirements placed on storage are correspondingly simple. If the range of human experience, the variety of human dilemmas that require directive help within family and village are less complex, the epic which supplies the directives will itself be less complex. Furthermore the transcription of this orality is conducted under different terms. In the Greek case the users of the language were themselves the discoverers of the new craft of transcription and applied it directly to what they themselves were saying without help of any foreign intermediary. Continuous oral recital of contrived speech and continuous transcription of such speech proceeded side by side for a long time within the same community; but for African and Polynesian cultures the alien anthropologist has to learn a language not his own before transcribing its sounds into a sign system which is not theirs. He cannot match and mate sign and sound with the same immediate and instinctive intimacy that the first Greeks employed. Lastly, as a translator, he will employ the idiom of his own speech, thus repeating and importing 2,500 years of literate development of the human consciousness, which comes between himself and the speech that he is translating.

The "moments" of mimesis

The conditions in oral society under which the Homeric poems came into existence make it impossible for the critic to distinguish between creative composition and mechanical repetition, as though these represented two categories mutually exclusive, the first of which was superseded by the second. To make the distinction, as is commonly done, is to rely on canons of judgment drawn from our experience of literature as a literate phenomenon. At all stages of the Homeric process, now lost in the mists of anonymity, we should speak only in hyphenated terms of the composer-reciter, the singer-rhapsode. Whether in individual instances the powers he commanded amounted to genius or merely skill, they consisted in the manipulation of two kinds of spell, or rather of one single spell directed in two different directions, one upon himself and his mouth, the other upon his audience and their ears. In both cases the spell was urgently required by the need to memorize verbal statements arranged in a fixed repeatable order, these extending in length from the formulas composing the parts of the hexameter, to the moral formulas incorporated in narrative situations, to the situations themselves, and to those series of situations which make up an episode, and to a given number of episodes which compose a total narration.

The mental effort required is difficult for the literate mind wholly to imagine, but it obviously meant a total absorption, a mental immersion in the act of recital. Plato described it by the term *mimesis*, which in this context comes close to meaning the "miming" of a mythos, its acting out by sympathetic identification with the characters and actions described.[6] The singer responding to a prompt in his mind—or one supplied by his audience—will proceed to tell us about Patroclus and Achilles, let us say, how Patroclus fought and fell in Achilles' place. He commits himself to recollecting the start of a given sound sequence leading into the mythos, and to a parallel recollection of what that mythos was all about. It was not indeterminate; it had its beginning, middle and end, which he is aware of as he begins the recital and which becomes more definite in realization as he proceeds, first to himself, and then to his audience who follow his song murmuring it to themselves. A modern audience at a musical recital likes to demonstrate its sophistication by preserving immobility as the strains reach their ears; no such intellectualized isolation was ever possible for the members of a culture of oral communication and oral memorization.

Such absorption controlled by rhythm of words, of instruments, and of body, meant that in the period of a given recitation the reciter remained totally indifferent to the existence of all mythoi other than the one that he happened to be reciting. He cannot think of them or relate to them unless and until the mythos he is committed to has been completed as a movement. Then and only then might his memory call up from its reserves a second one with linkage to the first. His rhythmic recollection proceeds by elocutions which are performed in intense self-absorbed moments of activity. Memory varies according to individual capacity. Singers therefore varied in their capacity to hold a single mythos without faltering and in their capacity to command a repertoire of such.

The sophistication of the verse technique, no less than the life style of the participants in the stories, argue for a period of oral composition which matured with the maturation of the Greek city state in Ionia. Homer's is not peasant poetry. For a century or more before the process of transcription began, a group of bards, or two groups, let us say, had become specialists not only in the Trojan War story but in two applications of the story known as the *Wrath* and the *Return*. Possibly some of them individually commanded the art of reciting all the parts, the individual mythoi which came to make up the *Iliad* and the *Odyssey* in our texts. This we shall never know. But a knowledge of the overall scene, the general *context*—(which is a literate term), or the "ideal epic" as some critics have called it,[7] was shared by all of them. An individual singer could break in on the overall scene when he pleased, without being aware of its sequence precisely as that is required in our present texts. Parts of what to us is a required sequential whole could be recited backwards from our standpoint, or told in what we with our fixed texts before us would call a string of *selections* (another literate term, as though speech consisted of alphabetized pieces to be picked up). A poet could switch attention to another mythos or piece of the epic—how many such pieces he might command would depend on his individual capacity—he would have to recall how to begin it and as he did so he would recall his prompting lines. But as he proceeded he would temporarily forget what he had just been saying as he continuously exchanged one set of absorptions for another, replacing one moment of memory by another.

In sum, the acoustic memory is associative but not comprehensive; it lives and works by temporary total commitment to a stretch of mythos before passing in transition to a different mythos constituting a fresh act of recollection. But the second will still share the same ethos as the first, for both in their expression must reflect and preserve the mores of the culture; both are parts of the same cultural encyclopedia, so that, digression and repetition aside, and allowing for some inevitable inconsistencies, style and substance remain uniform to a degree beyond anything that a "committee" of literate poets could manage.

It is to be concluded that our *Iliad* and *Odyssey* were recited sporadically in self-contained performances of individual episodes.[8] We cannot now disentangle what these were; the documentary organization later applied was extraordinarily skillful. Adopting the divisions of the text as we now have it, any attempt to imagine what these recitals might have been is tempted to envisage them as governed by the presents division into 24 books. We can only say that such a division represents the decisions made by the literate eye of later scholarship. In spirit, this was carried out in some sympathy with the original genius of oral performance—that is, episodes in the canonical text are separated from each other by natural breaks in most cases. There is no reason to suppose that this corresponds with fidelity to the original recitation process. We are asking in effect what were the separate pieces of each poem which after documentation were brought in all probability together in Athens, and arranged in the sequence we now have. We shall never know, though it is a little easier to guess what they may have been in the case of the *Odyssey*. The journey and return of Telemachus, for example, and the voyages narrated by Odysseus could be recited as self-contained mythoi in whole or in parts. To make some guesses about the *Iliad* is more difficult because its present arrangement is more intricate. In a very few cases a whole book or major part thereof stands out as a self-contained mythos. This is true of the twenty-fourth (the ransoming of Hector), and of the twenty-third, from line 259 (the funeral games), or of the tenth (an epic of night operations), or of the second, from line 87 to line 483 (the panic and rallying of the Greek army after nine years of war). A single recitation, of course, need not be confined to the length represented by a single book. There are a few sequences of books which could make up a recitation as they stand; 16 with 17 narrate the career and death of Patroclus; 8 and 9 describe the Trojan advance, the Greek retreat, and the Greek appeal to Achilles for rescue. More intricately, one can become aware of books now separated in our text which in continuity could have been recited as single thematic sequences. Thus Book One which describes the failure to resolve a quarrel with fatal effects predicted for the Greeks could be followed by Book Eight in which these effects occur and then by Book Nine where a second attempt is made to remedy the situation. The names of Achilles, Agamemnon, Nestor and Odysseus and their words and deeds dominate both Books One and Nine. Still more intricately, what would now be viewed as selections in our text could have been part of whole recitations now redistributed. This could be true, for example, of the domestic comedy acted out on Olympus, now distributed throughout the poem. The divine family presided over by its autocrat is presented in Book One, 493 to the end; later we see Hera and Athene descending from Olympus to interfere and then returning (5.711 to the end), whereat Zeus orders his household to maintain neutrality and then withdraws to Mount Ida (8.1–52), only to be seduced there by Hera (14.153–353), so that the family on Olympus can abandon neutrality while he sleeps, until he awakes in anger and despatches the orders which compel his willful household to restore the status quo (15.4–235). Such a combination would produce a single memorizable recitation of a mythos about the gods sung in a consistent key of comic realism.

Such are offered as examples, wholly hypothetical, of the kinds of recitations which lie below the continuities that we now call the *Iliad* and the *Odyssey*. The poems as we have them offer too many possibilities of permutation and combination for us to accept any one proposed arrangement as authentically original. Any one portion sung singly contains allusion in which the mythos of the whole epic is implicit. The reciter is aware of the existence of this ideal epic, it is present by implication. But the singer's attention is fastened upon his immediate theme; his memory is temporarily steeped in it to the exclusion of other considerations.

The echo-principle

Within this psychological commitment to rhythm and to the flow of rhythmic speech it is possible to determine an acoustic law at work which serves to supply connection as a kind of binding principle which ties bundles of recited situations together. It can be called the principle of the echo sounding in the ear with which is combined the principle of the mirror reflection presenting itself to the mind's eye. The first book of the *Iliad* provides a simple illustration: there at the beginning of the story is the priest on the seashore addressing Apollo with complaints; we wait awhile and the story proceeds and there is Achilles on the seashore addressing his mother with complaints. The formulas used in the first instance are repeated with necessary variation for the second and a physical scene once used is reflected in its counterpart. The principle can extend itself to include larger complexes of actions and situations. Thus in Book One the narrative relates how the *agora* met, how Nestor with suitable exhortation tries to mediate the quarrel, how Agamemnon despatches two emissaries to Achilles to take away Briseis. In Book Nine the mythos has moved on but the echo returns. The reciter narrates how the *agora* meets again, is superseded by a council in which Nestor with appropriate exhoratation once more mediates, and how Agamemnon dispatches emissaries to Achilles to restore Briseis. The echo principle is operative even to the point of re-using for three persons in the second instance the formulas which were appropriate for two persons in the first. This kind of mechanism is directly acoustic and only indirectly imagist. It is persistent in both poems and has been well documented by Homeric scholars, but with this difference, that the mechanism is interpreted in visual terms alone and is described as a pattern rather than as an echo, as though panels of matching series were arranged in sequences like aba, abba, abcba, and the like in the manner of painted altar-pieces.[9] But it was the ear, not the eye, that had to be seduced and led on by such arrangements, relying· on the actual sounds of identical or similar words enclosed in similar sounding formulas and paragraphs.

Echo is something that the ear of singer and audience is trained to wait for. Its mnemonic usefulness encourages the presence of anticipation. We can say of the second instance that it echoes the first or of the first that it prophesies the second. Oral mythos is continually stretched forward in this way as it is told in order to assist recall in the reciter's mind of how the mythos is to proceed, what the plot is to be. Echo, however, is modified. It is not a duplicate, for a duplicate would say nothing more than had already been said; the tale would degenerate into mindless repetition. The echo must accompany a fresh statement of fresh action, but this cannot be excessively novel or inventive; to accommodate the needs of memory there must be enough likeness to the prior statement to seduce or tempt the mind to make the leap from one to the other, and to tempt the mouth to follow with the appropriate enunciation. The constant need for a mechanism of anticipation and confirmation explains the prominence in oral epic poetry, among other things, of prophesy and prophetic statements put into the mouths of characters even in the moment of an action which they perform in the present. Achilles warns Patroclus not to go too far—so we anticipate that he will and maybe dangerously so; Apollo protests to the gods in council that Achilles' maltreatment of Hector must stop—so we know it is going to stop; Calchas must speak but he is afraid of offending somebody powerful—so we are warned that offense will be given and that a bitter feud is likely to follow.

Spoken language is a continuum, a soundtrack manufactured by the larynx and carried on waves in the air, divisible acoustically into moments but not spatially into extended panels. Moments which anticipate and echo each other are con-sonant, not symmetrical. An episode describing martial combat is filled with language noises which recall or are associated with fighting; a banquet scene with words of eating, drinking and merrymaking. Telemachus' journey in the Peloponnese is carried forward in repeated locutions which describe horses and chariots running, harness jingling as it is put on and taken off, cups of hospitality filled and drunk and emptied, greetings given and received. In the *Iliad*, a quarrel between two men is conducted in a series of responsions with similar epithets of hostility exchanged. There is a high element of onomatopoeia in orally memorized composition.

Such are the mnemonic mechanisms which control and guide the incantation of the verse and impose the necessary spell upon the consciousness of singer and audience. If we have dwelt on them in this place, it is to reinforce the conclusion earlier stated that oral composition and recitation both proceed in moments of intense activity, the moment being understood as a self-contained movement within a given mythos, during the performance of which the memory of other episodes is suspended. The reciter is absorbed in his present context and moves through it from beginning to conclusion in total indifference to other contexts outside the period that he is accomplishing.

The journey and the dream

Proto-literate Greece after Homer, at a time when the concepts of intellectual activity and the procedures of discursive thought were surfacing in the consciousness, found some difficulty in verbalizing them, in defining or describing the cognitive process. One word adopted to describe it was *hodos*, a journeying down a way, an itinerary; the word symbolizes both the route and the taking of the route. The philosopher Parmenides resorts to this metaphor and Plato revives it. As a piece of terminology it lives in the no-man's land between non-literate and literate habit; it catches the sense of the oral connective process and it is significant that both thinkers suggest that this route within the mind can be circular. It catches the sense of the oral reciter's commitment to a track of sound and speech which he follows rather than one which he himself directs. He is still the traveler with his feet moving along the road absorbed in marking the direction set for him, watching the signs set by the roadside; not the intellectual who calculates the steps that he is to take successively one by one in full consciousness. Often he will return on his tracks: "it is all one to me where I begin," says Parmenides, faithfully reproducing the plunge that the bard takes into a medium from which he also emerges having told his tale.

Another metaphor applied by Plato to the psychological situation of the poet and the audience is that of the dream from which both of them, bewitched by the images which pass before them, like sleepwalkers have to be awakened before they can become aware of "what is." [10] Platonism sets its foundations upon this awakened state of consciousness and calls the condition which precedes it by the Greek term *doxa*, which is not very happily translated as "opinion." One can appreciate the relevance of the dream-metaphor to the absorption of the oral poet both in composition and in performance (*mimesis*), bearing in mind that composition is itself an act of memory while performance is the act that seeks to imprint that memory on others. The dream is something which takes charge of us rather than vice versa. We surrender to it and our surrender while temporary is total in the sense that any connection with other mental states is broken, whether these are other dreams or the wakened state of controlled consciousness identifiable with intellection. An overall context of "meaning," or relevance to experience in general, is absent. Only by a restructuring of the language that one is using can one seek to establish such a context and this means a restructuring of one's psychology. The dream is equivalent to the moment of rhapsodic recitation.

The "dating" of "Homer"

The literate historian of archaic Greece just because he is literate when he approaches the problem of when and how Homer was written down is prone to visualize this as a single event; to postulate that the technology of the alphabet once invented would be applied wholesale to the transcription of a work previously existing in oral form; rather as a writer today commits his composition to paper and the typed paper is then transmitted to the printer to emerge from the press as a completed volume. Just so, the Greek "writer," whether visualized as rhapsodist or as scribe, is imagined to seat himself at a desk (tablets in his lap would not suffice) in order to transcribe on to rolls of papyrus (perhaps sheets of vellum, though this is unlikely) the *Iliad* and the *Odyssey* respectively.

This is an improbable picture; the invention of the alphabetic sign-code, by adding vocalics to the Phoenician series, was one thing. Its fluent application to the transcription of language in quantity was quite another. Writing on this scale would presume a habit developed into an art. We should rather ask: given the fact that the epic enjoyed a purely auditory existence, memorized and repeated orally, what was likely to be the original motive for bringing this contrived language into contact with the signs of the alphabet? The probable answer is one that is supplied in later notices in Pindar and Aeschylus: [11] it is also one that grows out of the oral operation itself. The motive was mnemonic, a response to the same psychological pressures that had inspired and governed the oral technique; the alphabetic signs offered a supplement to the energies required for memorization.

How was this to be done with a technique still in its infancy so far as fluent application is concerned? Surely by transcribing bits and pieces of the oral verse, such bits and pieces being used as prompters to remind a reciter how to start, or for that matter how to stop. They might perhaps grow into little epitomes of episodes which the reciter otherwise held in his head as his preferred repertoire. Gradually, and with recognition of the reduced effort required if they could be re-read, such transcriptions would extend themselves to the recording of whole portions of the verse. As a hypothetical illustration of this practice: the introductory lines to the *Iliad* could conveniently become a written piece, for they predict the course of the plot—prediction being the method of oral mnemonic—and so the bard might welcome the chance to read it over to remind him of the chief elements of his story before he launches into it. The catalogue in the second book was surely one of the earliest portions committed to writing. The two councils of the gods in the *Odyssey* which successively set portions of the action moving might be another example which if transcribed would be especially convenient. Details of this sort we shall never know but the hypothesis of partial transcription of "reminders," constituting the original use to which the alphabet was put, is surely not fanciful.

This amounts to saying that alphabetization was originally a function of oral recitation; the two were intermingled. If so, in order to understand the circumstances under which alphabetization was completed, we should consider the likely conditions of oral performance during the period when, according to our hypothesis, Homer was being partially and imperfectly alphabetized. The earliest inscriptions—a small group—cluster round the date 700 B.C. They are metrical, and widely dispersed. [12] On the other hand, the first lyric verse which we may be sure was actually transcribed in the lifetime of its author, by himself or through his dictation, was composed by Archilochus of Paros in the mid-seventh century. This perhaps is an over-cautious inference based on the extreme scantiness both of the remains of earlier poets and of the tradition surrounding their names. Is it possible that portions of the *Iliad* and *Odyssey* were transcribed not earlier than were the poems of Archilochus? We shall never of course know the precise answer but the question is not out of order. As for the terminus ante quem, the point at which we can assume either the *Iliad* or the *Odyssey* achieved that complete textual existence with which we are familiar, the tradition, already current before the end of the fifth century,[13] which stated that the Homeric poems were put in order after some fashion in Athens during the reign of Pisistratus or his sons, need not be disputed.[14] The alphabetization of Homer in the sense in which we know Homer might have been completed as late as 520 B.C., or earlier. So far as this tradition has been rejected, this has been due more than anything else to the presumption that Greece was fully literate at least as early as 700 B.C. and perhaps earlier, in which case the poems were likely to have been both written and read in what we call their cononical form much earlier than the reign of Pisistratus. But the presumption that Greece was fully literate before 500 B.C. (or indeed before 430 B.C.) would appear to be unfounded.[15]

The act of visual integration

As documentation takes place, a restless, moving sea of words becomes frozen into immobility. Each self-contained moment of recitation—an episode or a set of such—becomes imprisoned in an order no longer acoustic but visible. It ceases to be a soundtrack and becomes almost a tangible object. A collocation of such objects takes place as they are gathered and written. Because they are now preserved outside the individual memories of those who inscribe and gather them, the gatherer need no longer surrender himself totally and temporarily to absorption in any one of them. He is able to look at them in the mass and become aware of them as a sum, a totality. As he does this he begins to wake up from the dream. His relaxed consciousness allows his eye, not his ear, to rove at will over the sum total and as he does so he will begin to compare the parts with each other visually. Part of the attention previously concentrated on the recitation of any one of them becomes directed to a visual comtemplation of the whole.

An individual oral recitation, being a mythos, tells a tale in temporal sequence without flashback or major digression. But once the mythoi are *seen* together, it will be perceived that recitation A, describing the story of Odysseus' adventures, let us say, during his wanderings, and recitation B, the story of his detention by the nymph Calypso, his escape and shipwreck, and recitation C, the story of Telemachus going in search of his father, all deal with time periods which overlap with each other. Or let us say that the story of how the Greeks grew demoralized after nine years of war and broke ranks and then rallied and resumed the offensive needs to be related in time to the story of how Achilles and Agamemnon quarreled and how this brought about a Trojan offensive; and yet again to the story of Achilles' onslaught on the Trojans and how he routed them en masse and killed Hector. It naturally occurred to the reflective eye that the principle of temporal sequence which had been applied in individual recitations should be applied if possible to the whole mass. How place the pieces in a similar sequence? It cannot be done, very simply because these original recitations recited separate events many of which when viewed together can be seen to take place within overlapping time-spans. Moreover, in addition to the echo principle employed within each one, all recitations contain predictions or allusive statements which refer in passing to what is going to happen to a character or has already happened to him outside the context of a given recitation. These constiture fleeting memories of the fact that there is an ideal epic larger than any one single recitation. So a compromise is struck. The story pieces are sorted out and numbered so as to achieve the effect of a single overall time sequence which moves forward but with interruptions, flashbacks, and digressions to an appointed end. Thus arose the arrangement of our present text, correctly designated by Homeric critics as an *ordo artificialis*,[16] this *ordo* being the work of the eye not the ear, a work achievable only when the various portions of the soundtrack had been alphabetized.

It is at this point when visual organization is superimposed upon an acoustic one that an architecture of language becomes conceivable within which the phonetic principles of connection are accommodated. All the literate and the literary terminology now commonly applied to organized discourse begins to come into its own. The author of any preserved discourse becomes not just a singer but a "composer," his product becomes a "work" possessing "pattern" and "structure," controlled by "theme," "topic," or "subject." Even his actors become "characters." His activity in the case of the Homeric poems becomes "monumental."[17] These and dozens of other terms are drawn from the visual, tactile experience of handling alphabetized script. They lie outside the thought world of an oral culture and of the singers who originally sang the songs that we call Homeric. Henceforth it becomes possible that a Greek "literature" in the literate sense should come into being.

But it is to be stressed that the essence of language as a phonetic system could not be transcended and is not wholly transcended to this day. The works of Greek literature after the Homeric transcription occurred are composed in an increasing tension between the genius of oral and the genius of written composition. Because orality remained so close to the Greeks to the end of the fifth century, and indeed continuing into the fourth, the degree of this tension was unique in the literature of the period. Athenian drama, in addition to being rhythmic, obeys the associative and predictive rules of oral composition; it is composed on the echo principle and is conceived as a performance to be heard and seen and memorized but not to be read. It is also composed as a cultural record, an Athenian supplement to the Homeric encyclopedia. Yet it is very plain that it also employs the architecture of composition which only the writer's eye could supply. It represents an intermediate art retaining the specific energies latent in oral incantation, yet submitting to the reflective control exercised by a dawning intellectualism. As such, it could never be duplicated in any later culture unless our world were to collapse into total non-literacy and we all had to start again.

Documentation of discourse in Greece took time and originally was confined to inscribing what had previously been composed metrically according to oral rules. The invention of a prose which would realize the full potential of the word inscribed, the scope of expression available when the word no longer needed memorization to survive, took even longer. Its progress can be marked in the texts of Herodotus, Thucydides and Plato. The reasons for the delay lie in a law which is fundamental to the history of the human word: the modes of literate discourse whatever they may be cannot be understood apart from an understanding of the modes of non-literate discourse. Each is intimately bound up with the other, the oral because it would not exist for us without the literate resources; the literate because the sophistication of its own vocabulary and syntax grew out of changes and transpositions in the oral vocabulary and syntax and cannot properly be understood without grasping what these changes were. The very task which literate communication sets itself—the creation and the conservation of knowledge, technological and cultural—was first confronted and solved in the uncounted millennia of oral experience when man knew no knowledge other than that which was contained in the sounds of his language as they were pronounced.

NOTES AND REFERENCES

1 Problems surrounding the transcription of oral poetry came to scholarly attention with the publication of A.B. Lord's *Singer of Tales* (Harvard 1960) caps. 6 and 7. Cf. also G.S. Kirk *Songs of Homer* (Cambridge 1962) cap. 14; A.M. Parry, "Have We Homer's *Iliad?*" YCS XX (1966). Preparation of the present article has rested upon argument supplied in some of my previous publications: *Preface to Plato* (Harvard 1963) chaps. 1–4; "Prologue to Greek Literacy" in *University of Cincinnati Classical Studies Semple Lectures* Vol. II (Oklahoma 1973; *Origins of Western Literacy: Ontario Institute for Studies in Education Monograph Series* /14 (1976; "The Preliteracy of the Greeks" in *New Literary History* (*University of Virginia*) Vol. VIII, no. 3 (1977). See also Robert Kellogg "Oral Literature" in *New Literary History* Vol. V no. 1 (1973). Two articles by J.A. Davison on "Literature and Literacy in Ancient Greece" (*Phoenix* Vol. XVI nos. 3 and 4 (1962) are also relevant, as is the same author's support, given in A *Companion to Homer* (Cambridge 1962), for authenticity of the tradition which placed some consolidation of the Homeric text in the age of Pisistratus.

2 "Origins" (above note 1) pp. 22–50.

3 *The Ancient Near East: An Anthology of Texts edited by James B. Pritchard* (Princeton 1958), pp. 68–9.

4 "Origins" p. 34. G.K. Gresseth in "The Gilgamesh Epic and Homer" C.J. 70, no. 4 (1975) pp. 1–18, argues for closer stylistic congruence: the two "are cast in the same literary genre, the heroic epic" (p. 17).

5 A. Leo Oppenheim, "The Position of the Intellectual in Mesopotamian Society," *Daedalus* Spring 1975 p. 38.

6 *Preface* (above note 1) chap. 2.

7 I borrow the phrase from Kellogg (above note 1) p. 59.

8 The Homeric terms are *aoidē, oimē, muthos* and also *molpē* and *hymnos*. Frequent descriptions in both poems (especially *Odyssey*) of musical-poetic recitation allude always to performances of episodes.

9 C.H. Whitman *Homer and Heroic Tradition* (Harvard 1958), chap. 5, stresses the parallel between Homeric patterning and geometric art.

10 *Preface* pp. 190, 238 ff.

11 Pindar *Ol.* 10.1 ff; Aesch. *Suppl.* 179. *Choeph.* 450, *Eum.* 275, *P.V.* 460, 789–90.

12 Cf. "Preliteracy" (above note 1).

13 It is probably alluded to in Isocrates' *Panegyricus* and reported in Plato's *Hipparchus* (a dialogue included in the ancient canon and accepted by many Platonic scholars). Though these works were composed early in the fourth century B.C. their authors were born in 436 and 429 respectively.

14 Cf. Davison in *Companion* (above note 1).

15 Cf. "Preliteracy" and *Preface* chap. 3.

16 So Davison, in *Companion*.

17 Kirk *Songs* (above note 1) p. 316 would assign "monumental composition" to oral poetry of the 8th century B.C.

The Preliteracy of the Greeks

Eric A. Havelock

I T SOMETIMES HAPPENS in the course of scholarly investigation carried out over a long period of time that one is gradually pushed into accepting a view of the facts—an interpretation of them—which is not only contrary to received opinion but which is accepted slowly and reluctantly by the investigator himself. This has been the case with my own inquiries into the subject of Greek literacy. As some who have read my published work will know, I have concluded that the population of Athens did not become literate in our sense until the last third of the fifth century before Christ.[1] That is to say, while the historian of the time would fasten his eyes on the progress and consequences of a war—the Peloponnesian war—waged during those same years, which occupied the forefront of the historical stage, an event of greater social and cultural importance was quietly taking place behind the scenes.

Starting with an examination of the Greek alphabet and the precise way in which it functions as a symbolic system, and then proceeding to the first works inscribed in this medium, namely, the Homeric poems,[2] and then pushing on down through the course of what is called Greek "literature" (itself a misnomer), that is, rereading Hesiod, the lyric poets, Pindar, and finally Athenian drama, and asking myself fresh questions about the way these works were composed, their style and substance, and the kind of public to which it seems they were addressed, and the conditions of their performance—I have gradually approached a series of conclusions of which I have only recently appreciated the full consequences, and how drastic they may appear from the standpoint of traditional classical scholarship. At risk of appearing dogmatic, I think it will be best to expose them comprehensively, in something like their logical order, simply because the structure of the argument taken as a whole may carry greater conviction than would be true of the sum of its individual parts.

First: the invention of the Greek alphabet, as opposed to all previous systems, including the Phoenician, constituted an event in the history of human culture, the importance of which has not as yet been fully grasped. Its appearance divides all pre-Greek civilizations from those that are post-Greek. When all allowance is made for the relative success of previous systems of writing, and for the degree to which the Greek invention developed out of them, the fact remains that in the Greek system it became possible for the first time to document all possible forms of linguistic statement with fluency and to achieve fluent recognition, that is, fluent reading, of what had been written, on the part of a majority of any population. On this facility were built the foundations of those twin forms of knowledge: literature in the post-Greek sense, and science, also in the post-Greek sense.

Second: the classical culture of the Greeks was, however, already in existence before the invention took effect. That culture began its career as a nonliterate one and continued in this condition for a considerable period after the invention, for civilizations can be nonliterate and yet possess their own specific forms of institution, art, and contrived language. In the case of the Greeks, these forms made their appearance in the institution of the *polis*, in geometric art, in early temple architecture, and in the poetry preserved in the Homeric hexameter. These were all functioning when Greece was nonliterate.

Third: to understand what we mean by a "culture," the Greek included, we have to ask what gives it a structure, what is continuous and so identifiable. This question can be answered by borrowing from the cultural anthropologists the concept of the storage of information for reuse. The information concerned is not merely technological in the narrow sense, but also covers that body of directives which regulates the behavior patterns of individuals who are members of the culture. In a literate culture, it is easy to perceive this kind of knowledge taking shape as a body of law and belief, covering religion and morals, political authority ("the constitution," as we say), legal procedures of all kinds, especially those governing property, and also rights and responsibilities within the family. The civilization of the ancient Greeks is admittedly a rather startling phenomenon, but it may become less miraculous and more understandable if we are prepared to regard it as an ongoing experiment in the storage of cultural information for reuse.[3]

Fourth: a nonliterate culture is not necessarily a primitive one, and the Greek was not primitive. Once this proposition is taken seriously, one has to ask: in the absence of documentation in a preliterate society, what was the mechanism available for the storage of such information—that is, for the continuous transmission of that body of religious, political, legal, and familial regulation which already constituted, before literacy, the Greek way of life? This information could be carried only in the form of statements imprinted upon the memories of individual brains of living Greeks. How, then, could these statements preserve themselves without alteration, and so retain authenticity? The solution to this problem is supplied if they are cast in metrical form, for only as language is controlled by rhythm can it be repeated with anything like the uniformity that is available in documentation. The shape of the words and their place in the syntax are fixed by rhythmic order. The vernacular is therefore not used for any statements that require preservation.

Fifth: what we call "poetry" is therefore an invention of immemorial antiquity designed for the functional purpose of a continuing record in oral cultures. Such cultures normally follow the practice of reinforcing the rhythms of verbal meter by wedding them to the rhythms of dance, of musical instruments, and of melody. A poem is more memorizable than a paragraph of prose; a song is more memorizable than a poem. The Greeks identified this complex of oral practices by the craft term *mousikē*, and correctly identified the Muse who gave her name to the craft as the "daughter of Remembrance." She personified the mnemonic necessity and the mnemonic techniques characteristic of an oral culture.

Sixth: while the act of imprinting, considered psychologically, operates upon individual memories, its social function cannot become effective unless these memories are shared. Oral poetry therefore required for its existence an occasion which could supply a listening audience, large or small, ranging from an entire city to the company at a dinner table. Knowledge hoarded for reuse required not only rhythm, but constant performance before audiences who were invited to participate in its memorization. Truly private communication of preservable information becomes possible only under conditions of developed literacy. Only the documented word can be perused by individuals in isolation.

Seventh: the Greek alphabet, both at the time of its invention and for many generations after, was not applied in the first instance to transcribing vernacular statements but rather to those previously composed according to oral rules of memorization. That is why Greek literature is predominantly poetic, to the death of Euripides. This literature therefore will evade our understanding as long as we conduct its critique exclusively according to the rules of literate composition. These rules, whatever they are, can be said to intrude themselves by degrees, and slowly. High classical Greek literature is to be viewed as composed in a condition of increasing tension between the modes of oral and documented speech.

Eighth: the education of the Greek leisured classes throughout this period was oral. It consisted in the memorization of poetry, the improvisation of verse, the oral delivery of verse, the oral delivery of a prose rhetoric based on verse principles, the performance on instruments, string or wood, and singing and dancing. For a long time after the invention of the alphabet, letters were not included, and when they were first introduced, they were treated as ancillary to memorization and recitation. There is ample evidence that in the sixth and fifth centuries B.C. this curriculum was identified in Athens by the term *mousikē*, as previously defined, and no hard evidence that in.this period it covered reading. Organized instruction in reading at the primary level, that is, before the age of ten, cannot have been introduced into the Athenian schools much earlier than about 430 B.C. It is described in Plato's *Protagoras*, written in the early part of the next century, as by then standard practice, as it indeed had become when Plato grew up.[4]

Ninth: the inventors, and for a long time the only habitual users of the alphabet, were craftsmen and traders.[5] No doubt, as time went on, the leisured classes picked up some acquaintance with letters, but the extent to which they did so must remain problematic, for they had minimal motives for employing the skill until the middle decades of the fifth century. The craftsman's children went to work in the shop before puberty, and if they learned letters, that is where they learned them.[6] The upper-class boy, prolonging education into adolescence, had time to master the polite arts, which did not include reading. There are indications that a crude literacy among craftsmen was becoming common in the age of Pisistratus and after. This is consistent with the tradition that under Solon's policies craftsmen from overseas were encouraged to settle in Athens.

Such are the general conclusions here presented as an interconnected whole. They run against the grain of several common presuppositions from which classical historians find it difficult to escape, deriving as they do from our inherited experience of two thousand years of literacy.

The dominant one, from which all others flow, is the view that a nonliterate culture must be a nonculture, or at least marks a stage in human development which is better forgotten once literacy sets in. The two belong in different worlds. The prejudice is reinforced by the modern results of contact between literate and nonliterate cultures; the latter seem to collapse before the approach, the onslaught, of what is taken to be a superior and civilized mode of life.

Hence, in estimating the character and history of Greek literacy, which began from scratch, one is tempted to ignore the possibility that there may have existed prior methods of preserving information which were oral and antique, and in the Greek instance may have reached a high level of proficiency. One is forced to ask the unbelieving question: how could a culture as high-powered as the Greek have got its start in nonliteracy? To which one is forced to reply that it could not have. It must have had a proto-literate ancestry, thus kindling a continuing dispute about the date of the introduction of writing in Greece: either the alphabet must have been in use as early as the tenth century at the latest; or the Greeks never ceased to use the Linear B system of the Mycenaeans; or if a date of around 700 B.C. be admitted for the introduction of writing, then the Dark Age, so-called, was truly a dark age. Greek civilization can only be said to begin after 700. None of these three propositions is tenable.

Today persons and peoples are either literate or not: if semiliterate, this condition is viewed as a failure to become literate. This is because the alphabet is available, its full use is understood, a regimen for teaching reading to children is available, as also is an adequate supply of documented speech to afford practice in reading as well as a motive for reading. These resources are either used or not used, and the result is either literacy or nonliteracy. In dealing with ancient Greece, which started from scratch and had to learn the full use of the alphabet after inventing it, this simplistic view should be abandoned. Tentatively, let me suggest in its place a progressive classification, which would identify the condition of Athenian society during the seventh and as far as the last decades of the sixth centuries B.C. as craft-literate: the alphabet written or read represents an expertise managed by a restricted group of the population. During the latter part of the sixth and the first half of the fifth, the skill begins to spread, though I would suspect that the governing classes were the last to acquire it, but the skill is one of decipherment rather than fluent reading. The use of the written word is very restricted, and any reading of it is regarded as ancillary to the central function of culture, which still is, as it had always been, to memorize and recite the poets. I would classify this period as one of "recitation literacy." Only in the last third of the century is the average Athenian taught letters in such a way as to begin to pick up a script and read it through. It follows that testimonies drawn from fourth-century authors will take literacy for granted, for it has now been achieved. These chronological distinctions may seem fine-drawn, but they call attention to the basic fact that what we call the "literature" both of the sixth and fifth centuries is addressed to listeners rather than readers and is composed to conform with this situation.

Long experience of our own literate condition in the West has done more than merely convince us that all cultures depend upon achieving literacy as quickly as possible. It has had the indirect result of fostering two preconceptions about how any culture actually functions, both of which get in the way of a proper understanding of the original Greek experience. For the first of these let me quote, by way of illustration, what an eminent archaeologist has to say about one of the earliest alphabetic inscriptions we have, a craftsman's signature the lettering of which is well executed: "The fact of the signature at this very early date should imply that the artist was no humble *cheironax* but a person of social standing. On this evidence he would seem to have been a highly cultured person."[7] At first sight this statement seems perfectly natural and reasonable. Yet the way it is worded reveals a judgment unconsciously guided by the norms of our own society, in which the maximum of education is identified with the maximum of literacy. The cultivation centered today in the more privileged classes, to use a term which is snobbish but seems inevitable, is identified with a superior capacity to read and write, which diminishes as one goes down in the social scale. Therefore, if it be discovered that a Greek potter or carpenter or stonemason could use the alphabet, it is assumed a fortiori that the upper classes must have previously mastered this skill which had now filtered down to the artisan, or conversely, that the artisan was not really an artisan but a very educated type. The great bulk of the inscriptional material on which we rely for any material evidence of the alphabet's use in the early centuries is contributed by craftsmen. It may seem therefore inevitable to the historian of the period, and particularly the epigraphist, to conclude that if craftsmen wrote, then everyone did. But suppose, as I have earlier suggested, that the truth was rather the reverse of this, that the alphabet's use did not achieve what I may call cultural prestige for a very long time?

It is also a fact of life in literate societies that prose is the primary form in which experience is documented, while poetry is more esoteric and sophisticated, a medium to be reserved for special experiences outside the day's work. The notion runs deep in our consciousness, and continually colors the attitude we take up towards Greek literature in the first three centuries of its existence. Its poetic form prevents us from evaluating its functional role as preserved communication in the society of its day. More particularly, if we encounter in inscriptions a plethora of metrical statements, memorials, dedications, and the like, we are ready to read these in the light of what is believed to be an unusual degree of Greek cultivation. This conception has to be reversed if we are to understand early Greek poetry. In an oral culture, metrical language is part of the day's work.

Evidence for the date of the invention of the alphabet and its earliest use is supplied by epigraphy. But material evidence for literacy is something else. Reading is a habit which does not leave its impress upon a material object. Nor can you build it up upon the basis of a fund of inscriptions. What is needed is a body of documentation in quantity available in private houses, easily transmissible between persons, fluently and easily written. In short, a ready supply of material surfaces receptive to ink and light in texture. To be sure, schools in many parts of the world, Scotland for example, still use slates.·The Greeks used slates, wax tablets, and sand. But one learns to read not from a slate but from a body of documentation, and it is the existence of this body that supplies motivation.

Greek epigraphy cannot supply the material evidence, namely, the papyrus roll or book, which would have had to have existed in quantity and in ready circulation before 450 B.C. if Greece were literate before that date. Some rolls existed, of course, or our poets would not have survived at all. But how many copies of these works were there? Were they plentiful? Were they commonly read? Do the poets themselves speak as though this were so? No, they do not.

In deciding upon the existence or the degree of Greek literacy at any given time, the inscribed surface of clay and stone is in the nature of things neutral. It can be used on either side of the question. To give an example which is not epigraphic but drawn from epigraphic tradition, the laws of Solon were probably inscribed on the surfaces of some kind of revolving machine made of wood. This was in the early part of the sixth century. Was this for the benefit of the common reader, or was it a court of last appeal to be consulted in need and read by those who had the required expertise? The answer seems to lie in the practice of Solon himself. He propagated his policies in poems and even assumed the role of a herald to recite them at public gatherings.[8] Is this not an eloquent testimony to the existence in his day of a nonliterate public who were expected to listen, to remember, and to repeat—thus giving him incidentally political support—but not to read?

Even the inscriptions themselves, some of them, betray a few characteristics which are a little surprising if they were written for a literate society. If one takes the small group that are the earliest—datable, that is, to the period 700 B.C. plus or minus when the alphabetic invention first appeared in the Greek world—what one at once notices in this group, or at least in those that are decipherable as coherent statements, is that they are metrical. We then observe how meter continues to be used all through the next two centuries, not only for dedications and memorials but for less formal utterances. Is it fair to conclude that the first use to which the alphabet was put was indeed to transcribe, for whatever reason, sentiments which had been previously composed orally for memorization and recitation and that this use of the alphabet persisted for a long time?

The second characteristic observable in these early specimens and recurrent in later ones concerns the content of what is written. It is something that is being said aloud rather than silently stated or recorded. It has the quality of an oral announcement addressed to a particular occasion or a particular person. Third, in several early examples the statement is framed as the utterance of the object which speaks to the observer: "I am Nestor's cup" or "Mantiklos dedicated me." This habit of conferring a "voice" upon the object again recurs frequently in later inscriptions. What are we to make of it? Is it a mannerism? Or does it reflect the wish, in a society of oral communication where the spoken word is as light as the wind, that the statement to be remembered and repeated be the voice of the object because the object alone remains visible and permanent? In a few cases, the statement is even placed inside a balloon issuing from the figure's mouth, as in modern comic-strip illustration.

One more thing noticeable in the earliest examples is the epigrapher's desire to name a name as indicating owner, artificer, or dedicator. This was, of course, unavoidable in epitaphs. In the case of pottery, inscription is relatively rare and, when it occurs, most often carries a signature. Occasionally it takes the form of writing names attached to figures drawn in illustrated scenes, characters familiar from Greek myth and saga. One begins to wonder about this habit which fades out as the fifth century draws to its close.[9] May it represent an age-old custom in oral societies of naming the name, your own or your interlocutor's?[10]

In such societies the custom was a required formality in salutation and confrontation, greeting or challenge, and in particular in the taking and receiving of oaths. Your name pronounced was your identity, and without it you were a "nobody" like an Odysseus encountering strangers. It is noticeable how often, in pottery illustrations, the name of the character is attached to his figure and almost fastened to it.[11] This would mean, would it not, that in a society that had not yet achieved literacy you might still be expected to write names and recognize them, your own and others, when you could write and read little else?

There are some other indications observable in inscriptions which are more obviously negative in their import. The most revealing is the habit of manipulating the arrangement of letters for decorative purposes, to fit the surface chosen or achieve symmetry regardless of sense, and even of scattering isolated letters like trinkets to fill up empty spaces. The inscriber, when he does this sort of thing, is not thinking primarily of their phonetic but their visual values; he is not concentrated on reading them. A Picasso who plays games of this sort in a painting is imitating the antique. To be sure, a literate society will accept inscriptions arranged to fit an architectural shape, round an archway, for instance, but this is not quite the same thing. Architectural settings for letters do not conflict with word and sentence structure as these present themselves to a reader. The early Greek examples are much more extreme, for the confines within which the letters are manipulated are the small spaces, curved or flat, afforded by individual objects; they are not architectural. This same tendency to place visual above acoustic values can be seen in the retention of the so-called *boustrophedon* style of writing. Greek letters could be written right to left, in the Phoenician order, or left to right, which became the later standard. But both orders might be combined in a single inscription, a habit of arrangement which lingers into the fifth

Fig. 1. After A. Andrewes, *The Greeks* (1971),
Plate XIV.

century. Or else, the letters would be written vertically, up or down, or allowed to meander in accordance with the contours of a particular surface. Continual demands thus made on would-be readers to reverse images of words and sentences did not ask the impossible, but on the other hand they scarcely bespeak habits of fluency.

To bring these observations to life, a few epigraphic illustrations can be offered, a mere sampling from the vast reservoir available but one which hopefully will be typical enough not to be misleading.

The famous Dipylon Vase (Fig. 1) was recovered from a cemetery of geometric period outside the Dipylon Gate in Athens. It was dug up illicitly in 1871 before archaeology had become a controlled science, and the contents of the tomb in which it was buried, if any, were scattered and are unknown. The manufacture of the pot itself has been dated variously between 750 and 690;[12] it is "Late Geometric." It is famous not as a pot but as a surface on which someone scratched after manufacture, how soon after we cannot be sure, the earliest alphabetic writing extant, the letters being written in retrograde, i.e., Phoenician order. Reading them, one is entitled to reflect that here in this casual act by an unknown hand there is announced a revolution which was destined to change the nature of human culture, throwing the elaborate calligraphy of Egypt and the cuneiform records of Mesopotamia into the dustbin of history. The legible part of the inscription is metrical, consisting of a complete hexameter line in the Homeric manner, reading backwards: "who now of all dancers sports most playfully." This is followed by "an attempt at a second verse, which struggles up to stop near the handle."[13] The only certain thing revealed is a failure of composition. The site of discovery is Attic, but the lettering is not, which has prompted the question: "one may ask whether it is not Attic but was inscribed, perhaps to show his powers, by an outsider. . . ."[14]

The complete hexameter yields the reasonable inference that the pot was offered as a prize in a dancing contest, which one scholar, noting the word *atalotata*, has suggested was a contest in free style, as opposed to the formal styles required for choric performances.[15] This suggestion might give point to the adverb *now*. The formal part of the contest being concluded, the time has come to relax in a free-for-all performance. Being metrical, the statement inscribed is the kind that could have been composed orally for memorization, in which case its inscription is a historical accident. This is not of itself provable, but the style of the statement supports the inference, for it is phrased as an announcement. The generic wording "who now, etc." followed by an apodosis "let him, etc.," or words to similar effect, is in the style of an oral proclamation which enunciates a general ruling and its application, by a magistrate, herald, or other authority, to a populace or an audience.[16] And if this represents an announcement made at the contest and passed from mouth to mouth, we can understand why the inscription tails off. The original announcement geared to the occasion would have continued with something like "let him display his prowess" or "shall be honoured first among us" or "shall be awarded the prize of victory." But the contest is over, and the inscriber, or more probably his patron, was faced with the necessity of applying the statement to himself by way of a permanent memorial. His alphabetic ability held up as long as he could follow in his head its remembered rhythm, but it failed him when it came to continue a suitable apodosis, for the kind he needed was not supplied to him in the oral original. The alternative explanation, that a second and less skillful writer tried his hand at completing the statement,[17] would still be consistent with the view that once a remembered verbal rhythm failed, alphabetic fluency failed also.

For what reader or readers, if any, was this inscription made? Observing that this is a graffito, not an inscription formally designed and incised or painted, and remembering the decorations on the walls of the New York subway, as well as on those of less dignified structures, we might be tempted to infer that here was a device already within the casual competence of the common people, that is, of everybody. We remind ourselves, however, that when it comes to deciding who was to read a given inscription, the inscription itself is silent: qua inscription, it can offer no testimony. In the present case we note the oral idiom and the probable oral setting of the statement. Is it likely that the pot so inscribed was put on exhibition before the contest for an audience to read? I do not think so.

Let us imagine the audience at the dancing contest, a familiar feature of the oral culture. The donor or judge has issued the versified proclamation to be transmitted by word of mouth; that is his business. "There is a prize for free style. Here it is." Maybe the announcement is entrusted tó a herald. In the twenty-third book of the *Iliad*, as prizes are competed for in the funeral games for Patroclus, the donor (Achilles) is the main announcer, but a herald has a part to play also.[18] The inscription, however, was solicited by the winner. Either he happened to be alphabetically skilled himself or he commissioned somebody who was—the more likely alternative, for I do not think that accomplished dancers in this era, when *mousikē* was supreme and when its mastery was the mark of cultivation, were likely to bother with the alphabet. That would be left to artisans. But he knows that his victory can be memorialized in inscribed signs which still carry a flavor of the miraculous in this unlettered culture. The only way to report and record the victory formally is to echo the proclamation setting forth its terms. Perhaps he has the announcement scratched on before the audience has dispersed. Repeating it aloud, he points to the scratches: "Look, that is what the pot is saying." The curious gather round to inspect: "How does it say that? Show us. How can a pot speak?" "Oh, yes," he says, "it can speak," and he points his finger and spells out the letters one by one. The crowd is impressed. The value of the pot has risen. It is not just like any other pot. This one can speak. Or else he takes it home and proudly exhibits it to his family and friends. "What does it say?" He repeats the remembered hexameter to assure them that these letters are indeed speaking, though he cannot read them himself, and they in turn repeat the line to themselves. Such a scene may seem only a flight of fancy. Yet, to indulge the imagination in this way is not, I think, irresponsible, given the epoch and the material. I offer it as a warning: evidence for writing is one thing, evidence for literacy is something else.

A cup, badly smashed, close in date to the vase, has been found at the other end of the Greek world on the island (Ischia) near Naples which the Greeks called Monkey Island (Pithecoussa).[19] Like the vase, it carries an alphabetic graffito (transcribed in Fig. 2). Its appearance in Italy so early supports the view, advanced by Rhys Carpenter forty years ago,[20] that the invention was of a kind which, once achieved, was likely to travel easily, most probably in the course of trading. Need it surprise us that the lines are

Fig. 2.   After L. H. Jeffery, *Local Scripts of Archaic Greece* (1961), Plate 47, no. 1.

metrical? The first is a halting iambus: *Nestoros e[im]i eupot[on] poterio[n]* ("Of Nestor am I the well-drunk drinking cup"). The next two revert to the familiar hexameter: *hos d'a[n] tode p[ie]si poteri[o] autika kenon* ("Whoso drinks this drinking cup straightway him")/*himer[os hair]esei kalliste[pha]no Aphrodites* ("Desire shall seize of fair-crowned Aphrodite"). The first asserts ownership; it is like the stamp of a signature: "property of Nestor," to discourage theft. The statement serves a prosaic purpose, to which the iambic measure, like our blank verse, is appropriate, having closest resemblance to the style of the vernacular. But why use meter at all? The answer may be that it is the object which is speaking to us: it has a voice which has to perpetuate itself, and for such perpetuation, meter is the required medium in a non-literate culture. After this statement, what does one expect? The signature on another object found at Cyme on the coast nearby, and perhaps made fifty years later, supplies the answer, for it is followed by the warning: "Whoso steals me will go blind."[21] But on this cup, the writing breaks into grandiloquent hexameters with a Homeric ring to them, and though they open with the same generic phrasing, "whoso shall etc.," appropriate to an oral announcement, we have to ask to whom they may be addressed. A dedication can hardly be the explanation, for the verse seems to celebrate the delectation of the drinker rather than the deity. The speaker is no longer the object, now mentioned in the third person; he is therefore most probably the owner. The generic "Whoso drinks" cannot be himself, but must refer to others to whom he is addressing an oral invitation: "Drink of this cup (which is my cup) and you will have a certain experience."

Rather than suggest a religious motif, a less elevated explanation is more plausible. Drinking cups were manufactured for drinking out of, if I may be permitted the obvious. You drank not in seclusion but at the symposium, that regular social feature of Greek life. You drank not to some abstract god of love, as in Plato, but to the friend or favorite, the *kalos* sitting or reclining opposite you at the table. But you also did not just drink. The symposium was the occasion utilized by an oral culture for the performance and recitation of private poetry, encomia, love songs, invective, self-revelation, personal stuff, most of it sung to the lyre. Can we imagine the elderly owner of this cup, after taking a swig, passing it to the boy across the table? He says to him, "A great cup, isn't it? Here, please drink out of it. My man, Execestides made it. He's a good worker. But do you know what I did? After he made it, I got him to write down what the cup does to you. Can't read it myself but you can see it there. Shall I tell you what it says?" Leaning over, with a slight leer, "Whoso drinks of this cup shall be seized of desire. Here, boy, drink up, and I'll sing you more of it." It is to be accepted, I think, as a fact that Aphrodite's activities were not confined to the heterosexual.[22]

Whether this interpretation be viewed as probable, possible, or not worthy of its subject—and in its defense I would note that the author dwells upon the act of drinking with alliterative and possibly bibulous frequency[23]—the inscription bespeaks the idiom of a communication orally conceived and expressed before it is inscribed.

Another inscribed cup of the same period, and also badly smashed, was found on Ithaca[24] (the island of Odysseus). This time the words are not scratched, but painted on, and after firing. Putting them together, it is possible to decipher two thirds of a hexameter line: *[x]enfos te philos kai p[isto]s (h)etairos* ("guest-friend dear and loyal comrade"). There are perhaps two other verses undecipherable. Is this not a fragment of another symposiastic utterance, not an invitation this time but a compliment, perhaps a toast? One recalls Homer's description of how Telemachus and Pisistratos were welcomed at the court of Menelaus in Sparta.[25] The host salutes the guest: "My guest-friend dear, and comrade faithful," pronouncing this and other sentiments, perhaps at the table, and in any case presenting the cup as he speaks. The one act ceremonially accompanies the other. The verses of presentation are framed to be remembered orally. Hitherto, such verse has been the only way to keep the identification in memory. But either the owner or else the recipient can now use a second recourse. The services of a craftsman, perhaps the maker of the cup, perhaps another, are enlisted. The verses are recited to him, for him to paint them on the pot as a reminiscent memorial now permanently attached to the object.

Along with the vase and the cups, it is possible to include a piece of bronze sculpture (Fig. 3), about eight inches high, found in Boeotia and of about the same period. Stylistically it is "Early Daedalic"; its archaic character is obvious; presumably it represents a warrior who once wore armor, now lost. The lettering incised on it begins on the outer side of the right thigh at the bottom, proceeds upwards, reading left to right, turns across the crotch and

Fig. 3.   After L. H. Jeffery, *Local Scripts of Archaic Greece* (1961), Plate 7, nos. 1 and 2.

then down along the outer side of the left thigh, still reading left to right; then twists backwards and works upwards on the inner side of the left thigh, reading now right to left, crosses the crotch again, and descends on the inner side of the right thigh, still reading right to left. As has been pointed out,[26] this order of the letters, first regular and then retrograde, is a response to the surface space available and visible on the statue; they have to be fitted onto it. It is not therefore addressed primarily to the convenience of the reader: it is being thought of as part of the statue or, rather, as part of its decoration. The lettering is imprinted on the object, as it were, intimately, and it conforms with this convention that what the inscription records is once more an utterance voiced by the object. It speaks in hexameters: "Mantiklos dedicated me to the far shooter, the silver bowed one./For the gift do thou Phoebus grant gracious return." It was impossible to place these words near the mouth, as might be done on a vase painting. However, when the statue addresses Phoebus, we feel that it is the donor himself who is speaking. In effect, the inscription carries his signature, his claim to credit, his expectation of reward. Why then do it by indirection?

We are used enough to dedicatory inscriptions in verse to suppose that meter was used for hieratic or pious purposes, verse in our eyes being suitable for elevated sentiment. But in its period, this example is preferably viewed as once more cast in the idiom of orally preservable speech, even though when inscribed there would no longer be any theoretical need for using the meter, provided, that is, that most people could read it. I infer that most people could not. This inscription was memorizable and so repeatable.

In the nonliterate epoch which immediately preceded the manufacture of this statuette, how could the donor obtain credit for his gift in the eyes of god or man? This is a question we should ask ourselves, and we must reply that he could get it only by a ceremony before an audience in which the local poet memorialized in a few repeatable verses the act of the giver. This was the act of attestation: the statement made was designed not only to be heard by the audience but remembered by them. But a person is needed to supply the voice for the utterance, and if the utterance is to be recorded, to survive with a life of its own, then a person is required who is also preservable beyond the occasion and even the lifetime of those present. The person (or the voice) is supplied by the object which will continue to be around. Can we guess that under oral conditions the poet held the object in his hands or stood beside it as he pronounced the dedication? So when inscription becomes possible, it is written on the object to represent not the donor's voice but the object's. It will live on, still speaking.[27]

During the period when these inscriptions were made, the Greek alphabet was in its infancy. It was a trick that had to be learned and taught, and it would take time to settle on the proper procedure. Let us recall the procedure that gave it birth. Greeks in contact with Phoenicians noticed the ability of the latter to write down a Semitic tongue, and desired to acquire the same facility for their own Indo-European speech. The signs used by the Phoenicians symbolized linguistic noises made in their own tongue. The linguistic components of Greek were not identical: in some cases there was phonetic similitude, in others approximation, and in still others no phonetic relationship. If the Greeks had been linguistic scientists, they would have analyzed the components of their own tongue and invented a new set of signs to symbolize them. Instead, they borrowed the Semitic shapes and sought to fit their sound-values to the sound-values of Greek, incidentally making a drastic improvement by setting aside five signs to symbolize vocalizations.

In this act of transfer, the psychological factor common to both Semitic and Greek practice was the visual appreciation of the shapes of the letters. For the Semitic system already in long use, a successful teaching method had been devised.[28] You arranged the letters in a fixed visual order in a row and required the learner to learn this order visually, while at the same time learning acoustically the recitation of their names and sound values. Performing the two acts together, the one by eye, the other by tongue and ear, you matched and mated the two in your mind, to the point where you could read a piece of script, where the letters occurred out of series, by recognizing their values, and recombining them in the word order of what was being said: a Semitic ABC in fact, which the Greeks borrowed intact, as we from the Greeks. It was a visual object, the characters being inscribed in series on strips of ivory and the like. An example survives from the very earliest period. It was found in Etruria in Italy.[29]

This means that the Greeks mastered the system visually; their visual memory of it was complete. But because the acoustic values of the two languages could not be uniformly equated, when it came to memorizing the sounds, confusion and uncertainty set in. A literate mastery of any alphabet requires that visual shape and acoustic value or set of values be matched with lightning speed and certitude. But it is possible to tell from the epigraphical evidence that in some cases the Greeks were at first unable to make up their minds what precise value to assign to a given letter.[30] They were memorizing the ABCs not with phonetic but only with visual efficiency.

The early existence of graffiti either scratched or painted, as opposed to inscriptions formally executed on stone, clay, or bronze, has been taken as evidence that writing was from the beginning a casual act and so within the competence of everybody. The island of Thera, and Mount Hymettus overlooking Athens, have both yielded inscriptions of this character dating from perhaps the late seventh or early sixth centuries. According to the hypothesis put forward here, they would most probably be the handiwork of craftsmen trading insults or trying out their ABCs. The largest single group of such definitely attributable to the citizens at large appears in Athens in the first half of the fifth century. These were the ballots cast in an ostracism. According to this curious procedure, the people in assembly from time to time could pass a vote of exile upon a citizen considered dangerous. The names of several candidates for this penalty might be proposed, and a citizen cast his ballot by writing the name of his choice upon a piece of pottery and depositing it to be counted. It is commonly inferred by scholars that the practice implies general literacy in Athens in the first half of the fifth century B.C.[31] Let us take a second look at it, first as it possibly relates to previous traditional habits characteristic of nonliterate societies. Here surely is a conspicuous example of the requirement that a name should be named, but now besides being uttered or shouted aloud in the oral preliminaries in the assembly, where vote counting could become confused, it can be inscribed and so counted up as a body of visible objects, a procedure more deliberate and accurate. Moreover, this naming the name for such a purpose is like putting a curse on it, and this was one of the oldest oral procedures, followed in oaths and imprecations and maledictions before witnesses. Was ostracism an institution conceived midway between nonliteracy and literacy, expressing some of the habits characteristic of both, but doomed to obsolescence once full literacy set in in the last third of the fifth century, as actually happened?[32] Its psychology, so to speak, was oral. A fully literate people would stop thinking in this particular way about their political opponents.

This suggestion is not fanciful. On some of the ballots—admittedly few out of the hundreds surviving—the voter has actually inscribed his curse, and for good measure made it metrical. "May requital be upon Hippocrates": these are the words, forming half a pentameter, which one voter has taken the trouble to scratch on his sherd, and another, going even farther, has composed a complete distich, a hexameter followed by a pentameter: "Xanthippus son of Ariphron of the accursed prytaneis/Does this sherd declare to be most guilty."[33]

The institution called for the ability to write a proper name—just that. As earlier suggested, even a proto-literate society might require of its citizens that they be expected to write or to recognize a signature when they could do little else. When a voter wants to say more, he breaks into verse composed orally in his head. Ostracism considered as an act performed does not prove literacy.

In any case, with what efficiency was even this limited achievement managed? Misspellings are frequent, but this of itself proves nothing. Shakespeare varied the spelling of his own name. More to the point is the way the lettering is managed. Names can be written retrograde, or *boustrophedon*, that is, left to right and then right to left. Had the men who used these survivals of antique practice enjoyed the benefits of an elementary curriculum in reading and writing? I do not think so. In other examples, letters of names occur in rows written from bottom to top, or worse still, written higgledy-piggledy, at random. Their authors can never have had the benefit of that standardized school drill which alone makes literate practice possible.[34]

If finally, in defense of full literacy at this flourishing epoch of Athenian history, it be objected that such badly managed specimens are in the minority, what of the fact that many voters appear to have got other people to write the name for them? Large numbers of ballots inscribed with Themistocles' name provide a notorious but not unique example. Out of a total of 190, fourteen hands have been identified as authors.[35] It is possible to conclude that in the end Themistocles' luck ran out and he became the victim of ballot stuffing, a rigged election. Certainly a politician so famous for sharp practices himself could have less cause to complain about similar treatment from his opponents. But politics aside, is it not fair to conclude that such operations could not easily be carried out in the open circumstances of the balloting unless large numbers of voters could not trust themselves to write a name, or could not read a name when it was written for them? Was the institution discarded when it was because it had become less useful to politicians, because in turn more people were learning not just to write but to read the names which others might wish to write for them?

There remains one type of testimony so far not considered. The existence of an inscription of itself testifies only to an act of writing. The manner and degree of its reading remain matters of speculation. How many such, we may wonder, scattered by early man upon the earth's surface, remained for one reason or another unread except by the writer? Reading and writing are not subjects which normally get into sculpture and painting, but in the few instances where this occurs in early Greek antiquity, we may find that art can tell us a few things about literacy or its absence which epigraphy cannot say.

The Acropolis Museum at Athens contains three statues partially preserved, representing seated figures dressed alike. They are dedicatory, measuring close to three feet high. It was only when I personally noticed two of them that my attention was called to their existence. They have evoked little comment, perhaps because the unconscious prejudice in favor of Greek literacy has made their presence seem irrelevant (Fig. 4). What are they? They have been correctly identified as "scribes," and their date somewhere in the last third of the sixth century B.C. Humfry Payne, in his classic work on the archaic sculpture recovered from the Acropolis, spoke of them as "a

Fig. 4. After Humfry Payne, *Archaic Marble Sculpture from the Acropolis*, 2nd ed. (1950), Plate 118.

curious isolated group, unlike anything else in Greek sculpture; they have been thought to be based on an Egyptian model, but I cannot see anything really Egyptian about them, save the subject. And that after all might have occurred outside Egypt."[36] They are holding in their laps not papyrus but wax tablets, diptychs, and the existence of the statues might suggest some honorific status for the persons represented.

There exists a graffito found in Athens, of the same period, scratched in a fragment of a pot by a workman who, however, was not an Athenian, telling his mate where to leave the saw.[37] If we adopt the theory that literacy began at the top and penetrated to the bottom, we naturally infer that his betters who employed him were fully lettered and literate. But in that case, why did Athens at this time require the services of scribes? Surely their representation, in the form of dedicatory offerings, distinguished by special chair, clothing, and posture, argues for the fact that they commanded a craft which conferred social status on its possessors. This would be natural if it represented a prized monopoly available and valuable to the upper classes but one which they did not personally practice. We know from references in Pindar and Aeschylus,[38] the earliest we have on this subject, that in their time the written record was still regarded as supplying a reminder which preserved for the memory what had been orally pronounced. You went to a scribe and dictated a memorandum. Could you read it, or only he? The metaphors used by the poets imply that he had to read it back to you. To be sure, the scribe or secretary is in common employment in later antiquity— Cicero dictated to one—but in those literate centuries he had become what he still is today, a "secretary," a factotum whose function was auxiliary to other literates. Such people were no longer important enough to merit honorific representation in dedicatory statues.

A functioning literacy depends upon an elementary school curriculum designed to drill the small child in reading. We know nothing from literary sources about schools in sixth and fifth century Athens, and what little we do know does not point to the presence of reading drill in schools: rather, the reverse. There exists, however, a famous Athenian vase painted in red figure about 480 B.C., at the time when ostracism was coming into fashion, portraying a scene which is usually described as a "boys' school."[39] It was illustrated in a handbook on Greek education seventy years ago, has been reproduced frequently since, and, it is fair to say, has been made to do yeoman service in the cause of Greek literacy. The two sides of the cup (Fig. 5) have been interpreted as "one showing a reading lesson, the other a writing lesson."[40] Let us take a second look at them.

The action portrays a total of ten figures, of which four seem to be proportionately shorter and therefore younger than the six. Of the six, two seated, holding sticks, are probably spectators or listeners. They have been interpreted to represent parents or paidagōgoi. If it is agreed that the younger group are pupils under instruction, how old are they? Surely not small children being drilled in primary school but youths of fifteen and up, ephēboi. The actors in this scene are from the governing class; they are not working

Fig. 5. After Fürtwangler-Reichold, *Griechischer Vasenmalerei*, Series 3, Plate 136.

men's sons (who could not afford *paidagōgoi*); they enjoy leisure enough to afford advanced education. What precisely are they doing?

It is scarcely plausible that any of them are either reading or writing. One of them certainly is not; he is seated playing a lyre. The other three are standing. Their pose is that not of readers or writers but of reciters, even though artistic convention keeps their mouths closed; they are intended to be either speaking or singing. Each of the four, respectively, faces another man who is seated. These four older men therefore are plausibly taken to be instructors. What instruction are they giving? One listens to the pupil lyre-player. One is playing the flute in front of a standing pupil; one looks at the standing pupil in front of him while holding up a scroll which faces neither of them but the viewer of the vase. And one is holding tablets and stylus and is looking at the tablet while the pupil stands before him. Ignoring for a moment what may be going on between this last pair, what are the activities to be inferred as taking place between the other three? One is a music lesson in instrumental music, one is a singing lesson in which the pupil recites to the accompaniment played by his teacher—he would not be learning the flute standing up; one is reciting poetry to his teacher. The scroll held by the teacher contains an epigraph combining two fragments of different Homeric hexameters. The spelling is faulty and the combination incoherent, but each fragment is a hexameter opener, proclaiming the beginning of an epic theme. In one the poet invokes his muse, in the other he announces himself that he is starting. In placing the scroll in the picture, two alternative artistic intentions are possible. According to the more likely one, the artist tells the viewer of the vase by a rather cute device the passages which the pupil is supposed to be reciting. Or else, there is indicated a procedure whereby the pupil is given a cue in the opening line and is expected to go on from there.

What is going on between the fourth pair? The common interpretation is that the teacher is correcting with his stylus a writing exercise presented by his pupil. This would be more plausible if he were using the flat end of the stylus for elision rather than the point. Alternatively, using the point, he is supposed to be pricking out the shapes of letters for the pupil to fill in; this notion, based upon an interpretation of a passage in Plato which has been demonstrated to be erroneous, must be rejected.[41] If the action here bears any relation to what is otherwise transacted in these scenes, a different explanation is possible. The teacher is writing something himself. This is the most obvious interpretation. The pupil waits, standing. What is the instructor writing if not a theme, perhaps a free composition, which he is going to hand to the pupil to memorize? The latter will have to read it, that is admitted, but he will read in order to memorize and recite, and that is why he is portrayed standing. Aristotle tells us, in a later and more literate period, that the sophists did this for their pupils.

Whether or not this last explanation is correct, it is to be concluded that if this is a picture of instruction in a school, the overwhelming emphasis falls upon music, poetry, and recitation, to which writing is ancillary while reading is not portrayed at all. *Mousikē*, in short, was still central to the education of the Athenian upper classes in the first half of the fifth century. Reading was not. It is consistent with this view that the artist does not think it important to get his Homeric quotations alphabetically correct or coherent. They serve their purpose. Had his customers themselves been fully literate, he would have felt an obligation to meet their standards.

The existence of true literacy is a social condition. Yet curiously enough it is testable by a private activity. When a citizen reads something "to himself," as we say, and by himself, and does so habitually, he has become a member of a society which has divorced itself, or begun to divorce itself, from the audience situation. The content of preserved speech no longer depends for its publication and preservation upon oral communication and repetition by groups of persons. The silent solitary reader has accepted the full implications of documentation. His existence has a literary reference, which turns up in a comedy, the *Frogs* of Aristophanes, produced in 405 B.C. It takes the

Fig. 6.   After Theodor Birt, *Buchrolle in der Kunst*,
p. 15, fig. 90.

form of a remark placed in the mouth of one of the characters, the god
Dionysus: "As I sat on deck reading the Andromeda to myself." He goes on
to say that this act of reading brought to mind the author of what he was
reading, namely, Euripides.[42] This is the first explicit allusion to reading as
a private act. We can assume, if such a habit was taking hold and receiving
such casual notice in the course of this play, that Athens had become literate
in our sense, that is, was becoming a society of readers. In fact, the *Frogs* is
unique in containing several other allusions which point in the same direction.[43]

    This first mention of the solitary reader in Athenian literature occurs at
about the same time as a sculptor made the first physical representation of
him (Fig. 6). The subject is portrayed in relief on a grave stele in the developed High Classic style. It is as a reader reading to himself that this dead
person is now to be remembered and memorialized by the living who survive him. This is the earliest such representation in Greek art.[44]

So, as Athens enters upon the fourth century, her literate revolution, so much more significant for future history than all her political comings and goings, was being accomplished, with certain fateful consequences for Europe and the world.[45]

YALE UNIVERSITY

NOTES

1 Eric A. Havelock, *Preface to Plato* (Cambridge, 1963), p. 40.

2 I accept the consensus, disputed by M. L. West, ed., *Theogony* (Oxford, 1966), pp. 46 ff., that "Homer" preceded "Hesiod."

3 Havelock, "Prologue to Greek Literacy," in *Univ. Cincinnati Classical Studies*, II (Norman, Okla., 1973), 32.

4 *Protagoras* 325e, cf. 326c-e and *Charmides* 159c. Immerwahr (below n. 39) says: "The book roll is thus a mnemonic device facilitating recitation, not a real 'book' for reading alone" (p. 37). The "nuts and bolts" of Greek education have received scant attention from scholars, mainly because they were ignored by ancient historians. The handbooks cling tenaciously to the view that at the elementary level education began where we begin it. Thus Kenneth J. Freeman in his *Schools of Hellas* (London, 1907), noting the Platonic order "grammatistēs" "kitharistēs" "paidotribēs" (*Protag.* 312b), argues that "this system of primary education at Athens may reasonably be traced back to the beginning of the sixth century" (p. 52), placing reliance on the legend that Solon made the teaching of letters compulsory. This opinion has been recently repeated in Frederick A. Beck, *Greek Education* (New York, 1964), p. 77. Henri I. Marrou, in his *Histoire de l'Education dans l'Antiquité*, 6th ed. (1948; rpt. Paris, 1965), is more cautious. He notes evidence of illiteracy in the period of ostracism: "Néanmoins, dès l'époque des guerres médiques, on peut tenir pour certaine l'existence d'un enseignement des lettres" (p. 77)—an opinion supported by a mistranslation of a sentence in Plutarch, *Themistocles* 10, where it is said that the Troizeneans supplied the children of the refugee Athenians with "teachers," not "reading-teachers."

5 I now withdraw previous support (*Preface to Plato*, p. 51) for the hypothesis that the invention was the work of minstrels. Those supporting it (H. T. Wade-Gery, *The Poet of the Iliad* [Cambridge, 1952], pp. 13-14; Kevin Robb, *The Progress of Literacy in Ancient Greece* [Los Angeles, 1970], p. 13) rely on the assumption that composers of the first metrical inscriptions were necessarily minstrels and at the same time writers.

6 The apprentice relationship is described at Plato, *Protag.* 328a; cf. R. M. Cook, *Greek Painted Pottery*, 2nd ed. (1960; rpt. London, 1972), p. 271 (black figure illustration of a manager, painter, craftsman, and five assistants); and L. H. Jeffery, *The Local Scripts of Archaic Greece* (Oxford, 1961), p. 62 (masons learned to write and passed on knowledge to sons as part of craft).

7 J. M. Cook, "A Painter and His Age," *Mélanges . . . offerts à André Varagnac* (Paris, 1971), p. 175.

8 Solon 2 (Diehl): he refers to his inscription of *thesmoi* at 24.18-20. Epigraphical evidence so far uncovered exists for the practice of inscribing "legal texts" (it is misleading to call them "codes") on the walls of public buildings in Crete, one (from Dreros) datable 650 B.C. or later, the others inscribed in the sixth and fifth centuries, supporting the literary tradition that "the Cretans were pioneers among Greeks in establishing legal systems"; the island was "if not the birthplace at least one of the earliest receivers of the Greek alphabet" (Jeffery, p. 310). The best-known text, the so-called "Gortyn Code," was inscribed not earlier than 450. The "Constitution" of

Chios was inscribed on a stele c. 575-50. A codification of Athenian laws was inscribed in the last decade of the fifth century. This included a republication of some laws attributed to Draco, inscribed on a stele of which a mutilated portion survives. Some of the wording, so far as decipherable, is demonstrably archaic and the content very plausibly Draconian (Ronald S. Stroud, *Drakon's Law on Homicide* [Berkeley, 1968]). The title of E. Ruschenbusch's monograph *Solonos Nomoi: die Fragmente* (Weisbaden, 1966) is misleading. Of a total of 155 so-called "fragments," organized under no less than forty-two legal headings, three are taken from the epigraphical remains of the Athenian code, three from notices in fifth-century authors (Herodotus and Aristophanes), twenty-seven from quotations in fourth-century orators (Lysias, Demosthenes, Aeschines), ten from notices in Aristotle, four from notices in Cicero, thirty-nine from notices in Plutarch *(Life of Solon* and *Moralia)*, the rest being a miscellany of late notices in scholiasts, grammarians, and the like. Skepticism (cf., e.g., C. Hignett, *History of the Athenian Constitution* [Oxford, 1952]) has always surrounded these attributions to "Solon" (a number of which are anonymous). In Herodotus (I, 30-33, 86) he has already become the subject of moralizing legend. His name, like that of Moses, was liable to be invoked as authority for contemporary regulation, a comparison which is all the more to the point if Athenian society in the sixth and early fifth centuries, like the Hebraic in an earlier period, still relied heavily on oral record. Solon's surviving poetry is another matter, but it is noteworthy that it cannot be levied upon for any "fragments" of legislation. Noteworthy too is "the absence in archaic Greece of such records of public events as were erected in Egypt or Assyria or Persia" (Jeffery, p. 21).

9 R. M. Cook, p. 255, where it is also noted that "often the scene is self explanatory," i.e., the label *qua label* is not needed. Likewise, Attic signatures after peaking about 500 B.C. became rare by 400 (p. 256). I would infer that in a documented era the habit became obsolete. The object was no longer felt to require a "voice" imprinted on it.

10 W. D. Stanford, *The Odyssey,* 2d ed. (New York, 1959), pp. xxi-xxii; and Norman Austin, "Name Magic in the *Odyssey" California Studies in Classical Antiquity,* 5 (1972).

11 Jeffery, p. 47: "The name will naturally be written as close as possible to its owner, *as it were issuing out from him"* (my italics).

12 For the latest date once proposed, see Rodney S. Young, *Hesperia,* Supp. 2 (1939), 225-29; but now perhaps hedged? Cf. Jeffery, p. 16, n. 1.

13 Jeffery, p. 68.

14 *Ibid.,* pp. 16, 68. The treatment, unique in Greece, of alpha iota and lambda supports the suggestion that the inscriber was a visitor to an Athens still nonliterate at that time (late eighth century?), perhaps from Al Mina in Phoenicia, plausibly the original home of the Greek invention.

15 Kevin Robb, "The Dipylon Prize Graffito," *Coranto,* 7, No. 1 (1971), 12-14.

16 The conditional relative clause followed by apodosis (cf. also below fig. 4) recalls the conditional and participial constructions characteristic of early case law from Hammurabi onward (cf. R. H. Pfeiffer, *Introduction to Old Testament* [New York, 1948], pp. 211-18) which, though surviving in written form, demonstrably reflect the style of oral promulgation.

17 So Jeffery, p. 68.

18 *Iliad* 23.567-68. Actually, all the herald does in this context is to call for silence while placing the "sceptre" in Menelaus' hands, a ritual required to allow him to voice his protest. Cf. *Il.* 18.503 and 505.

19 Jeffery, p. 235.

20 *American Journal of Archaeology,* 37 (1935), 8-29.

21 Jeffery, p. 238 and pl. 47.

22 Cf. Pindar, *frag.* 108. On Attic *kalos* inscriptions see R. M. Cook, p. 258, where it is noted that the fashion (like the names and signatures, above n. 9) fades out in the last quarter of the fifth century.

23 Cf. *eupoton poterion . . . piesi poterio*

24 Jeffery, pl. 45.

25 *Odyssey* 4.613-19; 15.53-55, 69-74, 113-21, 147-51. Telemachus was truly a *xeinos philos.* The sentiment is a Homeric formula. Is it possible that the "trusty comrade" in the inscription refers to a second party accompanying the first—the "Pisistratus" of Homer's story?

26 Jeffery, pp. 46-47.

27 *Ibid.*: "Much of the earliest Greek writing consisted of explanatory inscriptions on existing objects." Yet were these inscriptions "explanations," that is, information separately coded in writing, a procedure understandable in a literate culture? Or are they not rather to be understood as "signals" uttered by the object?

28 Cf. *ibid.*, pp. 25-27.

29 *Ibid.*, pl. 48.

30 *Ibid.*, pp. 25-27.

31 E. Vanderpool, "Ostracism at Athens," in *Univ. Cincinnati Classical Studies,* II (Norman, Okla., 1973), p. 229: "Obviously the very existence of a law . . . presupposed that the electorate was largely literate."

32 The institution was last used c. 417 B.C.

33 Vanderpool, figs. 21 and 20. I borrow the reading of the distich from Vanderpool, p. 223; but see his footnote on the same page. The voter might even draw a profile of person named; cf. Vanderpool, p. 232 and figs. 46 and 47. Did this provide an "object" to which the "curse" (implicit in the vote) would be "fastened," and so made effective, as in later magical use of wax images and the like? No other motive for taking such trouble is discernible.

34 *Ibid.*, figs. 28, 24, 25, furnish typical examples.

35 *Ibid.*, pp. 225-26. The total represents a group found together in a well.

36 Humfry Payne, *Archaic Marble Sculpture from the Acropolis,* 2nd ed. (New York, 1951), p. 47 (with bibliography, p. 74).

37 Jeffery, p. 135 and pl. 22; also Mabel Lang, *Graffiti in the Athenian Agora* (Princeton, 1974), fig. 18. I have assumed the writer to be a *demiourgos.*

38 Pindar, *Olympian* 10.1 ff.; Aeschylus, *Prometheus Bound* 460, 789-90; *Suppliants* 179; *Libation Bearers* 450; *Eumenides* 275.

39 This unique scene appeared in Freeman's *Schools of Hellas* in 1907 (above, n. 4) (Fürtwangler-Reichold, *Griechischer Vasenmalerei,* Series 3, pl. 136). It is examined in H. B. Immerwahr "Book Rolls on Attic Vases," in *Classical Mediaeval and Renaissance Studies in Honor of B. L. Ullman,* ed. C. Henderson, Jr., I (1954), 19.

40 F. D. Harvey, "Literacy in the Athenian Democracy," *Revue des Etudes Grecques,* 79 (July-Dec. 1966), 631, no. 9.

41 This point is made by Harvey in an as yet unpublished article, "Greeks and Romans Learn To Write."

42 *Frogs* 52-67. Euripides, *frag.* 36(N) (datable between 424 and 421) is not so explicit.

43 *Frogs* 943, 1084, 1109-14, 1409-10.

44 Immerwahr, p. 37 with n. 2.

45 Havelock, *Origins of Western Literacy,* Ontario Institute for Studies in Education Monograph Series 14 (Toronto, 1976).

Thoughtful Hesiod

Οὐκ ἄρα μοῦνον ἔην Ἐρίδων γένος, ἀλλ' ἐπὶ γαῖαν
εἰσὶ δύω· τὴν μέν κεν ἐπαινέσσειε νοήσας,
ἣ δ' ἐπιμωμητή· διὰ δ' ἄνδιχα θυμὸν ἔχουσιν.
ἣ μὲν γὰρ πόλεμόν τε κακὸν καὶ δῆριν ὀφέλλει,
σχετλίη· οὔ τις τήν γε φιλεῖ βροτός, ἀλλ' ὑπ' ἀνάγκης   15
ἀθανάτων βουλῇσιν Ἔριν τιμῶσι βαρεῖαν.
τὴν δ' ἑτέρην προτέρην μὲν ἐγείνατο Νὺξ ἐρεβεννή,
θῆκε δέ μιν Κρονίδης ὑψίζυγος, αἰθέρι ναίων,
γαίης ἐν ῥίζῃσι, καὶ ἀνδράσι πολλὸν ἀμείνω·
ἥ τε καὶ ἀπάλαμόν περ ὁμῶς ἐπὶ ἔργον ἔγειρεν·   20
εἰς ἕτερον γάρ τίς τε ἰδὼν ἔργοιο χατίζει
πλούσιον, ὃς σπεύδει μὲν ἀρώμεναι ἠδὲ φυτεύειν
οἶκόν τ' εὖ θέσθαι· ζηλοῖ δέ τε γείτονα γείτων
εἰς ἄφενος σπεύδοντ'· ἀγαθὴ δ' Ἔρις ἥδε βροτοῖσι.
καὶ κεραμεὺς κεραμεῖ κοτέει καὶ τέκτονι τέκτων,   25
καὶ πτωχὸς πτωχῷ φθονέει καὶ ἀοιδὸς ἀοιδῷ.
ὦ Πέρση, σὺ δὲ ταῦτα τεῷ ἐνικάτθεο θυμῷ,
μηδέ σ' Ἔρις κακόχαρτος ἀπ' ἔργου θυμὸν ἐρύκοι
νείκε' ὀπιπεύοντ' ἀγορῆς ἐπακουὸν ἐόντα.
ὤρη γάρ τ' ὀλίγη πέλεται νεικέων τ' ἀγορέων τε   30
ᾧ τινι μὴ βίος ἔνδον ἐπηετανὸς κατάκειται
ὡραῖος, τὸν γαῖα φέρει, Δημήτερος ἀκτήν.
τοῦ τε κορεσσάμενος νείκεα καὶ δῆριν ὀφέλλοι
κτήμασ' ἐπ' ἀλλοτρίοις· σοὶ δ' οὐκέτι δεύτερον ἔσται
ὧδ' ἔρδειν· ἀλλ' αὖθι διακρινώμεθα νεῖκος   35
ἰθείῃσι δίκῃς αἵ τ' ἐκ Διός εἰσιν ἄρισται.
ἤδη μὲν γὰρ κλῆρον ἐδασσάμεθ', ἄλλα τε πολλὰ
ἁρπάζων ἐφόρεις μέγα κυδαίνων βασιλῆας
δωροφάγους, οἳ τήνδε δίκην ἐθέλοντι δίκασσαν.
νήπιοι, οὐδὲ ἴσασιν, ὅσῳ πλέον ἥμισυ παντός   40
οὐδ' ὅσον ἐν μαλάχῃ τε καὶ ἀσφοδέλῳ μέγ' ὄνειαρ.

Hesiod, *Works and Days* (Rzach), 11–41

If Hesiod is to be considered an oral poet in the same sense, and to the same degree, as Homer,[1] the metrics and vocabulary of these hexameters would be expected to obey Homeric rules of formulaic composition. In fact, they may contain hints to the contrary,[2] which might raise interesting questions concerning the technical conditions of composition. Rather than pursue these, I propose to focus on the character and content of the argumentative structure,[3] always bearing in mind that if this on examination shows a degree of novelty, in comparison with the habits of narrative epic, then parallel divergences in metrics and vocabulary would not be unexpected. Argumentation of course abounds in Homer, primarily in the speeches. The present passage, however, reads like an attempt to expound a formal thesis with a certain degree of logical rigor which measured by epic standards is unusual; it is to this attempt that present attention will be turned.

On the face of it, and making some concessions to the "roughness" of Hesiod's style, the content of these lines can be interpreted with reasonable coherence in the following paraphrase:

There are two varieties of contention among men; one of them is negative, provoking war, the other positive, rousing men to work through competition. Emulation of rich neighbors illustrates this kind of competition, (so does) quarreling between craftsmen and resentment between beggars or bards. You, Perses, must learn this lesson and so avoid wasting your time in (the wrong sort of) contention, which means listening in on the

1. J. A. Notopoulos, "Homer, Hesiod, and the Achaean Heritage of Oral Poetry", *Hesperia*, 29 (1960), 177–97.

2. For example, ἰθείῃσι δίκῃς (36), with word-end at position 3½, may be un-Homeric (but cf. Kirk, pp. 97 ff. below); the sense of ὀφέλλει (14) is Homeric, but ὀφέλλοις (33, the MS. reading, which may well be correct) might exemplify an adaptation of the Homeric formula for protreptic purposes (cf. also *W.D.* 213). ἐπιμωμητή (13), a *hapax leg.*, looks like a coinage formed to assist the poet's essay in definition.

3. For a recent discussion, see H. Munding, *Hesiods Erga in ihrem Verhältnis zur Ilias* (Frankfurt 1959).

wrangles in the agora. Sustenance is seasonal and must be adequately accumulated as a prerequisite for indulgence in disputes (of which, of course, I disapprove) aimed at the property of others (that is, of me). You (Perses) will not have a second chance to act in this way (that is, at my expense). We (Perses and I) should settle our wrangle (that is, lawsuit) justly. The allotment (I mean our patrimony) we (you and I) divided up (between us), but you (Perses) made off with much more (than your share), after honoring (that is, bribing) judges who like giving this kind of (that is, unjust) justice. Fools are they (the judges, the litigants, or Perses?), ignorant of the advantages of moderation (that is, legal compromise between Perses and me) and of a frugal diet (in preference to Perses' acquired wealth).

Suppose this is the sense and connection intended by the poet.[4] An initial difficulty then arises concerning the portrait of Perses who, on the one hand, it would appear, is exhorted to avoid the dangers of poverty, and on the other is accused of excessive acquisition. This inconsistency tends to support those who have argued that Perses, though he may have been a real brother, is used as a lay figure in this poem. This, though probable, is not the issue with which I wish directly to deal.

Behind the problem of personal identity in this passage lies another which cuts deeper. The air of logical connection which appears in our translation depends for its effect upon the bracketed portions added as supplements to the Greek text. Read without them, the argument tends to loosen up and even disintegrate. This is not true of the first fourteen lines (11–24), ending in examples of rivalry for wealth. But to these are then subjoined two aphorisms occupying a line each, the intent of which, taken by themselves, can be viewed as satirical: (*a*) the first object of a craftsman's criticism is always his fellow craftsman; (*b*) beggars resent each other, as do bards (hence, either: resentment is universal or: bards are like beggars). These rather

4. To assist this interpretation, the Loeb translator adopts the emendation τὰ for τε at line 37, and prints ἀλλὰ not ἄλλα.

cynical sentiments are linked to the previous gospel of work, but the logic of the connection is not very tight. Such activities would rather be proof of time-wasting than of hard work, that is, of the negative strife rather than the positive, especially in view of the implicit distinction previously drawn between *deris* and *zelos*.

At line 28, to maintain continuity with the previous passage, we have to interpret *eris kakochartos* as equivalent to the negative strife described in 13 ff., and as excluding the good strife of 24. But without this interpretation, the Greek more naturally reads as initiating a fresh argument, to the effect that strife of any kind can menace hours of labor; this happens if its attraction can lure one into joining the audience at disputes in the marketplace. On this showing, the poet at this point has abandoned the formal division with which he had begun.

Lines 33 and 34*a*, again, can be connected logically to the preceding by assuming that they are ironical, expressing a policy which from Hesiod's standpoint is immoral. But taken by themselves, without benefit of such moralizing interpretation, they could be read as another piece of proverbial cynicism advising the would-be aggressor in acquisition to be sure to have a secure financial basis from which to proceed.

From 34*b* onward, the continuity suggested depends on identifying the second person singular in the Greek as addressed to Perses, and the first person plural as including Hesiod and Perses. The *kleros* (37) then becomes their common patrimony, and the *neikos* of 35 becomes a lawsuit between Hesiod and his brother in which Hesiod had been worsted. The text supplies none of these clues. If they are withdrawn, the connection between 34*a* on the one hand, and 34*b* plus 35*a* on the other, falls apart, as is also true of the connection between 35*a* and 35*b* ff. and between 36 and 37, and between 39 and 40, and between 40 and 41.

It is not our intention to reduce the whole passage to a meaningless series of phrases, but rather to indicate that the poet is in fact aiming at an argumentative unity but that his unity is

very difficult for him to achieve; the reason being that he is
working with disjunct bits and pieces of verse drawn from his
oral reservoir which he is trying to put together in a new way.
However, before suggesting his method, it is fair to ask: How
far, supposing the original material does consist of disjunct
pieces of verse, can the process of disintegration of context be
pushed?

A good many units making up this composition consist of
self-contained proverbs. This is true of 23 *b* plus 24 *a*, of 25 plus
26—a pair linked by parallel syntax and assonance—of 28 (plus
29 if desired), of 30 plus 31, and of 40 plus 41. If syntax were
manipulated, one or two others could emerge from the text. This
is true of 22 (plus 23 *a* if desired) if *plousion* were changed to the
nominative, and of 32 if the first two words were changed to the
feminine and the last to the nominative, perhaps of 33 plus 34 *a*
if for the first three words some substitute were proposed:
plouton ktesamenos, though unlikely, would do. Further manipulation might produce similar effects on lines 20, 36 and 39. Not
the actual existence, but the latent possibility of such proverbs
is the point to be stressed.

Let us now return to what one feels to be the poet's sustained
intention. Though the passage can be analyzed and broken
down into these bits and pieces, when read as a whole it conveys
the impression of a single thread of sustained meaning, but the
thread, so to speak, is in spots very frayed, and almost broken.
The original impression is fixed for us by the first fourteen lines,
after which logical coherence begins to give way at 25 and
disintegrates faster as the poet proceeds. In these opening lines
he establishes quite firmly the antithetic concepts of a praise-
worthy and good *eris* and a blameable and bad *eris* (lines 12–13).
To each is attached a series of appropriate descriptive formulae.
The bad *eris* is a rouser of war, intractable, unloved, a burden
prized perforce (14–16). The good *eris* enjoys cosmic parentage
and divine status, is far better for men, and is a rouser of men to
work through emulation (17–24). So far, so good. But this
paragraph of fourteen lines in fact exhausts the capacity of the

poet (*a*) to maintain his antithesis with clarity and logic, (*b*) to define adequately its second half, that is, the functions and effects of good strife. The reasons for this double limitation will be suggested in a moment.

Thereafter, two things happen to the exposition. At first, Hesiod attempts to embark further on the attributes of the good strife, but the attempt breaks down into partial irrelevance (lines 25–7). Then he abandons the antithesis altogether and his verse is allowed to flow into a description of the evils of strife in general (28). But this strife is now viewed as centering not on war, but on litigation in the market-place (29); and it is to this topic that those formulas which fill up lines 30–2 attach themselves. Less clearly, the same topic seems to control lines 33–9, with 40 and 41 added as an appendix.

What is the reason for the initial failure of connection—the failure, that is, to sustain argument coherently beyond fourteen lines? I suggest the following: The oral reservoir, so to speak, as we can determine from Homer and from the *Theogony*, supplied our poet with familiar images of strife as the spirit of combat and of contention between individuals, as the child of Night, and as a dangerous element in human life. He applies his own creative genius to these formulas in order to split the single conception into two types, which he calls *gene*, and this constitutes a mental leap forward. The effect is to call into being a new topic of discourse, namely a good strife, a novel conception and one which he wishes to develop as a moral principle necessary to the economy of an agricultural society. But his formulas do not readily support either the antithesis or the existence of this new concept and he has to fight, as it were, mentally against the tradition, and his effort finally collapses. He becomes the prisoner of familiar formulas which have taken shape in an epoch of minstrelsy which was innocent of such a distinction, or at least had never formally recognized it; but he never entirely loses the thread of his new conception.

The first fourteen lines, then, give expression to a thesis which can be accepted as an act of new creation and a successful one.

They would nevertheless be expected to obey that familiar law of oral composition whereby any act of poetic originality is carried out by remodeling or reorganizing previously used formulas. The antecedents of these lines lie initially in those contexts of the *Iliad* where *eris* is portrayed as arousing the combative instincts of men in battle. Her Homeric image is a little complex. She is an affliction (*argalee*) and also possessed of passionate energy (*amoton memauia*), yet also is beneficial (*laossoos*). She casts *neikos* into the midst and arouses *ponos* and increases *stonos*, but she also puts *sthenos* into men's hearts. In particular, she encourages and enjoys an equal contest. Zeus and the gods generally let her loose on men. She can grow till she treads earth and strikes heaven.[5] Nor should we forget her role as that initial contention aroused by Apollo which sets the machinery of the *Iliad* in motion, particularly as Homer later makes a point of this when he represents his hero as condemning and discarding this *eris*.[6]

Echoes, as it were, of these attributes penetrate into Hesiod's divided account. As she who treads over the earth, the original *eris* turns into twin figures who do this (11–12). As the spirit of combat, afflictive (σχετλίη) and also god-directed (ἀθανάτων βουλῇσιν), she becomes the bad strife. But equally as the source of energy in the fighter and as the participant in equal contest and the source of *ponos* she helps to suggest the attributes of the Hesiodic good strife (20–4). Finally, as the source of *neikos*, she supplies a prototype for the lines following the antithesis which discuss or portray litigation in the agora.

Between the Homeric description of *eris* and the dichotomy achieved by Hesiod there intervenes the genealogy of *eris* supplied in the *Theogony* (225–32). The truth seems to be that the *Iliad*, the *Theogony*, and the *Works and Days* deal successively

5. IV.440–5 raging ceaselessly, a little wave which then extends from earth to heaven, casting equal *neikos*, fostering *stonos*; v.517–18 arousing *ponos*, raging ceaselessly; XI.3–12 *argalee*, discharged by Zeus, putting great *sthenos* in the heart; XI.73 *polustonos*; XVIII.535 companion of *kudoimos* and *ker oloe*; XX.48 arising as the gods mingle in battle, *kratere*, *laossoos*.

6. I.6, 8; XVIII.187; XIX.58, 64.

with *eris* as a topic of some significance and each enlarges on the preceding. Homer had described her as the spirit of war. In almost cosmic terms, she grows to such stature that she strides on earth while her head is against heaven. Her companions are *deimos, phobos, kudoimos,* and *ker oloe.* She is also the sister of Ares *androphonos.* She presides over or brings about *polemos, mache, neikos,* and *ponos.* The *Theogony,* rationalizing, we suggest, these images of *eris,* works her into the genealogical scheme by assigning her parentage to Night, thus giving her cosmic extension, and gives her a list of brothers and sisters which includes *Ker* (211), and a list of children which includes *Androktasiai, Ponos, Machai, Phonoi,* and *Neikea* (226–9). She herself is *karterothumos* (225), consistent with her Homeric portrait as the source of combative energy in men: altogether, a formidable and oppressive figure in the genealogical gallery of the *Theogony.*

Our present passage, then, begins by correcting this genealogy.[7] There are two *gene* of strifes, not one. But in using *genos* in this way, the bard has insensibly shifted its meaning. Two *gene* of *eris* (in the singular), if he had so phrased it, would mean two different generations or sets of children derived from *eris.* A man can have only one ancestral *genos,* but conceivably his descendants could number several *gene.* This would have been a genealogical correction, and in part Hesiod may mean this, since he is probably thinking of a strife who has good children as against the list of bad children in the *Theogony.* However, he does not say this. He speaks of "two *gene* of strifes" (in the plural) which can mean only two different strife-families, that is, two different people born (with the name) strife. The implication is that they are children of a common parent—either twins or at least sisters. Now this is not strictly a genealogical correction, but a typological one. *Genos* is being transmuted from its previous familial meaning into that of class or kind, and this is achieved by a change in the context in which an existing word

7. First noted in the commentaries *ad loc.* of Mazon (1914) and Wilamowitz (1928); see also other references in Munding, *op. cit.* p. 31, n. 41.

is used, not by using a new word. Once he has managed to double the name *eris* in this way, Hesiod splits one from the other conceptually by praising one and blaming the other. *Epimomete*[8] as an epithet is suggestive. An act of genuine mental creation has occurred and he is somehow aware of it. Is this why he insists on the participle *noesas* to indicate the effort of (mental) attention required? After that it becomes easy to muster some Homeric formulae, previously used to describe the combative *eris*, and here attach them to the blameworthy type, and to recall in the same context the Homeric designation of the gods, Zeus (xi.3) and Apollo (i.8–9) in particular, as the originators of *eris*. The divine *boulai* (*W.D.* 16) may even be another reminiscence of the preface to the *Iliad* (i.5).

But the sister *eris*, whose separate existence he so far tenaciously retains in his mind, requires a separate definition, and a more sophisticated one. This is his own mental creation,[9] and it is important, so he grounds the definition in that genealogy supplied in the *Theogony*, and then, remembering that Night is extended triple round Tartarus, above which grow roots of earth (*Theogony* 726–8), he exalts the importance of his new *eris* by giving it cosmic extension, thus preparing for the parallel assertion of the importance of its role in human life ("for men it is far better"). To define this role, he then successively attaches to the cosmic figure the formulas of three proverbs applicable to agriculture but recalling the Homeric spirit of emulation in combat which still lurks in the back of his mind as a contextual reference. Then, as if to reaffirm his mental grip on this dawning conception, he reasserts in a formulaic variant the importance of the role for men of this particular ($\eta\delta\epsilon$) *eris*.

If at this point his connection begins to give out and his coherence to fade, we can measure his partial failure against the initial success achieved by remustering traditional formulas in order to construct a new pattern, something we can properly

8. Cf. n. 2 above.
9. Munding, *op. cit.* p. 56, finds the notion of a good *eris* (but not the word) in the epic athletic contest.

style a new idea. A concept has been born, or rather given linguistic expression, which is the main battle. The effort is not sustained very long. The tight logic gives out because, we suggest, he is compelled to draw upon a vocabulary which is intractable for the purpose. Lines 33–9, on any interpretation, offer conundrums. 34b plus 35a are suspended in a vacuum. Do 35–6 appeal for a settlement out of court, as opposed to one adjudicated by a prince (39)? Would any such alternative be likely in Hesiod's society? The formulas of 36 surely refer to the normal administration of justice. And how could successful and greedy acquisition confer great prestige on princes, unless they were the beneficiaries?

A clue to these obscurities may lie once more in the *eris* theme of the *Iliad*.[10] Hesiod has moved from the good *eris* to *eris*-in-general by way of the agora. As *eris* is transplanted from the fields to the speaking place, she becomes the principle and process of litigation. The *eris* of the *Iliad* erupts and then subsides in two scenes laid in the agora.[11] Hesiod's participant in the agora, after gaining his fill, proceeds to provoke *neikos* and *deris* by going after other people's property. But he will not be able to do so twice. A distribution has been made, but he has made off with more. Honor is due to princes who are gift-gobblers.

With these sentiments compare some of the statements made by Achilles to Agamemnon:

> Ἀτρείδη κύδιστε, φιλοκτεανώτατε πάντων,
> πῶς γάρ τοι δώσουσι γέρας μεγάθυμοι Ἀχαιοί;
> οὐδέ τί που ἴδμεν ξυνήϊα κείμενα πολλά·
> ἀλλὰ τὰ μὲν πολίων ἐξεπράθομεν, τὰ δέδασται.   (1.122–5)

> καὶ δή μοι γέρας αὐτὸς ἀφαιρήσεσθαι ἀπειλεῖς   (1.161)

>   ἀτὰρ ἤν ποτε δασμὸς ἵκηται,
> σοὶ τὸ γέρας πολὺ μεῖζον   (1.167)

10. So Munding, pp. 25–41.
11. 1.54, 305; xix.45, 276.

ἦ πολὺ λώϊόν ἐστι κατὰ στρατὸν εὐρὺν Ἀχαιῶν
δῶρ' ἀποαιρεῖσθαι ὅς τις σέθεν ἀντίον εἴπῃ·
δημοβόρος βασιλεύς,[12] ἐπεὶ οὐτιδανοῖσιν ἀνάσσεις·
ἦ γὰρ ἄν, Ἀτρεΐδη, νῦν ὕστατα λωβήσαιο.   (1.229–32)

τῶν δ' ἄλλων ἅ μοι ἐστί θοῇ παρὰ νηῒ μελαίνῃ,
τῶν οὐκ ἄν τι φέροις ἀνελὼν ἀέκοντος ἐμεῖο·
εἰ δ' ἄγε μὴν πείρησαι, ἵνα γνώωσι καὶ οἵδε.   (1.300–3)

As for the proposal in Hesiod's lines that litigation between two parties (διακρινώμεθα) be settled, and the reference to the legal functions of princes, one may again compare, from the same scene in the *Iliad*, Nestor's unavailing attempt at mediation, including his remarks to Achilles:

μήτε σύ, Πηλεΐδη, ἔθελ' ἐριζέμεναι βασιλῆϊ
ἀντιβίην, ἐπεὶ οὔ ποθ' ὁμοίης ἔμμορε τιμῆς
σκηπτοῦχος βασιλεύς, ᾧ τε Ζεὺς κῦδος ἔδωκεν,   (1.277–9)

as well as the formal reconciliation offered by Achilles at *Iliad* XIX, where the *eris* now to be concluded is given thematic significance:

Ἀτρεΐδη, ἦ ἄρ τι, τόδ' ἀμφοτέροισιν ἄρειον
ἔπλετο, σοὶ καὶ ἐμοί, ὅ τε νῶΐ περ ἀχνυμένω κῆρ
θυμοβόρῳ ἔριδι μενεήναμεν εἵνεκα κούρης;   (XIX.56–8)
αὐτὰρ Ἀχαιοὺς
δηρὸν ἐμῆς καὶ σῆς ἔριδος μνήσεσθαι ὀΐω.   (63–4)

Acceptance of this offer is accompanied by the transfer of compensation previously promised (lines 140 ff., 238 ff.).

Are these echoes so slight as to be fortuitous? Or do they add up to a pattern of reminiscence? We recall the suggestion earlier made that, as Hesiod proposes the notion of a fruitful competitive strife, he may have the preface to the *Iliad* in his memory, among other contexts. Then he lets go of the antithesis and treats *eris* under another guise, as a single principle. But

12. Munding (p. 28) notes the coincidence between δῶρ' ἀποαιρεῖσθαι (230), δημοβόρος βασιλεύς (231), and βασιλῆας | δωροφάγους (*W.D.* 38–9).

in doing so, he does not simply repaint the epic portrait of her. Instead, she is translated into a legal context. The *neikos* which she arouses becomes akin to the principle of litigation, a topic complementing the notion of competition. Both are so to speak additions to the conceptual apparatus. But litigation has its epic prototype conspicuously in the engagement between Achilles and Agamemnon, a *neikos* to be settled not by war but by negotiation; it had launched the plot of the *Iliad*. Hesiod is using the same theme to launch his own poem. And so, as Hesiod proceeds to portray litigation, his phraseology evokes the scenes, of quarrel and reconciliation, between the two heroes.

If this be acceptable as an explanation of these puzzling lines, we see revealed another facet of the poetic process by which Hesiod, working within a fairly tight oral tradition, achieved his own creative ends. Besides the manipulation of epic vocabulary to yield fresh dichotomies, besides the loose grouping of aphorisms to furnish continuous discourse, we perceive also the evocation and exploitation of whole situations or scenes in the epic prototype, and ones which are familiar.

Ultimately, the method of Hesiod can be viewed as one of topicalization carried on within the existing matrix of narrative oral poetry. This is still some distance away from logically organized discourse, let alone abstract definition and analysis. The linguistic materials are still oral. They can be rearranged and regrouped and as it were "translated" to produce the semblance of discourse. Within these limits, the achievement of thoughtful Hesiod is surely not inconsiderable.

Pre-Literacy and the Pre-Socratics

by ERIC A. HAVELOCK

IT WILL, I think, be readily granted by an audience of classicists that our own discipline is not partial to the use of theory and distrusts an *a priori* approach to any problem. A self-restraint which in other fields of knowledge might be viewed as cramping the style of the investigator, by limiting the methodological choices open to him, is by ourselves felt to be a matter of pride. This accords with my own recollections of a Cambridge classical training which, so it seems to me in retrospect, actively discouraged the use of general concepts and working hypotheses lest they lead to imaginative reconstructions based on assumptions which were not amenable to strict proof or controlled by evidence what was specific and concrete.

And yet, as I look back upon the discipline of Greek studies of forty years ago, as it was taught to us and communicated through the books we read, it seems to me that it was in fact controlled by four related assumptions of the most general character, never explicitly stated, and all the more powerful as an influence over our minds because they were not. I think their influence is felt to this day and that an examination of them may still have relevance. Let me give them in what seems to me to be their related order:

The first was that Greek culture of the Classical period was a wholly literate phenomenon, much like our own. Homer, Pindar, and Aeschylus, no less than Thucydides or Aristotle, were writers whose works were composed for readers to take in their hands. It was proper to apply to them those criteria of composition which are appropriate to books silently read. One slight but rather neat illustration of this assumption is to be noted in Cornford's translation of Plato's *Republic*, where the word *poietes* is occasionally translated as "writer".[1] But a *poietes*, though he may have written and usually did write, is nevertheless not a *suggrapheus*. The distinction is a nuance, but perhaps an important one.

A second presumption could be stated as follows. While written Greek prose is extant only from the fifth century, and the earliest fluent Attic prose from the very end of that century, this is largely accidental. It is simply a matter of what has happened to survive. It was presumed that there existed a lost body of prose writing prior to Herodotus, both historical and speculative, at least as early as the beginning of the sixth century, and possibly earlier. The supposed existence of the Milesian school of philosophers, their works now lost, gave powerful support to this assumption. How tenaciously it is held can be seen if I quote a scholar who in other respects has proposed some interpretations of Greek culture which are non-traditional. Bruno Snell, in a monograph devoted to certain aspects of the vocabulary employed by the pre-Socratics, after noting that Xenophanes, Parmenides, and Empedocles wrote their philosophy in hexameter verse, then committed himself to this statement: "They did this despite the fact that the time had long gone by when it would have been necessary to render an idea of literary significance in verse form."[2] How does he know that? Where is this literary prose which preceded these philosophical poems? He cannot cite it for it does not exist, but its existence is presumed.

A third assumption which governed our classical studies was the most subtle and pervasive of all. It controlled our use of the dictionaries, our exercises in composition, and our style in translation. It was that the Greek language, roughly down to the spread of the Hellenistic *koine*, was constructed out of a system of interchangeable parts. I had better be careful here to clarify what I mean: not of course that the Homeric dialect was Attic, not that the style of a Thucydides resembled that of a Plato. I mean rather that the Greek language considered as a system of signs denoting meaning behaved roughly as a constant. What was logical or illogical for Homer was equally so for Aristotle. Varieties of dialect and style were the accidents that made literature interesting, but were not connected with any change in the denotative system as such. You could, so to speak, cross-translate, if you chose, between the main classical authors. Homer's idiomatic peculiarities, or those of Aeschylus, were due simply to the fact that they were poets who lived at particular times and places. The peculiarities of Thucydides were stylistic and grammatical, but his vocabulary and syntax were perfectly understandable in Plato's terms. The language in short had a common logic, finally formalized in Aristotle's canon. The best illustration of how this assumption worked was visible in the Greek lexicon itself. To elucidate the meanings of verbs and nouns, the analytical method was in the main followed, and it still is, for in this respect *LSJ* represents little if any advance upon *LS*. What seems to be conceptually the most generic meaning is cited first, quite often from prose authors of the fourth century. Then other usages, regardless of chronology, are listed as emanations derivative from this basic meaning. In short, no dictionary exists of the Greek language on historical principles. I have cited in another place[3] the instructive example of the article in *LSJ* on *gignomai*, "I am born". It can be noted in passing that the early compilers of dictionaries in the Roman and Byzantine periods were as analytically minded in this respect as we are. It is from their methods that we derive our own dictionaries, and I think it could be shown that their report on how the Greek language behaved was framed within categories which derived ultimately from the formal logic of the Academy and the Lyceum.

The fourth unstated assumption which informed our investigations of Greek literature and one which controlled the very way we thought about the Greeks was one which flows from the third, and indeed is part and parcel of it. If language be the mirror of thought, and if the semantics of the Greek language consist of a system of interchangeable parts, then the thought of the Greeks constitutes a similar system. By this I do not mean such an absurdity as that Homer's statements are to be equated with those of Pindar or Plato, but rather that Homer could have talked with Pindar, and both of them with Plato and Aristotle, in language the basic concepts of which would have been intelligible to all four. That is, they all knew, for instance, what morality and ethics were, and recognized the distinction between ethics and politics. They could have compared notes concerning education, virtue, justice, and the soul. They would have been able to compare their theologies and argue about them. They lived in a common world, and if pushed to it, they would have recognized this world as a physical phenomenon about which you could tell stories or in which you could see history taking place or upon which you could construct a metaphysics, if that is what you wanted to do. Greeks of any period could, if they chose, refer to what they saw and experienced in terms of space and matter, motion and rest, change and permanence, being and seeming, and the like. If Homer, Pindar, and Aeschylus do not indulge precisely in this sort of language, that is again because of the accident that they are poets. In the courtyards of their homes or in the agora or on the street, they would more or less understand Plato or Aristotle if they met them, even if they were not particularly interested in what they were saying, or even hostile to it. Indeed considered as representative voices of the Greek Golden Age, they were viewed as exponents of a common culture which was, roughly speaking, a constant. The dialect, rhythm, vocabulary might shift, but the same values were always there.

Habits of pedagogy contributed something to the spell of this assumption. You began with Xenophon, graduated to Plato's *Apology*, then perhaps a play of Euripides, and the Sphacteria episode in Thucydides. Later on came Homer, Pindar, Aeschylus, the lyric poets; latest of all, if ever, the pre-Socratics; and Hesiod never. The effect was to read the history of Greek literature backwards. The final statement of the Greek experience was to be found in Plato more than anywhere else. He provided the basic frame of reference, especially for the apologists, many of them eloquent, who wrote and lectured in defence of a classical education. Need I cite Lowes Dickinson from Cambridge in this connexion, or Sir Richard Livingstone from Oxford? A more recent example of this habit of treating the Greek mentality as a sort of Platonic constant can be cited by reference to the first volume of Werner Jaeger's *Paideia*.[4] Here a conception of Greek education, already introduced in the title of the work, is proposed as the preoccupation of the author of the *Odyssey*. The story of Telemachus and his relationship to Athena and to his father is retranslated, so to speak, into an essay on the theory and practice and problems of Greek education. This is of course a theme and a problem central to early Platonism. But could it have been so for Homer? Or was it not precisely the occurrence of basic changes in the institutions, and I will add in the language and thought forms, of the Greeks which were later to create the problem and make it a possible subject of discourse?

These then are the four unstated assumptions. Let me summarize them in terms which because of brevity will sound rather sweeping and which will omit many necessary qualifications. Greek culture from the beginning was built on a habit of literacy; Greek prose discourse was commonly composed and read at least as early as the Archaic age; the Greek language is built up out of a set of interchangeable parts; Greek thought-forms give expression to a common fund of basic values and concepts. I have tied them together because a generation ago I think they still formed an interconnected system in the minds of classical scholars, and because it is possible that they stand or fall together. If the first, for example, prove untenable, then it may be time to reconsider the other three. I put this tentatively, as a prospect to be viewed and explored. The present paper is intended to start the process of exploration, but no more.

It was in the late twenties and early thirties of this century that the first of these came under attack. Not, it is true, directly, for the scholars involved do not seem to have wished to raise such general considerations, but nevertheless their findings pointed toward the need of some revision of previous ideas concerning Greek literacy. The crucial publications were the work of two Americans. Milman Parry in 1928[5] demonstrated that the verse of the Homeric epics is an oral instrument, the character of which is comprehensible only on the assumption that it was designed and perfected by singers who themselves could neither read nor write. Rhys Carpenter in 1933 and again in 1938,[6] organizing the evidence already available to epigraphers, produced the conclusion that the

Greek alphabet could not have been invented earlier than say 720 B.C. One must I suppose tread here warily, particularly as fragments of earlier alphabetic inscriptions, or what appear to be such, continue to turn up, for instance as Sardis and Gordion. But since I detect a continuing and persistent reluctance among scholars of Greek literature to accept Carpenter's findings, let me quote a recent statement on this question from an authoritative source: "Nothing needs to be added to Carpenter's succinct comment, 'The *argumentum ex silentio* grows every year more formidable and more conclusive'."[7]

No attempt, so far as I am aware, was initially made to connect these two findings, nor to draw the conclusion that the Homeric poems despite their sophistication were in all likelihood a creation of a non-literate culture. One reason was no doubt that in the minds of Greek scholars the phrase 'non-literate culture' seemed to be a contradiction in terms. Greek literature by definition had to be a written literature composed for readers, and Greek poetry was assumed to be that kind of literary phenomenon that it is in our own culture, furnishing an aesthetic supplement to the prosaic statement, an embellishment as it were which beautifies and dignifies the day's work. The formulaic technique was therefore treated as poetic artifice in the modern sense of the word 'poetic', that is as a device of improvization designed to assist in telling a good story. It was viewed from the standpoint of its entertainment value.

The question looming over the horizon was patently a larger one. If the alphabetic script became first available only shortly before 700 B.C., and if it had no immediate predecessors, then do the Homeric poems survive as a massive exemplar of the *only* way in which, down to the time of their composition, any communication would be put on record and preserved? I say the only way because they alone survived to be written down. Without Parry's findings it would have been possible to argue that they came into existence only as a literary product, and after 700 B.C., but his conclusions, added to those of Carpenter, made it inevitable that the two epics must be accepted as the only available evidence of an oral culture, the conditions of which gradually disappeared from Greece at a rate to be determined by further investigation.

I have argued elsewhere[8]—and here I must ask forgiveness for offering certain propositions as working hypotheses without finding space to defend them in depth—that in fact the kind of composition we call poetic was *ab initio* a device invented to serve the needs of preserved record in an age of wholly oral communication. Preservation could occur only in the living memories of actual human beings. The syntax of the statements made in oral poetry had therefore to conform to certain psychological laws which operate to lessen the strain on the effort of the memory, and to guarantee some fidelity of repetition. This proposition is applicable in the first instance to the Homeric poems which on examination reveal the fact that they are indeed encyclopedias of 'typical information', necessary to preserve the practices and attitudes of a culture. The epic 'syntax' (using this term in the widest sense) in which the epic statement is made is not only essentially narrative in character, but repeats and reports all information so far as possible in the form of concrete and particular events which happen in sequence, not as propositions which depend on each other in logical connexion. The typical character of the statement made,[9] and yet its incorporation in a specific and narrative context, are, it is suggested, twin phenomena which betray a vehicle designed to preserve a culture in the living oral memory.

These observations, I should add, apply to Hesiod as to Homer, both of them composers very close to the oral culture, but while Homer is embedded in that culture, Hesiod is attempting a type of composition which for its organization avails itself of the help of the eye as well as the ear. He is looking at his papyrus as he sets down the lines of his material and he is able to rearrange this material in new ways.[10]

Nevertheless, the two poets stand together as representative of the kind of statement which was capable of preservation and transmission under pre-literate conditions, never more so than in the fact that they both employ a method of reporting and describing phenomena, which I have elsewhere styled the "god-apparatus". We are now edging nearer to the subject of this particular paper—the role of the pre-Socratics in the dawning age of proto-literacy. But before I actually reach them, let me dwell a little further on the gods of Homer and Hesiod considered not as objects of cult—and they rarely emerge in this guise in either composer—but as a necessary ingredient in the vocabulary of oral description and orally preserved record.

If all our knowledge of our environment—remember we are living in a wholly non-literate society—and all the moral directives we give our children have to be reported and preserved as a narrative series: if the facts have to be stated either as things that happen or as things that are done (and the latter form of statement is in fact preferred), then the preserved record must be populated by agents who perform acts regarded as important or produce the phenomena which require explanation. A moral principle is not stated as such, but exemplified as something that Achilles or Odysseus said or did or should not have done. Equally it may be exemplified as what Zeus or Apollo said or did. This latter theological form of report becomes inevitable when we deal with the physical environment: the weather, skies, and sea. Only Zeus and the other gods are available: they have to be super-agents, that is, divine, in order to be everywhere, in order to cover the territory.

Let me at this point illustrate from Homer himself. By the opening of the twelfth book of the *Iliad*, the Trojans under Hector have pressed their advantage until the Greeks quite literally have their backs to the wall—that wall the construction of which was described in Book vii. The bard chooses at this point to add a historical footnote. The wall no longer exists in his day. Time and the processes of nature have eroded and destroyed it:

That was the time when Poseidon and Apollo took
  counsel
To efface the wall, leading against it the might of rivers,
All that from the Idaean hills flow forth into the sea,
Rhesos and Heptaparos and Charesos and Rhodios . . .
[a catalogue of eight names of rivers] . . .

Of these all the mouths together were converted by
  Phoebus Apollo
And for nine days against the wall he discharged their
  flow. And Zeus rained
Continuously, that all the faster he might put the wall
  back into the sea-wash.
The Earth-shaker in person, holding trident in hand,
Was in the forefront, and from their place all the
  foundations did he despatch on the waves,
Even the beams and stones that the Achaeans, working
  hard, had placed there.
And he made things smooth by the strong-flowing
  Hellespont
And again the great shore with sands he covered,
Having washed away the wall. And then the rivers he
  converted to move
Down the flow by which before he had discharged their
  fair-flowing water.[11]

Several things are to be noticed about this method of description. In our language, it refers to a gradual and prolonged physical process of the years which eroded and removed the earthworks. But to be amenable to preservation
in the epic record, this kind of fact has to be compressed into
a single nine-day storm. That is, historical time is condensed
in order to achieve a single fictionalized episode which can
then take its place in that panorama of episodes which makes
up the bard's vocabulary. The single large episode in turn is
built up out of components which are events taking place in
the Troad. The adjacent rivers rise in flood: and the flood
waters wash against the obstruction. The force of their pressure, and their terrifying speed, are symbolized in the exaggerated and impossible statement that all rivers in the district
were combined to produce the effect. Upon the flood there
is then superimposed the rain storm. Conceptually speaking,
this was its original cause, but cause and effect come in reverse
order, because you feel and are afraid of the flood first before
you realize its cause in the falling rain. Flood and rain are

then supplemented by the current of the Hellespont, suggested in the epithet. In the context, the listener is encouraged to imagine the swollen waters of the strait joining in the task of levelling the earthwork. Finally, the normal peaceful order of nature is restored. The rivers resume their wonted channels, while on the now deserted shore the empty sand covers all.

We can replace this Homeric account by an equivalent. We can say that a construction of beams, stones, and earth-filling formed a rampart. This is standing near the Hellespont and a prolonged period of unusual precipitation in the adjacent hills results in the fact that the rivers normally flowing northwards overflow their banks and the countryside is flooded. The force of the flood washes out and demolishes the earthwork and the forces of the current in the strait subsequently deposit sand over the remains.

This kind of language takes the objects in the account and renders them in terms of categories and classifications, and then connects these together in a series of relationships. The earthwork is of a given type of contruct with given resistance. The flood is caused by a given and unusual quantity of water from given directions, and it in turn produces certain physical forces which have a given result through the application of physical pressures. The locale is defined and this includes the adjacent shore and currents of the straits, which develop a supplementary effect also physical, namely the silting-up. An episode has now been replaced by a phenomenon, and the events composing the episode have been rendered into sequences of cause and effect.

What is Homer's equivalent, in this instance, for our methodology of cause and effect? Surely it is to be found in the personal decisions and acts of persons. In this case, because Homer is dealing with physical phenomena, these have to be the decisions and acts of gods. First, a process which is historical—namely, the disappearance of the fortification—is represented by a personal decision of two gods to efface it. The subordinate events which compose the episode are then represented as the acts of gods. The accumulated destruction wrought by water erosion is replaced by Apollo's sudden conversion of the rivers as though he took their eight mouths and held them together like spouts. The pressure of the water on the wall is his personal discharge, as though he were bombarding it with a hose. The rainfall is Zeus' act, the loosening of the foundations under pressure is presented in the image of Poseidon picking and pushing at them and levering them out. The final slow silting-up is rendered as though it were a matter of taking a spade and a bucket and covering them over.

I suggest that we see here a demonstration of the basic functional purpose served by the god-apparatus as a recording device. Let us look at it backwards from the vantage point of our own more abstract habits, habits I suggest which could not mature in a pre-literate situation. For our abstract process, the orally-preserved record prefers a pictorialized image. For causal relations, there are substituted concrete acts represented as the decisions of persons and performed on objects by these persons acting as agents. The preference, I suggest, is dictated by mnemonic needs. The mind is allowed to avoid the impossible labour of rearranging events and materials in causal sequences which it would then have to memorize. Instead, the minstrel's medium short-circuits the experience and synthesizes it as an event so that it can be rendered in this 'theological' form. Just as in recording and repeating the terms of the human situation, and in describing or prescribing moral norms, the play of human habit and behaviour, reported in images of men acting, had to function in place of the ethical abstractions that we use ourselves; so also, in recording the situation of the external environment, the play of divine habit and behaviour had to function in place of causal accounts of relationships between forces and materials. Since there are no men extended through the environment to provide the behaviour, the consciousness demands that supermen be put there to supply the need. Otherwise it would be impossible to summarize with coherence the effect of storm and earthquake and flood, and the complex effect of the seasons, the warm sun, the spring winds, and winter cold. Nay, even the regular motions of the stars cannot be explained as motion for there is no such category in the mind. They will rise and set only as events occurring in narrative situations as the acts of persons.[12]

In a well-known story of Joseph Conrad's,[13] a primitive African is stoking the boiler of a river steamer as it slowly makes its way up the endless green vistas of the Niger. He knows he also has to watch the water gauge, for the powerful god inside the boiler is always thirsty; and if the supply runs short, the god will in his rage burst out of the boiler and overwhelm the industrious savage. This is a perfect though very simple paradigm of that efficacy with which even Homeric man could 'think'. The action of heat on water, to produce a resultant steam pressure and the action of heat on hot air to produce a resultant explosion are chains of cause and effect which describe what happens in terms of law and which utilize a language which classifies the facts under forms of matter and energy in order to do this. The animistic version of the same connected events short-circuits the explanation and makes it into a much simpler and more effortless picture of an agent with given powers and passions. His angry god bottled up in the boiler is something that the savage can both remember and express in his own vocabulary. But the concreteness of his vision does not prevent him from being an effective servitor of the god: that is, an efficient boiler-tender. As he stokes up the god to keep him comfortably warm, he also interrupts this process to pour water into him to keep him comfortably wet. This is the way the god likes it, and being continually placated by the proper ceremonies, he produces the results which his servant seeks. The boat's paddle-wheel revolves; the journey proceeds. Pictorialized comprehension has been carried far enough not only to live with a phenomenon, but within limits to use it. What of course the savage cannot do is to make an engine. His kind of language can express his acceptance of the engine and describe the proper way to live with it. It cannot help him to invent the machine in the first instance because he cannot rearrange his experience in terms of cause and effect. He lacks the know-how. To see and to recognize and to act is within his power, but to 'get on top of' the phenomenon, expressed in the Greek verb *epistasthai*,[14] is beyond him.

It is time to turn our attention at last to the pre-Socratics, for in them if anywhere should we surely seek for confirmation, if it exists, of the propositions concerning the character of Greek culture which have been put forward. Let us summarily restate them. Greek society before 700 B.C. was non-literate. In all such societies experience is stored in the individual memories of the members of the society and the remembered experience constitutes a verbal culture. The verbal forms utilized for this purpose have to be rhythmic to ensure accurate repetition, and the verbal syntax has to be such that statements, reports, and prescriptions are cast in the form of events or acts. The Homeric poems, and to an almost equal degree the Hesiodic, exhibit these symptoms. They constitute not literature in the modern sense, but orally stored experience, the content of which incorporates the traditions of a culture group and the syntax of which obeys the mnemonic laws by which this kind of tradition is orally preserved and transmitted. Finally, so far as the tradition formulates and transmits reports on the physical environment of the society, it will utilize a god-apparatus as the medium by which the phenomena to be described can be most easily cast into the required syntax, and so most easily recalled.

The pre-Socratics, by common consent, were thinkers whose speculations centred mainly (though not exclusively) on the character of the physical environment. Since they initiated this type of speculation in a field of vision, so to speak, that had hitherto been pre-empted by Homer and Hesiod, would we not expect their own early statements in the first instance to take the form of correction or contradiction of the Homeric-Hesiodic world view? If a new physical rationalism was to be introduced, then the previous traditional habits of looking at things stood squarely in the way and had to be removed.[15] Secondly, since they themselves were writers, it could be guessed that in the first instance they would find most objectionable or irrelevant in the Homeric and Hesiodic statements precisely those elements which resided there because of mnemonic necessity—that is, the rhythm, the verbal narrativization with its dynamism and its concreteness, and the use of the god-apparatus. The initial problems confronting the pre-Socratics would be syntactical, rather than philosophic in any larger systematic sense. They would be aware of the need of a new language and, it would follow, of a new mode of thinking, which could replace descriptions couched in terms of powerful and arbitrary agents and of acts performed by them, and could substitute a different mode of description, which, to judge by our own sophisticated speech, would be analytic and conceptual.

So far, so good. But we might also expect a good deal of ambiguity in their own attempts to break with their predecessors. Cultural change does not occur in neatly separable episodes with clear breaks in between. If they were seeking to change the traditional modes of describing the world, the tradition was still very much part of them. And it should be added that though the alphabet was in use by 700 B.C., while their own speculations were not undertaken until the 6th and 5th centuries, we would still be justified in asking whether the shift to literacy in Greece during the Archaic Age was sudden and automatic. On the evidence, it would not seem to have been so. The question here is not the availability of writing and of writers, upon which so much scholarly attention has been focused, but the availability of readers. Any diffusion of the reading habit would depend upon a reform of that ancient Greek school curriculum which had depended upon memorized recitation; a reform, if that is the word, which would enforce mastery of the alphabet as an automatic reflex at a tender age. This would take a long time—how long is a matter of dispute. But it is safe to conclude from the epigraphical evidence alone that Greece in the Archaic period was only craft-literate, if I may use the expression, not literate.[16] Under such conditions, the pre-Socratics would be expected to compose on papyrus, but under what I may call 'audience control'. In their own inner thoughts, they were trying to break with the oral tradition. But their public still had to memorize their statements and consequently these would reflect a transitional stage in the passage from pre-literacy to literacy. The philosophers would want to reach forward, but also be impelled to look behind, and their style of composition would be expected to reflect this ambivalence.

Do the pre-Socratic writings furnish evidence to support these expectations? I say their "writings", a term which should be used with the qualifications already suggested, but the very mention of it brings up an initial question of method. I cannot view any examination of the pre-Socratics as possessing much validity which does not in the first instance focus on their *ipsissima verba*, so far as these are recoverable. To quote from a recent text-book in this field: "It is legitimate to feel complete confidence in our understanding of a pre-Socratic thinker only when the Aristotelian or Theophrastian interpretation, even if it can be accurately reconstructed, is confirmed by relevant and well-authenticated extracts from the philosopher himself."[17] Now this means that, in determining the original lines of Greek philosophic activity, the so-called Milesians must be discarded. Our knowledge of them as speculative thinkers depends wholly on the later doxographies. Certainly, an imposing modern literature on the Milesian methaphysics does exist,[18] and no doubt certain concessions must be made to its existence. But I must make it clear for the purpose of the present treatment that Milesian evidence is not available. Our business in testing our propositions lies with Xenophanes, Heraclitus, and Parmenides, the three initial thinkers with whom I will try to come to terms. Viewing them as speculative pioneers who anticipate the literate future, let us mark in them the symptoms, if they exist, of their involvement in a pre-literate past.

Our knowledge of the statements of Xenophanes rests on a total of one hundred and nineteen lines and part-lines of poetry which are quoted in later authors. Forty-nine of these are hexameters, sixty-nine are in elegiacs, and one is an iambus prefaced to a hexameter. His more speculative statements seem to be concentrated in his hexameters. On the face of it, then, his composition is poetic, and favours rhythms which the oral style had rendered familiar, while demonstrating that greater metrical variety which we associate with the lyric poets. Is this accident? Did he cling to poetry by mere force of habit when a prose style existed which would have better served his purpose? His own verse supplies some indications that he sees his own role as that of an oral poet:

> By now there are seven and sixty years
> Buffeting my thought across Hellas' land.[19]

This has been taken to refer simply to the exile enforced upon
him after his native Colophon fell to Persia. But in what has
survived of him, he nowhere shows any sense of loss over this
event. His world is pan-Hellenic and these lines would seem
to describe that career proper to an itinerant whose method
of publication required him to move from audience to audience. To be sure, a Homer or a Hesiod would not have
referred to his poetry as 'thought' (*phrontis*). This interesting
new twist of vocabulary points forward to the discipline of
philosophy rather than backwards to the traditional themes
of epic.

But he still moves in the epic world. One of his stanzas runs
as follows:

> You sent the ham of a young goat. You got a fat leg
> Of a fatted bull, a prize for a man to obtain
> Whose glory will range over all Hellas nor give out
> As long as the family [*genos*] of Hellenic songs persists.[20]

The first two of these lines have baffled interpreters. I would
myself suggest that the exchange of gifts of meat is an elegant
metaphor for an exchange of poetic offerings.[21] These no
doubt were written on papyrus. Xenophanes thus is addressing a colleague who had originally addressed a poem to him—
a poem of merit, but Xenophanes has matched it with a better
one as a token of his affection for the recipient, and also of
his own superior prowess. For had not his poem celebrated
the colleague in a way which will make him, and therefore
also Xenophanes, forever famous? If this suggestion is correct,
the conceit is ingenious. As for the last two lines, they surely
presume that Xeonphanes' poem will be recited, for a man's
fame depended on this, and also that the recital depends on
an audience which uses the language, in this case Greek, in
which the poem is to be rendered. So Xenophanes visualizes
Greek poetry as a kind of single family of songs, even as
Homer and Hesiod had viewed the minstrels themselves as
members of the same tribe or family.[22] Hellas, and not any

particular city-state, is again evoked as the provenience of this kind of poetry. It is a Hellas not of readers but of listeners.

Xenophanes is of course a new kind of bard, and he is trying to dedicate his art to new and non-Homeric purposes. And it is congruent with his sense of new purpose that he is also more self-consciously aware of his own virtuosity or skill (*sophia*) as a bard,[23] a skill he contrasts with the mere brawn of the successful athlete, even as he contrasts the athlete's social prestige with his own undervalued merits:

> Better than brawn
> Of men or horses is my skill.[24]

The term "skill" is double-edged. It refers to the virtuosity of the poet, but it is going to be converted by the philosophers into a sign which shall index the new virtuosity of a special kind of poet—the poet turned thinker. We see the process beginning here. Xenophanes is a self-conscious master of skill-ful song but, a professional among professionals, he is turning upon his predecessors a critical eye, as our next examples show.

His own chosen vehicle of instruction and education is the symposiastic recitation which supplemented public recitation given in the arena or market-place. The evening banquet, ceremonially organized, leads up to the musical performance and Xenophanes now lays down some guidelines to indicate the kind of recitation he thinks is needed. It is still Memory, be it noted, as in Hesiod,[25] who inspires or assists the singer: that is, the sources of song are traditional. But the repertoire on which memory is to draw has now to be censored:

> Not battles of Titans or Giants
> Or of Centaurs, the fictions of our predecessors.[26]

This is a direct criticism of Hesiod's *Theogony*. Xenophanes has to move within the thought-world of the oral period, but in offering his own type of communication, he seeks to alter the direction of a tradition rather than to break with it. Thus also he acknowledges Homer's functional role in Greek culture:

> Since from the beginning according to Homer all men
> have been instructed that . . . [27]

The verse breaks off and we do not possess Xenophanes'
summary of the Homeric curriculum.

But he is himself committed to a discourse, poetic as it may
be, which yet must correct and revise the Homeric and Hesiodic prototypes. What is his central correction? Some would
find it in verses like the following:

> All things to the gods did Homer and Hesiod assign
> Which among human beings are a reproach and shame.[28]

In this fashion, he attacks the morality of the divine actors in
the epic narratives. Does he then offer to revise our conceptions of divine ethics? Does he propose a new theological
morality? Not so far as we know. The famous lines in which
he does offer positive doctrine of his own constitute a frontal
attack on what I have called the god-apparatus, considered
not as a moral system but as a mechanism of description.

> One *theos* supreme . . .
> Not resembling mortal men in shape or in intelligence
> [*noema*] . . .
> Always remaining in the same place without being
> disturbed.
> It is not appropriate for him to shift about from one
> place to another . . .
> Quite apart from labour he ordains all things by the wit
> of his intelligence . . .[29]

Discarding all those preconceptions we associate with theology
as a modern exercise, and explicitly those associated with the
doctrines of Hebrew and Christian monotheism, and regarding the sentences as wholly Greek and uttered in a contemporary context, what god or gods is Xenophanes talking
about, and what authors is he correcting? On the surface, he
is addressing himself in general to the anthropomorphic deities of Homer. But I think it can be shown that he has a more
specific target.

Hesiod's *Theogony* presents the era of the Olympians as marking the final supremacy of order in the cosmos and of the civilized virtues among men. These gods begin to emerge in their proper place in the succession at line 453, and their status becomes secure at line 885. In particular, the poet marks the advent of Zeus, whose own title of 'Counsellor' is matched by the poet's emphasis on the intelligence required to guarantee his safe birth and early nurture.[30] His ascendancy does not go unchallenged, first by the sons of Iapetus. Here it is his intelligence that is put to the test, and it is his intelligence that prevails.[31] The contest between himself and Prometheus is described as a battle of wits.[32] A second ordeal supervenes. He has to lead his faction of the gods in a battle against the Titans which shall end in their defeat and imprisonment. To win it he needs the physical prowess and the natural forces possessed by the three giants whom he frees from Tartarus. The crucial decision to free them is once more marked as an act of intelligence.[33] The prolonged character of the conflict for which their aid is enlisted is then described. The participants endured a labour which was exhausting.[34] All the gods were involved, as members of two confronting armies which, like the Greeks and Trojans, fought for ten years. The intensity, duration, and universality of the conflict are stressed three times over in variant formulae.[35] A last desperate effort wins victory for Zeus and his forces. This is preceded by a dialogue in which Zeus, appealing to his three allies the giants, reminds them that it was his counsels that gave them freedom to assist him.[36] They replying affirm the superiority of the intelligence of Zeus, and promise that they will try to match it with one of their own.[37] The last battle then erupts. Both sides use might and main. The cosmos is shaken. Zeus in person moves from Olympus and hurls his bolts. The shock nearly convulses earth and firmament as the gods collide. Earthquake and windstorm accompany the discharge of Zeus' shafts.[38] As the Titans are finally secured in Tartarus, the poet again reminds us that it is the counsels of Zeus which have achieved this.[39] Zeus faces one last challenge, from Typhoeus, and again, it is his intelligence that discerns the danger.[40]

After similar physical exertions, including a leap from Olympus,[41] he vanquishes his last adversary. The labour of the gods, adds the poet, was now completed, and Zeus is 'elected' or 'nominated' king at last, a consummation once more achieved through the aid of intelligence.[42]

When the surviving lines, admittedly few, in which Xenophanes records his 'theology' are compared with this Hesiodic account, it is difficult to resist two conclusions. On the one hand, when the philosopher asserts the primacy of the intelligence of one god, as a factor central to the successful exercise of power, he is being guided by Hesiod's assertion of the vital importance of intelligence as a quality of Zeus' own nature and as an instrument of his success in three crucial contests. On the other hand, the philosopher, in denying that this exercise of power involves any labour or movement from place to place, is explicitly correcting Hesiod's narrative, and demanding that so far at least as Zeus is concerned, he cease to be a physical agent achieving his will through physical acts. Xenophanes is as anxious as Hesiod to assert the supremacy of this god. But he probably intends also to correct Hesiod by asserting that this god's power is unique[43] and also not anthropomorphic. The role of other gods and allies in the struggle therefore disappears. In fact, comparing another statement of the philosopher already noticed,[44] we conclude that he intended to suggest that there never was a struggle. The epic story disappears, to be replaced by a statement of cosmic control exercised somehow outside events, through sheer thought.

These comparisons and contrasts between poet and philosopher serve to conform the hypothesis, first, that the Homeric-Hesiodic account of the physical environment dominated the Greek mind before the pre-Socratics, thus providing the pre-Socratics themselves with their frame of reference, and second, that in many vital respects they sought to break with this account. The thought of Xenophanes looks back to that entire context in Hesiod which comprehends the advent, struggles, and final triumph of Zeus. Here, in the formulaic style of oral epic, is stated an over-all world view which the still living oral culture of semi-literate Greece had accepted as a working model. This was the model that originally confronted and challenged the mentality of the pre-Socratics. The initial effort required was to attack what I have called the god-apparatus, considered as a narrative device for describing the purposes or forces or principles that control the cosmos. The idea of control itself is traditional, as also is the notion that this control requires intelligence. Xenophanes on the one hand is breaking with traditional modes of description, but equally he is using them and being guided by them. His relation to his prototype has all the ambivalence we should expect from a thinker in a period of crucial transition. He selects, refines, and rationalizes, but he does not altogether reject. For is he not himself still a child of a semi-literate culture?

Anaxagoras later was to repeat and reinforce this correction of Homer and Hesiod, and of their god-apparatus, with more sophistication.[45] It can be said of Xenophanes, however, that his attack on the god-apparatus was so decisive that his successors accepted the results. Greek philosophers after him never used the old method of polytheistic narrative to describe phenomena. Many of them, like Xenophanes, were conservative enough to retain *theos* as a useful descriptive symbol, but only provided it was unified and stripped of concrete and pluralized activities.[46]

The quotations on which we rely for our knowledge of the style and speech of Heraclitus appear to be taken from a manuscript collection of his sayings.[47] When precisely this was compiled it is impossible to say. The clues to the philosopher's own situation are to be sought however not in the existence of this book but in the verbal form in which he originally cast his doctrines. Making allowance in some cases for garbling in transmission, it is still possible to perceive the simple principles on which he constructed his style.[48] A few examples grouped in ascending order of complexity will suffice as typical demonstration:

1. Harmony invisible over visible prevailing
2. The beast that walks with blow is pastured
3. Law (verily is) obedience to counsel of one[49]

English and indeed any modern syntax cannot cope with the original compression. Numbers 1 and 2 consist of four Greek words, and number 3 of either four or five. With brevity there is also achieved a total autonomy. Each statement is self-contained and exhaustive; nothing can be added to it. Moreover, while each arrangement of words stimulates a reflective response, this comes as a kind of delayed reaction in the mind. The words evoke situations which are pictorial and concrete. The secret harmony, like an enemy in the dark, overwhelms its rival. A boy is driving the cows to the field with a stick. Zeus nods while Olympus quakes.[50] These are the kinds of events which are woven into the flow of the Homeric and Hesiodic pictorial consciousness, but they have now been somehow distilled out and concentrated. The Greek words also betray a kind of solemn lilt, as though we were hearing fragmentary dactyls, spondees, trochees. Occasionally the sayings even break into recognizable poetry which lasts but a few syllables. And while metre seems to persist occasionally as a sort of hangover, some equivalent of its rhythmic effect is supplied acoustically in the form of assonance, as in example 1, and also semantically in the form of paradox, as in example 2, where the beating and the shepherding, two contrasted operations, are juxtaposed contrapuntally.

Acoustic aids to memorization are supplemented by a type of mnemonic which relies on meaning and not on sound, that is through the construction of images which are antithetical in their emotional effects. We shrink from a blow but welcome the green pastures to which it guides us. This is a different kind of rhythm, but it is rhythm. The memory is encouraged to construct an associative chain which has the effect of making the mind jump from one position to its opposite.

We can take a more extended example which can be divided into five cola:

   a. The order here the same of all
   b. Neither any of the gods nor any of men has made
   c. Nay, it was ever and is and shall be
   d. Fire ever-living
   e. Kindling in measures and quenching in measures.[51]

The devices here employed, of repetition, assonance, antithesis, and symmetry, are of course more obvious in the Greek than in the English version. The vowels of the first colon, for example, exploit the repeated 'o' sound six times. Each colon has elements of symmetry within itself. What is more interesting is a further relationship of syntax, achieved not just by stark juxtaposition of two parallel aphorisms, as in a previous example, but by piling up several statements in series and linking them by devices which exploit both echo and antithesis so that a development and amplification of meaning is achieved. Thus colon (b) is placed in antithesis to colon (a), but colon (c) echoes and amplifies colon (a), and (d) is an echo of (c), which at the same time adds a new key term of "fire". Finally colon (e) completes but also amends the image of immortal fire of (c) and (d), for in place of the sameness and eternity it substitutes the see-saw image in which we watch the blaze light up, and then again on the same hearth there is only smoke and dying embers.

It is difficult to escape the conclusion that statements of this type were framed not to be read but to be heard and memorized.[52] Here is a variant of the formulaic style, a term hitherto confined to the cola of the Homeric hexameter. These Heraclitean statements have been characterized by scholars as oracular,[53] but this does not get to the genetic roots of the style. Oracles in fact were habitually expressed in the standard Homeric medium.[54] Here on the contrary the hexameter is discarded: that is, the help of the regular pulse, struck on a musical instrument to enforce the proper succession of memorized words, is also discarded. The fact that other kinds of rhythm are substituted should not obscure the essential point, that these rhythms are less regular, or more precisely that the pattern within any given statement is unique. One line in this style is not a variant of any other. The hexameter flow has been broken. For this reason it would appear that each statement to be retained in the memory can only last a given number of words—the fewer the better. The longest saying in the collection[55] is only two and a half times the length of the last example cited. Each statement therefore ends up as self-contained and autonomous. You cannot add to it or subtract from it. The memory recalls it complete but has to relax after recalling it. Hence also firm connexion riveted in the memory between different statements is abandoned. In the epic, all statements were narrativized and had been able to retain narrative connexion. The Heraclitean statements are hoarded separately. The hexameters of Xenophanes, Parmenides, and Empedocles, by retaining the metrical 'lead', made possible greater continuity of thought.

For confirmation that this Heraclitean style is an oral style, we can turn to those of the philosopher's sayings which reflect the conditions of communication in his epoch, and the situation in which he publishes. He never refers to readers or books; his world is that of the listening audience:

> While this my *logos* is forever
> Human beings become non-intelligent of it
> Both before they listen and at first after listening.
>
> They have no skill of listening or speaking.
>
> The non-intelligent after listening resemble the deaf:
> The saying testifies for them: present yet absent.
>
> Not to me but to the *logos* having listened
> It is skilful to agree that all is one.
>
> Of all whose *logoi* I have listened to
> No-one reaches so far as to recognize
> That the skilled is separated from all.[56]

This last saying is particularly striking so far as it implies that even Heraclitus did not think of himself as reading the works of his contemporaries or predecessors (Hesiod, the Milesians or Xenophanes may be in his mind),[57] but as listening to their recitation. In what situation might this occur? How does he visualize his own public and that of his contemporaries?

> What is the intelligence or wit of them?
> To the bards of the peoples they attend
> And make the conversation of the crowd their instructor
> Not knowing that the many are inferior and the few are
>   superior.[58]

This is an unmistakable vignette, sharply etched, of the epic

recital being given in a city square as a regular civic performance attended by the populace who in the intervals of the
recitation discuss the performance, compare notes on the
story, and thus renew for themselves that instruction in their
own traditions which Plato was later to characterize in his
descriptions of poetic performance in the *Republic*. The audience is pluralized as *demoi*; that is, the minstrel is presumed
to be moving from city to city.

Heraclitus himself is limited to similar conditions of communication. But how can his own speech compete with the
traditional poetry? He, like Xenophanes before him and Plato
after him, would like to purge the oral performance of its
Homeric elements altogether:

> What Homer deserves is to be flung out of the assemblies
> and beaten up
> And Archilochus too.[59]

The bards won their victories at these assemblies where the
populace gathered to listen to prize-winning recitations. Hesiod had commemorated a victory of his own under these
conditions. Heraclitus notes the self-exaltation, the bard's
power and desire to exploit his audience emotively, as fundamental to the poetic art, yet as constituting its major limitation:

> Only impressions are what the most impressive can be
> conscious of and keep (in his head).
> Yet Right shall indeed catch up with the artificers
> and testifiers of falsities.[60]

The man of "impressions" who also creates an "impression"
is the bard, who gains esteem and is honoured and talked
about for his performance. He is the artificer of his own poetry. The Greek term *tekton* became traditional in this context.[61] Likewise he carries his poem in his head, an enormous
memorized repertoire, but for all that a repertoire which, in
the view of Heraclitus, is only a series of visual impressions
and images. These compositions, in short, are misleading fictions.[62] Heraclitus returns to the same theme again:

One thing in place of all is elected by the best ones
Glory eternal from men who are mortal
The majority gorge themselves like domestic animals.[63]

"The best" I would interpret to be not the warriors or statesmen but the bards, masters of communication, aristocrats in
the sense that they sit at the right hand of princes.[64] But for
Heraclitus their vision is limited to gaining a.temporary fame.
As for the majority, they provide the passive and receptive
audience.

These sayings, in effect, report on the conditions of an oral
culture when Homer, Hesiod, and the poets still dominated
the whole arena of preserved communication, and provided
the thought forms and syntax in which, and only in which,
the Greeks could sum up their experience of themselves, their
history, and their environment. As Heraclitus himself says:

Of the most is Hesiod instructor:
Him they conceive to know most
Who did not recognize day and night:
They are one.[65]

Heraclitus, no less than his audience, is compelled to have
daily acquaintance with Hesiod's world. Yet it is precisely this
acquaintance that he would wish to disrupt. He does not want
to live in this world. No wonder, then, that he is obsessed by
the difficulty of making statements which shall be from his
point of view correct: and once a statement has been correctly
worded, it appears no less difficult for an audience to take in
what has been said or to communicate it to others. Out of a
total of some one hundred and thirty sayings, no less than
forty-four,[66] or thirty-four per cent, are preoccupied with the
necessity to find a new and better language, or a new and
more correct mode of experience, or are obsessed with the
rejection of current methods of communication and current
experience. This statistic is striking in a man who in later
tradition was represented as a philosopher of materialism and
fiery flux. Fire, in fact, is mentioned in only five[67] of his sayings
and has been inserted in the text of three more[68] by scholars
who perhaps have been a little overzealous to justify the tra-

ditional estimate of him. Clearly, if we take his *ipsissima verba* seriously, his preoccupation with problems of vocabulary, and of the psychological response to vocabulary, must be regarded as central.

I lack space in this article to extend to this thirty-four per cent the analysis and discussion that this group deserves. I will permit myself only two observations. The aphorisms of Heraclitus are framed for oral memorization. Yes, but in choosing the aphorism rather than the hexameter, he stylistically breaks new ground as a thinker and refuses the easier role of those who continued in the bardic metre and idiom.[69] It is possible to speculate that the restriction of his own metier to one city, and therefore to one public audience, thus avoiding the bard's itinerant role, may have made it possible for him to choose a style which offered greater challenge to memorization. The aphorism of course had a popular ancestry as ancient as the hexameter. And as noted above it employs characteristic formulas and rhythms of its own. But to employ it at all was to break with the easy and, one is tempted to say, mindless flow of the bard's metrical and musical spell. Particularly, as also noted, it was to discard the accompaniment of a musical instrument. It was to attempt exposition in a style more tough and more challenging. And so Heraclitus it was who, I suggest, furnished the prototype and ancestry for the achievement of the first philosophical prose. In the remains of Zeno, Melissus, Anaxagoras, and Diogenes, we can still see the self-contained statement, pregnant and often balanced, being strung with its fellows on a continuous string to provide a running logic, as the autonomy of the aphorism begins to break down. In the words of Diogenes, the thing to do was to construct a beginning and a continuous exposition.[70] This achievement was stylistically beyond the Ephesian pioneer, but in his break with bardic metre he was indeed a pioneer. Need we wonder at his obsession with the right way of speaking and the correct comprehension of it?

When he presents his own world-view—it would be a mistake to call it a system—he tries to unite the diverse phenomena of human experience and speech under the term *logos*. This is his over-riding principle, and its centrality in his thinking has at last been adequately and forcefully presented in a recent treatment of the subject.[71] But what is this *logos* if not a new principle of language and its use? It represents a way of speaking, a verbal formula, or finally the principle embodied in such a formula. It is a verbal secret, difficult to frame, pervasive in application, which shall comprehend states and conditions or situations which on the surface are antithetical. In demanding our attention to this verbal symbol, Heraclitus, I suspect, focuses his opposition to the Homeric language of narration, and asks that our statements be made timeless, nonparticular, and comprehensive. His foe is not the flux in the universe, but the flux in the Homeric speech.

Of the poem of Parmenides, there now survive one hundred and forty-eight lines and seven part-lines along with six lines of Latin translation. Taken as a whole, it must have been very close in style to that of traditional minstrelsy; for even among the surviving lines, the commentary of Diels-Kranz has been able to identify nineteen verbal echoes of the *Iliad* and *Odyssey*, and four of the *Theogony* and *Works and Days*. These can be supplemented by the addition of about twelve more reminiscences of Homer, and at least eleven of the *Theogony*.[72]

These preliminary statistics sufficiently reveal how traditional is his vehicle of communication. In fact, the philosopher's relationship to Homer and Hesiod goes deeper than this. As we shall see, he has his memory tuned to certain central situations in their poems. But what we should first ask is this: does he choose this epic style to be the matrix of his thought out of antiquarian zeal? Is his poetry merely an external embellishment which in fact complicates a task which he could better have undertaken in prose? Or is the style functional to his role in his contemporary society?

The poem supplies some internal evidence on this point. It is cast in the form of a dialogue, or rather a monologue. Parmenides in the first person discovers himself to us in the opening lines as a passenger in a horse chariot which is conducted by maidens to the gateways of night and day, guarded by the goddess of Right (*Dike*). The maidens persuade her to open the gates and the chariot passes through. The goddess takes Parmenides' hand and begins an address to him which appears to last through the remainder of the poem. Critics have tended to isolate these preliminaries as though they formed a kind of ornamental preface. They can, however, be understood much more naturally as the device by which Parmenides dramatizes his own relationship to his audience. If his mentor addresses him orally, this is only a reflex of that oral situation in which Parmenides continually found himself as he launched similar admonitions on his own public. It is a confirmation of this view that as we read the poem it is difficult to escape the illusion that it is we who are being addressed by the philosopher, rather than the philosopher addressed by the goddess. The illusion is deliberate. Its precedent lies in the familiar device of inviting the Muse to sing the wrath of Achilles.

Thus also the symbolism of the poem never once assumes a situation of books and readers, but always of reciters and listeners. The maidens parley at the gateway with the goddess in traditionally oral terms. The philosopher approaches, as it were, the throne of the goddess who graciously receives him in oral audience, as Zeus receives petitioners in Homer. And she speaks with the traditional formulas of Homeric oral address.[73] The verbs in which she describes the effort of cognition demanded by her pupil are all taken from the Homeric vocabulary, and therefore draw no sharp distinction between verbal inquiry and mental inquiry, between verbal declaration and mental cognition.[74] Twice she asks her disciple to "hear".[75] When she warns against the error of men who are uninstructed, she describes them as deaf and blind with mouths agape,[76] much as Heraclitus described the audience listening in the marketplace. She admonishes her pupil himself never to employ an eye unsteady, nor a noisy ear or tongue.[77] When the time comes for her to add an appendix to her doctrine in the form of a cosmology, which is regarded by her as a fiction, she describes it as though it were a poem composed in regular epic style.[78]

Like Xenophanes, Parmenides describes himself as an itinerant. His goddess, he says, "conveys the man who knows through all the towns".[79] His medium therefore has to be that

Homeric speech which Greeks of all dialects understood. Accordingly, we could reasonably expect that where he seems to borrow verbally from Homer and Hesiod, he need not in fact be imitating their particular poems, but rather borrowing from the common stock of standard epic formulae and epithets upon which any Greek minstrel could draw at will.

Nevertheless, it remains true that the great majority of his epic reminiscences exhibit a very specific relationship to the *Iliad*, the *Odyssey* and the *Theogony*. That is to say, he is still living in a thought-world controlled by these poems. Yet the relationship is often quite bizarre. On the one hand, it is as though this philosopher were forced to practise minstrelsy within a tradition wholly dominated by these three poems; as though he not only knew them by heart, but found all his own frame of reference in them. Yet on the other, it is as though, in spirit and purpose, he were quite remote from them, so that he uses their language clumsily and incongruously to mean things it was never intended to mean.

Sometimes his use of a Homeric formula has the quality of a bad pun. This in the *Iliad* (Book v) the Trojan Pandarus, disgusted with his marksmanship, avows that when he gets safely home, his head can be severed from his shoulders by "some foreign man", if he does not get rid of his bow once and for all. The Greek for 'foreign man' can, by a change of gender, also mean 'foreign light', and the metrical pattern of the two words determines them as suitable to form the clausula of a hexameter. Parmenides adopts the clausula and adapts it to signify the 'foreign light' borrowed by the moon from the sun, though he has to reverse the syntax to do this.[80] Or again, in the same fifth book of the *Iliad*, Diomede wounding Ares is said to "rend through his fair flesh". The phrase once more provides a metrical clausula. Parmenides, with a slight shift in syntax from indicative to infinitive, can keep the metrical pattern but adapt the formula to mean an exchange of bright colour:[81] the meanings of flesh, skin, and colour overlap in the same Greek word.

In these examples, the incongruity between original and adaptation is complete. They almost sound like acoustic accidents. But there is a large range of borrowings which exhibit a kind of verbal faithfulness to Homer while completely altering his context. For example, Parmenides uses an adjective in two variant forms which can be translated as 'unlearning', 'unlearnt', or 'unlearnable'. He also uses the corresponding verb 'to learn by inquiry'. He applies these positively to the task of learning through doctrine, and negatively to describe notions which are illogical, absurd, and so unknowable. Among these last is the notion of destruction: it is 'unlearnable'. The same phrase appears in the third book of the *Odyssey*.[82] Telemachus, in search of news of his father, comes to Nestor and says that while the fates concerning other Trojan heroes are known, in the case of Odysseus "his destruction (*olethros*) is unlearnt". The identical combination of noun and adjective is thus borrowed by Parmenides from a particular context to express a generalization: destruction is (in a logical sense) unlearnable and so illogical. In borrowing, we also note, he subtly alters the semantics of what he borrows. *Olethros*, one Homeric word for a man's violent end, now is coming to mean the principle of destruction or passing away. The word has been stretched and generalized.

Examples like these seem to reveal that the philosopher's memory is responding to controls which are purely acoustic. But the spell of epic upon him does not stop there. He seems to recollect certain central episodes and situations in both *Iliad* and *Odyssey*, and translate and transmute them, as it were, into statements of his own experience.

Elsewhere[83] I have presented the case for the influence, both verbal and thematic, of the *Odyssey*, an influence not confined to the preface of the poem where 'the man that knows' is conveyed through the cities of men, but furnishing also much of the later imagery of the poem: the doctrine of the three routes of thought, one of them portrayed as turning back on itself; the mental journey which requires sailing directions from an inspired source; and even the goal of imperishability—all these have their counterparts in the *Odyssey*. Parmenides, then, sought to represent himself as a new Odysseus, and his philosophic quest as a new *Odyssey*, in terms which his oral audience, it must be remembered, would immediately recognize.

No less purposeful, however, is the way in which he evokes
memories of the *Iliad*, with the implicit claim that he is also
another Achilles. Consider, for example, the horses that conduct him on his journey. These steeds are swift and can ascend
to portals in the sky. They carry him "to the full extent that
the spirit came upon them (or him)". They are intelligent, and
perhaps can talk, and are immortal, and he consorts with
them.[84] Man and beast seem to be linked in some intimacy of
relationship. Memory reverts to that part of the *Iliad* which
begins near the end of Book xvi and runs through to the end
of Book xix. As Patroklos falls, the charioteer Automedon is
borne from the flight by the swift immortal steeds which the
gods have so munificently given to Peleus. Hektor might have
captured them, but Apollo warns him not to try:

> They are the horses of Achilles the wise, hard for mortal
>   men to control
> Unless it be Achilles born of an immortal mother.[85]

Then, while the battle rages over Patroklos' body, the horses
themselves are discovered immobile and weeping, and Zeus
addresses them in a famous apostrophe:

> Ye twain are ageless and deathless
> Why then give you to a mortal man?
> However I shall cast might into your knees and your
>   spirit . . .
> So he breathed might into them and they sped along
> Over Trojans and Greeks with the careering chariot
>   behind them.[86]

Then Achilles hears the news and he is visited by his mother
who comes up from the sea to comfort him. He tells her he
must act, and she warns him solemnly, as she had already
done in the first book, what this will mean, and he accepts his
fate. The divine armour is procured for him. He receives it
and is momentarily transfigured, and at this point the divine
horses re-enter the scene. He harnesses them and admonishes
them to serve him better than they had Patroklos:

> Use your wits in a different way[87]

he tells them. Then Xanthos replies, for Hera put human speech into him, and prophesies to Achilles in the same terms in which his mother had spoken:

> Your day of death is nigh. A great god or powerful
> Destiny is the cause.

Achilles replies:

> Why do you divine that there is death for me?[88]

And he whips them up, and holds to his course, shouting as he drives towards the enemy.

Parmenides, the philosopher, is his own Homeric hero. He too is close to the gods and perhaps feels the transfiguration which removes him from the common run of mental experience. He could not wholly identify himself with Achilles, whose fate was so bitter, whose passions were so intense at the expense of intellect, but he remembers that the talking horses were by Zeus identified as symbols of that immortality that he was going to celebrate in his own doctrine as a principle of being, and that they were intelligent, and that they were the steeds of Achilles "the wise", and that only Achilles could control them. He has drawn here from Homer the implication of some secret understanding between the inspired horse and the inspired man, and has used it to suggest his own intellectual partnership with this divine equipage.

Those episodes in Homer where the divine horses play their role are centred around the climactic scene where Thetis rises up from the sea to comfort her son, and then goes to Hephaestus to get him his new armour. These scenes too are present in the background of Parmenides' memory, for as he is driven through the gateway he is greeted by the goddess Dike:

> She received me spontaneously and took in her hand
> My right hand and spoke to me and addressed me as
>   follows:
> My young hero, consort of immortal charioteers,
> Even of steeds that bear you as you come to our halls

Hail, for in nowise evil was the destiny that escorted you
forth to come.[89]

The reception of the young hero as the goddess begins to
speak to him could evoke the memory of that spontaneous
affection with which in the *Iliad* Thetis greets her son on the
three occasions when she visits him. However, Thetis is in
Parmenides' memory in a very special way. Was it not she who
had in Homer's story the solemn duty of grief, as she dwells
again and again on her son's short and bitter fate? She like
the divine horses had the gift of prophecy. And it is Thetis
who in the first book of the *Iliad* cries out:

To an evil destiny did I bear you in my halls.[90]

Twice more, at successive crises in the hero's career, we hear
of the same destiny.[91] Here is where Parmenides must separate himself from the prototype. So his own goddess explicitly
corrects the sorrowful Homeric announcement:

The destiny that escorted you forth was in nowise evil.

The influence of the *Iliad* is not limited to these examples.
My selections may suffice to prove the pervasive control exercised by the Homeric contexts. The philosopher, while moving within them, seeks to remould them in the image of his
own discourse. He has a conviction of heroic ancestry, but
also of great achievement in himself, and this achievement is
novel.

To symbolize its novelty, and the kind of place where he
thinks his own mind has finally arrived, he has to choose
another model. As the philosopher's chariot approaches the
superterrestrial gates, they encounter a lintel and a stone
threshold: Right keeps the alternating keys, and the gates
when they open reveal a yawning gap: the hinges revolve
alternately in their sockets,[92] and the philosopher is driven
straight through to receive from the goddess who awaits him
admonition concerning the character of his quest and the
correct route to take. On this route he will encounter many
directives[93] defining for him the properties of that 'being'

which constitutes the goal of his search, and she dwells on these properties at some length. A selection of them follows:

> Right cannot slacken the fetters to let it be born or perish
>   . . .
> It is all continuous . . .
> It is unshaken in the boundaries of mighty fetters . . .
>   Becoming and Perishing
> Have been banished far off . . .
> It remains the same in the same and abides in itself
> And so remains steadfast right there. Yea, mighty
>   Necessity
> Holds in fetters of a boundary which fences it around . . .
>   Yea, Destiny has bound it down
> To be whole and unshaken . . .
> Since therefore the boundary is outmost it is completed
> From all sides, like the bulk of a well-rounded ball
> Equipoised from the middle in every direction . . .
> From every direction equal to itself, it proves to be alike
>   within boundaries.[94]

We saw Xenophanes, as he approached the crucial problem of defining a cosmic consciousness in non-narrative terms, framing his thought within the context supplied by Hesiod which described the ascent of Zeus to supreme power. It is a context which overall comprises four hundred and thirty-three lines of the *Theogony*.[95] Parmenides, it would appear, as he similarly sought to frame the terms of his own central doctrine, reverted in memory to the same context, but since his own mental designs were not quite those of Xenophanes, he selected for recall certain elements in the context which we so far have not noticed, but which were appropriate to his own purpose. The Zeus of Hesiod has to prevail over Prometheus and over the Titans, whose final condition is one of stringent imprisonment. In the case of Prometheus, "of necessity, mighty bond does confine him in", and as for the Titans, their warders "bound them in grievous bonds". This amounted to banishment "in a dank place, at the very end of mighty earth. They may not go out. Poseidon slammed brazen doors upon them and a wall goes round them on either side", and again "Far from all the gods, they dwell across the misty gap". The poet also describes an earlier imprisonment of the three giants by Kronos: "They were set at the very furthest within the boundaries of mighty earth".[96]

So far a guess can be ventured that when Parmenides anchored his 'being' so firmly within bonds and limits of necessity, his formulae may recall the imprisonments described by Hesiod. The guess will be hazardous until confirmed by further linkage. The chain of memory association, if it exists, betrays once more an acoustic rather than a logical law. For if in the same breath the philosopher can describe the banishment of non-being, then he appropriates twin images of imprisonment and segregation, which in the original were applied to the same subject, and in his own version applies them to different and opposed subjects.

We can now proceed to note and compare further elements in the same Hesiodic context. Tartarus, the site of imprisonment, evokes from the poet a contemplation of the cosmic structure itself. In variant version thrice repeated he tells us that (a) this construct is symmetrical, earth being poised equidistant from heaven and Tartarus, (b) round Tartarus runs a fence, and above it grow the roots of earth and sea, (c) there also are in order springs and boundaries of all . . . a mighty gap . . ., (d) the dire halls of Night stand fast . . . and before them the son Iapetus holds up heaven standing fast . . . immovably, (e) where Night and Day greet each other as they alternately pass the mighty brazen threshold, (f) there are the springs and boundaries of all in their order . . . the shining gates and brazen threshold immovable, fitted with continuous roots, self-growing.[97]

Rearranged, and in part transmuted, these elements all seem to be echoed in Parmenides' own account. The philosopher reaches and passes through the gap, across the threshold. Acoustic memory supplied alternating keys and hinges in place of the alternating deities. The boundaries are there, and the limits and the continuity, and the immovable steadfastness, and the cosmic symmetry now firmly rationalized into the image of a ball. Even the compulsive repetition, in Parmenides, of the boundaries and limits recalls in his prototype the same compulsion to repeat in three versions the cosmic vision. These indeed heralded a conception of vital importance to both poet and philosopher. But now it is no longer the physical construct that in imagination is being anchored before the eyes, but an abstraction which Parmenides is seeking to anchor in thought, even if this abstraction be itself a notion of sheer space.

We conclude that Parmenides like his two predecessors composed within the context of an oral culture: that the world view of that culture was still furnished by Homer and Hesiod: that the philosopher's task was of necessity to revise this world view and the language in which it was expressed: and yet that at the same time he can argue for change only within a frame of reference supplied by his traditional prototypes.

This paper has inevitably avoided coming to terms with the philosophies of the pre-Socratics properly considered. It has concentrated more on the past which still controlled them than on the future to which their efforts pointed. Enough has perhaps been said to suggest that the significance of these early speculative systems—if that is the proper word for them—may lie centrally in the demand that they do make for a new syntax and a new use of language, a new method of making statements about our physical environment. We conclude then by a suggestion. It is possible that in this enterprise our three philosophers stand together. The one unmoving and untroubled *theos*, the one common eternal *logos*, and the eternal unmoved unbegotten *esti*—could all three of these constitute a frontal attack upon the narrative sequence of experience and the narrative portrait of reality so long enforced by the need of oral memorization? For such a conclusion, our survey of the pre-literate condition may have partially prepared us. But demonstration must await a further opportunity.[98]

1. As at *Repub.* 397 c 8 cf. 598 e 4 where ποιεῖν is rendered as 'write'.
2. B. Snell *Die Ausdrücke für den Begriff des Wissens in der vor-Platonischen Philosophie*, Philol. Untersuch. 29, Berlin, 1924, p. 8.
3. E. A. Havelock, *Preface to Plato*, Oxford, 1963, p. 191 n. 6.
4. W. Jaeger, *Paideia* (Eng. Trans.) Book 1 cap. 2 p. 29 "We have tried to show that the character of Telemachus in the first four books of the

Odyssey is so presented as to serve a deliberate educational end." The notion that Greek culture is homogeneous is examined critically by A. M. Parry, "A Note on the Origin of Teleology", *JHI* 26 (1965) 259-62.

5. Milman Parry, *L'Epithète Traditionelle dans Homère*, Paris, 1928: *vid.* also *HSCP* 41 (1930) 73-148 and 43 (1932) 1-50.
6. Rhys Carpenter, "The Antiquity of the Greek Alphabet", *AJA* 37 (1933) 8-29, and "The Greek Alphabet Again", *AJA* 42 (1938) 58-69.
7. L. H. Jeffery, *The Local Scripts of Archaic Greece*, Oxford, 1961, p. 16: the controversy over date is briefly reviewed in Havelock *op. cit.* p. 49 n. 4.
8. Havelock *op. cit.* pp. 42 ff.
9. *Vid.* A. M. Parry, "The Language of Achilles", *TAPA* 87 (1956) 1-7.
10. For a sample of Hesiod's method, *vid.* Havelock, "Thoughtful Hesiod", *YCS* 20 (1965) 61-72.
11. *Iliad* xii. 17-33.
12. As in Hesiod's star-calendar, cf. *WD* 417-419, 565-567, 619-620.
13. "Heart of Darkness", in *Youth and Two Other Stories*, Doubleday (N.Y.), pp. 110-111.
14. On ἐπιστήμη in distinction from other cognitive terms *vid.* Snell, *op. cit.* pp. 81-96.
15. W. K. C. Guthrie, *A History of Greek Philosophy*, vol. I, p. 141, "Yet until the rise of a more scientific outlook . . . there was no alternative explanation of the past."
16. J. A. Davidson, "Literature and Literacy in Ancient Greece" Parts I and II, *Phoenix* 16 (1962) 141-156 and 219-233.
17. Kirk and Raven, *The Presocratic Philosophers*, Cambridge, 1957, p. 7.
18. Hence presumably Kirk and Raven (*op. cit.* pp., 74-162) feel compelled to offer an elaborate reconstruction of Milesian doctrine, which does not meet their own stated criterion of evidence: *vid.* also Guthrie *op. cit.*, pp. 54-58, 76-88 and 115-151 on the presumed Milesian *archae.* The Theophrastean account of these seems to depend on Aristotle: *vid.* McDiarmid, "Theophrastus on the Presocratic Causes", *HSCP* 61 (1953) 1-156.
19. Diels-Kranz, *FVS* 21 B 8.
20. D-K. 21 B 6.
21. cf. the Aeschylean "slices from Homer's dinners" (*Ath.* viii. 347 e).
22. Hesiod, *Theog.* 94-5.
23. M. Bowra, *Problems in Greek Poetry*, Oxford, 1953, pp. 16-19.
24. D-K. 21 B 2, lines 11-12.
25. Havelock *op. cit.* p. 100.
26. D-K. 21 B 1, lines 21-22. The στάσιας σφεδανάς repudiated in the next line can also be referred to the ἔρις θεῶν of the *Theogony* (line 705, cf. lines 710 and 637, and also *Iliad* i. 6) rather than as in D-K *ad loc.* to Alcaeus.
27. D-K. 21 B 10.
28. D-K. 21 B 11.
29. D-K. 21 B 23, 26, 25.

30. *Theog.* 457, 465, 471, 494.
31. *Theog.* 537 Διὸς νόον ἐξαπαφίσκων, 613 ὡς οὐκ ἔστι Διὸς κλέψαι νόον οὐδὲ παρελθεῖν.
32. *Theog.* 534, cf. the parallel epithets in lines 545, 546 and 559, 561.
33. *Theog.* 626, 653, 658.
34. *Theog.* 629 δηρὸν γὰρ μάρναντο πόνον θυμαλγέ' ἔχοντες, 881 αὐτὰρ ἐπεὶ ῥα πόνον μάκαρες θεοὶ ἐξετέλεσσαν.
35. *Theog.* 629-634, 635-638, 646-648.
36. *Theog.* 653.
37. *Theog.* 656 ἴδμεν, ὅ τοι περὶ μὲν πραπίδες περὶ δ'ἐστὶ νόημα, 661 ἀτενεῖ τε νόῳ καὶ ἐπίφρονι βουλῇ | ῥυσόμεθα.
38. The physical convulsion, *Theog.* 678-682 and 702-704, and the physical activity of Zeus, 687-693 and 705-706.
39. *Theog.* 730.
40. *Theog.* 838 εἰ μὴ ἄρ' ὀξὺ νόησε κτλ.
41. *Theog.* 842, 855.
42. *Theog.* 881, 884.
43. With D-K 21 B 24 οὖλος ὁρᾷ οὖλος δέ νοεῖ οὖλος δέ τ' ἀκούει compare *WD* 9 κλῦθι ἰδὼν ἀίων τε, and *Theog.* 700-701 εἴσατο δ' ἄντα | ὀφθαλμοῖσιν ἰδεῖν ἠδ' οὔασι ὄσσαν ἀκοῦσαι, 661 ἀτενεῖ τε νόῳ καὶ ἐπίφρονι βουλῇ | ῥυσόμεθα, 644 κέκλυτέ μευ κτλ., and 664-5 ἐπήνεσσαν δὲ θεοί, δωτῆρες ἐάων | μῦθον ἀκούσαντες. There are no Hesiodic spectators, no thinkers, no listeners, other than the one god.
44. See above n. 26.
45. D-K. 59 B 12.
46. Heraclitus B 32, 67, 78, 79, 102; Parmenides B 12, B 13; Emped. B 31; Diogenes B 5. Empedocles' descriptions of cosmic process avoid using the four divine names (D-K B 6) of the elements.
47. Diog. Laert. ix. 5. cf. the excellent discussion in Kirk and Raven pp. 184-7.
48. *Vid.* K. Deichgräber, *Rhythmische Elemente im Logos des Heraklit* pub. by Akademie der Wiss. und der Lit. in Mainz, 1962.
49. D-K. 22 B 54, 11, 33.
50. B 33 in effect rationalizes the statements of Hesiod *Theog.* 881-885 and *WD* 1-8.
51. D-K. 22 B 30.
52. Kirk and Raven p. 185. "The surviving fragments have very much the appearance of oral pronouncements put into . . . easily memorable form." As Kirk notes, Diels himself first propounded this view. But see also below, note 69.
53. So Burnet, *Early Gr. Phil.* p. 132 and Kirk *loc. cit.*
54. Wallace McLeod, "Oral Bards at Delphi", *TAPA* 92 (1961) 317-325.
55. D-K. 22 B 1. Although Kirk *loc. cit.* calls this a "structurally complicated sentence", it in fact obeys the same laws of colometric composition noted of previous examples, *vid.* Deichgräber *op. cit.* p. 57.
56. D-K. 22 B 1, 19, 34, 50, 108.

57. cf. Heraclitus B 40.
58. D-K. 22 B 104.
59. D-K. 22 B 42: τῶν ἀγώνων refers to occasions of the type described Hes. *WD* 653-657.
60. D-K. 22 B 28.
61. *vid. LSJ sub voc.*
62. cf. Xenophanes (above, n. 26).
63. D-K. 22 B 29.
64. *Theog.* 94 ff. and the discussion in Havelock *op. cit.* pp. 110-111. Demodocus is styled a "hero" at *Od.* viii. 483.
65. D-K. 22 B 57. I take the correction to be specifically of *Theog.* 748 ff. (rather than also of *Theog.* 123 as D-K *ad loc.* and other scholars) where Day and Night are presented as coeval and occupying the same locale. That is, Heraclitus is preoccupied with the same Hesiodic context that engaged the attention of Xenophanes and Parmenides.
66. D-K. 22 B 1, 2, 5, 17, 19, 21, 23, 28, 29, 34, 35, 40, 41, 42, 45, 46, 47, 50, 51, 55, 56, 57, 70, 72, 73, 78, 79, 80, 83, 86, 87, 92, 93, 95, 101, 101a, 102, 104, 106, 107, 108, 110, 113, 114. To these could be added 13, 18, 22, 27, 54, 71, 74, 97, 117, 118, 123 if viewed in the same light. (I agree with others in rejecting 112 and 116.)
67. D-K. 22 B 30, 31, 61, 76, 90.
68. D-K. 22 B 14, 64, 67; per contra *logos* occurs in nine sayings, 1, 2, 31a, 45, 50, 72, 87, 108, 115.
69. Hence perhaps he is more aware of the written word as a medium than is Xenophanes or Parmenides, cf. B 59, retaining with Kirk and Guthrie the MS reading γραφέων, and cf. B 101a if the advantage of eyes over ears be taken to refer to reading (his sayings) as against listening to a recital. B 87 might then be taken to refer also to his own sayings heard, read and digested.
70. D-K. 64 B 1.
71. By Kirk in *Heraclitus, the Cosmic Fragments* and Kirk and Raven, *op. cit.* chapter 6.
72. I will not here burden the footnotes with a complete statistical review of epic reminiscences. Their frequency can be inferred from what is said in the rest of this paper.
73. D-K. 28 B 1 lines 23-25, cf. *Iliad* i. 361, xviii. 385, 424, *Od.* i. 120 etc.
74. φράζω D-K 28 B 2 line 6 and B 6 line 2, νενόμισται B 6 line 8, πολύδηριν ἔλεγχον B 7 line 5, φατίζω B 8 line 60, and the combinations of φράζω and γιγνώσκω B 2 line 9, of λέγειν and νοεῖν B 6 line 1, of φάσθαι and νοεῖν (reiterated) B 8 line 8, of ἀνόητον ἀνώνυμον B 8 line 17, of νοεῖν and φατίζειν B 8 line 38, of λόγος and νόημα B 8 line 50. πυνθάνομαι and its cognates, used frequently by the philosopher, signify ambivalently both hearing and learning.
75. D-K. 28 B 2 line 1, B 8 line 52.
76. D-K. 28 B 6 line 7.
77. D-K. 28 B 7 line 4.

78. D-K. 28 B 8 line 52, cf. line 60.
79. D-K. 28 B 1 line 3.
80. *Iliad* v. 214, Parmenides D-K. 28 B 14.
81. *Iliad* v. 858, Parmenides D-K. 28 B 8 line 41, cf. also Emped. D-K. 31 B 21 line 14.
82. Parmenides D-K. 28 B 1 line 28, B 2 line 6, B 8 line 21: *Od.* iii. 88, cf. *Od.* iii. 184 and the reiteration in the Telemachus-Nestor episode of the noun ὄλεθρος and the verb πυνθάνομαι.
83. Havelock, "Parmenides and Odysseus", *HSCP* 63 (1958) 133-143.
84. D-K. 28 B 1 lines 4, 24-25.
85. *Iliad* xvii. 75-78.
86. *Iliad* xvii. 444 ff.
87. *Iliad* xix. 401 ἄλλως δὴ φράζεσθε, cf. Parm. B 1, 4 πολύφραστοι ἵπποι and n. 74 (above).
88. *Iliad* xix. 409-10, 420.
89. D-K. 28 B 1, lines 22-26.
90. *Iliad* i. 418.
91. *Iliad* xviii. 95 and xxiv. 132, and cf. n. 88 (above).
92. D-K. 28 B 1, lines 12, 14, 18, 19.
93. cf. Havelock *op. cit.* on their Homeric character.
94. D-K. 28 B 8, lines 14, 25-27, 29-31, 37, 42-44, 49.
95. *Theog.* 453-865.
96. *Theog.* 616, 718, 731-733, 813, 622.
97. *Theog.* 720, 726-8, 738-40 (cf. 700, 814, 116), 745-748, 748-754, 809-813.
98. This paper was first delivered as a lecture to the Institute of Classical Studies on 24 January 1966.

The Oral Composition of Greek Drama *

Eric A. Havelock

1. *A Hypothesis*

The Greek alphabet, an instrument of symbolic efficiency greatly superior to the non-Greek systems from which it emerged, introduced itself into a culture which had for several centuries been completely non-literate. It is usually supposed that with the invention a condition of general Greek literacy resulted automatically and quickly. This after all is what has tended to happen in non-literate societies when colonized in modern times by representatives of literate cultures who arrive already equipped with the technologies of reading and writing. In the case of the Greeks, however, it may be incautious to draw this conclusion. One must distinguish the original act of invention from the methods required to realise its potential. At the time when it occurred, these did not exist. There were for example no primary schools for teaching letters, and no body of documentation large enough to provide the occasion, let alone the desire, to learn to read. Obviously a few people did learn the art. The question is How many, and where did they belong in the social scale? The existence of a general literacy depends upon the existence not of writers as such, but of a reading public large enough to form a majority. How to estimate the date at which this happened is admittedly difficult. The Greeks of the archaic and classical periods did not take note of their reading habits. What evidence there is — a considerable body — is indirect. A conservative estimate would conclude that a condition of

* An early draft of this paper was read to a colloquium held by the Institute of Classical Philology at the University of Urbino, Italy on June 2, 1978, presided over by Professor Bruno Gentili, whose assistance and encouragement in this enterprise the author gratefully acknowledges.

general literacy came about in Athens in the last third of the fifth
century B.C., at the close of the Periclean age, but not before that.
This means, in the case of the Greek mainland, a time lag of well over
250 years between the date of the original invention and its complete
social application. In Ionia, the period may have been shorter. Is a
delay of this length credible?

It may become so, if some factors of elementary physiology are
taken into account.

The 'natural' condition of human speech is acoustic. The raw
material of what is now written literature existed for countless mil-
lenia only as it was shaped by the mouth and heard by the ear. In the
centuries immediately preceding the introduction of the alphabet, the
Greek language had reverted to this purely oral condition if indeed
it had ever left it. To put the new invention to full use, its users
were now required to mate the inherited habits of mouth and ear to
acquired habits of hand and eye. A completely new factor was introduced into the act of verbal communication, namely vision. The
clash of the senses, it is suggested, required prolonged alignment of
hearing to vision. A psychological adjustment was required to bridge
the gap between them. The first inscribers of course managed this,
but slowly and painfully. Fluent application would take time, and
dissemination of such fluency, bearing in mind that we mean reading
fluency, longer still. We have been practising the application of the
Greek alphabet in the west for some 2300 years. The skills, habits
and institutions required to convert it into a complete cultural instrument have become perfected and familiar, obscuring the physiological problems created by its introduction, though by no means altogether removing them.

For the Greeks an additional obstacle to achieving the transition
lay in the formidable strength of their previous tradition. How formidable this was can be appreciated when it is realized that in any
oral culture — and par excellence that of the Greeks — important
communication must be an orally managed communication, a sophisticated art. The culture requires a body of tradition to live by, a
verbalized storehouse of information, custom and propriety. The only
place where this can survive is in individual memory. To survive
there, it has to be cast in rhythmic form, which in the Greek instance
is discovered in the epics of Homer. We read as texts what was

originally composed orally, recited orally, heard acoustically, memorized acoustically and taught acoustically in all communities of the early Hellenic civilization. The rules for this procedure were formulaic and sophisticated: they were nourished by an expertise and received some institutional support. They bred in the population a total habit of oral usage and comprehension. Is it likely that a culture long committed to these loyalties would readily substitute habits of the written word, and would cheerfully take to reading? and would welcome the book as a friend? There is some evidence to the contrary, that the book was greeted, if not as an enemy, at least with grave suspicion, a source of deceit, as against the integrity of the spoken word [1].

Athens, rising to importance (or perhaps regaining it) in the sixth century before Christ, was a city still proto-literate, or even, in a majority sense, non-literate. Where was the corpus of verbalized tradition to which she should turn, for the consolidation of her own institutions and the education of her youth? Obviously there was still Homer, treasured, recited, quoted and taught in school, market place, and on public occasions. But Homer's was not the native dialect; it was an artificial amalgam predominantly Ionic, and the tales he tells have a dimension and an appeal which is pan-Hellenic. Will a desire spring up in proto-literate Athens to acquire her own oral supplement to Homer, composed in the native speech, the dialect of Attica, and addressed to native Athenian concerns?

The outline of a hypothesis begins to emerge, to be tested against the plays themselves, but at present taking the following shape. Attic drama, an art form native to Athens, arose as tradition suggests in the last half of the sixth century, in order to provide the needed Homeric supplement. It continued and extended for the benefit of Athenian audiences the cultural functions hitherto performed by Homer for all of Hellas. These had been in the first instance didactic: the entertainment provided in the stories told in the *Iliad* and *Odyssey* was like a spell woven to clothe a running report upon the *nomos* and *ethos* of the Greek maritime complex. As it was reported, it was also recommended for conservation. In this way the epics had furnished the Greek-speaking peoples with an overall identity, moral, political, historical. The Athenians turned to drama to discover their own particular identity, which was that of a single city-state. Listening

---

[1] Below, nn. 57, 59.

and watching as the plays were performed, they recognized and absorbed a running commentary on their own *nomos* and *ethos*. Carrying out this function, Greek drama remains fundamentally didactic in purpose. Its many composers — a more accurate title than authors — applied their skills to combining oral education with oral entertainment. The three masters were those who in three different ways perfected the combination; that is why in their own day they were esteemed as masters. Their works became a kind of standard not only of performance but of instruction. They taught by indirection, as Homer did, because this is the way that oral support for cultural identity — the "tradition" as we say — is made memorizable and preservable. The plays were continual reenactments of aspects of the civic scene, with which the audience was invited to identify.

Content aside, the style was also essentially Homeric, in the sense that the basic rules of composition remained oral. Drama had to be poetic, or it was nothing, and its authors were recognized as poets rather than dramatists [2]. The chorus constituted the original and central element. As a replacement for epic recital, it had the great advantage that mimesis in language could be reinforced by mimesis in dance, and that mimesis of melody and rhythm could be exploited far beyond the range of the chanted hexameter. Into the choric performance was poured a mass of social commentary, directive and reflective, which continually reiterated and summarized the *nomos* and *ethos* of the civic community, its accepted and average attitudes and proprieties. The dialogue took from Homer's rhetoric its protreptic and admonitory color, counselling, commenting, directing, exhorting, praying, denouncing, repenting, poignantly exposing what was to be accepted and avoided, expressing the extremes of masculine and feminine response, dramatizing their penalties and rewards [3]. Finally, the "myth" of each play, locating the plot in an imaginary heroic past, continued the principle of the Homeric fantasy, clothing the contemporary message in an archaic aura, and so giving it distance and grandiloquence and survival value. But all this was to be done in

[2] Plato uses the appellation *anēr tragikos* (*Phaedo* 115a), but in the *Frogs*, as elsewhere in Plato (e.g. *Rep.* X: cf. Aristotle *Poet.* 1453a 29) the authors of plays are just "poets".

[3] "Slices from the great banquet of Homer" is the description of Aeschylus' plays ascribed to their author by Athenaeus (347e).

the Attic dialect, with a touch of Doric in the choruses to add a flavor of solemnity.

Yet compositionally, tragedy could never have started by being simply Homeric, and nothing else, and the longer it lasted, the more it would begin to place a distance between itself and the oral model. The required hypothesis becomes complex. The authors of these plays were in their own day described not as writers but as producers, "teachers of choruses". The phraseology calls attention to the part played by oral communication in their professional activity. Yet who shall doubt that even in protoliterate Athens groups of verses as they were put together were committed to writing, to be reviewed, enlarged, revised, as composition progressed? The rules for singing which had guided the hexameters of the Homeric bard were one thing. The procedures for putting together a stage play in a subsequent era were something else, physiologically more complicated. Whether the dramatist wrote himself or dictated — the more likely alternative [4] — either his own vision or more probably that of his amanuensis who read back to him came into play as a compositional control intruding upon the acoustic controls he had long been used to hearing and using. The eye was to share responsibility with the ear, but the activity of the eye was personal to the producer. For his audience he must retain the ear alone, that is, the acoustic rules, listening himself to his composition as it was spoken and sung. It is to be inferred that Greek tragedy was composed in a state of continuous physiological tension between the modes of oral and written communication. It can also be suggested that the secret of its genius, which sets the high classic apart from subsequent art forms, resides in this tension, peculiar as it was to its time and place, never to be repeated in quite the same way.

The audience, coterminous with the populace, to which the dramas addressed themselves, was becoming increasingly literate as the century wore on. Important communication could be frozen in

---

[4] When the *Oedipus Coloneus* (to give an extreme example) was "written", Sophocles could not have read the script by unaided eyesight; so at least I have been assured by ophthalmologists. Nothing in the Greek diet could have compensated for senility of vision. Unless it can be shown that this play is more "oral" in composition than its predecessors, the reasonable assumption would be that identical methods of composition were used for all of them.

script, read, re-read and referred to, instead of being drilled into the oral memory. By the logic of this progression what might be called the orality of Greek tragedy was bound to suffer erosion. The central didactic purpose wuold weaken, as the culture came increasingly to rely on written forms of stored information available for re-use. The nice balance between instruction and entertainment, a mnemonic necessity from times immemorial, would be altered in favor of entertainment. Traditional plots manipulated to celebrate and conserve the *ethos* of the community might yield to manipulation of a different sort, designed to express a personal vision on the part of the dramatist. Characters set in a Homeric world where they were required to express large community concerns might in the growing lapse of this need (now supplied by discussions in prose treatises) be supplanted by representations of men and women preoccupied with purely personal matters. Compositionally, as plays began to be written with the expectation of being read, the composer would feel a reduced pressure to conform to certain mnemonic rules. The invented would be freer to prevail over the expected. Finally, as the literate age set in with the fourth century, the tension would disappear, the function and style of high classical tragedy would become obsolete. Drama became what it has largely remained in literate societies ever since, an ingenious entertainment, not a contribution to the social encyclopaedia [5].

Such a hypothesis surely has radical implications which at first sight are difficult to accept. Greek drama has been written about from differing critical standpoints, literary, philosophical, psychological, but all presupposing that here is an art form which is autonomous, called into existence solely by the creative energies of its authors. To tie its style and substance so closely to a change in technology may seem aesthetically disagreeable. Nietzsche for one argued that high classic tragedy did indeed die for cultural reasons, but his observation seems acceptable because grounded in causes which were perceived in his day to be ideological, not technological, a matter of changing dispositions of the mind, not of mere communication.

Yet does our hypothesis reduce the genius of the authors and the historical stature of their plays? If anything, their achievement be-

---

[5] Shakespear's plays, both in plot and sentiment, retain some resemblance to the encyclopaedic character of Greek classic drama, and for the same reason, being composed in a time of popular transition from oral to written word.

comes larger than life, with a comprehensiveness denied to their modern counterparts. The problems and objectives surmounted by their art became more complex and subtle than anything that could now be envisaged for the stage. The social condition which provoked and called forth these compositions was historically unique and can never recur.

If all this is true, evidence which fits and supports the hypothesis is surely available in the texts of the play we have. That is the place to look for it, bearing in mind however that all we can do now is to read them, without hearing and watching the performance as originally presented and without sharing in the response of the original audience. For the investigator who presupposes that composition and production were undertaken for a community of oral communication, and governed by this fact, this is a genuine difficulty. Ancient authorities offer some help. They report for example that on the one hand, in the era of Pisistratus and his sons, Homeric recitations in Athens were regularized, the purpose being educational [6], and on the other, that in the same era Greek drama was perhaps invented, certainly established as an Athenian institution [7]. These events occurred as matters of public policy, and performance was given continuity through the instrumentality of two public festivals, the Panathenaea and the City Dionysia, the first being a quadrennial celebration (supplemented by the lesser Panathenaea in the missing years) but the second an annual one, affording, one would guess, an opportunity for the new art of drama to propagate and extend itself as supplement to the already established art of epic. The educational intentions attested for Homeric recital should be understood as applicable to drama also, the production of which was financed by public arrangement [8] and rewarded by the judgment of state officials. Performance was preceded in the theater by a ceremonial procession of a patriotic character, in which orphans of veterans received armor presented by the state. These are familiar facts duly noticed in histories of the Greek theater, but without

---

[6] Plato, *Hipparchus* 228b-c; cf. also Isocrates *Panegyr.* 159; Lycurgus *in Leoc.* 102; Diog. Laert. 1, 57.

[7] *Marmor Par.* ep. 43; Plut. *Solon* 29; Diog. Laert. 3, 56; cf. Pickard-Cambridge, p. 58.

[8] A *choregia*, as a form of indirect taxation, had the same status as a *trierarchia*. Both were *leitourgiai*.

realization of their sociological significance. Such elaborate civic patronage must have been inspired by something more than a mere love for the theater. It surely reflected a conviction that the stage was somehow performing a vital public service. This would make sense if tragedy was felt to be a process of public education, to be fostered by state support. This is how Plato describes its role, drawing no distinction between tragedy and Homer. It is not a role he approves of: tragedy he says performs its educational functions badly. As for the historical reasons why it may have assumed such functions in the first place, these do not concern him. His interest in the matter is philosophical, not literary.

By fortunate accident, however, there survives an extended critique of Greek tragedy as an art form, the first of its kind, framed for the understanding not of the modern reader but a contemporary audience, and existing not in a written treatise — the time for such has not yet come — but as a stage performance. The stage itself is exploited to offer commentary upon the stage, but this time in comedy, not tragedy. The critique, in one way or another, covers the progress of drama in the fifth century. For all its comic disguise, it has things to say about the kinds of plays produced in that period which indicate that our hypothesis may be well founded.

2. Testimony of a Contemporary

The *Frogs* of Aristophanes was produced about four months after the death of Euripides. Of the various characters who at one time or another occupy the stage, only one is there both at the beginning and the end. This is Dionysus, patron of tragedy [9], represented early in the play as a devotee of Euripides whom he would like to fetch back from the underworld. Finally admitted to Hades, the god disappears briefly from view [10] until discovered shortly after inside, present as a guest in Pluto's dining room, where he has been

[9] And therefore the logical choice for the role of presiding over what is essentially a critique of tragedy's developmental history. There is no need to posit "uncertainty" (Stanford, *Introd.* p. XXX) surrounding the symbolism of his role.

[10] ll. 669-673.

invited to arbitrate a fierce dispute between Aeschylus and Euripides. Aeschylus has been living there now for over fifty years, an honored guest at the head of the table. Euripides has on entering taken Aeschylus' chair and proposes to sit in it permanently. Though the company present (who bear a strong resemblance to the people of Athens living and dead) have supported his decision, Aeschylus will have none of it [11]. The prolonged and acrimonious wrangle in which the two poets presently engage, disputing their rival merits as professional dramatists, takes up the second half of the play [12]. The chorus at suitable intervals adds fuel to the flames. Dionysus contributes running commentary in a series of asides mostly irreverent and irrelevant.

The Art of Euripides

Euripides, seizing the initiative, asserts his superiority on the ground of professional skill (831). The key term is *techne*, strictly untranslatable unless in a periphrasis which fuses the modern senses of technology and art into a single notion. The scene in Hades previously described has already brought it into prominence. Dionysus' servant, parleying with the doorkeeper, overhears a hubbub within. What is going on? The doorkeeper explains. A public argument has erupted in Hades between two "craftsmen" competing for the title of "master-craftsman" in their respective skills with a public pension as the prize. This kind of troublesome social disruption (*stasis*) is always going on among the dead, any time craftsmen are admitted. That is why Dionysus' presence is required in the present instance, to settle the matter, since he presumably, as patron of tragedy, is an expert in the particular skill now in question (762-821: *techne* and its derivatives occur ten times in this passage, linked with *sophos* in the sense of "skillful").

Euripides warms to his work. If there is going to be a dog fight, in which the respective merits of diction, music and "the sinews of

[11] This portion of the action is transacted through "verbal scenery" (755-813), in the course of a dialogue held in front of the proscenium.

[12] This reversal of previous practice (Lesky, pp. 442-444) effectively focusses dramatic attention upon the poetic contest.

tragedy" may get mangled [13] (861-862), he is ready for it and will give
as good as he gets. The chorus gleefully seconding both sides calls
on the Olympian muses to come down and take seats at the ring so
that they can enjoy the fun (876-884). The contest will be between
two types of diction, one "civilised and finehoned", the other "tearing
up the ground with root and branch expressions" (901-904). So they
begin. Euripides, after dealing a glancing blow at the reputation of
Aeschylus' predecessor Phrynichus, launches a two-pronged attack
on his rival's use of stage mutes and bombastic diction (909-935).
As for himself, inheriting the art of tragedy from Aeschylus (931) he
has "taken the inflammation out of it" and "added extract of fluencies
filtered out of papyri (941-943), afterwards adding monodies to the
mixture to give it nourishment" (944). All characters were given
plenty of things to say (948-950) "and so I taught the present audience
to talk" (954). His stage action was contemporary — "the kinds of
things we all do and are familiar with" (959-960) without benefit of
mythological equipment (963-967). "You have only to compare our
respective pupils to see the difference" (964). Aeschylean types
(pointing to the audience?) are crude, the Euripidean ones are cute
(965-967). "This is the kind of thinking (*phronein*) [14] I introduced
to the present audience, inserting reasoning and inquiry into (dramatic)
technique (*techne*), which made them begin to cerebrate (*noein* 974)
and able generally to think things through and in particular to improve
management of households and investigate and question" (971-978).

The Art of Aeschylus

It is now Aeschylus' turn. The chorus give him his cue, hailing
him ambiguously as "the original Hellenic architect of towering
solemnities and author of the order of tragic trumpery" (1004-1005)
and invite him to "let go" (1005) which he promptly does. His
opponent is a man he cannot stand (1006-1007). He will challenge
him on fundamentals. "What is the real basis of a poet's standing
in the community [15]? Answer, please" (1008). The reply given is

[13] The scholiast interprets the language as referring to a cockfight.
[14] Below, n. 67.
[15] For this sense of *thaumazein* see Herod. 3, 80, and *LSJ* s.v.

double-barrelled: One thing is his virtuosity (*dexiotēs*); the other is
his moral guidance (*nouthesia*) and his improvement of human beings
in cities. "Very well, this is exactly where my opponent has failed.
From me he inherited noblemen, six footers, not shirkers but citizens
(1013-1014). They were great fighters to boot (1016-1017) and look
what he has done with them!" (1013, pointing to the audience).
Euripides wants a better answer than that: "Pray, precisely what was
the 'action' [16] you put on which produced such 'instruction' in no-
bility?" (1019). The question is put superciliously; it offends the
older poet, and he hesitates, until Dionysus prompts him: "Come on,
tell us the answer" [17] (1020). The answer when it comes make the
audience rise in their seats. "The 'action' I composed was full of
fight — It was the *Seven Against Thebes*, and when they viewed it,
every man in the audience conceived a passion to prove himself [18] a
warrior (1021-1022) ... My next 'instruction' was *The Persians*. That
taught them to set their hearts on winning and never losing (1026-
1027) ... That's the exercise that real poets should be practising
(*askein*). Go back to the beginning and see how the great poets were
those who made themselves beneficial (*ōphelimoi* 1030-1031) ...
Divine Homer himself won fame and fortune only from the fact that
he gave useful (*chrēsta*) instruction [19] (1035) ... It was from his imprint that my mind took its stamp in the creation of many worthy
characters, Patrocluses, Teucers, the purpose being to inspire the
citizen warrior to stretch himself out to match them" (1040-1042).
Eroticism and incest, he adds, are not fit subjects for the poet (1043-
1052). He should "suppress reference to immorality (*apokruptein
to ponēron*) and avoid exhibiting it and giving instruction in it (1053-
1054). The man who explains things to children is the schoolmaster,
but for adolescents [20] it is the poet (1054-1055). What we say should
be useful (*chrēsta*; 1056) ... Important maxims and reflections (*gnōmai, dianoiai*) require corresponding diction. In general verisimilitude
(*eikos*) requires that the speech of demigods be elevated and their

[16] Below, n. 47.
[17] I follow here the division of speaker proposed by Rogers and Stanford.
[18] On the force of *einai* here, see Havelock, *Greek Concept*, pp. 237-239.
[19] Plato, *Rep.* 601d-602a.
[20] As had been represented in the so-called "School Scene" on a vase of
Duris: Havelock, 'Preliterary of the Greeks', pp. 385-387.

clothing statelier (1059-1061)". Euripides' instruction, he argues, has encouraged verbal fluency at the expense of physical exercise (1069-1070). Things have gone wrong generally "and my opponent is the cause of it" (1078), with his scenes of prostitution, illegitimate births, and incest combined with general cynicism (1079-1082). "As a result, the city of Athens has become crammed with scriveners [21], shysters and scamps continually victimizing the demos (1083-1086)".

Stylistic Comparisons

During a brief pause the contestants catch their breath. The chorus would spur them on. To be sure, it is only a battle of wits and words, but requiring some sophistication on the part of the audience. Will they feel a lack of education (*amathia*) preventing them from following the nice points (*lepta*) as they are made? (1109-1111). No need to worry; that is no longer the case. "They are equipped. Every one of them is holding a papyrus [22] and able to take in the verbal niceties" (*manthanei ta dexia*, 1112-1114). The contestants need have no fear, so far as the audience is concerned; the intelligence is there (*sophoi*, 1118).

The argument reverts to fine points of dramatic technique. Euripides launches an attack on Aeschylus' prologues, their style and substance, with suitable quotation (1119-1176). Aeschylus counter-attacks in kind (1177-1247). Comparisons then shift to matters of melody and meter (*melē* 1248: cf. 861-862). Those of Aeschylus are parodied to expose their epic monotony (1262). Retaliating, their author defends his own style as Homeric in source [23] (1298) and delivers a frontal attack on the music and meters of Euripides. They are foreign (1302), sentimental (1322) and meretricious (1308-

[21] Below, nn. 58, 59.

[22] On *biblion*, see n. 55.

[23] I so interpret the phrase *ek tou kalou* (1298; as also the Loeb, note *ad loc.*). Aeschylus has already laid claim to Homeric diction and adoption of Homeric character models. It is his dactylic, i.e., epic, meters which have been selected for special satiric treatment by Euripides. Accordingly at 1299-1300 he defends his Homeric style as an alternative to the flowery meadows of Phrynichus. Editors guided by a scholiast's note on 1282 have preferred to identify Terpander as the "source" intended.

1327). The attack concludes with a long satirical parody of that kind of solo performance (*monōdia*, 1330), emotional and personal, and therefore judged to be trivial, which occurs in some of Euripides' later plays. In the present example, a poor spinning girl has had a bad dream, warning her that a neighbor has raided her hen roost.

A decision is needed. To fight so far has been a draw. A gigantic pair of scales is produced to weigh the lives and merits of two dramatists — a parody of a Homeric episode which in turn had been imitated in an Aeschylean drama. In fact neither protagonist is weighed personally. Decision is to depend on the weight registered by spoken lines as they are deposited [24] by the protagonists into the two scale pans. Competing lines are duly discharged. Aeschylus has the advantage in ponderosity. There is no doubt of that; he even proposes to wind up the competition by letting Euripides and his entire family get into one of the pans and sit down — "he can take his papyri with him too". All his rival needs to do to outweigh them is to pronounce just two of his own lines into the other pan (1407-1410).

A Final Exam

Dionysus however is baffled. "I can't choose", he says, turning to the audience: "I do not want to alienate either of them. One I consider an intellectual, the other I enjoy" [25]. But without a decision, what is to become of his original mission to Hades? "Pick a winner and take him back with you", says Pluto. The time has come for the ultimate test. Before meeting it, the two candidates

---

[24] Is this hilarious scene (aside from its obvious purpose to parody Homer) also intended to recall a favorite but indecent after dinner amusement? There is mock gravity in lines 1369-1377, hailing this tour de force of ingenuity.

[25] I agree with Stanford (note *ad loc.*) that the poet he enjoys is Aeschylus. The pleasure is that of direct response to oral poetry, as opposed to a "formed opinion" about the "intelligence" of Euripides (1413). Dionysus voices the divided allegiance of contemporary Athens, hesitating between the claims of traditional oralism and the new literate rationalism; so also at 1934.

must be informed as to the true purpose of Dionysus' visit to
Hades. He is not primarily interested in an argument over aesthetics.
"I came down here to fetch a poet [26]. If you ask me why, I wanted
the city to be rendered secure, and so continue to conduct choric
performances. Which of you two is likely to give the city counsel
which is really useful? (*chrēston*). He'll be the one I take back
with me" (1418-1421). The god then sets the candidates two examination questions [27] to answer. The first is a specific one: "The
topic is Alcibiades. How do we deal with him? I want a brief
statement (*gnōmē*) from each of you" (1422-1423).

The replies given are each in character. Euripides the radical
says in effect "Repudiate him". Aeschylus the conservative says
"You should not have raised him. But now you have, you must
tolerate him" (1424-1432). The styles correspond. Euripides frames
two antithetical definitions, covering the true patriot and the disloyal
citizen, ingeniously expressed by arranging in sequence four pairs of
antithetical terms. Aeschylus offers a vivid image [28] of the lion cub
growing up in the house as a dangerous pet.

Different as they are, the two answers still make a decision very
difficult; one is intellectual, the other easy to understand (*sophos . . .
saphōs* 1434). A second question is needed to break the tie, this
time a general one: "I want one more brief statement (*gnōmē*)
from each of you, giving your formula for the city's security".
Euripides, who has only recently left the upper world, has his
answer ready: "Get rid of the present government" (1443-1450).

---

[26] The sense of lines 1417-1419 and 1469-1471, when compared with what
had been said in 52-54, 66-68, 71-72, 96-97 (with the parody of 1471 recalling
that of 101) does not justify the view (Stanford, *Introd.* pp. XXIV and XXXIX,
with n. 23) that Dionysus' motive for visiting Hades as originally stated, namely
to fetch back Euripides, is "entirely ignored". To succeed in restoring him to
upper air would automatically achieve continuation of the tragic choruses (1419)
and the advice he is required to give for preserving the city is judged to be as
satisfactory as that of his rival. The final substitution of Aeschylus with its appropriate encomium is a comic reversal.

[27] Discernible in this portion of the plot may be an intention to parody
the Socratic elenchus of the poets, as described in Plato's *Apology.*

[28] It had been used at *Agamemnon* 717 ff and appears to have been
traditional.

Aeschylus, long absent from it, is more cautious. He needs information. "What kind of people is the city using for a government?
Are they useful types?" (1455) "No". "Does it prefer vicious
types?" "No, it employs them only perforce". "A city so undecided
cannot be made secure, I'll give my views when I get up there"
(1454-1461). "No, you don't", says Dionysus. "Your blessing must
be pronounced here and released upwards". So at last the pronounce-
ment comes: "Go after the enemy's territory even if he occupies
yours" (1463-1465).

The answers are again in character. The first proposes the
radical solution; the second would revert to the original war policies
of Pericles. Both are framed antithetically, conforming to gnomic
style. The first is introduced by a completely abstract epistemological
formula: "When present unbelief shall be considered believable, and
that which is believed become unbelievable" (1443-1444). This on
request has to be replaced ("Please", says Dionysus, "use words
less educated and more understandable": cf. 1111, 1434) by a
slightly more specific equivalent, which then runs: "Assume we
cease to believe in the citizens we now trust, and use those we
now refrain from using — security will follow. Or again, assume
we are at present in a bad way, and then that we reverse our
present course — security will follow" (1446-1450). The second
version is as conceptual as the first, but now spelled out, in a
parody of propositional argument. It satisfied Dionysus ("Well done,
O Palamedes, O nature intellectual!"), but so do the concrete expressions used by Aeschylus: "How give security to a city which
finds profit neither in custom-tailoring nor ready-mades [29]? . . . when-
soever enemy's land becomes their common usage [30] and theirs the
enemy's; when ships are income and income is non-income" (1458-
1465, where the parody is at the expense of his imagist diction and
verbal assonances) [31].

[29] The Greek expression contrasts a tailored cloak for city wear with rough
homespun.
[30] For this rendering of *nomizō* see Havelock, *Liberal Temper*, pp. 122,
411, 413.
[31] There is no need to obelize these lines (Wilamowitz) merely because they
recall a vanished policy.

The Winner

The long contest thus ends in a draw. Dionysus cuts the knot by announcing he will follow his heart (*psychē*) and choose Aeschylus, thus nullifying that deep affection for Euripides which he had announced early in the play. The loser reproaches him for this betrayal, but to no purpose.

While Aeschylus withdraws to Hades for one last dinner with Pluto, the chorus in nine lines acclaim that keen comprehension (1483, 1490, *xunesis* and *xunetos*) which in his person will now "go home" in the upper world to the benefit of the citizenry and his own family (1483-1490). In nine more they decry the Socratic habit of "throwing away music" and "ignoring the greatnesses of the tragic art" in favor of a pursuit (*diatribē*) which concentrates on big propositions and fancy talk (1491-1499).

Aeschylus, now dined and wined, reenters, to receive from Pluto and chorus their final farewells, which bid him "Secure our city with worthy maxims and educate the witless" (1501-1503, pointing to the audience), and express the general hope that "the gods of the land will furnish to our city those goodly sentiments (*epinoiai*) which produce major goods" (1529-1530).

3. The Testimony Interpreted

At first sight, this whole comic confrontation, conducted as it is in an exchange of quotations and parodies, is likely to be read as a comparison of styles rather than substance. The two poets are introduced unambiguously as "craftsmen", encouraging the view that the issue will turn less on what they say than how they say it. Euripides' initiative seems to confirm this, when he challenges comparison in terms of "diction" (*epē*) and meter-with-melody (*melē*), though he also adds "tragedy's muscle" (*neura* 862). The contest as it gathers momentum is identified by both poets, as also by Dionysus and the chorus, as one between competing varieties of virtuosity (*sophia, sophismata* 872, 882, 896, 1104, 1108; cf. 1519) and verbal dexterity (*dexiotēs, ta dexia, dexios* 1009, 1114, 1370).

These are cited as hallmarks of achievement on both sides[32] of the dispute (cf. 780), whether applied to the elegancies of one poet or the heroics of the other. Euripides however in the finale emerges as the *sophos* par excellence (1413, 1434, 1451: cf. 776).

The Art of Civic Instruction

But when Aeschylus at his first opportunity takes the floor to challenge his opponent, he elicits a proposition which in fact both of them accept[33]. Virtuosity aside, a poet's chief business is education. Phrased as "improvement of human beings in cities" (1009-1010), this reproduces a cliché describing the educational process as envisaged for example by Plato's Socrates[34]. As a conception of the poet's function, it is presented in the *Frogs* not in the guise of something thought up by sophistic theorists, but as a view shared by society in general, which honors poets for doing so. It is not surprising that Euripides so readily concedes this to be the case. He had already defended his own dramatic style as an effective method of "instructing" his audiences to "express themselves" (954), to which Aeschylus had retorted that such "instruction" might better never have been given (955). The audiences, replies Euripides, have been the "pupils" of both dramatists[35] (964). As these exchanges develop, there is no hint that the argument is leaving the poet's "craft" out of consideration. On the contrary, civic instruction emerges as one of its central components.

Aeschylus, warming to his theme, and defending the instruction given by his own dramas, places it squarely within the context of that instruction given by the four great traditional poets of Greece[36]

---

[32] The entire choric "invocation" (875-882) makes this clear. The tone of Dionysus' instructions to both contestants (905-906) is Euripidean rather than Aeschylean. Though the *xunesis* of Euripides is satirised (893), the same "accurate" faculty is in the conclusion assigned to Aeschylus (1483; cf. 876).

[33] Below, n. 48.

[34] *Apol.* 24c-d; *Protag.* 318d, cf. 316c, 318a.

[35] And therefore in this particular comedy partnership between players and audience is unusually prominent; see below, n. 45.

[36] Norwood p. 260 sees in this passage only a bias which "leads to the absurdity of praising 'divine Homer' because he taught military science". For a

(1030-1036) and in a notable aphorism (1054-1055) defines the poet as the man who takes over from the schoolmaster [37]. The verbs *didaskō* and *ekdidaskō* reverberate like drumbeat through his eloquent lines, no doubt playing deliberately upon the special sense of the "instruction" given by a poet to his chorus (1026, 1035, 1054, 1055, 1069; the same verbs on Euripides' lips 1019, 1057) [38]. Notably, after turning to the audience and reproaching them for failing to "practice" (*askein*) the required discipline, he then applies the same verb to describe the poet's proper "practice" (1025, 1030). Verb and noun have educational overtones [39].

After a pause to allow the contestants to recover breath, the comedy reverts to light hearted parodies of style (1099-1413). But that concluded, the issue upon which the two poets are to be judged is restated in terms of what they can do to assist the city, by way of political and moral guidance (*parainein* 1420; cf. *nouthesia* 1009). This is the subject of the final examination for both of them, and while the answers offered are typically different in style, there is no thought of disavowing their didactic function. The objective is to produce citizens who can manage their affairs efficiently — to produce in fact what Plato later calls "civic excellence". "Benefit" and "utility" are the measures applied to the poet's services, not the communication of aesthetic sensibilities. Significantly, these utilitarian terms are stressed by Aeschylus (1030-1031, 1035, 1054, 1455), not, as a modern critic might expect, by his supposedly "sophistic" opponent. The counsel which in the finale both are challenged to supply is the practical one of making

collocation of Homer, Hesiod, Orpheus, Musaeus (with addition of Simonides) as sophistic educators in disguise, see Plato, *Protagoras* 316d.

[37] Plato, *Protag.* 325e-326a describes the literate situation in which the poets instead of being communicated orally and directly are memorised out of written sources.

[38] At 1026 the prefix *ex-* has been supplied (first by Bentley) to render the MS reading metrical (cf. 1019). I agree with Stanford (*ad loc.*) that "taught fully" catches the sense here, but would add that the play on the verbs would not appear artificial to contemporaries; "teaching choruses" was part of the accepted programme of oral education.

[39] Stanford notes ambiguity between "poets should practice" and "poets should train men".

the city secure [40], and in their parting accolade the chorus hail the winner as the likely source of "what is good for it" (1487).

The recipients of such instruction are not referred to as an audience of playgoers drawn to the performance by their special interest in the theater. They are any and all members of the community, who have to learn to manage society at two levels, the civic one, which is primary and in which *politai* are involved with their *polis* (1010, 1014-1017, 1027, 1419-1433, 1435-1450, 1454-1465) and the domestic, involving relationships within the *oikia* [41] (976-977, 1489).

If drama today can be used as an educational instrument as it is inserted into the curricula of schools and colleges, this is done in the interest of literary appreciation and aesthetic sensibility. Very different are the Greek objectives, as understood by Greeks. Both poets, accepting their role as instructors in social utility, assume a burden on behalf of the Greek stage which its modern counterpart has not been called upon to bear (unless perhaps in Japan). Such a function makes sense however in the context of the hypothesis previously offered that Athenian drama came into existence as a supplement to Homer, designed as a storage mechanism for the oral re-enactment and consolidation of the mores of an essentially pre-literate community. Such instruction must be socially oriented, with utilitarian intention; its ancestry is Homeric: its method of communication is restricted to the spoken word, framed and pronounced as such, and existing for repetition in the memory. In short, behind the parody, the slapstick, the claims, the retorts, the recriminations, lurk a set of assumptions peculiar to one period and only one in the history of European literature. Greek drama is a disguised corpus of oral wisdom contained within a narrative matrix, the mythos which preserves it.

[40] This concern is obviously inspired by present perils (1531-1532). The notion of civic *sōteria* is thematically repeated (1419, 1433, 1436, 1448, 1450, 1458, 1501). Is the poet also recalling a formula of contemporary political theory? Cf. Democritus B252 (with Havelock, *Liberal Temper*, p. 92).

[41] The claim to teach better household management is not made "absurdly" (Stanford *ad loc.*); the language is that of Protagoras *apud* Plato, *Protag.* 318e-319a.

The "Orality" of the Contest

The competition of quotation and parody carried on between the two contestants makes a demand on the sophistication of an audience which by modern standards is unparallelled. How could such wealth of allusiveness, often turning on niceties and nuances of verbal expression, be grasped understood and savored by an audience drawn from the civic population? The debate in the *Frogs* has in fact played a role in building up that modern conception which would view ancient Greece as the home of an ideal culture never since equalled. Yet the required sophistication becomes understandable and assumes a more common human dimension if it is linked to the assumption that an oral culture is served by an oral memory of a rather specialised sort. The knowledge on which this audience of non-readers relied was not what we would call a "literary knowledge" [42]. They were used to the recitation of remembered verse, and had received an education which concentrated on the cultivation of this practice. Their acquaintance with drama was not confined to the original single competitive performance. Large numbers of the populace had over the years received training as members of choruses in tragic recitation [43]. If as is probable, the auditions held in Pericles' Odeum included rehearsals of dramas, this again spread an oral knowledge of them. The plays went on circuit in the countryside, and most importantly, were incorporated into the oral curriculum of the schools, and quoted in social intercourse. The proposals of Plato to censor the curriculum makes this clear. Presumably there were favorites among the mass of dramatic material available, and it was presumably these that Aristophanes preferred to draw on for the tragiparodies that occur generally in his plays.

At the same time, in this particular play, he has the chorus say on his behalf that now oral memory can be supplemented by

[42] This problem is well treated by Sedgwick.

[43] Dionysus, restating his motive for going to fetch a poet from Hades (1418-1419) explains that it is "to ensure that the city be rendered secure and continue to hold choruses (i.e., choric dramas)". The explanation need not seem "perfunctory" (Stanford *ad loc.*) once the sociological role of the dramatic festivals is appreciated. The comedy pleads half humorously and perhaps nostalgically for the continuity of a traditional institution of oral education now threatened not more by war than by the technological shift towards literacy.

[281]

instruction from a written source in the possession of members of the audience [44]. The dramaturgy of the *Frogs* is unique in that it is able to exploit the mnemonic resources both of the traditional oralism and the new literacy.

There are some particulars in the text which point in the same "oralist" direction. They would not have been expressed quite in the way they are, if the subject of the *Frogs* debate was a fully "literate" literature. For example, the debaters will step out of dramatic character in order to involve the audience in what they are saying, almost as though the theater population were being treated as partners in the critical give and take. This kind of relationship, aside from its obvious employment in the parabases, expresses itself as an occasional feature in all Aristophanic dialogue, but is especially conspicuous in this play [45].

Again, Aeschylus, before the battle of wits is formally joined, protests (866 ff.) that the location (Hades) in which it is to be staged puts him at a disadvantage: his own poetry has not died with him, but Euripides' poetry has. Commentators from antiquity onwards, alert to see in this sally only a compliment to one poet at the expense of the other, involving also a mistaken judgment of Euripides' powers of survival, have missed the main point of the joke. The disadvantage for Aeschylus is that he does not have his poetry with him; it is available elsewhere. But Euripides has his with him "and so he will be able to recite it" (869). The assumption behind the joke is that poetry is not a written medium but a spoken, and its resources are the intimate property of its maker. Euripides' situation is the normal one — he takes it with him when he dies. Aeschylus' situation is the abnormal. Unluckily for him, his poetry has stayed behind him in the upper world, to be recited there, leaving him in Hades high and dry. The joke turns things upside down — a *paraprosdokian* in the best Aristophanic manner.

In similar vein, when the weighing scene promised at 797 is finally carried out, it is not any written works of the two poets that are placed in the scales, but spoken lines projected (one might almost say "spat") like winged words (1388) into the pans. Aeschylus is con-

[44] Below, nn. 60, 62.
[45] 783, 954, 960, 962, 964?, 972, 1013?, 1025, 1084, 1086?, 1109-1119, 1446-1450?, 1458?, 1476, 1484?, 1503.

fident his quotations will prevail because they have more acoustic "weight" (1367); he is the better "oralist", as indicated when he caps the contest by challenging his rival to climb into the pan himself and take his family and his papyri with him. The mere utterance of two more Aeschylean verses will still be enough to outweigh them (1407-1410).

The stage is a place which by its very nature requires performers to behave as talkers, not (except intermittently and rarely) as readers. It is not a library or lecture hall. If the poetry discussed, quoted and satirized in this comedy comes through as a purely oral phenomenon, this may be thought due to the mere fact that it is being quoted in drama. Nevertheless, if a similar comic confrontation can be imagined under modern conditions, expressing itself in such a virtuosity of quotation and misquotation, would one not expect occasional and casual reference to textual sources in published works or unpublished scripts, particularly if the material is to be used for teaching? Such references, with one exception already noted, are conspicuous by their absence. Quoted verses are not repeated or read out from given contexts, but are cited or alluded to as *gnōmai, dianoiai, epinoiai* (1059, 1423, 1430, 1435, 1502, 1530: cf. 877) or as *dexia, sophismata* and the like. That is, they are thought of as maxims, aphorisms, sentiments, conceits, orally framed and delivered. These are solicited from both poets in the climax of the competition.

The Greek poetry referred to in this way comes through as though it were a performance rather than a body of "literature", and it is consistent with this impression that Aeschylus explaining how his teaching has been communicated describes the effect on the audience in terms of psychological identification. The *Seven Against Thebes* makes them want to "stand up and fight". Watching (and listening to) the *Persians* fills them will "burning ambition to win". The Homeric prototypes on stage become an inspiration to the citizen to "stretch himself out on them" [46] (1042). This becomes possible because Aeschylean drama is a "doing", an enactment (1019, 1021,

---

[46] An Aeschylean predilection for manic characters and scenes, satirised in 816-817 (Stanford, *Aeschylus in His Style*, pp. 13-14 and 129-131) may reflect a parallel tendency to exploit oral-mimetic relationship with audience, as for example might a Homeric rhapsodist reciting the grief of Achilles or Priam.

with a play upon the word) [47]. Euripides in a different context claims the existence of an intimacy between his plays and their audience (959-961).

Intrusion of Literate Idiom

So far a common ground is shared by both poets [48]. Is their confrontation then purely personal? Assuredly not. Signs are not wanting of a collision not only between two styles, but two epochs. One of the differences is fortuitous, meaning that its emphasis derives from the military and naval situation of the moment. The naval battle of Arginusae has recently been fought and won at heavy cost. A second one is still to come. It will bring disaster and the surrender of the city. The times are critical. War weariness is general. Can one last effort be made? In this context the military instruction of Aeschylus receives especial emphasis, as against Euripides the "civilian", the mouthpiece of a purely political solution.

But there are deeper differences, which can be charged to a change in the cultural condition. Aeschylus stoutly defends the artificialities of heroic language and archaic costume and supernatural status (*hēmitheous*, 1060) for his characters, as appropriate to the importance of what is being said. A style closer to the heroic ethos of Homer is one which exploits to the full the element of mythic fantasy characteristic of oral didacticism. The same style calls for the suppression of what is vulgar in common life. In contrast, the plays of Euripides, chronologically removed by a gap ranging between forty and eighty years (depending on the play chosen), show signs of a willingness to discard the fantasy. True, the characters, so far as names are concerned, are still not contemporary. But in behavior they are. In particular the debate brings out a shift in his plays away

---

[47] In classical usage, the literal sense of *drama* was always close to the surface; cf. Plato, *Apol.* 35b, *Symp.* 222d, *Rep.* 451c.

[48] The contrary views of Wilamowitz, Murray, Page, Sikes, Rhys Roberts, that the comedy constitutes a bitter attack on Euripides, suggests the difficulty of understanding the impartiality of Aristophanes' humour. Stevens reviewing and rejecting such opinions justly observes that the play's basic conception was "the idea of exploiting the dramatic possibilities inherent in the clash between two playwrights so conveniently antithetical"; see also Wycherley.

from large political concerns towards those of the household (976-977) and its life style, the life style of masters and servants, the relations both legitimate and otherwise between the sexes, and the status of infants and young children. The mythoi of the older master are costume pieces formal in style and rigidly presented. Their Homeric rhetoric is dramatically monotonous. Euripides' characters are given much more to say. He claims merit for his monodies, and they are indeed solos, magnifying the presence in the plot of individuals whose roles do not depend upon social importance. The concerns are private, which for the old style means they are trivial, to be satirized as such. The same contrasts show up in diction. Metaphor has always been a favored tool of critical appreciation, and Aristophanes is no exception. His stylistic terminology draws upon medicine (942-943), carpentry (799), masonry (801), brick making (800), naval construction (824), as well as armor (818) and animals (815, 822). Thus, for Euripidean diction he prefers brews and infusions (942-943), filings and shavings [49] (819, 881, 902), squares and triangulations (956), while for Aeschylus, it is tree trunks (805, 907), timbers, beams and bolts (824), battlements (1004), and also crested helmets (818) and shaggy bulls (822, 925-926).

In part, these are chosen to dramatize a comic contrast between two idiosyncratic styles. But there is more to it than that. The genius of a strictly oral style is formulaic; it encourages the formation and use of vocabulary syntax and rhythms which are seductive of oral memorisation. The statements it prefers to make are specific rather than general, activist rather than analytic. It delights in similitudes which are themselves episodes. The requirements encourage a performative syntax favoring the concrete over the abstract, the image over the proposition. Sound effects may prevail at the expanse of simple sense, as in the use of imposing but semantically cumbrous compound words, and exploitation of euphony through alliteration

---

[49] Rendering *paraxonión* (819) as cognate in this instance to *paraxeó, paraxoé*, a connection suggested by the next word *smileumato-ergón*; cf. also *parapeismata* (881). Rogers (Loeb) translates "whirling of splinters and phrases smoothed down with the plane". Editors prefer to follow the scholiast by connecting with "axle" (*LSJ* s.v.). Stanford accordingly (note *ad loc.*) imagines a competition between heroes mounted on chariots. I prefer to think Aristophanes brought two incompatibles into absurd combination, like "The Walrus and the Carpenter".

and onomatopoea. Statements are enlarged upon by variant repetition [50]. These are not matters of stylistic idiosyncracy, but give expression to the need for mnemonic enforcement. Much of Aristophanes' own poetry has this quality, which may incline him towards a bias in favor of Aeschylus. But it is hard to detect this in the actual course of the dispute, for at the same time he constructs in skillful parody (and not only in this play but several others) a very full representation of a quite different type of diction and syntax. The words of this style are "smaller", and more accurately "shaped". Their hallmark is the adjective *leptos* [51], a reiterated term. They are also more plentiful; fluency is increasing [52]; that is, additions are being made in some profusion to an existing vocabulary, and this is arousing resentment from traditionalists. Finally, narrative modes of syntax, concrete and activist, are being converted into statements of an analytic character. The form in which the final examination of the two candidates is cast reveals what is happening. Aeschylean images are being replaced by Euripidean abstractions. Both are still "gnomic", using alliteration, parallelism, antithesis, onomatopoea. But the accidence and syntax of Euripides' terms can be perceived as an anticipation of the dialectic of a Plato insisting that we say what things are, not what they do or is done to them.

In parallel, the dispute between two poetries begins to uncover a widening gap between two mentalities. The winged word or more correctly the feathered phrase is turning into a "notion" or "idea" (*gnōmē, dianoia, epinoia*). The content of what is uttered is being directed away from the mere event or happening towards the topic or subject of a discourse, for example, "the case of Alcibiades" (1422), or "the case of the city" [53] (1436). The narrator's or actor's role is interrupted by the dialectical question: What do you think? and the framing of alternatives, one of which may be rejected. The speaker

[50] Stanford (note on 1154) appropriately labels this habit "liturgical". Euripides criticises two examples of it, 1154-1157, 1173-1179. Division of opinion among rhetorical theorists over its merits (Stanford *ad loc.*) may indicate confusion of judgment when later and literate standards of composition are applied.

[51] See Radermacher and Stanford *ad loc.*

[52] Frequently derided as "mouthings" (841, 1069, 1071, 1310) as elsewhere in other comedies, but defended by Euripides at 943.

[53] *Repub.* 449c-450c is one of many passages which illustrates this common philosophic usage.

or respondent uses calculation (*logismos* 972) where previously an intuitive grasp of a whole situation would have sufficed. Narrated sequences of actions as they are performed are rearranged in terms of causes and their effects. The mythoi employed by Euripides now call for more extensive explanation offered in descriptive prologues [54]. The old style plunged into the assumed story-situation, and that was that. The new wonders about the negative side, about what is and is not the fact (1443-1444).

As we have said, these differences between two poetries are not likely to be the result of mere personal choice, reflecting the kind of contrast we might expect between two strong but divergent artistic personalities. The Homeric qualities of Aeschylean composition, noted but not explained by Aristophanes, are consistent with the thesis that Aeschylus had been composing for a society of oral communication, which means that the Athens of the first half of the fifth century was such a society. Both poets accept the didactic function. On this count, Euripides is still accepting the presuppositions of an oral society. Yet the manner of his discourse is different. Is this perhaps because his verse is beginning to respond to an altered condition of communication, in which the habits of literacy are invading those of orality? Is he composing in a writer's idiom, increasingly dependent on a reader's response?

The Documented Word

The question points towards a drastic conclusion, which one would hesitate to draw were it not for some encouragement which Aristophanes himself provides. His Euripides represents himself as a poet whose "fluency of diction" is "an infusion strained out of papyri" [55] (943). The remark has been understood by later and literate

[54] At 1122 Euripides characterises Aeschylus' prologues as "unclear in the expression of events". The line is defended by Merry but obelised by other editors. The use of the tag "lost his bottle of oil" (1200 ff) satirises not only homely vocabulary (so edd.) but also the prosaic result of expounding a play's plot in logical sequence.

[55] On this as the proper translation of *biblia* in the fifth century (as also at lines 1113, 1409) see Havelock, *Preface to Plato*, p. 55 n. 16.

interpreters to refer to a supposed library in the poet's possession [56]. More correctly, it is phrased to suggest that Euripidean poetry draws upon expressions favoured by the idioms of documented speech. What precisely these are is not explained except to describe them as fluencies" (*stōmulmata*) which presumably are found by some to be disagreeable though Euripides here presumes they are acceptable. "Aeschylus", to judge from the challenge with which he concludes the weighing scene, would not agree. His spoken verse can outweigh not only the corporeal presence of Euripides and his family, but also his "papyri" (1409). Oral and literate styles are juxtaposed as adversaries, to the advantage of the former [57].

That it may be proper to draw this general conclusion (rather than restrict the reference to an eccentricity on Euripides' part) is indicated by two other things that are brought out in the course of the debate. Aeschylus concludes an extended critique and condemnation of his adversary (1006-1072) with a peroration (1078-1088) which identifies the immorality of his plots as the source of general social and civic corruption. The evidence is there to see (pointing to the audience), in the swarm of rascals, shysters and decadents. So far so good; the terms of abuse are the common coin of comedy. But heading the same company, acting as agents of the same demoralization, are numbered "the scribes" [58], another class that has infested the city [59].

[56] This supposition originates in Athenaeus (3A), where the author of the *Deipnosophists* is credited with a library surpassing the collections of previous famous book-collectors, ranging from Polycrates to Ptolemy Philadelphus. Euripides is included in the list.

[57] Cf. also Eupolis 304.

[58] In the 6th B.C. apparently a privileged profession, as could be expected when literacy was restricted; cf. Havelock, 'The Preliteracy of the Greeks', pp. 384-385.

[59] The vulgate reads *hupo grammateōn*. The scholiast explains that these were exempted from military service, which looks like a guess inferred from conditions in a later and literate epoch. Merry observes that "the reference is obscure", but that the noun may have meant "scribblers dabbling in philosophy", a suggestion which comes nearer the mark than those based on emendation (below). Demosthenes uses *grammateus* pejoratively (*De cor.* 269, *De fals. leg.* 371) and the verb *grammateuō* derisively (*De cor.* 261, 265). Lysias (*Or.* 30, c. 399 B.C.) describes a certain Nicomachus as appointed and paid (in 411 B.C.), and also re-appointed (in 403 B.C.), as a *nomothetēs*, to inscribe (*anagraphein*) the laws of Solon, and denounces him for amending and distorting them to suit his own purposes private and political. He made himself, says Lysias (27),

The chorus follow up this sally by inviting the protagonists to match wits with excerpts from their works [60]. Dramatically this will be a tour de force. Will the audience be bright enough to spot the quotes and parodies (1111)? Yes, things have changed (1112). Every member is equipped [61], holding a papyrus so that he can take in the poetic virtuosities [62] (1113-1114).

"into a *nomothetēs* instead of a *hupogrammateus*". At *Frogs* 1504-1514 Pluto sends Aeschylus on his way with a parting denunciation of certain contemporary characters among whom is a Nicomachus. This has encouraged editors to read at line 1084 *hupogrammateōn* as one word; and to interpret the noun pejoratively as "underclerks". But the sense of this noun in Lysias (27 and 28) and of the verb *hupogrammateuein* (29) appears to be professional and not pejorative, and to mean literally "underwriter", "subscriber" in the sense of an official charged with adding commentary or paraphrase to the existing texts. The verb is also used professionally, not pejoratively, by Demosthenes (*De fals. leg.* 70). Lysias in the same speech (*Or.* 30) refers to *suggraphai* "according to which sacrifices should be performed out of the *kurbeis* and *stēlai*". What these *suggraphai* were is disputed, but a possible meaning would refer to written versions prepared on papyri, which were "out of" the monuments, meaning they derived from but interpreted or amplified the oral sense of the archaic originals. Whether or not this suggestion is acceptable, the hesitancy of editors to accept the notion that "writers" as such could be regarded as a nuisance in Athens at this time is removed, once the reference is interpreted in the context of an uneasy transition from protoliteracy to literacy. The same uneasiness coloured the popular attitude towards the spreading use of written documents (cf. Havelock, *Preface to Plato*, p. 40 with nn. 14, 15).

[60] At 1104 the chorus announce "There is a supply of *eisbolai sophismatōn*" available on each side (of the contest). These are not "introductions" (Merry and Stanford) but "verbal thrusts" (the English 'sally' employs the same metaphor), as also at 956. The scholiast on 1208 uses the noun differently to indicate the "introduction" offered by a prologue; *ta dexia* are "verbal dexterities" (including *gnōmai*) on which a composer might pride himself: cf. *Clouds* 547-548. On the practice of anthologising, Havelock, *Preface to Plato* (n. 55 above).

[61] "Having served in war" (*estrateumenoi*) and so retaining the accoutrements previously acquired for service, these being humorously identified with the papyrus copies in their hands. Citations in *LSJ* s.v. do not however illustrate this interpretation. Does the participle mean "having fought a campaign of reading lessons", "served in schools of reading?". With the implication that such training was recent and arduous? Stanford interprets "veterans in literary criticism", as experienced in previous comedies. But what comedies would these be?

[62] Was this *biblion* a version of the whole play procurable by the time of a second production for which a whole antistrophe (1109-1118) was added or substituted? This seems very unlikely. Or was it a version of lines 1119-1363,

Commentators have labored over these references. They become immediately explicable on the theory that from two different points of view they reflect the effects of an infusion of literacy and literate habits into the Athenian body politic. Negatively, the change is creating a deep disturbance in the popular consciousness. Euripides is seized on as the cause when in fact he represents only the effect — an effect which Aristophanes accepts and is prepared to exploit. Both poets (1109) have to be reassured that a rather intricate competition of quotations will work, in the highly verbalized episode (1119-1247) which will follow. The availability of readers in the audience is recent.

In the opening scene of the play, Dionysus, explaining his motive for a journey to Hades, describes his longing to see Euripides. This had come upon him "when reading the Andromeda to myself" — the first indication of the existence of the solitary reader, divorced from any audience situation, in Greek literature [63].

Language uttered and remembered has no corporeal existence (unless as airwaves, of which the culture was unaware). Language written and read becomes an object, a thing, separated from the consciousness that creates it, and immobilized in a condition of physical survival. The metaphors applied to describe both styles mirror the notion that words are becoming material objects. The brews and notions perhaps seek to catch the quality of liquidity in spoken speech. But the bricks, frames, beams and boards suggest objects that are almost tangible, certainly visible. Archaic terminology had described human language synthetically, as song, speech, utterance, saying, talk. (Neither *epos* nor *logos* originally signified the separated word) [64]. In the Aristophanic critique one detects an increasing tendency to view

---

provided (at the poet's expense) for the original production? or was it an anthology (n. 60) of well known passages of drama which Aristophanes intends to exploit?

[63] Havelock, 'Preliteracy of the Greeks', p. 388.

[64] The *orthoepeia* of Protagoras need not mean more than "correct expression", i.e. pronunciation of words in combination. But Prodicus' study of synonyms indicates a conceptual isolation of the single "word" (for which the original equivalent was *onoma*; Heraclitus B23; Parmenides B8, 38; cf. Havelock, *Greek Concept*, p. 268). Rogers and Stanford render both *rhēma* and *epos* variously as "expression", "phrasing", "line", "verse", and also as "word" (799, 862, 924, 929, 1161, 1198, 1379, 1381, etc).

language as though it were broken up into bits and pieces of separate passages (1199), divided into lines (1239), measures (1162-1163), feet (1323), stanzas (1281). These can be weighed and tested like coins of varying but determinate values [65] (802, 1367 etc.). This kind of terminology, it is suggested, is being fostered by new habits of seeing language as a physical thing, a medium which for a majority of the population had in previous generations been only spoken and heard and listened to.

A Shift in the Greek Consciousness

The new vocabulary exhibits a growing intellectualism, another symptom of the same silent revolution. As speech written down becomes separated from him who has spoken it, so does the content of the statements made. These become objectified as thoughts, ideas, notions existing in their own right. Correspondingly, as separate entities, they seem to require a separate source, not a linguistic one associated with the speaker's tongue or mouth, but a mental one of a different order located in his consciousness. To produce them this consciousness is required to activate itself, by question, search, investigation, examination and the like. There are presumptions here which go beyond style and border on philosophy, or at least intellectual history. Aristophanes' critique perceives them as basic to the style of Euripides. His parodies caricature a whole register of cognitive language now invading the Greek tongue [66] (957-958, 978, 982 ff., 1422, 1430, 1454 ff.), a delayed result, it is suggested, of increasing

[65] The phrase *basanizein kata epos* (802; cf. also *epōn basanistria* 826) was introduced to describe the critical procedure reported as the one Euripides will adopt. At 1121 he promises the procedure himself, using *meros* as direct object of the verb. Both idioms signify a testing of physical parts one by one, rather than torturing a slave (but cf. 616). The weighing scene, ending with a challenge to pit *biblia* against two spoken lines, adroitly combines the notions of language as utterance, i.e., weightless, and as written, having corporeal weight.

[66] Stanford on *perinoein* (958) notes that this verb does not recur in what survives of literature of the 5th or 4th centuries; *kompsos* (967 al.) was coming into fashion at this time to describe an "intellectual", whether in literature or philosophy (cf. its use in Plato *passim*). Chantraine (cited by Stanford on 967) translates "bien soigné".

literacy. The traditional style had "kept men from thinking" [67] (962, 971).

Such symptoms of increasing linguistic sophistication are often attributed to the experiments of the sophists and the teaching of Socrates. It is true that the chorus, in their final commentary on the debate, blame abuses of language, to the detriment of tragedy, upon association with Socrates (1492). The question however remains whether the dialectical enterprise of the philosophers sprang like Athena newborn from the head of Zeus; or was it a response to an existing situation, created by an incipient but accelerating change in linguistic habits, brought on by the literate revolution?

Growth of Invention

Language aside, the plots themselves might in their structuration show some response to the new literate possibilities. Aeschylean plots are accused of being static and dull. He does not make enough dramatic use of his characters; his choral lyrics are prolonged and monotonous; he keeps his audience waiting; they know what to expect (919) and how to be patient. Euripides offers livelier dialogue; he inserts a contemporary, that is non-mythic, life style into his plots. He is pilloried as par excellence the inventor of twists and turns, the artist of surprises (even though this is what Dionysus and chorus often seem to prefer, 905-906). His monodies, which he has added as novelties, are selected for special satiric attention.

The Aristophanic critique does not suggest that this contrast between the expected and the unexpected is connected with the introduction of the written word. But the connection may be there. In our original hypothesis, it was argued that the word orally preserved was for mnemonic reasons required to be familiar, the written word being more hospitable to the unexpected and the invented. In Euripides it may be possible to perceive this latter effect at work; but only in an incipient stage [68]. He is not accused of tampering with

[67] On the sense of *phronein* see Havelock, *Preface to Plato*, pp. 212-213.

[68] A parallel effect is observable in Aristophanic comedy. Lesky p. 446 notes "the increased scope allowed to pure invention" in the *Ecclesiazusae* and *Plutus*.

the *mythoi* themselves (1052-1053). We are not at the stage of true fiction in literature, and will not be for several centuries. But it is permissible to speculate that the Euripidean conversations and lyric solos, so agile and topically diversified, are directed towards listeners who are growing used to reading, often in prose, what is no longer necessarily familiar, that is, traditional, and therefore old-fashioned.

Summing up: the testimony of Aristophanes can be interpreted to this effect. Overall, during the fifth century, a shift in the Greek consciousness was taking place, so far as Athens was representative of that consciousness. Possibly because the shift was focussed in Athens, her people were able to seize the philosophical leadership of antiquity. One might of course extend the beginning of the change as far back as the days of Solon and Pisistratus. It was a delayed reaction to the materialization of the Greek tongue at the turn of the seventh century. But it takes place in a condition of ambiguity. Euripides is still for practical purposes an "oral poet". Image and abstraction are locked in a relationship of tension. Contemporary Athenians do not know quite what to make of it all. Between the two competing styles, which are also states of minds, Dionysus cannot choose: "One is more intellectual, the other easier to understand". Which is which? Surely the Euripidean analysis is clearer. No, not to the orally conditioned mind, which grasps with immediacy the import of the Aeschylean similitude, concrete, dynamic, affective, acoustically memorizable. The modern reader, inheriting as he does the habits of a million years of acoustically preserved speech, still feels this is true.

Yet Aristophanes is composing at the end of the story, and he is aware that this is so, as he looks back to what he regards as the beginnings of tragedy, for him only seventy years earlier. It had grown, in function and style, out of a tension unique to its epoch between the word orally remembered and the word written down. The latter was now winning — had indeed won. Its Athenian users were "discarding music" [69], and the chorus condemns them for doing so. But in the same breath it sings the swan song of tragedy and perhaps of comedy also [70].

[69] On the social significance of "music" see Havelock, 'Preliteracy of the Greeks', p. 371.
[70] "In the world of literature the deaths of Euripides and Sophocles in the previous year may have seemed to mark the end of a great epoch. In fact only

4. *The Seven Against Thebes: A Tract For Its Times*

Inviting Aeschylus to reply to his rival, the chorus of the *Frogs* had hailed him as the original Hellenic master of tragedy (1004-1005). Challenged by Euripides to produce his credentials as the exponent and instructor of civic valour, he cites the production of the two earliest extant plays we have, the *Persians* (472) and the *Seven Against Thebes* (467). That is their supposed chronological order, as recorded in antiquity. But it is not the order of the Aeschylus who speaks in this play. He gives priority to the *Seven*, perhaps as the leading exemplar of drama in its didactic role, as viewed in retrospect sixty two years after its first production. Does the text of this play support any of those conclusions which we have elicited from the Aristophanic critique?

The text as we have it has been tampered with. There is no dispute that this begins at line 861. The extent of tampering after this point can be variously estimated. The drama celebrated in Aristophanes' text for its martial inspiration corresponds only to the untampered portion. This is true regardless of whether an original ending has been lost and replaced, or whether it may still survive as reconstructed from portions of the ending we have.

The Seven, Part One (it we may so style the first 860 lines) is a very static play, a dramatization of a single situation, that of a city under siege, and the urgent need to defend and preserve it. Civic morale, dependent on decisive leadership, is the paramount issue, dwelt upon in the prolongue and reiterated in the subsequent exchanges between protagonist, chorus and messenger. Fear of captivity and enslavement for the civilian population, particularly the women, is vividly expressed and as sternly repressed. Protection from the city's gods is passionately implored — their images are on stage — and their possible desertion of the city despairingly envisaged. Besiegers and defenders are reviewed in their martial panoply. Defiant challenge is met with counter-challenge. The protagonist arms himself and leaves for battle, foreseeing his own doom as he does so. But though he falls, the victory paean is raised. The city is saved.

one great masterpiece of the high classical period remained to be written — the *Frogs* of Aristophanes" — Stanford, *Introd.* p. XV.

Listening and watching, an Athenian audience would find it easy to respond to an action infused with so many Homeric memories: Troy under siege, its king and queen distraught, its wives and children under threat of enslavement and exile (cf. not only 78-180, but 321-368); Hector its doomed defender, but equally the doomed aggressor Achilles, victim of a premonitory oracle, "straightway after Hector is death ready and waiting for you" (cf. Eteocles 683-704). Chorus and actors together by their spoken words recreate the battle scene: the Homeric challenge, the warriors arming, the duels to the death. The attackers are even given Homeric titles: Achaeans (28, 324) and Argives (59 etc.). Only the latter fits the professed Theban situation.

But prevailing over recollection of the *Iliad* there is the contemporary civic reality. All the city states of Hellas knew what the threat of attack meant; they lived with it and had to cope with it, even as they were also schooled to attack in their turn. Thebans and Argives in this play are positive and negative of the same experienced history. The defenders are that hoplite citizen army (717) already celebrated and commended by Tyrtaeus' adaptations of Homeric verse. The instructions given by Eteocles are a paradigm of the duties required of any civic body in such a crisis. The panic of the chorus is at once a sympathetic evocation of what is likely to happen, and an object lesson in what is not to be allowed to happen.

Behind this general awareness of the facts of life as lived in the Greek city states there lurk some specific memories. A contemporary audience was aware of one catastrophe that had befallen less than a generation ago, and of another very recently and narrowly averted. In 494, Miletus, the largest and wealthiest city in Ionia, had fallen to the Persians. Her fate was a premonitory signal. Was it going to be Athens' turn next? The sack had been memorialized by the Athenian dramatist Phrynichus, twice recalled by Aristophanes as Aeschylus' predecessor (*Frogs* 910, 1298). His *Taking of Miletus* (*Milētou Halōsis*) had earned him a heavy fine and the banning of the play, so emotional was its effect on Athens: the mother city of Ionia had failed to save her daughter. Fourteen years later, the same foreign foe took Athens, heroically abandoned by almost the entire population, who were able to reoccupy the ruined acropolis only after risking all on the hazard of an encounter by sea. The message of the *Seven* is: Never again! The mythos of Thebes provides the clothing within which these concerns are disguised. They lurk close to the surface of the composition. The city whose gods are invoked for protection is described as one which is Greek-speaking and free, and must be preserved from slavery's yoke (72-75). The same gods are implored never to betray it to a foreign-speaking army (166-170). Language like this recalls the Persian threat, not a situation in which Greek meets Greek as in the Theban story. In the herald's announcement of victory (792-794) "Be of good cher . . . this our city has escaped slavery's yoke; the bombasts of monstrous men have been cast down" we hear the accents of triumph and relief after Salamis, and perhaps after Marathon too. The recipients of this announcement are addressed as "Children of mothers nursed and nurtured", on the face of it an otiose cliché, until we realike that the messenger in imagination is speaking to the non-combatant population segregated for the occasion in Salamis and the Argolid. In these expressions, scattered through the action of the play, a present and vivid consciousness temporarily breaks through the archaic framework of the myth. This is nowhere more evident than in the prologue, addressed to Cadmeian citizens who, given the dramatic conventions of the period, can be none other than the Athenian audience themselves.

The plot of the *Seven Against Thebes* is bifocal. The major theme is positive: a city successfully defended and saved, the besiegers vanquished. But success has its negative price. Attackers and defenders are led respectively by two brothers who in the event commit mutual fratricide. This denouement is represented as the inevitable effect of a previous tragic family history, starting with their paternal grandfather, and involving a curse (or several curses) placed upon them by their own father.

The necessity of the confrontation between them begins to emerge only at 631 ff. Both brothers betray an awareness of what the result is likely to be (616, 683 ff.). Up to this point only a single solitary hint of the existence of this family burden has been spoken, at line 70. The protagonist initially speaks in the role of a commander in confident charge of a Cadmeian city; and his messenger addresses him in the same terms (1-2, 39). His familiar identification "Oedipus child" is postponed till the chorus use it at 203, repeating it at 372 (with an ominous pun on the name) and 677. The child names his own father only at 654, at which point the theme of the fatal family history takes over; but even then not exclusively. As the protagonist leaves the stage to go to his death, the chorus break into a dirge commemorating the history and the fratricide now seen as inevitable. Even while doing so, they make it clear that whatever the fate of the family, the city's concerns have priority in their minds (758-771). News of its rescue when it arrives takes precedence (792-802). The messenger brings bad news as well; the fears however which he rekindles are still for the city; the fate of the brothers is something of a distraction. As it dawns on the chorus what has happened, their first cry is a brief hymn of triumph to the city's gods for protecting it (822-824). They then realize an emotional dilemma: shall they rejoice and cry Hurrah! at the city's salvation, or weep for its "polemarchs"? (825-832). The dead must have their obsequies (835-838), performed in a brief funeral dirge (840-860), in the course of which the two bodies are brought in and exposed on stage. The concluding farewell consigns both brothers to the darkness of Acheron's shore, a journey which awaits us all. Even while they sing, the chorus digress to confess that the city remains their chief concern (843).

Later tradition reported the *Seven* to be the last of three plays assumed to form a trilogy, the first two being named after the brothers' grandfather and father respectively. The fact predisposes modern interpreters to insist on a close relationship between the three, leading to the conclusion that the theme of the family curse inherited from the first two is intended to play a larger role in the third than in fact appears to be the case (that is, if the tampered text is left out of account). If the plot postpones treatment of the curse and its effects, this is viewed as designed to furnish the play's climax. This theory ignores the fact that the construction of classical drama, as opposed to its successors, is normally not climactic. From the way "Aeschylus" refers to the *Seven* in Aristophanes, we would not guess that the play formed part of a trilogy, or dealt with the house of Oedipus, just as a later mention in the *Frogs* (1124) of an "Oresteia" seems intended to refer to "a play about Orestes" meaning the *Choephoroi* (which alone is quoted), not the trilogy now known by that name, of which the *Choephoroi* forms a part in printed texts. If the Aristophanic critique is any guide, the Athenian audience of 405 B.C. may be judged to have been indifferent to trilogic composition.

The fratricide, then, forms an appendix, not a climax, to civic defence and rescue. But it is treated in a way which associates it directly with the city's welfare. The theme of military defence against a foe without is supplemented by the prospect of faction within, and the need to avert it. Attacker and defender are blood brothers. In this simple fact is symbolized the threat of civic stasis; both are members of the city and rivals for its leadership. It is a situation no less endemic to the Greek city states, and one experienced within the previous generation in connection with Persian threat of conquest. The threat is first exposed in a portion of the play (568-596) which even by the standards of oral storage is unusually and explicitly didactic. Conceivably it formed the center piece of the original text. Paragons of virtue are rare among the stage characters of Greek drama, and when Aeschylus presents Amphiaraus on the Argive side in such a guise, he has special intentions in mind. The utterance of this man (as reported by the messenger) first condemns the aggressive and militaristic *ethos* of the attacking army, which he blames on one Tydeus who has been the Argives' "teacher" (573). Then, turning on Polyneices, he charges him with the intention to lay waste his native city and its indigenous gods with a foreign army. "Take your native land with the sword, and it will never be your friend again" (585-586). This is not the kind of achievement to be celebrated orally and transmitted to posterity (581). Explicitly, the language condemns the act of treason, and is spoken by an authority who is labelled "a man sober, just, stalwart and pious" who "desires the reality of excellence, not its appearance" (592).

The treason is internecine, of brother against brother. Warning against civic *stasis* is a lesson which enters into the Greek gnomic tradition with Solon. Eteocles, commenting upon the messenger's report, voices a variant upon the same theme: this man of justice, alas! is forced to keep company with fellow citizens (*politai*, 605) of a different stripe and may suffer their fate. Such language once more recalling Solon translates the situation of Amphiaraus from a military to a civic context.

The mutual death that follows both averts the city's peril and redeems the protagonists; it is in the nature of an act of absolution. This is Aeschylus' way of recommending the healing of faction and restoration of civic harmony, a theme touched on later in the *Eu-menides*. Evidence for this interpretation lies in the linguistic treatment given the two rivals after their death. In life, Eteocles had condemned his brother in moral terms (664-667). But in death the two are spoken of as a pair of equivalents without moral distinction and given titles which implicitly incorporate them into the city now preserved by their passing. "The city is rescued but the earth has drunk the blood of its pair of kings" (820-821). "The city fares well, but its presidents, the pair of generals, have cast lots and divided their possessions" (815-816). "Shall I cry Hurrah! for the city . . . or bewail its polemarchs?" (825-828). "Here are twin sorrows (i.e. the bodies exposed for obsequies), twin deeds of valour" (849).

At the point where the protagonist realizes that his opponent is likely to be his own brother (653), the full force of his family history, as it will control future action, explodes upon the stage. He cries aloud "O god-maddened and by gods abhorred! O family of Oedipus and mine own, most lamentable!". The dramatic situation becomes paradoxical; in this fix he can protect the city only by being killed himself; the family history so requires. Even as he arms himself to repel the invader, following here the logic prescribed by all previous preparations, the chorus would now fain deter him. They quail before the perceived power of the demon of the family's destiny now approaching (687). He resolutely accepts destiny and leaves for battle. As he does so, they break into a long meditation upon the fatal history of the house of Laius (745) and Oedipus (752). It is this second stasimon that rivets the attention of the audience upon the family story. Sung in a mood darkened by fear and foreboding, it reflects uncertainty over the fate of a city which is embroiled with the fate of the two brothers who lay claim to it. The calamities of the house are like an angry sea threatening to overwhelm the ship of state and there is so thin a defence between (758-763): "My fear is that the city be vanquished in company with its kings" (759-765). These specific fears are followed by general reflections, once more recalling Solon's civic meditations: "Destructive effects (fortunately) pass by the needy. But prosperity waxing thick induces headlong jettisoning".

Once the chorus learns the city has been preserved, there is grief for the brothers, but no more fear; only joy at rescue.

In sum, while the drama includes a celebration of a family curse, its preoccupation is with the civic good. In the words of the Aristophanic critique, the drama becomes an admonitory lesson, a *nouthesia* or *parainesis*, directed to this end. The vehicle employed for this purpose is an archaic mythos, which in Homeric fashion enlarges contemporary concerns by placing them in a grandiose and heroic setting, making the message the more effective by distancing it from the present.

5. *The Language of Oral Instruction*

The "Euripides" of the *Frogs*, proposing the grounds on which a meaningful comparison of rival dramatic skills should be made, had spoken of the "sinews of tragedy". Leaving aside the mythos and its overall thematic structure, does the language of the *Seven* as it is welded together line by line reveal any modalities of oral composition operating within the composer's mind and responding to an oral relationship with his audience? We can begin where the audience began, with the prologue, an element in Aeschylean drama which Euripides selected for specific attack. "He has been difficult to understand in the exposition of what goes on" (*Frogs* 1122). This contrasts with Euripides' own method, previously described (945-946): "I didn't plunge in abruptly and mix things up. At the first entrance, at the very beginning I had a speaker state the substance of the drama to come".

The way the contrast is drawn is from Euripides' standpoint a just one. His plays start by providing information directly. In the Aeschylean style this is done indirectly. The fact that the information is required at all indicates the presence of certain needs on the part of the audience which were being modified when Euripides wrote. There were no theater programmes to consult (or perhaps, by the time of the *Frogs*, these have just appeared?). That the spoken prologue in some sense took their place has long been observed. But it was not just a programme. Accepting the assumption that the drama invited its audience to identify with the action, we can view the prologue as telling us where we are, who we are, what has happened or been done in the past, and what is going to happen or be done in the present in order to cope with the past. Euripides complains that the prologues of Aeschylus are not explicit. This is precisely true of the prologue to the *Seven* (1-77). It is divided between two speakers who introduce themselves as participants in the drama, and voice concerns which supply background information. Rendered directly and explicitly, the information takes the following form:

1   the locale is Thebes; the participants are the citizen body; the speaker is their ruler Eteocles (lines 1, 2 and 6)

2a   orders to be given must be appropriate (1)

2b   as befits any watchful guardian of the ship of state (2-3)

3a   if one succeds, credit goes to the gods (4)

3b   if mischance supervenes, the commander will become the object of dire lamentation (5-8)

4   which may Zeus forfend (8-9)

5a   all of military age are required to defend city, altars, children (10-16)

5b   and earth which has nurtured them to be reliable inhabitants and shield-bearers (16-20)

6a   so far heaven has been favorable (21)

6b   a siege is in progress so far with heaven's favor successfully resisted (22-23)

7   but an unerring soothsayer relying on hearing and sagacity gives intelligence (24-27)

8   that the Achaean enemy plans a major assault (28-29)

9a   so total mobilization is required to man walls and gates immediately (30-35)

9b   god will accomplish (things) favorably (35)

10   meanwhile visual intelligence has also arrived reliable and certain (36-41)

11a reporting that seven heroic enemy champions have sworn a blood oath to destroy Thebes (42-47)

11b or perish in the attempt, and have dedicated personal memorials to their descendants; they are pitiless, breathing fire like lions (48-53)

12a events are moving swiftly; they have just finished allotting gates to themselves (54-56)

12b which requires an immediate counter-assignment of (seven) picked defenders (57-58)

13   the Argive army is advancing en masse (59-61)

14a which requires the commander of the ship of state to take measures for immediate defence (62-64)

14b the first opportunity must be seized (65)

15a provision of visual intelligence from the field will continue (66-67)

15b accurate reporting will ensure effective measures for defence (68)

16a gods of Greece, earth and city (69)

16b and also the avenging spirit of a father's curse (70)

16c are implored to avert utter destruction of a Greek city and enslavement of its inhabitants (71-75)

17a this plea is made on common ground (76)

17b a prospering city honours gods (77).

In this rewritten version of the text, speech rhetorically framed, expressive of reactions and attitudes of engaged persons, has been rendered analytically, "its inflammation reduced", to use Euripides' phrase, in order to extract from it that body of information which the audience actually acquires while listening to it. To examine the contrast between the two versions is to uncover a basic difference between communication as orally composed and its literate counterpart. In the latter, information has been separated out from its context and turned into a series of "facts", impersonally stated. Put back into oral context, they become the component parts of addresses delivered by two living persons visibly present on stage. Since drama by definition is that particular art form which exploits human address, we have so far not learnt much except the obvious difference between the dramatic and the non-dramatic — until one observes that while the information in the play may be said to be aimed at "us" as audience, it is not, in the original, spoken to "us" at all, and the speakers are not motivated by any desire to inform "us". They are informing each other, or more properly, engaging with each other, since the exchange with the citizen body is one-sided. It would be possible to place a speaker at the head of the play who in effect spoke his piece, his prologue, to "us", framing it as a series of facts about the play, but presented in an aloof separation from the action. This in fact is the form of prologue which later gained preference with Euripides. The speakers in an Aeschylean prologue speak as characters already involved in the action directly they open their mouths, and consequently the information aimed at the audience is mixed up with the action, inherently woven into it. This is what the Euripides of the *Frogs* means by plunging in abruptly and confusedly. An explanatory statement is incorporated into a dramatic scene by which the information is conveyed indirectly and implicitly.

This dramatic method follows that law which had previously governed epic poetry whereby didactic content had to be incorporated into narrative contexts in order to render it memorizable. Statements of informational fact resemble statements of moral rules or habitual patterns in this, that so stated they lack any involvement in dynamic action or quick-moving event. The living oral memory prefers the panorama of act and event; it prefers the tale in whatever form, short or long, epic, lyric, dramatic. So even the initial informational programme of an Aeschylean play is cast in this form.

The Euripidean separation of the prologue marked a stage in dramatic development in which the rule of oral composition is weakening. It is difficult to see what could have caused this, other than a release from memory's demands created by increasing literacy. The plot-content of a play begins to take on the quality of words as they are read in separation from what is said and done. It becomes objectified and separated from the action of the play itself. From the Euripidean standpoint, the effect is to increase clarity and logic. From the Aeschylean and oral standpoint, it is to substitute a new fangled self-conscious and bookish drama in place of an instinctual and truly poetic one; it is a way of replacing a poetry of the organic consciousness by a prose of the intellect.

Elucidation of the difference can be pushed further by penetrating into the specifics of syntax. As reworded in item 1, the text is represented as telling us what the city *is* and who the participants *are*. But no such verbs of veridical statement are used. They are elicited from a dramatic vocative, the first two words of the play "Citizens of Cadmus!". The "facts" are there but only as celebrated in a dramatic posture. One more essential fact, the identity of the speaker, is postponed till it becomes a name incorporated into a short vivid narrative of an act of civic lamentation (3b). "All of military age" in (5a) adequately states the substance of the item in a conceptual summary. But the original Greek vividly and concretely describes three different 'ages of man', identified by verbs and adjectives expressive of what they possess or lack. A performative syntax is used to relay veridical fact.

The same syntax is required to clothe the expression of general sentiments which in one way or another serve to report, to recommend and to conserve the community's life style. This "wisdom" is an inherent component of Homer, and no less so of drama, betraying by its continuous presence in the plays their function of oral instruction. We recall how the two poets in the *Frogs*, facing the final competitive examination, were required to submit rival *gnōmai*, that is, maxims or aphoristic pronouncements. Though today we would not think of testing dramatic expertise in this way, the text of the *Seven*, as of any Greek play, demonstrates that the test was reasonable at the time, because applied to a rooted characteristic of Greek tragedy. If it has escaped some of the attention it deserves from critics, this is only because, obeying the oral law of narrativization, the "wisdom" is not only woven into the action, but is itself expressed as action.

As specimens of detached aphorisms, the prologue offers a few brief recognizably distinct clauses (9b, 14b, 17b). More important are the disguised forms, less recognizable for being attached to the specifics of what is happening. The first occurs in the first lines of the drama. Items 2a, 2b are actually spoken by the protagonist who says "To speak to the point is incumbent upon any man who keeps watch over state affairs, managing a city's rudder from the poop, refusing to allow his eyes to slumber".

The standing "literary" (and literate) view of such language is that it gives an initial indication of personal character. Eteocles is here posturing as a responsible but perhaps over-confident ruler, in contrast either to the frenzied chorus, or to his own later doomed and manic self. This latter possibility encourages the critic to look for "irony" on Aeschylus' part, using a term much in vogue in modern studies.

But a functional approach to the poetics of Greek tragedy would estimate that, after the manner of the Homeric encyclopaedia, a narrative (or in this case rhetorical) context is being used to incorporate a piece of the "wisdom" of the society, adjusted to be plausible in the mouth of the character concerned, but with direct reference to what the population of a city state would consider plausible generally.

Isolation gives the aphorism visibility, but more often it appears in disguise. Memorisable oral speech, favoring the specific over the general, instead of saying "Honesty *is* the best policy" prefers to phrase it as "an honest man is he who reaps profit". So far the aphorism is still perceptible in isolation. But the same oral tendency will prefer to carry specificity further: "If I do good to friends will it not profit me?". Here a given person is speaking, and what more suitable context is there in which to place such a person than that supplied by a Greek drama? Accordingly, the utterance of the protagonist continues as follows: "If success should crown our efforts, credit (will go) to the gods" (3a), a statement tied to the participants in the action, while at the same time expressing a general if rather cynical observation — what people in such circumstances are always ready to say. This is followed up with a remark applied specifically to the speaker's own person (3b), but again implying a general rule: that when things go wrong people look for the appropriate scapegoat.

The two varieties of aphorism, overt and latent, persist throughout the drama as a fundamental component of the text. They are among the factors responsible for that quality we feel to be "classical" in the antique sense. To be sure, the Shakespearean plays exploit the same resource and make considerable play with it. But there is a difference of degree which amounts to a difference in kind. Post-classical commentary on the human scene is just that, a commentary. It tends to case itself in epigrams rather than speak sayings; it is more self-consciously framed, less woven into the action.

Much of the prologue continues in this vein. Item 5a voices the standard duty of civic defence; 5b celebrates the debt to native soil which justifies 5a, with an echo of similar sentiments framed by Solon. 7 describes a particular soothsayer, but in formal terms which define the expected credentials of any soothsayer who is blind. 9a restates the civic duty of 5a, and 14a restates the commander's duty of 2b. 15b, though cast in a form promising personal safety to the protagonists, conceals a cliché describing correct military procedure. 16a and 16c, which in the original are voiced by the protagonist as he apostrophises the gods, dramatize a propriety of behavior in such circumstances; this is what any Greek would and should do. 17a is worded to combine the two senses of what the protagonist shares with the chorus and what is common custom shared by all.

The proportion of such generalities concealed as a deposit in the text does not lessen as the action proceeds. The drama becomes in part something geared to a specific time and place and circumstance, in part a kaleidoscopic mirror of the thousand facets of the life style of the culture. This renders inapplicable many of the canons of criticism derived from the kind of understanding supplied by a literate culture. For example, if Eteocles reprimanding the chorus indulges in anti-feminist sentiments (187-190, 195, 200), recalling similar expressions in Hesiod. it is a mistake to interpret these as a sudden revelation in depth of his own character. When in dispute with the chorus he exchanges clichés over the relative merits of divine help as opposed to self help (216-244), this is not a character conflict between pious believers and a committed agnostic, but an extended and poignant expression of the ambiguities of popular wisdom on this issue, and of popular attitudes in dealing with it.

Space forbids further extended review of this embedded material. It is·not too much to say that the text of any Greek classical play placed under similar scrutiny will yield similar results. Read from this perspective, and listened to, the language of Greek tragedy comes through as the language of a preliterate consciousness. To understand it we have to bridge a gulf between ourselves and the oral antique. Testimony that the gulf exists is unwittingly contributed by those textual critics who would amend originals where they can by excising aphorisms as well as repetitions as irrelevant to context.

The Aristophanic critique of Euripides had made much of unwanted stylistic innovation in his plays. In riposte, Aeschylus was charged with static rigidity and a kind of immobility of plot; the audience was always kept waiting for what they already knew enough to expect (*Frogs* 919-924). Our interpretation suggested that the stylistic difference reflects a difference between methods of oral and literate composition. The latter is more free to indulge in the fictional and the invented; the former eschews the unexpected, prefers the know and familiar, and tends to guide the memories of its audience by anticipation, prediction and responsive echo.

Support for this thesis emerges once more in the prologue to the *Seven*. Its business being to supply information, one asks: what sort of information in this? How much of it deals with facts antecedent to the action, which help to bring it about, supplying necessary background for the plot? Item 1 is unambiguous in this respect and is supplemented by items 6a and b, 7, 8, 10, 11a and b, 12a. These tell us that the city of Thebes, under the command of one Eteocles, whose father has cursed him, has successfully resisted a prolonged siege, but has just received intelligence that it is threatened by a last desperate assault led by seven champions. Against this background, the present action as it gets under way is indicated. The defences are to be suitably manned (items 5, 6, 9a, 12b, 14a, with a hint in 5b that the population to be defended is earth born). The enemy is advancing (13). Intelligence will continue to be provided (15a). Heaven's protection is solicited (4, 16a, 16c).

When however the character of this information (including some items so far omitted) is considered in relation to the future as well as present and past, it becomes evident that the purpose of a great deal of it is not merely to supply an existing framework within which the future will take place, but to prepare the audience to expect what the future will in fact be. The prologue is not only retrospective but predictive. Thus item 3 forecasts by indirection the complex denouement of the play. The city will be rescued with due credit given to the gods (3a); the protagonist will suffer disaster followed by lamentation (3b). Item 11a summarizes what will be more fully described by the messenger in the body of the play. 11b refers to what will actually happen to the champions, and its reference to their aggressive temper is expanded in later descriptions. 12b prescribes and so anticipates what in fact the protagonist will carry out. 15a warns us that much of the "action" will be cast in the form of messenger's reports. 16a and 16c provide a foretaste of the more frenzied appeals to heaven which will be voiced by the chorus. 16b throws out a brief hint of the future fatality of the family curse.

This phrasing of what is now happening to suggest or hint at what is likely to happen is a device by which lengthy oral communication can be grasped comprehensively when it is uttered and more easily recalled afterwards. The mind is led on by a series of statements which overlap each other. Part of the future is contained within the present, producing a sense of time characteristically oral, in which past, present and future interpenetrate and flow into each other, unseparated by formal divisions into fixed moments. The technique and the sense it creates is responsible for that strong impression placed upon the mind of the literate reader that the plots of Greek drama are conceived fatalistically, expressive of a peculiarly Greek belief in the power of overriding destiny. In fact the Greeks were not a fatalistic people to judge from their own dynamic history. It is possible to trace the cause of this impression to a technological necessity which required the use of forecast in oral composition to serve purposes which were mnemonic rather than ideological.

The same requirement operates to burden the verse with restatements of what has already been stated. The role of decisive leadership, brought into immediate prominence in items 2a, 2b, is revived with rewording in 14a, 14b. The muster of defenders first proposed in 5a, 5b is reiterated in 9a, as is the imperative need for divine assistance (3a, 4, 6a, 6b, 9b), culminating in the concluding apostrophe to named gods (16a). Intelligence of enemy plans and moves is provided twice (7, 10) and will be provided again (15a). These last three are cumulative rather than repetitive; two are linked by echo-pattern: the use of ears (7) is balanced by that of eyes (10).

All these should be viewed as responsions (rather than mere repetitions, for none are identical), guided by an economy of vocabulary which recalls the formulaic technique of epic and is uncharacteristic of literate composition. They function to drive home the salient "facts of the case", imprinting them upon the consciousness of the listener, to be retained in the memory with a degree of automatism. We perceive in them part of the reason for the static quality of Aeschylean drama (and indeed of all Greek drama). Thus programmed, it moves deliberately, even ponderously, but inevitably towards its prescribed end.

For the methodology is not confined to the prologue. It prolongs itself throughout the subsequent episodes, maintaining a kind of acoustic programming of echoes and responsions. Thus, though the *parodos* of the chorus, supervening immediately upon the prologue, is sung in a different key, fiercely emotional, at once an appeal, a protest and a cry of panic, yet thematically speaking it stays carefully within the boundaries of statement already expressed. The protagonist had warned against panic; they respond by voicing it. There have been warnings of impending assault; they give it lively and detailed description. Stress has been laid on the need to protect the city's inhabitants and its children; they respond in the role of the inhabitants themselves, appealing for protection. The help of Zeus and the city's gods has been invoked; they amplify and intensify the invocation, and extend it to include a catalogue of who these gods are (128-165). At the mid-point of their song they restate the arrangement of the 7 champions which is to govern the plot of the drama (124-126).

Once completed, the song prompts a responsive denunciation from the protagonist. His reproaches in part echo the things they have been saying and doing (185-186, 190-191), in part reproduce the warnings he himself had pronounced and which were pronounced to him (182-183, 196-198), but which now include an addition, the threat of stoning. These contrary attitudes are then repeated by being brought together in contrapuntal dialogue (203-259), ending in a kind of reciprocal reconciliation (260-287), leading into a choric lament

(288-368) which revives fears previously expressed at the prospect of the city's fall, but sung now in a lower key appropriate to the new mood achieved at the close of the previous dialogue.

The audience with the accents of the prologue still in their ears are waiting for the renewed optical intelligence previously promised (item 15a). It is accordingly produced (369 ff), with some repetitive emphasis, expanding on what the prologue had already indicated. An arithmetic count of seven warriors previously proposed is matched by a corresponding count of seven, also previously proposed, producing an arrangement of seven sequential pairs, along which expectation and memory are guided, accomodating the varieties of description within each pair. The list culminates in two matching brothers, whose conjunction automatically triggers the story of their family, related at length in the second stasimon, with premonition of mutual fratricide. The action briefly pauses, for the only time in the play, as the audience, suspended between hope and fear, waits again for promised intelligence. The news when it arrives offers matching correspondence to previous expectation. The city has escaped the fate described in the first stasimon; the brothers have succumbed to the fate predicted in the second. Such double tidings logically provoke double celebration: the victory paean first, and then the ritual lament.

Such are the sequences which as they are heard in performance attract the attention to move easily forward, and in retrospect to remember them in their order with a minimum of effort. Behind all the artistry of language, character and plot lies the persistent control imposed by the rules of the orally exercised memory.

6. *From Aeschylus to Euripides*

The hypothesis initially proposed has now been tested against a text, which under examination has revealed the presence of a didactic purpose carried out at two levels. The first of these is thematic, requiring the plot of the play overall to be so manipulated as to provide a disguise for contemporary social concerns and an indirect lesson in how to manage them. The second is aphoristic, a level at which the rhetoric and songs of all participants are linguistically contrived to contain copious fragments of the *ethos* and *nomos* of the society, its oral "wisdom". Such instruction, to be effective, must be given a continuing life in the oral memory. The basic linguistic tool to achieve this is the contrivance of a narrative situation expressed in the mythos or 'plot' of the play, and the use of a performative syntax applied to particular statements made in the course of the play. A supplementary tool is visible in the way the plot is forwarded, through the successive statements of the participants, by the free use of anticipation and prediction followed by repetitive echo and fulfillment of expectation.

These characteristics, regarded as fundamental to the original nature of Athenian tragedy, have been extracted from the text of the first eight hundred and seventy five lines (as numbered in the *OCT*) of the *Seven Against Thebes*. It is instructive to match them against the tampered conclusion of the play, covering the next two hundred and eighteen, representing an addition or substitution, partial or complete. The two are not in accord, as the following considerations indicate:

1. Three new characters are introduced (Antigone, Ismene and a Herald) without any previous warning or any reference to them, indirect or direct, casual or openly predictive. This would violate that law of oral composition, deduced from the previous text, which we may style the law of aroused expectation.

2. In the text of this sequel one misses an infusion of that kind of aphoristic wisdom, overt or concealed, hitherto characteristic of the composition. One can detect four examples, all confined to a concluding section introduced by the entrance of the herald, but this will not help any argument for oral authenticity, since this section has been rejected by general agreement. All four lack imagery and are rather prosaic and flat. Three (1011, slightly disguised, and 1044, 1051) are one-line epigrams which could be subtracted from the verse without loss. One may say there is a "Euripidean" ring to them (the third may be making a political point by substituting *demos* for *polis*), and this is equally true of the fourth (1070-1071) which reflects a consciously relativist moral philosophy.

The long antiphonal lament over the two brothers, shared (in the MS) by Antigone, Ismene and chorus (875-962), is a passage which scholars have been inclined to attribute to the original. A comparison with the preceding second stasimon, belonging to the authentic text, may point to a different conclusion. That stasimon, maintaining fidelity to the thematic complexity of the play, had hailed the city's victory before turning to celebrate the brothers' death, and had then as it were dismissed them both to the dark shores of Acheron (822-860). Why, one may ask, the necessity for a second celebration of them? Is it even appropriate after such a dismissal? And why one which disturbs the balance of the play by restoring their fate to center-stage? Possibly there is a stylistic problem as well. The original lament terminates in a *gnōmē*, disguised to be sure, but a genuine fragment of traditional wisdom: "the boat keeps crossing Acheron: it is a dismal mission: the obscure shore receives us all": the condensed imagery is characteristically Aeschylean and oral. There is not a trace of such reflection, or of such imagery, in the supplemental lament.

It is to be concluded that suspicion falls on the whole of this last part of the *Seven*. The grounds are not merely external (e.g. the apparent use of Sophocles' *Antigone*). There is the specific objection that its composition violates the canons of a genuinely oral style of composition as revealed in Part One. The original, we suggest, conforming to its main thematic intention, may have terminated on a note of celebration, somewhat after the manner of the *Eumenides*, saluting the city and its gods now rescued and secure. Simultaneously, the history of the House of Oedipus had ended with the mutual fratricide. That was the version adopted by Aeschylus and for all we know it might have been the original one. A correction was later supplied extending the family history, in which the influence of a literate period of composition can be seen at work. Manuscripts of the original had been in circulation, were read by actors and audiences, and amended to suit contemporary tastes. Family matters, rather than civic education, have become the business of the stage. The constraints imposed by a culture of purely oral communication have been lifted. Restatement of traditional material, and the devices of programmed anticipation and response, are no longer required for either didactic or mnemonic purposes. Remove them, and novelties of construction become possible, such as the sudden intrusion of the two sisters. The whole emphasis has shifted from tradition to entertainment. This was not done, we suggest, earlier than the fourth century.

The early date of the composition of the *Seven* gives it an advantage in our demonstration. Here if anywhere the original genius of preliterate or more correctly proto-literate tragic composition will be found at work. The *Seven* is possibly the simplest example of the type; Aeschylus' style is a developing one. He could be relied on to extend and elaborate the range of his composition — as conspicuously in the *Oresteia* — while retaining the underlying oral strategy we have elucidated. That strategy has been considered to the exclusion of any other arising from the use of writing. Yet let us not forget the complexity of our original hypothesis. It assumed that there existed in Greek drama from the beginning an initial tension between the ear which listened as the audience had to listen, and the eye whose architectural vision of language was private to the composer or mediated to him by an amanuensis. Our examination of the *Seven Against Thebes* has concentrated on the former while ignoring the latter, and is therefore incomplete. But of the two tasks, it has performed the more urgent one, since any critic who estimates the plays as works of literature written for literate audiences covers familiar and well-trodden ground. The tension is of course there, already in Aeschylus, and increasing in his successors, but its exploration lies beyond the limits of this paper. Briefly it can be indicated that the Sophoclean diction, for all its marked differences, is still infused with gnomic material which in Sophocles' reflective choruses sometimes takes over completely. The *Oedipus Tyrannus*, to take as example perhaps the most famous of all Greek plays, seems from one point of view to be a model of personally contrived art, tightly designed and controlled by its author's personal genius. Yet even as the protagonist speaks his mind in the prologue (as Eteocles, in the *Seven*) he also speaks the aphorisms of power and of statecraft. These are not his personal inventions. May it be true, as has been suggested, that just as the Athens of 480 B.C. lies behind the *Seven*, so does the Periclean administration lurk behind the image of Oedipus. The poet, in the words of Aeschylus, is still the voice of what is "useful" to the community. Nor does any other play of the Greek canon so relentlessly exploit the mnemonic apparatus of anticipation and prophecy followed by the fulfillment of previous expectation in emphatic and repeated sequences, reinforced by punning conjunctions. And yet also, competing against these factors of mnemonic control, one observes in the *Oedipus* the growth of architectural design, particularly in the placing of choruses between spaced intervals of dialogue, symptomatic, it is suggested, of the increasing intrusion of the reading eye upon the process of composition. As the century moves towards its close, the prologues of Euripides separate themselves bookishly from the action, the plot becomes objectified and in the later plays more fictional, exploiting surprise at the expense of prediction, while in the choruses, as if to compensate for the growing rationality of the dialogue, emotional and personal release encroaches upon social and traditional meditation. It is often said of Euripidean choruses that they are severed from the action and become dramatically non functional. Their role in either the *Hippolytus* or the *Bacchae*, to take two conspicuous examples, disproves this contention. In the modern sense of the dramatic, they become more functional, not less. What they progressively lose is their role as the carriers of the cultural tradition. The reenactment of the *ethos* of an oral community through words, melody and dance had been their original reason for existence, one which under conditions of increasing literacy they were bound to lose. But to the end tragedy never discarded the chorus, choosing instead to modify its content. Structurally, the chorus had once been the central component containing the core of the oral message. Even in its latest and altered condition, it remained as a reminder that the literate Athens of 400 B.C. was the child of protoliterate Athens of 500 B.C.

Such are the kinds of conclusions concerning the history and character of Greek drama whicht might be expected to gain support from a more extended examination of the extant plays. The present study has already exceeded its allotted space. Imperfect after its fashion, if it has succeeded in opening up a problem which others after me will feel prompted to pursue in depth, it will have performed its task.

Yale University

Bibliography

E.A. Havelock, *The Liberal Temper in Greek Politics*, New Haven-London 1957.
—, *Preface to Plato*, Oxford 1963.
—, 'The Preliteracy of the Greeks', *New Lit. Hist.* 8, 1976-1977, 369-391.
—, *The Greek Concept of Justice*, Cambridge Mass. 1978.
A. Lesky, *A History of Greek Literature*, London 1966.
Liddell-Scott-Jones (LSJ), *Greek-English Lexicon*, Oxford 1940.
W.W. Merry, *Aristophanes The Frogs*, Oxford 1905.
G. Norwood, *Greek Comedy*, London 1931.
A. Pickard-Cambridge, *The Dramatic Festivals of Athens*, Oxford 1968[2].
L. Radermacher, *Aristophanes' Frösche*, Wien 1954[2].
B.B. Rogers, *Aristophanes Frogs*, Cambridge Mass.-London 1950.
W.B. Sedgwick, 'The Frogs and the Audience', *Class. et Mediaev.* 9, 1947, 1-9.
W.B. Stanford, *Aeschylus in his Style*, Dublin 1942.
—, *Aristophanes: The Frogs*, London 1958.
P.T. Stevens, 'Euripides and the Athenians', *Journ. Hell. Stud.* 76, 1956, 87-94.

Aftermath
of the Alphabet

The Greek invention has worked its will upon the later cultures, although the effects were confined until very recently to Europe and to those parts of the world colonized by Europe, including America. If these can be seen to be revolutionary, this is possible only in retrospect. The course followed has not been a straight line. A kind of energy was released in human affairs which was not there before, a driving force which has operated upon many spheres of human activity besides communication itself, and which indeed has changed somewhat our habits of thought. But the impact has been registered at long range, with fitful application and erratic progress. The precise character of this cultural energy can be understood only when the original genius of the invention and the manner of its application in ancient Greece are more closely examined. But before returning to the eighth century before Christ, it may be profitable to cast a quick glance down the centuries from the inception of the alphabet to our own day, taking a survey which will help to place the invention in the perspective of later European history.

I have characterized it as a breakthrough at the qualitative level when compared with all previous attempts at script.

One would have thought that, if the original system possessed the atomic efficiency that has been claimed for it, if it provided a genuine table of elements of linguistic sound, exhaustive and precise, this should have been done once and for all. No need to repeat the invention. Why then, as the centuries of European history unfold, do we find that three main alphabetic systems have competed with each other: the original and modern Greek, the so-called Roman used by western Europe and by those areas of the world colonized by western Europe, and the Cyrillic used by Russia and other Slavic communities? The historian, replying to this objection, will point out that both Roman and Cyrillic derive directly from the Greek original. But this does not answer the question: why tamper with the original if it was so satisfactory? Why again does it come about that even the Roman alphabet when applied to some modern tongues has been supplemented by accents in some cases, by diacritical marks in others, or even by additional letters?

Why again have the descendants of the supposedly inferior North Semitic systems managed to hold their own in those Mediterranean lands where Arabic in one form or another is still spoken? Why, for that matter, was one of them, the Turkish, able to supplant the use of the Greek alphabet in Constantinople after the Turkish conquest, thus reversing history? Why is the Hebrew alphabet, a North Semitic derivative, now able to supplant the supposedly superior Roman in modern Israel?

Why again, after the fall of Rome, did it come about that the use of the Roman alphabet contracted to the point where the general population ceased to read and write so that a previous socialized literacy reverted to a condition of virtual craft literacy, once more reversing history? Is it not in fact true that the habit of identifying general literacy as the essential basis of civilized life, a habit which came to prevail in the period of the Roman Empire, re-established itself only in the nineteenth century?

And, finally, why today do professionals in the field of linguistics and phonetics require their own separate system of signs to indicate accurately the phonemes of a spoken tongue? Have I exaggerated the extent of the breakthrough achieved by the original Greek system? Was the invention theoretically such a foolproof system for identifying phonemes?

The law of residual ambiguity

To assert that it was is fair enough, given the historical context of the invention. That is the way the matter deserves to be put, if one is to define the distance that separates the Greek from all its predecessors. It represented indeed a quantitative jump. But the vicissitudes to which the invention has later been subjected during the course of its European history point to the fact that the system could not have been quite as foolproof as these claims for it would suggest. They have to be qualified, and the qualification usually takes the form of pointing out that the Greek system was invented to symbolize a given language, the ancient Greek, and was therefore limited by the phonetics of that particular language. Certain sound values required for other tongues were not available. But this answer does not expose the basic limitation. The Greek system itself, despite its atomization of the phonemes of the Greek tongue, provided in some cases a less than exact register of them. Some residual ambiguities remained. Some unavoidable choices were still required of the reader, though to be sure these were drastically limited compared with what had been true of all previous systems.

This could arise from two causes. To begin with, if the task of atomizing linguistic sound was to be carried out exhaustively, twenty-three letters were not quite enough, so that some double duty performance was still required. And again, there were undoubtedly idiosyncracies of pronunciation in ancient Greek, as in modern tongues, which eluded the standardized values attached to the signs. But more fundamentally, a single sign of an alphabet in *actual use* cannot be expected to represent a single phoneme on a one-to-one basis of correspondence. Linguistic science would like to formulate a sign system with agreed values which would automatically represent the phonemic structure of a given tongue. Ultimately, it could be said that this objective relies on a "Platonic" conception of language and also of the representation of language in script. No actual script can meet this formal requirement. Once this limitation on perfection is empirically even if reluctantly accepted, the question arises: Was it really necessary to invent new letters, as time went on, to represent the phonemes of languages other than Greek? Could this requirement not have been met by using combinations of existing Greek letters to symbolize a given phoneme? This would introduce some fresh ambiguities, but not at the cost of changing the sign system. In short, admitting that man lives in a linguistic tower of Babel, does he also have to live in a Babel of scripts?

It would be possible, using merely the twenty-five signs (counting in the breathing) of the ancient Athenian, or the twenty-three of the late Republican Roman, to construct a usable table of phonetic values for a Russian alphabet of thirty-six signs. The table would adequately convey a recognition of the linguistic noises of the Russian. All that is required is that the original atoms of the Greek system, that is, the letters, be arranged in groupings in which the corresponding sound values whether vocalic or consonantal are modified by combination to produce new values. Some ambiguities will remain. They can be supplied only by the memory of the spoken tongue, that is, of spoken Russian. But to revive this memory is all that any alphabet is expected to do, anyway.

The function of the original model was not to replace a prior knowledge of spoken speech but to trigger a recall of that knowledge. Its effective use depended upon the requirement that the oral vocabulary of the reader first be fluent and educated. The alphabet was and is an instrument of acoustic recognition, and only that. It happens to be the most efficient so far devised by man.

The Greek letters used in printing modern texts of ancient Greek represent the "East Ionic" version of the original system, standardized in Athens by decree in 403 B.C. Even assuming that this official act responded to a contemporary sense that the values of these Ionic letters represented the readiest equivalent of spoken Attic, the fact remains that exact equivalents in countless spellings of words had been sought without success for three previous centuries. Most conspicuously in the case of the vowels there was the problem of distinguishing the "quantity" or time length of the vibrating breath. The signs alpha and iota left this to the reader to decide, and in the case of iota lengthening actually produced a phonemically distinct sound, that is, a different vowel, for which there remained no separate letter. Similarly, epsilon, eta, and the diphthong epsilon iota failed to cover the varieties of the "e" sound that could arise in pronouncing the language. Consonantal ambiguities again could show up, for instance, in the application of zeta or theta or double sigma or double tau or combinations which included the aspirant chi, and when Athens by opting for the East Ionic transferred the sign for the aspirate to the value of eta (H), the aspirate symbol had to be reinvented by using a modification of eta shape. The inscriptional evidence from the time when the alphabet was introduced indicates that a continuing process of trial and error was going on over the Greek world. It is impossible to explain all varieties of spellings as due solely to dialectical differences. Those that are not should not be stigmatized necessarily as "mis-spellings," for this involves the assumption that the orthography of ancient Greece should be judged by the standards of Byzantium. Yet the Ionic-Athenian alphabet "worked," as also in its turn did the western version which became the Roman. Once this point is grasped, while recognizing at the same time that it could not have caught all the nuances of pronunciation of spoken Attic or any other Greek dialect, one becomes prepared to recognize that the same qualification should be applied to Roman or Cyrillic as they are employed to render the various tongues that use them. This handicap, if it is the best word, has remained endemic in the system in all its derived forms. We do not now know and presumably never will know precisely how Plato's dialogues were spelt when they were composed or even whether their orthography was standardized. All one may be sure of is that a reader of Plato in the first half of the fourth century was left with many acoustic choices. The orthography of printed Greek, in modern texts, reflects phonetic decisions adopted by the Alexandrian scholars of the Hellenistic age, supplemented by certain further conventions adopted in Byzantium one thousand years later. When we attempt to pronounce ancient Greek, having only these signs to guide us, and following the hypothesis that their values are rigidly fixed, with no supplemental help given to us by any memory of the living tongue, we (a) tend to overstandardize the original pronunciation and (*b*) do this by substituting phonemic variations which are characteristic of our own native tongue.

The fact that the invention could never be perfected as an instrument of recognition, that is, that it never did or could achieve in practice what it was designed to achieve theoretically, goes a long way to explain the checkered and uneven history of the alphabet, starting initially in ancient Greece itself. The initial shapes of the letters, modified from the Phoenician model, varied with local choice, which produced the so-called epichoric alphabets. Even the elementary problem of standardizing the orthography was left to be settled by the vagaries of political and cultural influence. The same accidents of usage, rather than any rational empiricism, decided what letters of the original Semitic system were to be discarded, and which new ones to be added. Aside from the choice of shapes, there was also some variation in the assignment of sound values to given shapes, with the result that, as the Greek world approached literacy, two main competing systems had emerged, labeled Eastern and Western by modern scholars. Final standardization for the Greek world was reached only in the fourth century, and it is of significance to note that the driving force behind it when it came was not orthographical logic promoted by a group of Unesco intellectuals but the political and cultural power of Athens. This it was that settled the matter. For in Athens both Eastern and Western systems had been competing until it was decided that the Eastern orthography corresponded more readily to the needs of Attic pronunciation. During the Hellenistic Age the prestige of the Attic, that is, of Athenian, writings, their sheer quantity and quality, insured that the Eastern system was to prevail without benefit of any further decree and regardless of dialect. It became the alphabet of all literate Greeks. The end result was that a choice technological in character imposed itself through influences political and cultural.

The Roman version

The Greek story is instructive, for it shows how an invention which was theoretically indifferent to any spoken language which it was required to serve, that is, which could be put at the service of any dialect, in fact pursued a career which entangled it in a given dialect of the spoken speech. Similar entanglement has been characteristic of its later European history and explains some of the vagaries of that history noted earlier. My insistence that the spoken tongue and the sign system used to represent it are theoretically independent of each other has to be qualified by what man in actual history has done with the invention and how he has handled it. Thus if the political and cultural primacy of Athens was to settle the orthography of all ancient Greek, we need not wonder that when the problem arose of applying the system to the Latin tongue the choice made was once more determined by similar historical accident. The Western version of the Greek alphabet had prevailed in Magna Graecia through the influence of colonizers who brought this Western system from their homelands. These Italian Greeks in turn had neighbors who were speakers of Italic tongues and experimented in using the Greek signs to represent their own speech. Whether the Latin speakers used the Etruscans as an intermediary, adopting an Etruscan version of the Greek system, is not entirely certain.[10] In any case it is a safe inference that these speakers were non-literate, in the same condition as the Greeks themselves had been before 700 B.C., and relying therefore on an oral and poetic tradition now lost. If they had had any pre-alphabetic system of writing, which is to say, a syllabic system, they would scarcely have accepted the Greek invention so readily when we consider the fact that the cultures of the Near East which used the North Semitic systems have resisted the influence of the Greek invention until modern times.

The assumption, conscious or otherwise, which is usually followed in explaining the use of the Western version of the Greek alphabet for Latin is that the choice was governed by the genius of the Latin language. The use of crossed x to signify the sound of "ex" in the Western and Latin versions, as opposed to the aspirate "chi" in Eastern Ionic, represented a mere accident of orthographical choice. Both Eastern and Western systems identified this sound value, but used two different signs for it. Latin could have used either indifferently. But in addition, the Western version can be viewed as supplying signs for certain phonemes not symbolized in the "East-Ionic" alphabet, and presumably not used in Attic Greek therefore. Reasoning on these lines one can argue that Latin phonetics required separate signs for values represented by the aspirate h, and by q as opposed to k, and found them available. On the other hand, the Western model supplied no sound for Latin f, which had to be borrowed by approximation from the digamma sign, a Greek survival. In this particular instance, Plutarch in a later age, transliterating Roman names into the East-Ionic Athenian, had less trouble with Latin f by using East-Ionic phi than the early Latins must have had when using the West Greek system.

The development of the Latin alphabet after its initial adaptation from the West Greek could be viewed as a process governed by a mixture of logic and accident. There was a time when a "k" sound was represented variously by k before a, q before u and o, and c before i and e. To achieve a less redundant notation by choosing c for this purpose can be viewed as the work of logic. But why in that case keep q

unless *qu* represented a single sound rather than a cluster? Zeta of the Greek system, originally present, was first dropped and then added again at the end of the letter-series as taught mnemonically, because of the cultural infusion of Greek words. A modification of the letter *c* was introduced as *g* to represent the original sound of gamma. The letter *y* came into the register as another late addition because of attention to Greek influence. Ambiguities between long and short vowels were met for a time by doubling the vowel, a conscious modification which did not last. However much phonetic logic there may have been in such changes, the point to be made is that both the choice of the original system to be copied and much of its subsequent modification were governed by what one might call "cultural politics" rather than by the mental processes of linguistic science.

As the same system has been attracted into the task of representing English phonetics, the *i* shape becomes split into two, to render the *j* sound separately. On the other hand, the letter *c* is restored to ambiguity by being asked to represent both soft and hard sounds, as also is the case with *g*, and the letter *w* is invented by Norman scribes to give separate visual identity to one of the values of *v*, a sound not unlike that of the ancient Greek digamma, which thus lost its separate signification for many centuries, only to have it restored. Phoneticians may object that the anomalies of English spelling are merely the result of sound-changes in the language which have not been kept up with in the spelling. But their presence is only an extreme illustration of the fact that flexibility of relationship between script and spoken tongue has been endemic in the history of the alphabet ever since the Greeks invented it.

A detailed history of these matters is not to our purpose. Our only objective is to bring out the element of arbitrariness and sheer accident in the choice of variations imposed upon the original Ionic system, which itself when standardized represented an arbitrary choice imposed not by phonetic logic but by politics in the general sense of that term. What I have so far stated to be true of the Greek, the Roman, or the English adaptations is equally true of the Cyrillic system or of the minor modifications that are employed in symbolizing the Scandinavian or some of the Slavic languages. All systems using the Greek principle must leave some residual approximation and therefore ambiguity. The original Greek invention achieved the essential task of analysis and it has not been improved upon.

But suppose the original Ionic system had been retained and used to transcribe the sounds of modern English. Could it not have been made to serve with no more residual ambiguity than the Romanized letters and values that are actually used? Take the sentence: "These are the English shoes which are worn out quickly by Christian scholars." In reading "these," "the," and "English," residual ambiguity requires the reader to supply three different vocalizations all represented by the letter e. The words "shoe" and "worn" require vocalics which do not resemble the conventional values of either o or e. Confronting the combination ch in the words "which" and "Christian" the reader is required to make disparate choices besides making allowance for a purely orthographical convention which supplies an unwanted letter c in front of k in "quickly." Attic Greek on the other hand lacked the sounds represented by sh and soft ch in our example, and the Ionic alphabet therefore did not use conventions to represent them. The same applied to the noises represented in our example by the Roman qu and by w. The Ionic system also lacked the letter y. But there is theoretically nothing to stop these being made up for another language by suitable combinations of Ionic letters already available. Thus one possible rendering of the sentence phonetically in Ionic would run as follows:

θιες ἀρ θε ἰγγλισχ σχυς υἰτσε ἀρ ὑορν αὐτ κυικλι βαι χριστιαν σχολαρς.

To be sure, this would require two phonetic interpretations of σχ, and the acceptance of the conventions that the combination ιτσε could represent a (non-Ionic) "breathed" consonant, and that upsilon could render consonantal *w* in certain positions. But the residual ambiguity would be less than is true of the transcription into (English) Romanized letters. If the learned reader protests that such a retention of the Ionic system would have been untrue to the etymological history of Anglo-Saxon, one must reply that etymologies are part of the history of sound, not of letters, even if, when examined by the literate scholar today, the letters take on the appearance of being a function of the language. The conventions of the script, to repeat, are theoretically one thing: the behavior of the spoken tongue is something else altogether.

The battle of the scripts

If the effect of this transliteration appears grotesque to the reader, this reminds us that not only do the users of a given language form as it were an addiction to it so that it requires an effort of education to accept the reality of any other ("Why don't these foreigners learn to speak English?") but also that this affection can transfer itself to the script in which the language happens to be read. Habits of orthography governing the mere shapes of written symbols can attract to themselves fierce loyalties and equally impose themselves as instruments of control over peoples. The identity of the visible script becomes fused with the identity of the spoken tongue and so with the national culture. This is a fact of life, however illogical it may be, as earlier I have pointed out. The hold exercised by the Chinese characters upon the mind and emotions of educated Chinese is only the most striking example of this tendency. The present writer still remembers addressing a seminar of Chinese nationals at Yale University in 1943 at a time when the necessities of war were pointing to a closer diplomatic and technical collaboration between China and America; and how cordiality in the audience changed to hostility when the suggestion was made that the writing of Chinese could profitably be placed on a phonetic basis and Romanized in the interest of more fluent written communication. It is reported today of modern Yugoslavia that the differences between the dominant Serbs and their Croatian compatriots are rendered all the more acute by competition between rival alphabets in which the Roman version used by the non-Serbs appears to be prevailing over the Cyrillic, thus aligning Yugoslavia with the West rather than with Russia. The result is often offensive to Serbian patriots and even Serbian intellectuals. The mental and moral gulf which separates Westernized peoples from the Chinese on the one hand and from the Arabic-speaking peoples on the other is reinforced by a feeling that the scripts of the non-Westernized nations have a value of their own linked with some traditional wisdom or esthetic sensibility. In the case of the Arabic nations this conviction is reinforced when the script is elaborated for calligraphic purposes as in patterns imposed on woven materials developed as a substitute for the graven image forbidden by Islam. Such manipulation of script as it embodies esthetic virtue can also be regarded from the standpoint of communication as a technological vice, becoming a divisive obstacle to readership and so defeating the theoretic objective of any script, namely, readiness and speed of recognition. It may indeed be true that loyalty to a given script, usually to be identified with national feeling of some kind, increases in direct proportion to the difficulty with which the script is read. This same fact may have some effect even within the restricted domain of scholarship. Thus the scripts descended from the Northwest Semitic shorthand syllabaries, ranging from Phoenician through Aramaic to Hebrew and Arabic, have limitations which have already been described. But this does not sometimes prevent Semitic scholars from advancing claims to their historical importance and present relevance which seem designed to disguise from view the unique character of the Greek invention by representing it as merely a minor improvement upon a previously achieved system already phonetically mature.

The modern state of Israel has been set upon a course which would revive the use of square Hebrew, thus providing an instructive instance of the way in which script "follows the flag." But there would appear to be no doubt that if the continuing identity of Judaism as a nationality rather than as a religion is thought to depend upon an artificial revival of the Hebrew language, then this revival in turn will be greatly assisted in catching on if it is wedded to the use of the antique script, thus placing not a single but a double barrier of language and of calligraphy between Israel and the rest of the world. One may contrast the indifferent success which the revival of Erse has met with in Ireland, noting that the revival is attempted in a script which gives no unique reinforcement to the tongue, for it is shared by all Europe and particularly by the hated English, as would be inevitable considering that historically speaking the original craft literacy enjoyed by Ireland was founded upon the Romanized alphabet.

Calligraphic virtuosity of any kind fosters craft literacy and is fostered by it, but is the enemy of social literacy. The unlucky careers of both the Greek and Roman versions of the alphabet during the Dark Ages and the Middle Ages sufficiently demonstrates this fact. Styles of writing the letters multiplied, their shapes became elaborated and disguised, by the activities of different scribal schools centering on competing capitals of learning. This fractionating of the alphabet would not have occurred on such a scale but for the collapse of social literacy in the West upon the fall of Rome. The so-called Roman Rustic or popular style of writing, gaining ascendancy from the second to the fifth centuries of our era, as a response to literate needs and practices, then vanishes from the scene. Europe, in effect, reverts for a time to a condition of readership analogous to that which obtained in the pre-Greek Mesopotamian cultures. Scripts become hieratic and also political in the sense that kings and emperors seek to consolidate their power over the bureaucracies which serve them as instruments of government by insisting upon the usage of a given style of script. When we speak of the "King's writ running" over a given area, the idiom testifies to the alliance between script and political power.

Such conditions, from the standpoint of European culture, were anarchic. It was not merely a matter of the divisions created by the dialects which replaced Latin. The scripts themselves in their refined diversity made socialized literacy impossible. In this context, the Carolingian empire can be viewed as coming to Europe's rescue, establishing through political power a cultural dominance which in turn could foster the idea of a "European" script. To be sure, progress was erratic, and Renaissance scholars in a sense had to rediscover the idea and implement it, but tendencies thus set in motion were in the long run to bring back to Europe the blessings of a single cursive hand; illustrating once more the relationship existing between politics and the alphabet, a relationship which was first demonstrated in the case of antique Athens.

Literate culture in the classical age

To look back beyond Medieval Europe to the literate urbanity of classical civilization is to realize that the Greeks and Romans, though committed to competing versions of the original invention, handled the scripts as literate peoples would handle them. That is to say, given the fact that they served as instruments of two competing languages, they were made also to serve as vehicles of cross-translation to create a community of readership in both tongues, and one might say almost a joint bilingual literature. Allowing fully for the obvious differences between the geniuses of the Greek and the Latin writers of poetry and prose, it remains true that if we identify them today by the common title "classical" this usage reflects a reality of cultural history. This community of taste, theme, and outlook was made possible by partnership in that shared instrument of readership, the alphabet, Eastern and Western. It was not just that Rome, the inheritor, used Greek models, significant as that may be. Plutarch in turn, as a Greek writer, was able to Hellenize Romans, as had Polybius, living among Latin speakers, and as Lucian. If Lucretius could Latinize the Epicurean documents that he read, Marcus Aurelius could Hellenize the Roman experience of Stoicism. Roman and Greek, to repeat, shared a common readership. The scope and variety of their readership was originally made possible by the phonetic perfection of the Greek invention. The Romanized version of the system added a set of sounds and sound values theoretically unnecessary and therefore complicating, but the joint phonetic superiority exercised by the two was an adequate foundation upon which to build a classical literacy. Once Greek and Latin, two separate tongues, were both successfully alphabetized, fluent and accurate reading of one by the other became automatically possible.

This form of literate communication was not open to any of the pre-Greek civilizations. There was no joint or shared readership between overlapping cultures, the Semitic, Egyptian, Anatolian, or Mesopotamian. The calligraphic instruments available and in use in all tongues were too limited in efficiency. Correspondingly, neither Greek nor Roman literature owes very much to the Levant, despite the current attempts to demonstrate that they did. The task of decipherment, common to all the syllabic scripts, placed a barrier too high to be climbed.

Latin literature is unique among world literatures in the depth of its debt to a foreign tongue, carried even to the extent of borrowing the formal rules of prosody. The reason is surely to be sought in the fact that the Greek tongue was the first to be alphabetized and the Latin was the second. The Greek books that had come into existence were the first books which recorded the full literate experience possible to the human mind. No wonder that the Romans, as they read them, fell under their spell. After all, they were finding themselves as, so to speak, "present at the creation." If therefore they created what in a sense is a library literature, the first of its kind, this is understandable. The Greek works of the archaic and high classical periods which they most admired were very different and far closer to the genius of oral composition. But they had been alphabetized. That was enough for Virgil to compose a whole epic written out of a library shelf of Greek manuscripts, and to make it a work of art.

Readership before the printing press

There were limits set to classical literacy by the character of the materials and the methods employed to manufacture the written word. The alphabet did not fully come into its own until Western Europe had learned to copy the letter shapes in movable types and until progress in industrial technique made possible the manufacture of cheap paper. So-called book production in antiquity and the various styles of writing employed have received substantial scholarly attention, the results of which need not be recapitulated here except as they throw light on the material difficulties which any extension of popular literacy was bound to encounter. For literacy is not built upon a fund of inscriptions. In Greece, where stone and baked clay initially provide our earliest testimony to the use of the alphabet, what we would like to know more about is the availability of those perishable surfaces which could perform the casual and copious services now supplied by the paper which we moderns so thoughtlessly consume and throw away. Herodotus reports that the earliest material of this nature in use was parchment, that is, animal skins, obviously a very limited resource, quantitatively speaking, though qualitatively superior as later antiquity was to realize. The other basic surface was that of the papyrus sheet available in Egypt. How soon did Greece import papyrus in quantity? The texts of Homer, so we were told by late tradition, received a recension of some sort in the period when Pisistratus ruled Athens about the middle of the sixth century. In what form were these texts available? Were they inscribed on papyrus? Certainly the first half of the fifth century saw the increasing use of papyrus in Athens, and also of the waxed tablet for making notes on. References in the plays of Aeschylus make this certain. But it is possible to deduce that the references are there because the use of such items was novel rather than familiar. The words "biblos" or "byblos" are translatable as either "papyrus" the material, or as the object consisting of papyrus on which writing is placed. The common translation "book" is misleading. Individual sheets of papyrus, as is well known, could be gummed together at the edges in series, thus forming a continuously extended surface which could be rolled up. To find the place you had to unroll until you came to it. "Biblion," the diminutive, meant neither book nor roll but a simple folded sheet or conceivably two or three such, folded once over together. Such details as these, coupled with the certain scarcity of material when judged by modern standards, serve to remind us that the would-be reader in ancient Athens encountered certain obstacles to his reading which we would regard as constricting. In estimating the degree of literacy and the rate of its spread, how far should such material limitations be taken into account? Should they not make us more cautious in this matter than Hellenists usually are? To give just one example: Plato in his *Apology* makes Socrates refer to the *biblia* of Anaxagoras the philosopher, "purchasable for a drachma at most," which he says "are chockfull" (*gemei*) of such statements (*logoi*) as the prosecution has referred to. Are these books? Of course not. The reference is to those summary pronouncements of the philosopher's doctrine which still survive in quotation from later antiquity and which we now call the "fragments" of the philosopher. They are compressed in style and even oracular and, we suggest, were published as a guide to the philosopher's system to be used as a supplement to oral teaching. Such summaries could be inscribed in installments upon separate sheets of papyrus purchasable for a drachma per sheet. But a good deal has been made of this reference in describing the supposed Athenian book trade of the period and also in affirming a sophisticated literacy which is presupposed by the misleading translation "book."

This is not to discount the degree of literacy achieved in Athens in the last third of the fifth century before Christ but to emphasize that however general the management of the alphabet became, the habit of rapid reading which we are accustomed to identify as the hallmark of a verbally competent person would be very difficult to implement. There was no large volume of documentation to practice on. If Plato's Academy in the fourth century B.C. had a library, how many shelves were filled? The very term "library" is almost a mistranslation, considering the modern connotation, as when we are told that Euripides possessed the first library. This tradition appears to base itself upon an inference drawn from a piece of burlesque concocted by Aristophanes in his play *The Frogs* at the poet's expense. Euripides and his poetry, in a contest with Aeschylus in Hades, have to be "weighed," so he is told to get into the scale pan, after "picking up his papyri," indicating that the poet could be expected to carry a parcel with him. He is satirized as a composer who had turned himself into a reader and who made poetry out of what he had read, in supposed contrast to his antagonist who is orally oriented.

On what materials did Athenian children in elementary school learn their letters? Probably sand and slate, rather than papyrus, both being media quantitatively copious, since they admit of continual reuse through erasure. A "school scene" which predates the age of social literacy in Athens portrays an older man using a waxed tablet. Such waxed tablets but not paper are actually featured in the plots of a few plays of Euripides produced in the last third of the century when the delivery of a message or letter is called for. Aeschylus is aware only of their use for memoranda. In either case the material used would favor brevity of composition. It also could of course be reused, which again implies continual erasure of the written word. Documents can be flourished in a comedy of Aristophanes to back up an oral statement with the implication that only shysters would use this resource; the written word is still under some suspicion or is a little ridiculous. All in all, one concludes that the reading of the literate Athenian was confined within limits that we would think narrow, but what he did read he read deliberately and carefully. Speed of recognition, the secret of the alphabetic invention, was still likely to be slow relative to modern practice, and this likelihood bears on the acknowledged attention which writers and readers of the high classical period gave to words and their weighing. Inscribed language was not being manufactured at a rate great enough to dull the attention or impair verbal taste. The written word carried the value of a commodity in limited supply. The literature of the period bears the hallmark of a verbal nicety never excelled and rarely if ever equalled in European practice.

As a corollary to this verbal sophistication (which was reinforced by residual habits of oral composition), the writers of the classical period consulted each other's works and wrote what they had to say out of what others had written before them to a degree difficult for a modern author to appreciate. The world of literature, because quantitatively so restricted, could constitute itself a sort of large club, the members of which were familiar with each other's words even though separated by spans of historic time. A good deal of what was written therefore called upon the reader to recognize echoes from other works in circulation. If the modern scholar thinks he is able to trace influences and interconnections which seem excessive by modern standards of free composition, he is not necessarily deluding himself. The world of the alphabet in antiquity was like that.

Books and documentation multiplied in the Hellenistic and Roman periods. Papyrological discoveries indicate that papyrus was in ready supply in Hellenistic Egypt, where indeed one would expect to find it. But up to the end of antiquity and beyond that through the medieval centuries, extending through the invention of the codex or book proper, so much easier to handle and consult, the distinction between our modern paper literacy, if I may call it, and the literacy of our ancestors still holds. It is a distinction determined in part by the sheer quantitative limitations placed in antiquity upon the materials available for inscription. The use of the palimpsest — the document hoarded and then erased and reused, sometimes twice over — is eloquent testimony to the scarcity and the preciousness of the material surfaces upon which alphabetic script could be written.

But scarcity of materials aside, the production of script and hence the resources available for readership were bound to remain restricted beyond the imagination of any modern reader as long as such production remained a handicraft. This set a second quantitative limitation upon the creation of all documentation, whether for literary or business purposes, as is obvious. A decree or law could not be promulgated in a newspaper; copies of accounts could not be distributed to shareholders; an author could not commit his manuscript to a publisher for mass manufacture and sale.

But the qualitative restrictions thus imposed were if anything more drastic. Strict uniformity of letter shapes was rendered impossible by the vagaries of personal handwriting. A degree of standardization was theoretically possible and certainly aimed at in the Graeco-Roman period. It quickly broke up thereafter. A handicraft may and does produce a custom-made product of fine quality, and in the case of those artifacts that we use and consume in daily living such competitive excellence becomes esteemed and valuable. But the production of custom-built products on the same lines when the goal is the manufacture of communication becomes self-defeating. To the extent that the scribes formed schools or guilds, formal or otherwise, to foster the elaboration of local hands and embellish competing styles of writing, readership of that sort which alone furnishes the basis of a literate culture was bound to be impaired. Calligraphy, as already noted above, becomes the enemy of literacy and hence also of literature and of science.

Alphabetic literacy, in order to overcome these limitations of method and so achieve its full potential, had to await the invention of the printing press. The original achievement, the Greek one, had solved an empirical problem by applying abstract analysis. But the material means for maximizing the result required the assistance of further inventions and had to await a long time for it. Such necessary combination of technologies is characteristic of scientific advance. To realize that there is energy available when water is converted into steam was one thing. To harness the energy successfully was another, requiring the parallel construction of machine tools capable of producing fine tolerances to fit piston to cylinder, the manufacture of lubricants capable of sealing the fit, the parallel invention of slide-rod mechanisms to control the periods of steam pressure, and of crank and connecting rod to convert the thrust into rotation. The energy of the alphabet likewise had to await the assistance provided by the dawning age of scientific advance in Europe in order to be fully released.

Politics and the alphabet
The difficulties to be overcome were not confined to the technological front. Great hazards confronted the alphabet

in the era of politics. I have described the initial split between the Greek Eastern and Western systems resulting in
the adoption of two versions, the Athenian and the Roman.
This situation, itself determined by political arrangements
rather than technological logic, was to perpetuate itself in
the centuries after Constantine as the alphabets of the Western and Eastern Empires competed with each other. The
division of course rested, or seemed to rest, on the existence
of two competing languages. It is of some significance that
attempts were made by calligraphers to construct a joint
alphabet suitable for both. Nothing theoretically stood in the
way of this. But the facts of political rivalry and schismatic
cleavage within Christendom rendered it abortive. In place
of the original, classical, bilingual literacy of a Plautus, a
Cicero, or a Plutarch, there emerged within the European
cultural complex two self-contained worlds of readers, one
Latin and one Greek, leading to a situation in which by the
eleventh century even the use of the Latin tongue and alphabet was proscribed on Byzantine coinage.

Meanwhile the activities of Greek Christian missionaries
to the Slavs on the northern borders of the Byzantine Kingdom had resulted in the unfortunate decision to invent a
third variety of the Greek system for the Slavic tongue and so
for the Slavic church. The Cyrillic alphabet that thus came
into existence in due course became the liturgical alphabet
of the Russian people, first of the educated classes and now,
in the twentieth century, of the populace at large. It was a
disastrous accident of misplaced ingenuity which, reverting
to the methods of pre-Greek syllabic empiricism, thought it
necessary to identify non-familiar sounds in the barbarian
tongue, that is, the non-Greek tongue, by inventing new
signs for them, rather than using fresh combinations of the
Greek signs which were already available. The political and

spiritual gulf between Western and Eastern Christendom widened. Byzantium was left to fend for herself against the Turks and when she fell her alphabet fell with her. The Arabic script of the invaders which supplanted it brought about a reversion to the inefficient syllabic shorthand, thus ushering in a new age of craft literacy, a severance between rulers and ruled, a revival of bureaucratic despotism and of religious monopoly of authority, while among the vulgar, habits of purely oral communication and preservation were re-established. It remained for Kemal Ataturk in the twentieth century to reverse this historical regression and restore Byzantium to the alphabet, this time the Roman version. His intention was to make Anatolia literate and he perceived that only alphabetization would do it. It is to be observed that he could do this only after the previous establishment which had used the Arabic system had been politically discredited.

The Greek system continued in use in that place where it had been born, namely, in Greece. It is scarcely to be doubted that, reversing the usual logic of phonetics, the stubborn survival of this readable script has in turn protected the Greek tongue and the Greek sense of nationality under centuries of Turkish rule, as is true also of the Slavs under Turkish rule who have retained the use of the Cyrillic.

In the Western Empire also political changes occurred which set back the clock of literacy, though the pattern of disturbance was different. After the fall of Rome, the Latin tongue upon the lips of the peoples of the Empire became gradually bowdlerized and broke up to form the Romance languages of modern Europe. In Britain and Germany the native speech, allowing for the retention of some common Latin words, displaced Latin altogether. While these vernaculars became the tongues of the common people, Latin remained the international language of the educated, which meant to a major extent the officialdom of the Church. For this Latin the use of the alphabet was reserved. Rulers and their bureaucracies and their intelligentsias, whether clerical or lay, conducted correspondence, drafted legislation, and composed prose and poetry in the Latin alphabet, as imperial Rome had done. But the tongue employed in this way separated itself from the usage of the common people to the point where any member of the governing class reserved his vernacular, whatever it was, for oral use only. He had a second language as his literary language and devoted to this alone the prestige of inscription. Europe therefore, during the formative period of the Romance languages, reverted to craft literacy, and the professional separation between the craft-elite and the commonality attained a dimension it had never had in those Mediterranean bureaucracies that preceded the Greek. The scribe who had managed the syllabary at least was using it to symbolize the common tongue except in those few cases where a scribal regime was used as the instrument of rule over an alien people.

During the period in which the alphabet remained imprisoned in this way, the intellectual energies of Europe remained dormant. The written word was used to repeat familiar themes and ideas by way of affirmation, refutation, or explication rather than to invent novel statement. The awakening occurred well before the Renaissance when at last the alphabet was restored to the service of the vernaculars, so that vernacular statements, poetic or prosaic, were allowed the status of the preservable. For this step forward Europe owes a large debt to the Normans. In Italy the *Divine Comedy* heralded the replacement, gradual but inevitable, of Latin literacy by vernacular literacy, as did Chaucer for England. Once more, as long ago in ancient

Athens and Rome, a European person would at last start to be a habitual reader of his own tongue.

The bygone usage of Latin as an international language has been esteemed by historians and scholars and its passing has been regretted. This is proper enough provided one takes account of the price paid when "letters" on the one hand and "learning" on the other were allowed to form a closed alliance. In England, neither the Tudor grammar school nor the King James version of the Bible would have been conceivable until this alliance was broken. It is no accident that the most literate of our poets, the master of the written English tongue, knew little Latin and less Greek and retained the habit of spelling words with that phonetic freedom characteristic of North American college students.

The folios of Shakespeare's plays like the King James version of the Bible were printed books, not manuscripts, reminding us that the technology of movable types, initiated two hundred years earlier, had been able to supplant two thousand years of handicraft, giving to alphabetized speech a new dimension both quantitative, in the sense that the written word was now duplicatable with speed, but also qualitative in that the letters at last could escape the bondage of scribal style and whim and could become standardized and legible as never before. The theoretical objective of the original Greek invention, namely, that the letter shapes would be such in their relationship to sound that they could sink into the unconscious and cease to be objects of knowledge, would at last be achieved. Though early typography continued for a while to employ calligraphy, the two were natural enemies. The Venetian printer and publisher Aldus Manutius (1450-1525) put posterity in his debt when he printed his books with classical capitals and Carolingian minuscule. A serviceable humanist script had to be one easily written and easily identified. This objective was achieved in Italy by the middle of the fifteenth century. The age of modernity, of modern literature, of modern thought and modern science, was at hand, leading to the knowledge explosion of our own day.

Arithmetical "literacy" and musical "literacy"
The modern scientific era, commonly dated from Newton, did not depend for its coming of age uniquely upon the advantages of the printed page, important as these were for the compilation and distribution of theoretic reasoning and empirical information. It relied also upon a revolution in the symbolization of quantitative measurement. A brief digression is in order to note that an effective system of notation for recording linguistic sound required to be married to a partner before the two in combination could lay the foundations of mature scientific discourse. The partner proved to be a system of notation effective for recording numerical as opposed to verbal relations.

It appears that the Babylonians had preceded the Greeks in achieving arithmetic computation and hence a fairly accurate measurement of the heavenly motions. The notation used included the sign for zero, perhaps as early as the time when the Greeks invented their alphabet. (I do not mean to suggest that there was any connection between these two inventions.) They had also invented positional values for numerals and organized them within a system which combined decimal and sexagesimal bases. What they failed to do with numbers was to reduce and simplify the required number of signs and so arrange a convention which, by simple combination, could produce a value for any number whatever,[11] just as a combination of alphabetic signs could produce a value for any linguistic sound whatever. In short, they failed to do for the act of counting what the Greeks did do for the act of speaking. The Babylonian system worked but with the same slowness and ambiguity of interpretation which was characteristic of the syllabic systems of writing that preceded the alphabet.

The Greeks contributed nothing to the solution of this problem. Compared with the Babylonians their arithmetic, unlike their geometry, was regressive. The numerals that we now use are due to Hindu-Arabic invention and were introduced into Europe perhaps in the twelfth century. They have supplanted all previous number systems just as the Greek alphabet supplanted all previous writing systems. The invention consists of an agreement to use only ten symbols, which used singly indicate the integers from zero to nine. To achieve any other number, two or more of these are placed in a visible row and the eye is then required to read backwards — the reverse of usual alphabetic usage — in order to assign to the individual figures ascending values in multiples of ten, these being governed by the relative distance of any figure from the end figure in the line. Positional value, in short, an abstract conception, rather than empirical imitation, symbolizing given quantities on a one-for-one basis, provided the secret of modern enumeration which allows all numbers to be related quickly to each other by addition, subtraction, multiplication, and division because the rule of position holds the same for all of them.

The system, considered as an invention which converts the invisible into the visible using an atomic system of ten elements, represents an intellectual achievement comparable to that of the alphabet. And once again the symbols are so reduced in number that they can be taught by rote to children. The recognition of a number can become as swift and automatic as the recognition of a sentence, in fact, it may be easier for a child to recognize a number than to recognize a sentence. Arithmetic like reading could now be democratized.

The age of Newton, as previously noted, is usually identified as marking the initiation of modern science. This event, I suggest, owed a joint debt to the technology of the Hindu-Arabic system of numerals and to the technology of the Greek alphabet, both being multiplied in their effects by the printing press. It is true that the numerical invention appeared three hundred years before the printing press. Its effects therefore took longer to register. Yet if either invention were to be subtracted from our story, it is difficult to see how modern science could have arisen. There are psychological laws which are in parallel, perceived to be at work in both instances. The dependence of science, Greek or modern, on the usage of the Greek alphabet lay in the area of scientific conceptuality, if I may use the word, in the rationale of classification embodied in scientific terminology. But when it comes to counting, the alphabet as a recorder of speech can properly speaking record only the names that men use to identify separate numbers. (The use of individual letters to indicate numbers in a series which happens to be that of an abcedarium has nothing to do with their alphabetic function.) When an act of calculation is performed by the brain only a very limited set of combinations of numbers can be put together by remembering the names for them and the quantities or values they represent. To dispense with such a burden on the memory a separate visual medium was required to match quantities with shapes as sound is matched with the shapes of the alphabetic letters. Thus there was achieved in the act of calculation that same speed of recognition which I have identified as the secret of the Greek alphabet.

To complete the story of the notational systems upon

which Western civilization relies would require notice of algebra and of the algebraic refinements employed by sophisticated science. Such systems if they become such are properly the province of specialists whereas the alphabet and the cardinal numerals are tools of general human communication. There is however one system of notation which considered as a tool of general communication can be viewed as a supplement to letters and numbers. That is the one employed in the musical score. Modern polyphonic music as we have been accustomed to know it from the sixteenth century onward can be viewed as an "invention" which depended upon the perfection of an adequate visual notation. From this point of view, a comparison can be drawn between the appearance of "music," considered as a complex art form employing sound, in modern times, and the emergence of "literature" as an equally complex art form employing diction in classical antiquity. Linguistic, numerical, and musical "literacy," so to speak, can be thought of as forming a tripartite foundation of western culture, built upon three technologies each of which is designed to trigger mental operations with automatic rapidity by using the sense of visual recognition.

The original Greek music was composed to accompany oral recitation of verse, and was the servant of the diction not its master. It was required to conform to the rhythm of the words, rather than have the words laid on the rack to conform to the music. In the latter relationship, the one we are used to, music can be seen to have achieved its own identity apart from diction. Rhythm and pitch are arranged in a series of wordless relationships which have their own rationale. "Music" however as the Greeks used the term comprehended the combination of diction with melody, and even when Plato proposed censorship of certain musical modes, in addition to censorship of content, it is not clear that he is able to conceptualize the music in sharp distinction from the diction. Indeed, his sharp disapproval of certain types of "rhythm" and "harmony" on moral grounds gains credibility if he is thinking of the kind of things the singer or player would be saying while performing them.

The union thus taken for granted was inherited from the previous non-literate culture. Given music's function as the servant of diction, it can be seen why the Greeks may never have achieved a satisfactory notation for their "music" considered in isolation, because they were inhibited from conceptualizing it in isolation. However, the achievement of what may be termed an autonomous music in western Europe can be viewed as a delayed result of the achievement of verbal literacy. As the written word gaining its own identity became increasingly prosaic, freed altogether from the trammels of verse rhythm, rhythm could be conceptualized and manipulated in mere sound independent of diction, and could be increasingly thought of not as an accompaniment to words but as a separate technology with its own laws and procedures.

The alphabetic cultures of the modern world

Armed with the Arabic system of enumeration and with a true alphabet — whether Greek, Roman, or Cyrillic is a matter of indifference — now applied to symbolize the actual spoken speech of the vernacular, and equipped also with a system for manufacturing and multiplying and mass producing the alphabetic script in printed books, Europe was ready to move into modernity. Elitism of readership and of calculation was on the way out. Beginning about the fifteenth century there slowly grew up a European literary and scientific culture shared across the boundaries of national states, nurtured by the development of a cross-readership and a cross-translation. Its prototype long ago had been the Helleno-Roman joint culture. Both rested on the implementation of alphabetic literacy. If today we are so often tempted to speak of the "European mind" or the "Western mind," vague as these determinations are, they have a factual basis insofar as we mean those cultures which have continued to employ the Greek invention in its three main varieties. For in the first place the reader of a given tongue is afforded automatic recognition of all possible inscribed statements made in that tongue. He is also supplied with an endless flow of such inscription. And in the second place, since all alphabetized tongues are theoretically recognizable with the same speed, he can after learning another language phonetically reach equally direct acquaintance with the same language in its written form.

Since popular literacy as earlier noted depends not alone on the alphabet but on instruction in the alphabet given at the elementary level of child development, and since this is a political factor which varies from country to country, the alphabetized cultures are not all socially literate. But at least nothing stands in the way of their becoming so.

Confronting them across the world are those cultures which still employ non-alphabetic scripts with which we should include that group, fast disappearing, which has employed no script at all and has remained until recently culturally wholly in the oral epoch. The closest neighbors of the alphabetic cultures are those that use the Arabic or Sanskrit scripts descended from the North Semitic shorthand syllabaries. In the other hemisphere the Chinese offer a special case of a script neither alphabetized nor phonetic. The Japanese use a syllabic system of their own. Can it be an accident that in the contemporary world during the last century we are able to observe the non-alphabetic cultures striving with might and main to catch up with and emulate that science and the thought which we call "Western" or "European" but which can receive the more accurate technological definition of "alphabetic"? It may be objected that they appear to be able to catch up without changing their calligraphic system. But is this really true? The interrelations between the two groups which, in historical justice, I shall call the Greek and the pre-Greek is quite complex and the catching up is managed by various devices which in fact reveal how the historical value of the pre-Greek systems is compromised when they are considered as systems of communication. The devices are as follows:

First, the concept of vocalization may be borrowed from the Greek system and supplied as an addendum to the script in the form of assists to reading (the *matres lectionis*) or by way of diacritical marks to assist the reader in making the correct acoustic choices. This makes the script more adaptable to novel statement. Or secondly, and more commonly, the information, scientific and thoughtful, available in the Greek script is borrowed and translated into the local script. The process is continual. As it occurs it testifies to the historical priority of the alphabetized information. This acts as the leader and the non-alphabetic culture becomes the follower. Since the abilities of all spoken tongues to conceptualize are theoretically identical across the world, a Japanese can orally express what the West has taught him. Transferring the statement to his own script, he will then be able to recognize and to read what he already knows, as did the scribes of antiquity. But the free production of novel statement in his own script will remain difficult.

Or thirdly, a tongue which is alphabetized is introduced alongside of the local one by an invader or conquerer, commercial or imperial. The script thus introduced competes with the local script and either wholly displaces it or supplies the educated classes with the concepts and know-how needed for modernization. This is the case, for example, with India and is partially true of all cultures coming into contact with the Greek system and trying to make terms with it — the Japanese, the Chinese, the modern Egyptian and Syrian, and so forth. The foreign information can be supplied in Roman script or in Cyrillic script — it makes no difference. Europe and America on the one hand, and Russia on the other, united by their common alphabetic advantage, now are in the position to supply both ideas and technology as foreign influences, resented perhaps but greedily accepted by their non-alphabetic clients.

It is no accident therefore that purely oral habits of thought and experience and oral forms of literature have survived so much more tenaciously in the Arabic countries, in China, and in Japan. The Sayings of Chairman Mao, for example, are indeed "sayings" even if written in Chinese script, oracular and terse in the manner of Homeric aphorisms. So are the statements of the Koran. The concreteness of this kind of speech, its poetic simplicity and its directness, can prove attractive to the literate mind, reminding us that we may have paid some price for the conquest of the West by the Greek alphabet. This raises a large and dubious question which cannot be answered here.

What our story, however, has demonstrated is the astonishingly checkered, not to say hazardous, career of a reading device which we in the West now take so much for granted. Historians have acclaimed the "triumph of the alphabet," but the triumph was often compromised, sometimes bitterly contested, and to this day is only half won.

Having cast a glance down the centuries since the Greek

invention first made its appearance, the time has come to return to a consideration of what actually happened in Greece when it appeared. Our narrative would be obliged to revert to the eighth century before Christ, and since, as previously noted, the literate grew out of the non-literate and was built upon it, the character of the non-literate would demand prior examination, as a prerequisite for understanding the literate. The laws of oral composition must first be grasped, if we are to understand the laws of literacy. This means starting with Homer, the encyclopedic recorder of the Greek oral experience. But my time has run out. To deal with such a topic would exceed the limits set by these four lectures.

10. The distinction between "Eastern" versus "Western" does not accurately describe the complex history of the spread and distribution of the archaic Greek scripts (Jeffery, *The Local Scripts of Archaic Greece* [Oxford: Clarendon, 1961]. It does, however, usefully indicate two facts. (1) From the alphabet's inception there existed an "eastern Ionic" version (Jeffery, p. 325) in which long *e* and long *o* were distinguished by separate signs (eta and omega). The sign shaped like the Roman H, the aspirate, was used for eta; the script lacked any sign for the aspirate (missing in the Ionic dialect) and the sign shaped as an X was used exclusively to symbolize the sound which we in English would spell as "chi." These usages were standardized by Athenian decree in 403 B.C. for the script used to transcribe Attic Greek, and later, because of the political and cultural influence of Athens, they became standard for Greek script generally. Such usages had, however, already penetrated beyond the area of Ionia proper, spreading westward (cf. for example Jeffery, pp. 241, 346, apropos of Naxos and Rhodes) so that they became "western" as well as "eastern." (2) However, the earliest version of the Greek sign system to reach Italy was that used in Euboea in the late eighth or early seventh century and transmitted to the Euboic colony of Cyme near Naples. This Euboic version (Jeffery, p. 79) did not distinguish long and short *e* and *o*, used H for the aspirate, and used X for the sound "chs" (our *x*). These features are all reproduced in the Roman alphabet, borrowed probably from the Etruscans, who in

turn had presumably borrowed theirs from Cyme. The end result has been that usage both in antiquity and to the present day has been divided between a "Roman" version (i.e. Euboic equals "western") and a "Greek" version (i.e. Athenian equals Ionic equals "eastern").

11. Cf. O. Neugebauer, *The Exact Sciences in Antiquity*, 2d ed. (Brown University Press, 1957), pp. 5, 17–18, 27.

Index

abecedarium, 12, 26, 27, 61, 99, 198, 343
abstraction, 230, 256, 285, 336, 342
Academy, 222, 333
Achilles, 122, 131, 132, 142, 143, 158, 176, 177, 181, 194, 251, 252
acoustic control, 262, 263, 307
acrophonic, 84
Aeschylus, 29, 37 n. 48, 124, 180, 184, 201, 220, 222, 257 n. 21, 269-312, 331, 333
Africa, 23, 231
Agamemnon, 131, 142, 143
agent, personal, 137-39, 176, 177, 181, 227, 229, 232, 239
agonisma, 148
agora, 177, 210, 217
agrammatos, 48
agriculture, 124, 128
Alcibiades, 274, 285
Aldus Manutius, 340
Alexander the Great, 163
Alexandria, 17, 25, 29, 30, 319
alliteration, 195, 284
Al Mina, 206 n. 14
alphabet: ambiguity, 316-21, 324, 325; and politics, 323, 324, 336, 337; and designation, 7; as mnemonic, 180, 201; Cyrillic, 318, 319; date, 15, 16, 34 n. 22, 89, 92, 188, 225; "eastern" v. "western," 82, 318, 320, 349; effects, 82-88, 100; efficiency, 167, 168, 315; fluency, 185; in Athens, 318; letters, 26, 27, 48, 67, 199, 317; modern Greek, 315, 325; of Homer, 166-84; Phoenician parentage, 12; recorder of orality, 103, 105, 106, 120, 144, 151; Ro-

man, 315, 319, 321-23, 327, 328; technology, 77-88; v. syllabary, 63-70
amathia, 271
America, 150, 314, 348
Amphiaraus, 297
anagrapheus, 287
Anatolia, 330, 338
Anaxagoras, 31, 37 n. 49, 107, 240, 246, 331
Anderson, W. D., 34 n. 21
Andromeda, 289
anthologies, Greek, 288, 289
anthropology, cultural, 107-12, 150, 186
anticipation, 141, 177, 178, 305, 311
Antigone, 130, 131, 309
antistrophe, 164
antithesis, 242, 247, 274, 275
aoide, 184
aphona, 82
aphorism, 116, 139, 162, 219, 246, 274, 275, 278, 282, 298, 302-5, 309, 311
Aphrodite, 195
apoikismos, 36 n. 35
Apollo, 142, 143, 177, 178, 197, 214, 251
Apology, 223, 331
apprentices, 205 n. 6
Arabic: numerals, 47, 342; script, 48, 49, 53, 66, 71, 319, 326, 327, 345, 346, 348
Aramaic, 66, 70, 76, 327
archaistic sculpture, 25
Archilochus, 17, 19, 35 n. 30, 35 n. 31, 103, 123, 180, 244
architecture: Greek, 43, 44, 105;

architecture (*cont.*)
  verbal, 183, 311. *See also* integration
Ares, 215, 249
Arginusae, 283
Arias and Hirmer, 37 n. 42
Aristophanes, 28, 29, 122, 123, 126, 136, 139, 268-92, 333
Aristotle, 11, 14, 23, 25, 31, 34 n. 21, 36 n. 37, 38 n. 49, 48, 133, 220-22, 234
arithmetic, Babylonian, 46
arithmetical literacy, 341-43
Armayor, G. K., 36 n. 38
arming scenes, 126
Armstrong, J. J., 126
Artemis Orthia, 105
askein, 271
aspirate, 319
assonance, 241, 242
Assyria, 206 n. 8
atalotata, 193
Athena, 176, 181, 224, 263
Athenaeus, 287
Athens, 318, 320, 329, 333
atomic theory, 81, 82, 315, 342
Attic, 21, 147, 193, 221, 319, 349
audience, 146, 187, 233, 243, 244, 248, 271, 276, 279, 281-83, 287, 295, 301
Austin, N., 206 n. 10
authorship, 120, 144
Automedon, 251
Avesta, 153-55, 161, 163

Babel, 109, 317
Babylonia, 46, 47, 168-70, 341
Bacchae, 312
Baker, Sir Samuel, 22
Balkan singers, 9, 13, 150, 164
bard, 13, 168, 175, 179, 209, 235, 236, 244, 245
Barron, John, 36 n. 41
basanizein, 290
Becatti, G., 105
Beck, E. A., 205 n. 4

biblion, 286, 288, 290, 332
biblos, 33 n. 12, 332
biography, Greek, 24, 25
Boeotia, 196
book rolls, 27, 28, 205 n. 4, 332
books, 263, 330-33, 335; printed, 340
boulai, 216
boustrophedon, 191, 199
Bowra, M., 36 n. 37
Briseis, 137
Britain, 338
brothers, pair of, 295-98, 308
Burnet, J., 258 n. 53
Byzantium, 222, 319, 337, 338

Cadmus, 295
Caesar, Julius, 137
caesura, 154
Calchas, 178
calligraphy, 26, 53, 54, 192, 326, 327, 336, 340
Callinus, 36 n. 35
Calypso, 181
Cambridge Ancient History, 12, 33 n. 16, 34 n. 22
Cambridge University, 30, 220
Carcinus, 36 n. 35
Carolingian, 328, 340
Carpenter, R., 31, 89 n. 1, 89 n. 5, 89 n. 6, 92 n. 12, 194, 257 n. 6
case law, 206 n. 16
catalogue poetry, 162, 163, 169, 173; in *Iliad*, 180
cause and effect, 229, 231
Centaurs, 236
Cerri, G., 20
Chadwick, J., 90 n. 7
Chalcas, 142, 178
Chamoux, 34 n. 24
character, dramatic, 303
Chaucer, 339
Cheiron, 189
Cherniss, H., 38 n. 49
China, 49, 51-53, 86, 326, 346
Chios, 206 n. 8

Polyneices, 297
Polynesia, 102, 173
Pomeroy, S. B., 32 n. 3, 34 n. 22
poneros, 271
Presocratics, 30, 31, 220-60; vocabulary of, 245, 246
Priam, 131
principle, 139, 227, 247, 250
printing press, 83, 331, 336, 340
Pritchard, J. B., 97, 183
Prodicus, 32 n. 5, 125, 289
prologue, 272, 286, 295; Euripidean, 302; informative, 305-7; to *Seven Against Thebes*, 299-304
Prometheus, 160, 238, 254
prophecy, *see* anticipation
proprieties, 127, 130, 132
prose v. poetry, 21, 87, 90, 91, 147, 183, 189, 221, 224
Protagoras, 32 n. 6, 125, 279, 289
proverb, 72, 96, 97, 116, 139, 162, 212
Proverbs, Book of, 116, 117
psyche, 276

quantity, metrical, 154, 155, 318

Radermacher, A., 313
reading: as recognition, 60-62, 101, 318, 327; as reflex, 62, 83; democratization of, 62, 83, 95, 101; evidence for, 190; private, 203, 204, 289; v. speaking, 47-50; v. writing, 56-59, 95, 101. *See also* literacy
readership, Graeco-Roman, 329, 330, 345, 346
recitation, 59, 188, 203, 244, 267
religion, 111, 123, 125, 127, 128, 153, 186
Renaissance, 328, 339
responsion, 157, 158, 307
rhapsode, 33 n. 20, 174, 179, 283
rhapsodos, 33 n. 20
rhaptos, 33 n. 20
rhema, 32 n. 5, 289

rhesis, 32 n. 5
rhetoric: Homeric, 137, 284; tragic, 264, 303
Rhodes, 349
rhythm, 116-19, 132, 232, 262, 345; pleasure of, 134-36, 164; thematic, 142, 241, 242
Richter and Hall, 37 n. 46
Ritter and Preller, 30
ritual, 72, 73, 153, 170, 308
Robb, Kevin, 12, 205, 206
Robinson Crusoe, 58
rock and roll, 165
Rogers, B. B. (Loeb), 313, 254
Romance Tongues, 333
Romanization, 48, 326
romantic poets, 20
Rome, 29, 31, 39, 47, 83, 85, 151, 222, 315, 316, 324, 338, 339, 345, 349
Rossi, L., 35 n. 29
Ruschenbusch, E., 206 n. 8
Russia, 53, 66, 105, 315, 317, 318, 348

Salamis, 295
Samaritan Pentateuch, 97
Samos, 105
Sandhi, 154
Sanscrit, 66, 152, 154, 161, 163, 346
saphos, 274
Sappho, 19
Sardis, 225
saying, 116, 117, 139, 242
Scandinavia, 324
schools: primary, 21, 27, 28, 62, 83, 95, 101, 187, 201, 205 n. 4, 261, 333, 342, 343, 346; Tudor, 340
school scenes, 27, 28, 37 n. 45, 201, 203
science, modern, 343
scribe, 76, 83, 95, 102, 167, 168, 172, 272, 287, 336, 339, 340; Norman, 323; statues of, 200, 201

Library of Congress Cataloging in Publication Data

Havelock, Eric Alfred.
   The literate revolution in Greece and its cultural
consequences.

   (Princeton series of collected essays)
   Includes bibliographical references and index.
   1. Greek language—Alphabet.   2. Oral tradition.
3. Greek literature—History and criticism..   I. Title.
PA273.H27   481   81-47133
ISBN 0-691-09396-2   AACR2
ISBN 0-691-00026-3 (pbk.)

Eric A. Havelock is Sterling Professor of Classics Emeritus, Yale University. His numerous publications include *The Liberal Temper in Greek Politics* (Yale), *Preface to Plato* (Harvard), and *The Greek Concept of Justice* (Harvard).